Routledge Revivals

Pre-Capitalist Modes of Production

First published in 1975, this book investigates the various pre-capitalist modes of production briefly indicated in the works of Marx and Engels, and gives an examination of the conditions of the transition from one mode of production to another. The fundamental concepts used in these investigations, including those of mode of production, of necessary labour and surpass labour, of politics and state, are derived from Capital and from other works of Marxist theory. The primary aim of the analysis is to raise the conceptualisation of pre-capitalist modes of production and of transition to a more rigorous level. This book will appear controversial to both Marxists and non-Marxists alike.

Pre-Capitalist Modes of Production

Barry Hindess and Paul Q. Hirst

Routledge
Taylor & Francis Group

First published in 1975
by Routledge and Kegan Paul

This edition first published in 2018 by Routledge
2 Park Square, Milton Park, Abingdon, Oxon, OX14 4RN
and by Routledge
711 Third Avenue, New York, NY 10017

Routledge is an imprint of the Taylor & Francis Group, an informa business

Publisher's Note
The publisher has gone to great lengths to ensure the quality of this reprint but points out that some imperfections in the original copies may be apparent.

Disclaimer
The publisher has made every effort to trace copyright holders and welcomes correspondence from those they have been unable to contact.
A Library of Congress record exists under ISBN: 75324798

ISBN 13: 978-1-138-56146-5 (hbk)
ISBN 13: 978-0-203-71069-2 (ebk)

Pre-capitalist modes of production

Barry Hindess
Department of Sociology
University of Liverpool

Paul Q. Hirst
Department of Politics and Sociology
Birkbeck College, University of London

Routledge & Kegan Paul
London and Boston

First published in 1975
by Routledge & Kegan Paul Ltd
Broadway House, 68–74 Carter Lane
London EC4V 5EL and
9 Park Street
Boston, Mass. 02108, USA
Set in 10 pt Times on 12 pt body

ISBN 0 7100 8168 5 (C)
ISBN 0 7100 8169 3 (P)

Contents

Introduction

This book is a work of Marxist theory. Its object is to investigate the various pre-capitalist modes of production briefly indicated in the works of Marx and Engels and to examine the conditions of the transition from one mode of production to another. The fundamental concepts used in these investigations – the concepts of mode of production, of necessary-labour and surplus-labour, of politics and the state, and so on – are derived from *Capital* and from other works of Marxist theory. The aim of the analysis is to raise the conceptualisation of these modes of production and of transition to a more rigorous level. For each of the modes of production discussed in the book we attempt either to construct a general concept of that mode of production or else to show that such a general concept cannot be produced. Some of our conclusions, for example, that there is no 'Asiatic' mode of production, that the feudal mode of production requires neither serfdom nor seignorial power, and that the transition between one mode of production and another must be conceived in a non-evolutionary form, will appear controversial to both Marxists and non-Marxists.

1 Theoretical abstraction and concrete analysis

This book is a work of theory. Its approach is abstract and theoretical and it is concerned to determine the theoretical status and validity of certain specific concepts. There are two points here and it is essential that they be clearly distinguished. To say that our approach is abstract and theoretical is to say first that it consists in the application of the concepts of a determinate problematic, that of the Marxist theory of modes of production, to definite problems posed within it. All concepts are abstract in a very specific sense: they are defined by the place which they occupy and the function which they perform within a determinate field of concepts, a problematic. Concepts are formed and have their existence within knowledge. They are not reducible to or derivable from any set of 'given', 'real' conditions. The concept of the feudal mode of production, for example, is not the product of a generalisation from a specific set of historically 'given' feudal societies nor is it a Weberian 'ideal-type', a construction based on the deliberate and one-sided accentuation of certain 'real' conditions in accordance with the idiosyncratic values and interests of the investigator. On the contrary, the concept of the feudal, or any other, mode of production is the product of theoretical work. Its theoretical status and validity can be determined only within the field of concepts which specify the general definition of mode of production. It is a valid concept if it is a possible mode of production, if it is constructed according to the concepts of the Marxist theory of modes of production.

It will be apparent from these remarks that we are completely opposed to the theoretical empiricism which characterises the academic social sciences and history. In these disciplines scientific knowledge is alleged to be reducible to 'given' facts, either to the 'given' real conditions or to the 'given' experiences of human subjects. Science, therefore, begins with the careful observation and collection of facts: it ends with their correlation. Knowledge is a construction based on empirically given elements and the empirically observed correlations between them. One of the most influential methodological orientations in the academic social sciences, for example, is characterised by the deliberate use of observationally defined empirical categories and the determination of relations between categories by means of empirical research. This means that observed 'facts' are analysed according to more or less systematic sorting procedures based essentially on John Stuart Mill's methods of agreement and difference in order to determine empirically valid relationships or causal laws. This positivistic and statistical empiricism has been subjected to a brilliant and devastating critique by David and Judith Willer in their book *Systematic Empiricism: Critique of a Pseudo-Science*.

Empiricism represents knowledge as constructed out of 'given' elements, the elements of experience, the 'facts' of history, etc.[1] Unfortunately for these positions facts are never 'given' to knowledge. They are always the product of definite practices, theoretical or ideological, conducted under definite real conditions. To pretend otherwise, to represent certain elements of knowledge as given in the real, is to denegate the central role of scientific practice, of experimentation and of explicit theoretical construction and argument, in the production of scientific knowledge. Facts are never *given*; they are always produced. The facts of the sciences are products of scientific practices. In the academic social sciences and history and also, it must be admitted, in the bulk of Marxist scholarship dealing with pre-capitalist societies the situation is quite different. The latter tends to be historical and descriptive in orientation and to treat the brief indications of, say, feudal or slave production in the works of Marx and Engels as more or less adequate descriptions of the structure of particular historical societies.[2] The theoretical problem of the validity of the concept of a particular mode of production thus tends to be reduced to the empiricist problem of the correspondence between the concept and the 'facts' of history. For example, the problem of the validity of the conception of the 'Asiatic' mode of production tends to be discussed in terms of the 'facts' of Indian or Chinese history.

The empiricism of the academic social sciences and of much Marxist scholarship has serious theoretical effects. In so far as certain facts are represented as 'given' in the real or as 'given' by history they must fall below the level of theoretical determination: they cannot be the product of an explicit theoretical practice. The empiricism of these disciplines therefore ensures that these 'facts' are ideological constructs and that their 'theories' are, at best, sophisticated theoretical ideology.

In contrast to the empiricist practice of theoretical ideologies, the sciences proceed through the explicit theoretical construction of their concepts and the theoretical definition of their objects. This book is a work of Marxist scientific theory. It must be judged in terms of that theory, in terms of the field of concepts and forms of proof specific to its problematic. We attempt to construct the concepts of certain pre-capitalist modes of production and, in the case of the 'Asiatic' mode of production, to prove that there can be no such concept within the Marxist theory of modes of production. Our constructions and our arguments are theoretical and they can only be evaluated in theoretical terms – in terms, that is to say, of their rigour and theoretical coherence. They cannot be refuted by any empiricist recourse to the supposed 'facts' of history.

To say that our approach is abstract and theoretical, then, is to say that we proceed by means of explicit theoretical argument and explicit theoretical construction and that we work with theoretical forms of proof and demonstration. All theoretical practice involves theoretical abstraction: it is a process that takes place entirely within knowledge. In this sense Lenin's investigations of a concrete social formation and of specific concrete conjunctures – in, say, *The Development of*

Capitalism in Russia and *The Agrarian Programme of Social Democracy in the First Russian Revolution* – are works of theoretical abstraction. They are no less theoretical and no less abstract than Marx's *Capital* which investigates the concept of the capitalist mode of production and uses particular social formations merely as the source of illustrations. The Marxist analysis of a concrete situation is always a work of theoretical abstraction.

There is, however, a second sense in which our approach is abstract. It is the sense in which the abstraction of *Capital* differs from that of *The Development of Capitalism in Russia.* Both are works of theoretical abstraction but they have different theoretical objects: one investigates the concept of a particular mode of production and the other investigates the conditions of a determinate concrete social formation. Scientific practice involves both the construction and investigation of abstract, general concepts and the investigation of particular real conditions: the latter is always misrepresented in empiricist conceptions of knowledge as the application of concepts to particular 'given' phenomena. In fact, as we have argued, nothing is ever 'given' to knowledge. What empiricism represents as given is always the product of a definite theoretical or ideological practice.

The abstract general concepts of Marxist theory – the concepts of the various modes of production and of their conditions of existence, the concept of social formation, and so on – are means for the production of knowledge of concrete social formations and of concrete conjunctures. It is these general concepts that provide the means for the determination and theoretical definition of particular current situations and which determine the criteria of the construction and validation of the concept of particular social formations. The general concept of, say, the capitalist mode of production is not confined in its application to any particular social formation. It is not a description of a particular structure of social relations but a means for the analysis of social relations. Concrete conditions are not 'given' to theory in order to validate or to refute its general concepts. On the contrary, it is the general concepts that make possible the analysis of the concrete.

This book is abstract and general, then, in the sense that its object is to determine the theoretical status of certain abstract general concepts within the Marxist theory of modes of production. It is abstract in the sense that it makes no attempt to analyse particular concrete social formations. If we do not investigate the specific conditions of the class struggles of the present situation in, say, the societies of

Africa or Latin America it is not that we consider those struggles unimportant, nor is it the product of an academic ideology of 'pure' and 'distinterested' scholarship. On the contrary, if we do not enter the terrain of concrete analysis in this book it is because the problems we investigate here cannot be settled at that level.

2 Can there be a general theory of modes of production?

Our investigations in this book are restricted to particular pre-capitalist modes of production and the transition from feudalism to capitalism. We do not investigate the concepts of the capitalist or the advanced communist (i.e. socialist) modes of production. The decision to restrict the book in this way requires some explanation. It is the result not of any antiquarian interest on our part but of our initial conception of the book as contributing towards the project of constructing a general theory of modes of production. Our investigations compel us to reject that project as scientifically unfounded, as the effect of a teleological and idealist philosophy of history. The Marxist theory of modes of production involves abstract and general concepts – the concepts of mode of production and social formation, of ideology and of politics and the state, and so on – but there is no general theory of modes of production. This section of our Introduction outlines the project of constructing a general theory of modes of production and gives our reasons for rejecting it.

In *Reading Capital*, part III, 'The Basic Concepts of Historical Materialism', Balibar defines a mode of production as a *combination* of elements: labourer, non-labourer, means of production. These elements are combined according to both a 'property' connection and a 'real appropriation' connection which correspond respectively to the relations of production and the forces of production. Now, consider Balibar's comments on Marx's 1857 *Introduction*:

> Marx's aim was to show that the distinction between different modes is necessarily and *sufficiently* based on a variation of the connexions between a small number of elements which are always the same. The announcement of these connexions and of their terms constitutes the exposition of the primary theoretical concepts of historical materialism, of the few general concepts which form the rightful beginning of his exposition and which characterize the scientific method of *Capital*, conferring on its theory its axiomatic form; i.e. the announcement of

> a determinate form of this variation, one which directly depends on the concepts of labour-power, means of production, property, etc., is a constantly necessary presupposition of the 'economic' proofs in *Capital* (p. 225).

In principle, then, the different modes of production must be conceived as variant forms of the same general structure: the different possible combinations of a small number of elements define the concepts of the different possible modes of production. In Balibar's conception the different modes of production constituted in this fashion may be divided into two types: those in which the two connections *correspond* and those in which they do not. In the first type the action of each connection serves to reproduce the other: the correspondence may therefore reproduce itself indefinitely. In the second type the action of the property connection (relations of production) transforms the real appropriation connection (forces of production). These are the transitional modes of production: their concepts are the concepts of their dissolution.

Now, the constitution of such a general theory of modes of production appears in Balibar's text as a project that has yet to be realised. In *Capital* we are given the elaborated concept of a particular variant form of the general structure of production, namely, the capitalist mode of production. For the concepts of the other modes of production we are merely given a series of brief and partial indications which are mostly in the form of illustrative comparisons designed to highlight certain features of capitalism.

On this interpretation, then, there appears to be a serious discrepancy between what we are promised in the shape of a general theory of modes of production and what we are actually given in the works of Marx, namely, the concept of one mode of production and a few suggestions for the rest. This book was originally conceived as a contribution towards that projected but unrealised general theory of modes of production. By producing the concepts of several distinct modes of production it seemed that we could investigate different possible forms of Balibar's two connections, the relations and the forces of production, and of the correspondence which unites them in the non-transitional modes of production. In this way it might be possible to establish a more exact concept of the general structure of production and of the conditions which determine its variant forms, the different possible modes of production.

But this project for a general theory of modes of production is idealist and teleological. It would reduce Marxism to the level of a philosophy of history. The teleological character of *Reading Capital*'s reconstruction of Marxism, of the concept of structural causality and of Balibar's concepts of transitional and non-transitional modes of production, is demonstrated in chapter 6. It has also been demonstrated in Balibar's own 'Self-Criticism'. These demonstrations need not be repeated here. For the purposes of the Introduction the essential points may be summarised as follows.

A general theory of modes of production must represent each particular mode as a particular variant form of a single general structure. The general theory is therefore a structuralism: it is a theory of a *structure* and of the possible forms in which it may be realised. In this case the structure is *the* mode-of-production-in-general and its possible historical realisations are the different particular modes of production. The difference between one mode of production and another is the effect of variation in the form of combination of the relations and forces of production. This variation, this difference between one combination and another, therefore appears capable of explaining real historical effects. In this conception a difference between concepts is supposed to function as the origin (the cause) of differentiation in the real.

The idealism of this position is apparent. The general theory of modes of production projected in *Reading Capital* can be realised only by reproducing the essential structures of the idealist philosophies of history. These doctrines conceive history as a rational order in which determinate historical phenomena are each represented as the expression (the effect) of a determinate idea. Relations between phenomena may therefore be represented as expressions of relations between ideas and the movement of history as the working out, the realisation, of a pre-given complex idea. The idea is the essence of its phenomena. History is a rational order in the sense that an adequate knowledge of a determinate historical phenomenon is identical to its essence, the idea which is expressed in that phenomenon. In such conceptions the essential structure of history (the relations between essences) appears as a structure of relations between ideas – a rational order.

The most developed and most coherent of these positions is undoubtedly that of Hegel. In his *Philosophy of History*, for example, determinate historical unities (the Greek world, the Roman world, etc.) are each represented as expressions of a determinate Spirit, and each Spirit is but a moment in the development of the World Spirit.

Here determinate historical phenomena are expressions of determinate essences while the movement of history is an effect of the contradictory structure of these essences. Thus the Egyptian Spirit is represented as a *problem* whose solution is the Greek Spirit.

What has Hegel to do with *Reading Capital*'s attempted reconstruction of the Marxist theory of modes of production? Althusser and Balibar explicitly reject teleological interpretations of Marxism and they are particularly concerned to differentiate between Marxist and Hegelian conceptions of history. The Hegelian philosophy of history, it seems, is quite alien to *Reading Capital*'s Marxism.

Now, the essential structure of the philosophy of history is determined not by the use of such words as 'Spirit' or 'idea' or 'essence', but by the conception of history as a rational order, an order, that is to say, which is governed by an expressive causality in which determinate phenomena are to be explained by reference to the essences which they are thought to express. It makes no difference to this essential structure if the essences are conceived as 'ideas' or 'Spirits' or, as in *Reading Capital*, as the correspondence between the relations and the forces of production. It matters little if the movement of history is an effect of the contradictory structure of a Spirit or of the non-correspondence between relations and forces of production. What is crucial is not the precise character of the essence but the mode of causality and the forms of explanation which it entails. The realisation of a general theory of modes of production must involve a collapse into the expressive causality of the idealist philosophies of history. The 'structural' causality of *Reading Capital* is no less expressive because the essence in question is called a structure.

These arguments are developed at greater length in chapter 6. For the present it is necessary to indicate what is involved in the rejection of a general theory of modes of production and of the expressive (or structural) causality which it entails. There are two points here. First, it must be emphasised that the absence of a general theory of modes of production does not mean that there can be no general concepts. There is no general structure from which the particular modes of production can be deduced as the variant forms in which that general structure may be realised. There *is* a general concept of mode of production but its function in Marxist theory is to specify certain conditions that must be satisfied by any concept if it is to be the concept of a determinate mode of production. The general concept of mode of production and the other general concepts of Marxist theory are theoretical means of production of the concepts of determinate modes of production. These latter may be constructed by means of certain general concepts but they cannot be deduced from them.

Second, expressive or teleological causality has no place in scientific theory. On the contrary, it is the product of essentialism, a philosophical and ideological mode of analysis in which determinate real phenomena are 'explained' by reference to the essence – 'Life', 'Man', 'the Greek Spirit', or what have you – that they are held to express. In essentialist distortions of Marxism, for example, determinate historical phenomena may be reduced to effects of the consciousness of a class-subject (as in Lukács) or to the expression of a determinate inner principle. In chapter 6 we show that Balibar's position reduces the transition from one mode of production to another to the expression of a contradictory essence.

In opposition to these essentialisms we insist that the social formation must be analysed in terms of a determinate material causality with real relations producing certain definite effects. In taking this position we emphasise what has always been essential to Marxist theory, namely, the role of the class struggle in history. The reproduction or the transformation of a determinate structure of social relations is the outcome of specific class struggles (political, economic and ideological) conducted under certain definite conditions. It is for this reason that Marxism insists on the necessity of a concrete analysis of the current situation. The general concepts of Marxist theory are theoretical means for the production of knowledge of concrete social formations and of concrete conjunctures. They are not a substitute for concrete analysis. They are the tools that make it possible.

3 The concept of mode of production

The general concept of mode of production specifies the general conditions which must be satisfied by a concept if it is to be the concept of a determinate mode of production. In this final section of our Introduction it is necessary to outline this general concept and to consider its implications with regard to the mode of proof we adopt in our investigations of the concepts of determinate modes of production.

A mode of production is an articulated combination of relations and forces of production structured by the dominance of the relations of production. The relations of production define a specific mode of appropriation of surplus-labour and the specific form of social distribution of the means of production corresponding to that mode of appropriation of surplus-labour. For example, capitalist relations of production define a mode of appropriation of surplus-labour which works by means of commodity exchange. Capitalists buy means of production and items of personal consumption from each other. They buy labour-power from labourers in exchange for wages. With these wages the labourers buy items of personal consumption from capitalists and must then sell their labour-power for a further period in order to be able to buy further means of personal consumption. Appropriation of surplus-labour here depends on a difference between the value of labour-power and the value that may be created by means of that labour-power. Surplus-labour takes the form of surplus-value. This appropriation of surplus-labour presupposes that means of production are in the hands of the capitalists, since otherwise there is no necessity for the labourers to obtain means of consumption through the sale of their labour-power. Thus capitalist relations of production define a mode of appropriation of surplus-labour in the form of surplus-value, and a social distribution of the means of production so that these are the property of non-labourers (capitalists), while the labour-power takes the form of a commodity which members of the class of labourers are forced to sell to members of the class of non-labourers.

The concepts of necessary-labour and surplus-labour are examined in the first part of chapter 1. There we show that surplus-labour is a necessary element in all possible modes of production. They differ not in the existence of surplus-labour but in the mode in which it is appropriated. It may be appropriated collectively as in the primitive communist and advanced communist (socialist) modes of production, or it may be appropriated by a class of non-labourers as in capitalism or feudalism. In the second case the mode of appropriation of surplus-labour constitutes antagonistic relations of production and a social division of labour between a class of labourers (wage-labourers, peasants, etc.) and a class of non-labourers (capitalists, feudal lords, etc.). The mode of appropriation of surplus-labour governs the mode in which the social product is distributed among the agents of production.

'Forces of production' refers to the mode of appropriation of nature, that is, to the labour process in which a determinate raw material is transformed into a determinate product. 'The elementary factors of the labour-process are 1, the personal activity of man, i.e., work itself, 2, the subject of that work, and 3, its instruments' (*Capital*, I, p. 178). Forces of production differ according to the manner in which these elements are combined into concrete forms of the production process: the forms of co-operation and co-ordination of the labour of several individuals, the forms of articulation of the means and the object of labour with the activity of the labourers, and so on. For example, in *Capital*, I, part IV, Marx examines different forms of the capitalist labour process and in particular the transition from manufacture to modern industry which constitutes the so-called 'industrial revolution'. Very schematically we may say that the transition from manufacture or craft production to modern industry involves a complete transformation in the form of combination of elements of the labour process: from the unity of means of labour and labour-power constituted by the tool to the unity of means of labour and object of labour constituted by the machine. In this example the new system of productive forces formed by capitalist mechanised industry involves a transformation of the articulation of the elements of the labour process. 'Productive forces' refers to this articulation of elements, not to the elements themselves. In this sense it is not the craftsman's tool or the industrial machine as such that define the productive forces, but the specific form of their articulation into a concrete labour process.[3]

Now the concept of mode of production as an articulated combination of relations and forces of production precludes the construction of the concept of a particular mode of production by means of the simple juxtaposition of a set of relations and a set of forces. On the contrary the concept of a particular mode of production is the concept of a determinate articulated combination of relations and forces of production. This means that there can be no definition of the relations or of the forces of production independently of the mode of production in which they are combined. In the analysis of the concept of primitive communism, for example, in order to show that the concept of the appropriation of surplus-labour by the mechanism of the redistribution of the product defines a set of relations of production, we have to establish that a determinate set of productive forces corresponds to that set of proposed relations of production. Where, on the contrary, no set of corresponding productive forces can be deduced from a proposed mode of appropriation of surplus-labour, this latter belongs to no mode of production and cannot define a set of relations of production. We show in the chapter on the supposed 'Asiatic' mode of production that the concept of the appropriation of surplus-labour by the mechanism of tax/rent cannot define a set of relations of production since it belongs to no possible concept of an articulated combination of relations and forces of production.

A conceivable mode of appropriation of surplus-labour, then, defines the relations of production of a determinate mode of production only on condition that a determinate set of productive forces is deducible from the concept of this mode of appropriation. Here we treat the relations of production as the primary element in the concept of mode of production. In fact there is no alternative. It is impossible to construct the concept of an articulated combination of relations and forces of production starting from the primacy of the productive forces. The concept of a determinate labour process is sufficient to define a technical differentiation of functions between the agents of production, but it is impossible to deduce a determinate social division of labour from these functional differences.[4] In chapter 1, for example, we show that Meillassoux's definition of mode of production in terms of the primacy of the labour process must imply an arbitrary and contingent variation at the level of relations of production. The analysis of the labour process in isolation from the relations of production precludes the concept of the mode of production as a determinate articulated combination of relations and forces of production.

VARIANT FORMS OF THE MODE OF PRODUCTION

The concept of mode of production as an articulated combination of relations and forces does not preclude the possibility of variation at the level of the relations or of the forces of production. On the contrary the structure of a determinate mode of production specifies a complex space of variation and the variant forms that are possible within that space. Variant forms are not contingent empirical deviations from the purity of the general concept of the mode of production in question. The concept of a determinate mode of production defines the specific variant forms that are possible as a necessary effect of its structure. For example, the general concept of the feudal mode of production specifies that surplus-labour is appropriated in the form of rent. The payment of this rent may be in kind, in money or in labour. The concept of the feudal mode thus defines a space of variation in the forms of rent. The concept of the feudal mode as an articulated combination of relations and forces of production ensures that this variation has definite conditions and effects in the structure of the mode of production. Labour-rent, for example, corresponds to a specific form of feudal labour process, namely, the combination of independent tenant production with demesne production under the supervision of the feudal lord or his agent.

The space of variation and the variant forms that are possible are inscribed in the general concept of the mode of production in question. This concept of variation must be clearly distinguished from the arbitrary variation that appears in the conception of the supposed 'Asiatic' mode of production or with Meillassoux's technicist conception of mode of production. In these conceptions variation at the level of the relations or the forces of production is strictly arbitrary since it is impossible to specify the conditions of variation in terms of the structure of the mode of production as a whole. Thus in the case of the supposed 'Asiatic' mode the variation between individual and communal production is entirely arbitrary since it has no effects or conditions at the level of the relations of production. Such arbitrary variation is anathema to the Marxist concept of mode of production.

MODE OF PRODUCTION AND SOCIAL FORMATION

'Social formation' is a Marxist concept which may loosely be said to correspond to the ideological notion of 'society'. It designates a complex structure of social relations, a unity of economic, ideological and, in certain cases, political structural levels in which the role of the economy is determinant. It is determinant in the sense that the conditions of existence of the dominant relations of production assign to each of the levels a certain form of effectivity and mode of intervention with respect to the other levels. If the dominant relations of production are antagonistic, involving a social division of labour between a class of labourers and a class of non-labourers, then the social formation contains a state and a political level as the necessary space of representation of the antagonistic classes. Otherwise, there is no state and no politics. The concepts of 'state' and of 'politics' are examined in chapter 1.

The relation between the concepts of mode of production and of social formation may be understood in terms of the conditions of existence of particular modes of production. The concepts of the relations and the forces of production are economic concepts whose articulated combination defines a particular type of structure of economic social relations. The concept of each particular mode of production defines certain economic, ideological or political conditions that are necessary to the existence of that structure of economic social relations. For example, if the relations of production define a certain distribution of the means of production to different classes then certain legal and political conditions will be necessary to ensure the maintenance of that distribution. Similarly, if a mode of production presupposes the existence of commodity relations then definite legal and contractual forms are required for that mode of production to exist. To take a slightly different example, it is clear that the capitalist and the slave modes of production require that certain forms of monetary calculation are performed by particular agents of production. The existence of these modes therefore depends on the maintenance of the ideological social relations in which these forms of calculation are developed and individuals are trained in their use.

The precise character of these necessary economic, political, and ideological conditions of existence must of course depend on the structure of the mode of production in question. In particular, the mode of production determines which of the structural levels is to occupy the place of dominance in the social formation. With the capitalist mode of production the economy is both dominant and determinant, but in other modes other levels occupy the dominant position as an effect of the specific conditions of existence of its relations of production. For example, in both the primitive communist and the slave modes of production the ideological level is dominant although the conditions of its dominance and the structure of the dominant level are very different in the two cases. Finally, the different variant forms of the mode of production imply a variation in its structural conditions of existence. Thus the simple redistribution and complex redistribution variants of the primitive communist mode of production have quite different structures of ideological social relations as their necessary conditions of existence.

It is important to be clear as to what is involved in this conception of the mode of production and its conditions of existence. A particular mode of production exists if and only if its conditions of existence are present in the economic, political and ideological levels of a determinate social formation. If these conditions are not secured then the mode of production cannot continue. Conversely, the existence of a particular mode of production requires that economic reproduction should take place. Economic reproduction is secured only if the economic level is structured by the dominance of a specific set of relations of production and the corresponding productive forces. Otherwise the distribution of the social product must fail to provide for the reproduction of the agents of production or to provide the particular means of production which are the necessary conditions of their labour. If economic reproduction does not take place then the social formation must cease to exist.

Two further points must be made here. The first is that the structure of the social formation is not deducible from the concept of its determinant mode of production. The conditions of existence of a particular mode of production prescribe the limits of variation in the structures of the economic, political and ideological levels if the mode of production is to survive. Thus the structure of the economic level of a particular social formation must be governed by a variant or set of variants of a determinate mode of production but it may also include certain elements of other modes – provided only that the presence of these elements does not contradict the conditions of existence of the dominant relations of production. Second, it must be emphasised that the presence of a particular mode of production is not sufficient to secure the reproduction of its conditions of existence. To suppose otherwise, to suppose that the existence of a mode of production entails the reproduction of its conditions of existence, would mean that the transition from one mode of production to another could never take place. The mode of production would then be eternal. The effects of such a teleological conception are examined at length in chapter 6. The economic, political and ideological conditions of existence of the mode of production are secured, modified, or transformed as the outcome of specific class struggles conducted under the particular conditions of the economic, political and ideological levels of the social formation. The particular structure of economic, political and ideological conditions in the social formation determines the possible outcomes of the class struggles conducted under such conditions. Such a structure will be called a *conjuncture*. Movement from one conjuncture to another is the outcome of class struggle: it involves the modification or transformation of existing relations and of the specific conditions of the class struggle. A transitional conjuncture is one in which the transformation of the dominant relations of production is a possible outcome of class struggle conducted under the conditions of that conjuncture. The analysis of the conjuncture and the determination of the transformations and displacements made possible by its structure is the objective of concrete analysis in Marxist theory. The concepts of the social formation, of the mode of production that governs the articulation of its levels, and of the particular structures of these levels are necessary instruments for the theoretical definition of the structure of the conjuncture.

THE NOTIONS OF BASE AND SUPERSTRUCTURE

By this point the reader may be concerned about the fate of terms such as 'base' and 'superstructure' or of the equivalent formulations that appear in so many summary expositions of Marxist theory. Consider, for example, the formulations of Marx's 1859 Preface to *A Contribution to the Critique of Political Economy*:

> In the social production of their existence, men inevitably enter into definite relations, which are independent of their will, namely relations of production appropriate to a given stage in the development of their material forces of production. The totality of these relations of production constitutes the economic structure of society, the real foundation, on which arises a legal and political superstructure and to which correspond definite forms of social consciousness. . . . At a certain stage of development, the material productive forces of society come into conflict with the existing relations of production or – this merely expresses the same thing in legal terms – with the property relations within the framework of which they have operated hitherto. From forms of development of the productive forces these relations turn into their fetters. Then begins an era of social revolution. The changes in the economic foundation lead sooner of later to the transformation of the whole immense superstructure (pp. 20–1).

Nothing could be more misleading than the reading which finds in this passage an economic determinism, that is, a position which asserts the primacy of the economic factor above all others in history. This reading, beloved by Weberian sociology, finds in Marx a factorialist theory of history and counterposes to Marx's 'one-sided' emphasis on the economic factor the liberal position that other factors too (non-economic, non-material) must have their turn.[5]

There is nothing in the quoted passage to legitimate such a reading: the economic structure is the '*foundation* on which arises a legal and political superstructure and to which *correspond* definite forms of social consciousness'. The notions of *foundation* and of *correspond* can hardly justify the conclusion that the content or the form of the superstructure has a direct economic *causation* in the sense of the anti-Marxist factorialist polemics. Rather, the economic structure is the foundation on which the superstructure rests and which therefore defines certain limits to what can be erected upon it. This passage says nothing about the *origin* or *cause* of the superstructural forms or of the corresponding ideologies. It does, however, suggest the existence of distinct structural levels, economic, political–legal, ideological, within the social formation.

Nevertheless, while the economic determinism reading has no justification it can hardly be said that these rather cryptic formulations provide a rigorous basis for the construction of the concepts 'mode of production' and 'social formation'. In many respects, indeed, Marx's formulations in this passage are seriously misleading. The notions of *foundation* and *correspond* or of the forces *coming into conflict* with the relations of production may not justify an economic determinism but they may well suggest the existence of a single general structure of the social formation in which the articulation of levels is the same in every case and of a universal mechanism of transition from one mode of production to another so that each specific transition exemplifies the same universal process. In short these notions suggest – although they do not require – precisely the general theory of modes of production which we have already dismissed as teleological.

It is for this reason that we have preferred to formulate the relation between mode of production and social formation in terms of the concepts of political, economic and ideological levels and of the conditions of existence of the mode of production. Far from suggesting the existence of a single general structure these concepts ensure that the precise articulation of levels in the social formation is specific to the structure of each determinant mode of production. Similarly, far from suggesting a universal mechanism of transition these concepts require that transition be analysed in terms of the crucial role of the class struggle conducted in the specific conditions of particular transitional conjunctures. In short, these concepts preclude all teleology and all essentialism. Marxism is not a philosophy of history.

MODE OF PROOF

The general concepts of mode of production, social formation, and conjuncture outlined above govern the mode of investigation we adopt in our analyses of the concepts of particular modes of production and of the problems involved in the analysis of periods of transition between one mode of production and another. Our investigations of the concepts of particular modes of production or of transition are abstract and theoretical. We attempt to determine the theoretical status and validity of certain abstract general concepts within the Marxist theory of modes of production but not to analyse particular concrete social formations or particular conjunctures.

For each of the pre-capitalist modes of production briefly indicated in the works of Marx and Engels we may pose the following question: 'Is it possible to construct the rigorous concept of that mode of production as a distinct and determinate articulated combination of relations and forces of production?' We proceed in each case to answer the question either by constructing the necessary concept or by demonstrating that no such construction is possible. If the concept can be constructed in accordance with the general concept of mode of production then it is a valid concept of the Marxist theory of modes of production. Otherwise the concept has no validity in terms of Marxist theory.

Our proof of the validity of the concept of a particular mode of production therefore involves the specification of its relations of production, the deduction of the corresponding forces of production, and the demonstration that the relations and forces form an articulated combination in the sense outlined above. The conception of the 'Asiatic' mode of production is invalid since, as we show, the proposed relations of production allow an entirely arbitrary variation at the level of the productive forces. These relations and forces cannot therefore constitute an articulated combination.

There is a partial exception to this procedure of proof by construction in the case of the 'ancient' mode of production. This was the object of our earliest investigation. The concept of the ancient mode of production constructed in chapter 2 defines the relations of production in terms of a concept of the appropriation of surplus-labour by *right of citizenship*: citizens extract surplus-labour by virtue of their rights as citizens with respect to the operation of the political, legal and ideological apparatuses of the state, for example, through their access to the distribution of taxation and other appropriations levied by the state on citizens themselves and on the subject communities. Without going into the details of this construction we can specify the inadequacy of its conception of the relations of production as follows. The concept of appropriation of surplus-labour by *right of citizenship* conflates the (economic) concept of the mode of appropriation of surplus-labour with the concept of its (political) conditions of existence. Consequently, neither the economic nor the political levels of social formations governed by the ancient mode can receive a rigorous examination. First, the absence of a rigorous definition of the relations of production precludes the theoretical definition of the variant forms of this mode of production. Second, the definition of relations of production in terms of a specific form of political intervention in the economy fails to establish the necessity of that intervention in the concept of the economy itself. This means that there can be no rigorous determination of the limits to the variation in the political forms that are possible in social formations structured by the conditions of the existence of the ancient mode of production.

The inadequate conception of feudalism current in Marxist theory is the result of an error of this kind. In defining feudal relations of production in terms of a relation of lordship and servitude, a political subordination of one class to another, Marxist discussions of feudalism have conflated an economic relation with its political conditions of existence. The limitations of and the difficulties involved in such a conception are demonstrated in chapter 5. Our construction of the concept of the feudal mode of production as an articulated combination of relations and forces of production in the strict sense outlined above enables us to determine the specific character of the political and ideological relations that are possible in social formations dominated by the feudal mode.

It cannot be claimed that the concepts of the pre-capitalist modes of production outlined in this book in any way approach the level of rigour and the complexity of Marx's concept of the capitalist mode of production elaborated in *Capital*. The concept of the ancient mode is, perhaps, the least satisfactory but, even for the other modes, we have not developed a specific analysis of economic reproduction from the concept of the articulated combination of relations and forces of production. Our less than adequate conceptualisation of these modes of production has two major causes. In the first place, these concepts cannot be elaborated further unless many crucial theoretical problems of Marxism are resolved and, in particular, until adequate theories of the political and ideological instances have been developed. This is especially important in the case of those modes of production which assign the place of dominance to the political and ideological instances. Second, the level of conceptualisation in which the construction of an articulated combination of relations and forces of production provides an initial proof of the validity of a particular concept of a mode of production is sufficient to deal with the questions currently raised about pre-capitalist modes of production. To attempt to develop these concepts further would be a formalist and antiquarian exercise, a pursuit without justification in terms of its contemporary theoretical and practical relevance.

One

Primitive communism, politics and the state

In the concept of any given mode of production the economy plays a double role. It is determinant in the sense that its conditions of existence assign to each of the levels of the social formation its precise effectivity and mode of intervention with respect to the other levels. In this respect the economy plays what might be called a matrix role in determining the structure of the articulated hierarchy of levels in the social formation. The economy is also represented as a level within this articulated hierarchy. The place of dominance within the hierarchy of levels must not be confused with the matrix role of determination. In the capitalist mode of production the economy is both dominant and determinant but in other modes of production other levels occupy the dominant position. The economic level is itself structured by the double articulation of the mode of appropriation of surplus-labour, which defines the structure of relations of production, and the mode of real appropriation, or productive forces, which defines the forms of organisation of the labour process. The mode of appropriation of surplus-labour is the dominant articulation which governs the character of the corresponding productive forces.[1]

The appropriation of surplus-labour always presupposes a determinate mechanism of extraction which is articulated on a determinate set of corresponding productive forces. The precise significance of this concept of correspondence between relations of production and productive forces in the concept of mode of production is discussed in chapter 6. For the present it is sufficient to note that the mechanism of extraction of surplus-labour governs the structure of the productive forces and that the variant forms of this mechanism correspond to variations in the forms of organisation of the labour process. For example, the concept of the capitalist mechanism of extraction of surplus-labour through the production and appropriation of surplus-value involves a labour process that is also a process of self-expansion of value. This mechanism requires a certain form of separation of the labourer from his means of production in order that labour-power and means of production may both enter the labour process in the form of commodities, that is, as values. The concept of the appropriation of surplus-labour necessarily involves the articulation of determinate mechanisms of extraction of surplus-labour on to determinate forms of labour process. Conversely, the reproduction of the forces of production necessarily requires their articulation on to a mode of appropriation of surplus-labour. Forces of production 'correspond' to relations of production as the indispensable conditions of the functioning of a determinate mechanism of extraction of surplus-labour. The precise form of the correspondence is an effect of the structure of the mode of appropriation of surplus-labour. The form of correspondence of relations and forces of production in the capitalist mode of production is quite different from that in, say, the ancient or the feudal modes.

If, as a first approach to the subject of this chapter, we define primitive communism as a mode of production governed by a mode of communal appropriation of surplus-labour two immediate consequences may be deduced. First, there can be no social division of labour between a class of labourers or direct producers and a class of non-labourers. Second, the absence of a political level is a condition of existence of the economy in this mode. The mode of production must then consist of two levels only, the economic and the ideological. If there is no political level there can be no state and no state apparatus.

Nevertheless, it is clear that a definition of this kind requires considerable further elaboration before it can be taken seriously as giving the concept of a mode of production in the above sense. In particular, it fails to give us the concept of the communal mechanism of appropriation of surplus-labour and it is impossible therefore to deduce the structure of the corresponding productive forces or the necessary form of articulation of the economic and ideological levels. We shall see that there are two distinct communal mechanisms of appropriation, corresponding to the primitive communist and advanced communist (socialist) modes of production respectively, which involve quite distinct forms of ideological intervention in the economy. We shall see also that there are two major variants of the primitive communist mechanism of appropriation of surplus-labour and that the development of productive forces within primitive communism corresponds to the dominance of one of these variants.

Before proceeding to the theoretical elaborations required to establish these points it is necessary first to examine the concepts of necessary-labour and surplus-labour and to show that the presence of a determinate mode of appropriation of surplus-labour is a necessary condition for all modes of production without exception. Second, we must examine the concepts of politics and of the state and demonstrate that the existence of a political level is an effect of the structure of those modes of production characterised by a social division of labour between a class of labourers and a class of non-labourers. Where there is communal appropriation of surplus-labour there are no classes, no state and no politics. We shall therefore have to consider the question of 'government' in classless societies.

These discussions will lead on to a more precise definition of the primitive communist mode of production and of its distinction from the mode of advanced communism. The remainder of the chapter is devoted to the systematic elaboration of the theory of the primitive communist mode of production and to the specification of the two major variants of its mechanism of appropriation of surplus-labour. In the course of this discussion it will be necessary to examine recent Marxist analyses of the nature of the economic structure of lineage and segmentary societies with particular reference to the question of whether these societies are characterised by the exploitation of cadets by their elders. Here we shall see that the failure to work with an elaborated concept of the primitive communist mode of production must have grave consequences for any attempt at a Marxist anthropology. In the absence of such an elaborated concept any conclusions regarding exploitation in lineage societies are, at best, seriously misleading. Finally we shall comment on the difference between Marxism and anthropology with particular reference to the question of kinship and to Morgan's theory of the gentile constitution.

1 The concepts of necessary- and surplus-labour

> Thus we may say that surplus-value rests on a natural basis; but this is permissible only in the very general sense, that there is no natural obstacle absolutely preventing one man from disburdening himself of the labour requisite for his own existence, and burdening another with it, any more, for instance, than unconquerable natural obstacles prevent one man from eating the flesh of another. No mystical ideas must in any way be connected, as sometimes happens, with this historically developed productiveness of labour. It is only after men have raised themselves above the rank of animals, when therefore

> their labour has been to some extent socialised, that a state of things arises in which the surplus-labour of the one becomes a condition of existence for the other. At the dawn of civilisation the productiveness acquired by labour is small, but so too are the wants which develop with and by the means of satisfying them (*Capital*, I, pp. 511–12).

In this passage Marx rejects all concepts of surplus derived from the postulate of irreducible human needs. The concepts of necessary- and surplus-labour are strictly economic concepts, they are not concepts of physiology or zoology and are not derived from any extra-economic concept of given human needs. In addition, we are told that surplus-labour appears whenever 'labour has been to some extent socialised'. The division into necessary- and surplus-labour is an effect and a condition of existence of all forms of social production. Surplus-labour therefore appears in all modes of production without exception. There can be no social formation, however primitive, without surplus-labour and the mere fact that surplus-labour exists and is appropriated cannot distinguish one type of economy from another.

Marxism therefore rejects not only those concepts of surplus that are defined with respect to the physiological needs of the individual human subject but also those in which the surplus is thought to consist of an excess over the basic consumption needs of a society. Conceptions of this latter type are too often presented as Marxist. For example, Baran defines 'potential economic surplus' as 'the difference between the output that *could* be produced in a given natural and technological environment with the help of employable productive resources, and what might be regarded as essential consumption' (*The Political Economy of Growth*, p. 22). Two elements should be noted in this definition. First, it refers to what '*could* be produced' under different conditions and it therefore depends on 'the less readily visualised image of a more rationally ordered society' (*ibid.*, p. 23). The utopian and ideological character of this notion is evident. It depends on a difference between the real and the ethical ideal of a more rationally ordered society.[2] In that respect it may allow Baran and those who take a similar position, e.g. Sweezy and Gunder Frank, to launch into an ethical critique of capitalism but it has nothing whatever to do with science.

The second element is 'what might be regarded as essential consumption'. The surplus is defined as whatever is left over. This is a very common position. Herskovits, for example, defines surplus as 'an excess of goods over the minimum demands of necessity' (*Economic Anthropology*, p. 395), while Gordon Childe defines social surplus as 'food above domestic requirements' ('The birth of civilisation', p. 3). In these positions there are presumed to be very simple societies with no surplus at all while the presence or absence of a surplus and its size is thought to govern the possible forms of institutional development of a society. Herskovits, for example, explains the failure of the Bushmen of South Africa to develop a specialised ruling apparatus on the grounds that 'the Bushmen produce no surplus' (*op. cit.*, p. 399).

In his critique of such positions Pearson has shown that there can be no absolute standard in terms of which any excess provides a surplus for institutional development. If the concept of surplus is to be used at all, he maintains, it must be in a relative or constructive sense:

> A given quantity of goods or services would be surplus only if the society in some manner set these quantities aside and declared them to be available for a specific purpose. . . . The essential point is that relative surpluses are initiated by the society in question ('The Economy has no Surplus', p. 323).

This concept of surplus is properly economic; its existence and, if it exists, the form that it takes are effects of the structure of the economy. It can be defined only in terms of the manner in which the circulation of products is instituted in a given society. In this way Pearson elaborates a concept of surplus on the basis of Polanyi's theory which proposes to differentiate the types of economy according to their mode of distribution of the social product.[3] We will examine this theory in chapter 2 and will show there that an adequate theory of the types of economy cannot operate at the level of circulation. Thus while Pearson correctly recognises the importance of constructing a purely economic concept of the surplus his attempts to do so are less than successful. These arguments need not be repeated here. If Pearson's position is an advance over all extra-economic concepts of the surplus he nevertheless leaves open the possibility of an economy without surplus.

The errors of the substantive view of the economy elaborated by Polanyi and his associates are avoided in the Marxist concept of the economy as the double articulation of a mode of appropriation of surplus-labour and a mode of real appropriation. Here the appropriation of surplus-labour is a central element in the definition of any possible economy. The Marxist concept of necessary-labour is defined as that labour time necessary to secure the conditions of reproduction of the labourer. Surplus-labour, that is, labour over and above necessary-labour, exists in all modes of production because the conditions of reproduction of the labourer are not equivalent to the conditions of reproduction of the economy. This is a fundamental distinction but it cannot be recognised in a problematic such as Polanyi's which defines types of economy without reference to the process of real appropriation.

Why is surplus-labour a necessary element even in communist society? Marx provides a clear answer to this question in his *Critique of the Gotha Programme.* Paragraph 1 of this programme maintains that 'the proceeds of labour belong undiminished with equal right to all members of society'. The central part of Marx's comment on this phrase is given below:

> Let us take first of all the words 'proceeds of labour' in the sense of the product of labour; then the cooperative proceeds of labour are the *total social product.*
> From this must now be deducted:
> *First,* cover for replacement of the means of production used up.
> *Secondly,* additional portion for expansion of production.
> *Thirdly,* reserve or insurance funds to provide against accidents, dislocations caused by natural calamities, etc. These deductions from the 'undiminished proceeds of labour' are an economic necessity and their magnitude is to be determined according to available means and forces, and partly by computation of probabilities, but they are in no way calculable by equity. There remains the other part of the total product, intended to serve as means of consumption.
> Before this is divided among the individuals, there has to be deducted again, from it:
> *First, the general costs of administration not belonging to production.*
> *Secondly, that which is intended for the common satisfaction of needs,* such as schools, health services, etc.
> *Thirdly, funds for those unable to work,* etc., in short, for what is included under so-called official poor relief today (pp. 322–323).

Thus even in communist society where there is no class of non-labourers or of their functionaries to consume the surplus-product the conditions of reproduction of the economy are not reducible to the reproduction of the individual labourers. Thus, no surplus-product, no mode of production and therefore no social formation.

While surplus-labour is a necessity in all modes of production it is clearly not sufficient that this surplus-labour be performed. If the economy is to be reproduced together with its conditions of existence, then surplus-labour must always be appropriated by means of some determinate mechanism of extraction. The precise form and content of surplus-labour is therefore an effect of the mechanism by which it is extracted. It follows that necessary- and surplus-labour must always be defined with respect to some determinate mode of production. Surplus-labour exists only in its different forms and the concept of each form is internal to the concept of the mode of production in question.

It should be clear that surplus-labour does not exist solely to provide for a class of non-labourers. A class of non-labourers may or may not exist but non-labouring individuals can be found in all social formations, children, the old, the sick. In addition to those who are incapable of productive labour there may also be those who perform unproductive but socially necessary functions, for example, medical workers, teachers, ideological functionaries. In this respect the existence of a technical division of labour according to function in no way presupposes a social division of labour between classes, between a class of labourers and a class of feudal lords, capitalists, or other non-labourers. Individuals in some of these categories may also be productive labourers but it is necessary to the existence of all social formations that some functions which are not directly productive be performed. The reproduction of the economy requires that the conditions of reproduction of those who perform these functions be satisfied.

In all cases the appropriation of surplus-labour is necessary to secure the reproduction of the economy and of its conditions of existence in the totality of social relations. In some cases, namely the primitive and advanced communist modes of production, appropriation is collective. There are therefore no classes, no state and no political level. In all other modes of production the mechanism of appropriation is not collective but involves a class of non-labourers. The conditions of existence of the economy and therefore of the mode of appropriation of surplus-labour must then involve the presence of a determinate form of state and a political level in the social formation since the reproduction of the existing forms of real appropriation, i.e. the concrete labour processes, depends on the corresponding mechanism of extraction and distribution of surplus-labour. In these cases control of the conditions of production must be in the hands of the ruling class and its functionaries.

2 Politics and the state

In chapter 1 of *Ancient Society* Morgan distinguishes the two basic forms of government of human societies in the following terms:

> all forms of government are reducible to two general plans, using the word plan in its scientific sense. In their bases the two are fundamentally distinct. The first, in the order of time, is founded upon persons, and upon relations purely personal, and may be distinguished as a society (*societas*). The gens is the unit of this organisation; giving as the successive stages of integration, in the archaic period, the gens, the phratry, the tribe, and the confederacy of tribes which constituted a people or nation (*populus*). At a later period a coalescence of tribes in the same area into a nation took the place of a confederacy of tribes occupying independent areas. Such, through prolonged ages, after the gens appeared, was the substantially universal organisation of ancient society; and it remained among the Greeks and Romans after civilisation supervened. The second is founded upon territory and upon property, and may be distinguished as a state (*civitas*). The township or ward, circumscribed by metes and bounds, with the property it contains, is the basis or unit of the latter, and political society is the result. Political society is organised upon territorial areas, and deals with property as well as with persons through territorial relations. The successive stages of integration are the township or ward, which is the unit of organisation; the county or province, which is an aggregation of townships or wards; and the national domain or territory, which is an aggregation of counties or provinces; the people of each of which are organised into a body politic (pp. 6–7).

This passage contains Morgan's formulation of one of the fundamental theses of the Marxist theory of history, namely, that the existence of politics is indissolubly tied to that of the state and that both are necessarily present in some types of society and necessarily absent in others. Morgan attributes the necessity of the political organisation of society to the dominance of the idea of property which poses problems that are beyond the capacity of the gentile constitution. Where the idea of property is not dominant there is no politics. 'It is evident that the failure of gentile institutions to meet the now complicated wants of society originated the movement to withdraw all civil powers from the gentes, phratries and tribes, and re-invest them in new constituencies' (*ibid.*, p. 263).

In Morgan's text the stages in the evolution of the idea of property and the various arts of subsistence serve as indices of the structure of the economy in different societies.[4] Indices, however, are no substitute for theory. Morgan's indices, in particular, are not derived from an elaborated theory of the structure of the economy as a determinate system of social relations. For that reason the sequence of arts of subsistence in Morgan's text appears to be somewhat arbitrary while the nature of the connection which he attempts to establish between economic changes and the movement from a gentile to a political form of government remains obscure.[5] In his own presentation and analysis of Morgan's discoveries, in *The Origin of the Family, Private Property and the State* Engels finds it necessary to note: 'the forms of the changes are, in the main, described by Morgan: the economic content which gave rise to them I had largely to add myself' (p. 538).

Where Morgan refers to the growth of the idea of property which led mankind to 'establish political society on the basis of territory and of property' (*Ancient Society*, p. 6), Marxism maintains that the existence of the state and of politics is an effect of a social division of labour which is specific to certain modes of production only. In the two communist modes of production where appropriation of surplus-labour is collective, the agents of production are not divided between a class of labourers and a class of non-labourers. No state apparatus is required to maintain the mechanism of appropriation of surplus-labour and the social formation consists of two levels only, the economic and the ideological. All other modes of production are characterised by a social division of labour into classes. In these cases the political level exists as the necessary space of representation of the interests of the various classes and the presence of a state apparatus is a necessary condition of the maintenance and functioning of the mechanism of appropriation of surplus-labour by the ruling class. The presence of a political level and of the state is therefore a condition of existence of all modes of production in which the appropriation of surplus-labour is not collective. If the relations of production distribute the agents of production into classes there must be a state and a political level. If there is no state there is no political level and no politics.

Before we return to these points it is worth noting that this conception of politics and the state is fundamentally opposed to all functionalist theories in which politics is conceived as a necessary functional component of any social system. Consider, for example, Talcott Parsons's comment on the status of political science as a discipline.

> Neither power in the political sense nor the operation of government as a sub-system of the social system can be treated in terms of a specifically specialised conceptual scheme of the same order as that of economic theory, precisely for the reason that the political problem of the social system is a focus for the integration of *all* of its analytically distinguishable components, not of a specifically differentiated *class* of these components. Political science thus tends to be a synthetic science, not one built about an analytical theory as is the case with economics (*The Social System*, pp. 126–7).

In functionalist sociology and anthropology the necessity of politics is abstractly determined as a universal functional requirement through analysis of the concept of social system in general or of society in general. If politics is always with us societies may nevertheless differ in the extent to which necessary political functions are performed by structurally differentiated institutions. Parsons observes, 'There is a very wide range of variability with respect to the extent to which such a differentiated structure emerges' (p. 162). This variability with respect to the development of a differentiated political structure allows functionalists to reserve the term *state* for such a differentiated structure while *politics* refers to the abstractly defined social functions that may be performed by the state when it exists and by less differentiated structures when it does not. Thus it is possible for functionalist accounts of politics to distinguish between societies with the state and simpler, less differentiated societies without it.[6]

What must be emphasised here is that even where a distinction of this kind is made between stateless societies and the rest by functionalist writers the theoretical basis of the distinction is completely opposed to the positions of Marxism and of Morgan. For functionalism the distinction, if it is made at all, refers solely to the different institutional means for performing the same universal functions. This position is clearly stated in the concluding sentence of Krader's *Formation of the State*: 'The state achieves the same ends as societies without the state, thus affirming the continuity of human existence, but it does so by different means, thus affirming its discontinuity' (p. 110).

Here, as in Parsons's work, the emergence of specifically political institutions is conceived in terms of structural differentiation with respect to universal social functions. The teleological character of this conception is evident. The concept of structural differentiation with respect to a limited number of universal social functions implies both a fundamental directionality in social change and the existence of a more or less elaborate rank-ordering of societies according to their level of differentiation. Thus the seeds of all possible future societies are already present in the most elementary and least differentiated of societies. Since structural differentiation may be conceived with respect to distinct functional universals and the precise form and nature of functions differ according to each society's response to specific problems of adaptation to its environments Parsons must reject any simple linearity. Nevertheless he retains an overall principle of directionality in the process of rationalisation. 'We have the virtual certainty that there is an inherent factor of the general directionality of change in the process of rationalisation. . . . ' (*The Social System*, p. 501).

In Parsons's sociology the process of rationalisation is inherent in the very concept of the social system although whether any given concrete society will take any of the evolutionary paths often seems purely contingent. In this respect he reproduces the essential structures of the speculative philosophies of history in which the process of history is conceived as the realisation of a supra-historical idea. Parsons, of course, is quite exceptional in the rigour and coherence which he gives to the functionalist conception. It is clear, however, that any attempt to conceive of political or other institutions in terms of structural differentiation must exhibit a fundamentally teleological structure.

Two further effects of such a teleological conception may be briefly noted. The first is that it must imply the notion of a community of interest in the state. The state is an institution which serves the interests of society as a whole. Thus while the state may intervene to regulate or to control the conditions of class conflict it cannot be conceived as representing specifically the interests of a ruling class in that conflict. Parsons's analysis of political power as a social resource is a clear recent example of this tendency.[7]

Second, since the state is conceived as performing a universal social function, the distinction between state and stateless societies cannot be made in terms of this function. In that case the state must be conceived as universal or be defined in terms of the appearance of a certain complex of differentiated political institutions. The choice here is essentially arbitrary and has no theoretical significance since there is nothing in the concept of the function that requires the distinction between state and non-state to be sited at one level of differentiation rather than another. Thus functionalist theory, if it acknowledges the existence of stateless societies, tends towards a multiplicity of juridical and administrative conceptions of the state, towards, for example, Weber's conception of the state as having a monopoly of the legitimate use of force, or Fortes's and Evans-Pritchard's definition of the state as a type of political system with centralised authority, administrative machinery, and juridical institutions.[8] These various conceptions differ in the arbitrary choice of which specific differentiated institutions are sufficient to constitute the minimal definition of the state.

Far from defining politics and the state in terms of a teleology of the functional prerequisites of society in general, Marxism establishes the necessity of a political level as a condition of existence of certain determinate modes of production, namely, those in which the relations of production impose a social division of labour into a class of labourers and a class of non-labourers. In other modes of production there is no state and no political level. The presence of a state and a political level are, then, conditions of existence for any mechanisms of appropriation of surplus-labour by a class. We have seen that the reproduction of the conditions of real appropriation in any social formation must be affected by means of the corresponding mechanism of appropriation of surplus-labour. Raw materials, the means and conditions of production must always be distributed among the agents of production so as to enable existing forms of real appropriation to continue. It follows that in all class societies the state is a condition of existence of the process of real appropriation itself. In that respect the state, where it exists, does indeed perform functions that are absolutely necessary to the existence of society as a whole. It does not serve merely the interests of the ruling class. In this case, however, the necessity of the social functions performed by the state is itself an effect of the structure of a determinate mode of production.

It has nothing to do with the teleological necessity of the functionalist universals.

We are now in a position to examine more carefully the concepts of the state and of the political level of the social formation. Unfortunately there is as yet no systematically elaborated theory of the political level to compare with Marx's analyses of the economic level of the capitalist mode of production. We are therefore compelled to rely largely on the indications to be found in the political writings of Marx, Engels and Lenin. In the present text we can give no more than the beginnings of a theory of the political level. The following analysis differs in a number of important respects from the interesting position of Poulantzas. In particular we argue below that Poulantzas takes a formalist position in which the relative autonomy of the political level is affirmed but the conditions of its specific effectivity are not established.[9] Consider first the following passages from *The Origin of the Family, Private Property and the State* (pp. 586–7):

> As distinct from the old gentile order, the state, first, divides its subjects *according to territory*. As we have seen, the old gentile associations, built upon and held together by ties of blood, became inadequate, largely because they presupposed that the members were bound to a given territory, a bond which had long since ceased to exist. The territory remained, but the people had become mobile. Hence, division according to territory was taken as the point of departure, and citizens were allowed to exercise their public rights and duties wherever they settled, irrespective of gens and tribe. The second distinguishing feature is the establishment of a public power which no longer directly coincides with the population organising itself as an armed force. This special public power is necessary because a self-acting armed organisation of the population has become impossible since the split into classes. . . . This public power exists in every state; it consists not merely of armed men but also of material adjuncts, prisons, and institutions of coercion of all kinds, of which gentile society knew nothing.

These points may be taken separately. The first suggests that the gentile constitution became inadequate with the formation of classes because it 'presupposed that the members were bound to a given territory'. This is an unfortunate formulation. The essential point concerns the breakdown of the gentile constitution as a result of its incompatibility with the appropriation of surplus-labour by a class.

Class society requires the existence of a state and a political level as the space of representation of class interests. A number of authors have suggested the possibility of segmentary states and of nomadic states organised by clan and bound to no specific well-defined territory.[10] We cannot discuss these possibilities here but, it must be noted, the formation of such states also involves the breakdown of the gentile constitution since kinship organisation is preserved only to the extent of its integration within the political organisation of the state.

Second, the armed men together with 'material adjuncts, prisons and institutions of coercion of all kinds' constitute the coercive apparatus of the state, the 'public power'. Such an apparatus is necessary if the state is to impose and maintain the mechanism of appropriation of surplus-labour by a class. This position must not be confused with the juridical and administrative conception of the state. These institutions may be necessary to the state but they do not define it. The situational and impermanent police organisation of the Crow Indians is not, as Lowie suggests in the *Origin of the State*, an emergent form of state organisation. It is only when coercive apparatuses are organised and co-ordinated as an apparatus for the maintenance of exploitative relations of production between a class of labourers and a class of non-labourers that they are constituted as specifically state apparatuses. The absence of a state does not therefore imply the total absence of coercion:

> Only communism makes the state absolutely unnecessary, for there is *nobody* to be suppressed – 'nobody' in the sense of a *class*, of a systematic struggle against a definite section of the population. We are not utopians, and do not in the least deny the possibility and inevitability of excesses on the part of *individual persons*, or the need to stop *such excesses* (*The State and Revolution*, *Collected Works*, 25, p. 464).

The coercive apparatus of the state is necessary to its role in the maintenance of exploitative relations of production:

> Because the state arose from the need to hold class antagonisms in check, but because it arose, at the same time, in the midst of the conflict of these classes, it is, as a rule, the state of the most powerful, economically dominant class, which, through the medium of the state, becomes also the politically dominant class, and thus acquires new means of holding down and exploiting

> the oppressed class. Thus, the state of antiquity was above all the state of the slave owners for the purpose of holding down the slaves, as the feudal state was the organ of the nobility for holding down the peasant serfs and bondsmen, and the modern representative state is an instrument of exploitation of wage labour by capital (Engels, *op. cit.*, pp. 587–8).

Two essential theses may be distinguished in this passage. In the first place the conditions of existence of the state and of the political level are given in the division of society into classes with irreconcilable class interests. No classes, no state and no politics. The formation of classes with the development of a social division of labour entails an antagonistic division of interests that cannot be represented within the framework of the means of reconciliation of differences of the gentile constitution. The antagonistic division of classes cannot be contained within the system of social distinctions constituted by the structure of gentile society. The gentile constitution is therefore unable to represent or to regulate class conflict. The state and the political level emerge as the necessary mechanism of regulation of the class struggle and as the field of representation of class interests. This field of representation of interests constitutes a level of the social formation distinct from the economic and ideological levels. While these latter are present in all social formations the political level appears in class societies only.

The state is therefore a condition of existence of class society as such and is by no means reducible to its function as an instrument in the hands of the ruling class. Nevertheless, Engels insists that the state is indeed an instrument in the hands of the ruling class of non-labourers which 'through the medium of the state' is in the position of political domination. How are we to understand the character of this instrument or 'medium' through which the interests of the ruling class are represented? The essential point is that the state apparatus is not a neutral medium with respect to the interests that it represents. Marx emphasises this point as one of the fundamental lessons of the Paris Commune and he reiterates it in the 1872 Preface to the *Communist Manifesto*: 'One thing especially was proved by the Commune, *viz.*, that "the working class cannot simply lay hold of the ready-made State machinery and wield it for its own purposes".'[11] This point is of the greatest importance for the Marxist theory of the state and of politics. The working class 'cannot simply lay hold of the ready-made' machinery of the capitalist state but must replace it by a different type of state apparatus. Marx and Lenin interpret the decrees of the Commune in precisely these terms:

> The Commune, therefore, appears to have replaced the smashed state machine 'only' by fuller democracy: abolition of the standing army; all officials to be elected and subject to recall. But as a matter of fact this 'only' signifies a gigantic replacement of certain institutions by other institutions of a fundamentally different type (*The State and Revolution*, *Collected Works*, 25, p. 419).

The position expressed here is perfectly clear and there is no need to multiply quotations. If class interests are represented in the state apparatuses the relation between interest and means of representation is not one of expression. The means of representation themselves have their own specific effectivity in determining the conditions of political practice. Failure to recognise this point is one of the characteristics of reformist interpretations of Marxism.[12] It follows that the content of the class struggle cannot be simply read off from the behaviour of political organisations since the very structure of these organisations determines the conditions of representation. The capture of state power does not consist in replacing the top men in existing apparatuses but in the transformation or destruction of the apparatuses themselves. State power does not, therefore, relate to the state apparatuses as an external and controlling agency. It consists in the apparatuses themselves.

We can now formulate the definitions of politics and the state which must suffice for the present text. We begin with the concept of state power which, as a result of the preceding discussions, may be defined as the organised set of state apparatuses which together constitute the conditions of the maintenance and imposition of a determinate mechanism of extraction of surplus-labour by a class. These apparatuses may be economic, political or ideological. It is their unity as an instrument of class domination that constitutes them as a state power. The state is therefore tied, as a necessary condition of their existence, to relations of production which distribute the agents of production into classes. State power serves to maintain, or, in periods of transition from one mode of production to another, to transform, the overall structure of relations between classes.

The concept of state power leads in to that of political practice. By practice we refer to any process of transformation of a determinate given raw material into a determinate product by means of determinate human labour using determinate means.[13] The raw materials of political practice are social relations between classes. The transformation of the overall structure of these relations clearly involves the capture of state power; their preservation involves the retention and exercise of this power. In this sense the objective of political practice is always and necessarily the control and exercise of state power. Marxist political texts have always insisted on making the structures of the state the specific strategic objective of political practice. Here, for example, are the opening lines of Lenin's *One of the Fundamental Questions of the Revolution*: 'The key question of every revolution is undoubtedly the question of state power. Which class holds power decides everything' (*Collected Works*, 25, p. 366).

The political level, as we have seen, is the site of political practice in the social formation. Its existence is therefore an effect of the structure of the economic level of the dominant mode of production. If the appropriation of surplus-labour is collective there are no classes, no state power and no politics. Otherwise classes, politics and the state are necessarily present. The political level is the space of representation of class interests. It is constituted as the totality of the means of political practice of the various classes, the forms and instrumentalities of their political representation. It is necessary to insist on the importance of the means and instruments of political practice in the general definition of the political level. Political practice can take place only by means of determinate political apparatuses, parties, state apparatuses, armies, in which bodies of men are gathered into determinate organisational structures. We have seen in our analysis of the concept of state power that these apparatuses cannot be conceived as being merely formal channels for the expression of class interests that are determined elsewhere – for example, in the economy. The state apparatus itself is the primary instrument of the political practice of the ruling class. Other classes are represented at the political level in state apparatuses, parties, and other organisational forms.

It is his failure to consider the *means* of political practice that ensures the ultimate formalism of Poulantzas's sophisticated attempt at a systematic elaboration of the Marxist theory of politics and the state. Poulantzas notes, quite correctly, that the specificity of the political cannot be defined solely by reference to the object, i.e. the raw material, and the product of political practice.

> They need to be completed by an adequate conception of the political superstructure. For if we define the political simply as

> *practice* with clearly defined objects and products, we risk diluting its specificity and finally identifying everything which 'transforms' a given unity as political (*Political Power and Social Classes*, p. 42).

So far, so good. We cannot define the political solely by its object without examining political structures. How does Poulantzas conceive of these structures? 'We must also locate inside a social formation the specific place and function of the level of political structures which are its *objective*' (*ibid.*). Thus the political structures are not defined as the *means or instruments* of political practice but as its *objective*.[14] Poulantzas then proceeds to the following definition: 'the political structures of a mode of production and of a social formation consist of *the institutionalised power of the state*' (*ibid.*). Poulantzas is therefore compelled to distinguish between the field of political practice whose objective is the state and the political structures themselves. Political practice is defined by its objective without reference to its instruments. This ensures the formalism of Poulantzas's conception of politics, which, in the end, is no more than a complicated form of reductionism.[15] The relative autonomy of the political level is affirmed in this position but the conditions of the specific effectivity of the political in the determination of class interests is denied. It follows that the means of political practice must be conceived as formal and indifferent channels of transmission of class interests having no specific effectivity with respect to the form or content of the interests themselves. Thus political practice is reduced to a mere reflection of class interests that are determined solely at the economic level. In Poulantzas's text reductionism is complicated by the assertion of the relative autonomy of the political level. That autonomy, however, does not refer to the field of political practice which, as we have seen, is conceived as distinct from the political level. The complication of this reductionist conception of politics therefore consists in the effective denial of the autonomy of political *practice* combined with the affirmation of the autonomy of the political level.

A particularly clear example of the effects of this position can be found in his *Fascism and Dictatorship* where a crisis of political representation is equated with the manifest withdrawal of support by fractions of the ruling class from the parties which represent them and even from the system of political parties in general. Here one political form fails to serve class interests and another form is adopted instead. Representation is displaced from the party to branches of the state apparatus. Here the means of representation are conceived as being determined by what has to be represented. In effect they are taken to be indifferent forms that are available to class interests that are pre-given to them.

Thus, in contrast to Poulantzas's conception, it is necessary to conceive of the representation of class interests at the political level as the product of a determinate political practice with determinate means of representation in the apparatuses of the political level and determinate conditions of existence in the structure of that level and the forms of intervention of the economic and ideological levels within it. It is the necessity of political representation in determinate political apparatuses and their articulation in the structure of the political level as a whole that governs the specific effectivity of politics in the determination of class interests. There is therefore no contradiction in supposing that the state is the primary instrument of the political practice of the ruling class and that the state apparatuses also furnish the means of representation of other classes. The means of representation have their own specific effectivity and cannot be conceived as merely expressing interests that are given to politics from elsewhere. The importance of this point will be apparent in our analysis of the place of the army and of patron–client relations in the political conflicts of the later Roman Republic in chapter 2. As another example we may cite the case of parliamentary parties in the democratic variety of capitalist state. These parties represent the interests of the various classes under conditions of representation which serve the interests of the bourgeoisie. The political apparatuses of the bourgeois-democratic state certainly provide instruments for the political representation of the working class in the form of trade-unionist politics whose objective is the modification of the conditions of the economic class struggle. But, as Lenin observes, there is politics and politics. 'Trade-unionist politics of the working class is precisely *bourgeois politics* of the working class' (*What is to be Done?*, *Collected Works*, 5, p. 426). The effectivity of the means of representation, trade unions and their political representatives, is particularly striking in this case. The conditions of representation of the working class serve the political interests of the bourgeoisie. For that reason Lenin's answer to his rhetorical question: what type of organisation do we require?, is that we require not a legal or parliamentary party but 'a single All-Russian organisation of revolutionaries' (*ibid.*, p. 511).

This discussion of the Marxist theory of the political level and the state has, of necessity, been formal and abstract. We have considered the general conditions of existence of the state apparatuses and the political level of those modes of production characterised by a social division of labour into a class of labourers and a class of non-labourers. This structure governs the necessity of a political class conflict but it does not, at this level of generality, determine the precise forms and apparatuses in which this conflict is to be fought out. For that we must refer to the analysis of the concrete conditions in determinate social formations. Such an analysis itself involves the theory of the mode of production dominant in that formation which establishes the general character of the state (feudal, capitalist, etc.) as a function of the specific articulation of instances given by the matrix role of the economy. The differential analysis of political forms cannot be attempted here but some discussion of politics will be necessary in connection with the other modes of production examined in this text. It is sufficient here to insist that the characteristic features of bourgeois-democratic politics must not be treated as defining characteristics of politics in general.

Finally, in this discussion, we must add a few brief remarks on the question of the formation of the state. It follows from the preceding argument that the process of the formation of the state is identical to the process of transition from primitive communism to some other mode of production. The problem of how the periods of transition from one mode of production to another are to be conceived is examined in chapter 6, in connection with the transition from feudalism to capitalism. That discussion need not be repeated here but it is necessary to note that there can be no theory of transition in general and that the transition from one mode of production to another cannot be conceived either as a unitary event or as an evolutionary development. There can be no question therefore of conceiving the formation of the state as being the singular effect of a single cause, such as conquest, or combination of causes or as an evolutionary growth resulting, say, from the quantitative increase in trade or private property.

As far as the question of the formation of the state is concerned we are not faced merely with the problem of transition from primitive communism to one determinate mode of production. Instead we must consider transitions from primitive communism to feudalism, to the ancient mode of production, and possibly to others. In *The Origin of the Family, Private Property, and the State* Engels examines two of these transitions. Thus his text presents not an analysis of the formation of the state in general but separate analysis of the formation of the feudal state among the Germans and of the ancient state in Rome and Athens. Here again Engels discusses the Athenian and the Roman states separately and quite correctly refuses to provide an analysis of the formation of the ancient state in general. Each concrete transition is effected in its own specific sequence of transitional conjunctures and the theory of transition consists in the analysis of the conjunctures and of the displacements involved in the movement from one conjuncture to the next.

It is true that all transitions from primitive communism to class society have the following in common. They all involve the formation of a social division of labour between a class of labourers and a class of non-labourers, and the formation of a state apparatus and a political level. However, this should not be taken to imply the possibility of a theory of the formation of the state or of the political level in general. We are always concerned with the formation of a determinate political level of a determinate type during the period of transition in which a determinate social formation moves from the dominance of the primitive communist mode of production to that of some determinate exploitative mode of production.

3 The primitive communist mode of production

It will be recalled that our preliminary definition of primitive communism as a mode of production characterised by a collective appropriation of surplus-labour merely specifies (1) that there are no classes, no state and no politics, and (2) that the mode of production consists of the articulated combination of the economic and the ideological levels. We have shown that the concept of politics is not defined by reference to certain universal social functions of integration and co-ordination. It follows that the absence of politics and of the state by no means implies the absence of organisation and co-ordination. Collective appropriation of surplus-labour in no way precludes the existence of administrative apparatuses or of individuals who perform unproductive but socially necessary functions.

We have yet to define the economic basis of the primitive communist mode of production as a determinate articulated combination of a mode of appropriation of surplus-labour and a corresponding mode of real appropriation. The abstract and formal preliminary definition given above does little more than assert that there is a primitive communist mode of production and that it consists of two levels only, the economic and the ideological. Assertion cannot take the place of theory. It is one thing to assert that primitive communism exists, it is quite another to establish it in its concept. As we have seen it is the structure of the economy in its matrix role of determination that defines the necessary and specific form of articulation of instances in the concept of the mode of production. In the absence, therefore, of the elaborated concept of the economic level of the primitive communist mode of production we have no theoretical basis for differentiating between primitive and advanced communism, two modes of production that have always been distinguished in the Marxist tradition. The remainder of this chapter is concerned to establish the concept of primitive communism as a determinate mode of production and to examine some of the theoretical effects of this concept. First it is necessary to show that primitive and advanced communism are quite distinct articulated combinations of a mode of appropriation of surplus-labour and a mode of real appropriation.

Briefly, advanced communism is characterised by Marx by the slogan 'From each according to his ability, to each according to his needs' (*The Critique of the Gotha Programme*, p. 325). The mode of appropriation of the product under advanced communism transcends those limitations of bourgeois right that remain under socialism. In particular the proportionality of labour-time expended to rewards is absent. The distribution of the product under advanced communism is precisely according to needs and not relative to the amount of labour. Determination of the distribution of the social product is collective and based on production planned according to the calculation of social needs. Thus advanced communism involves a complex division of labour, centralised and scientifically planned production and highly developed forces of production. Without these conditions it is impossible for social production to be organised without coercion. Thus, under socialism the distribution of rewards in proportion to labour-time is itself a clear form of coercion: 'If he does not labour neither shall he eat.'

The advanced communist mode of appropriation of surplus-labour may be defined as that of scientifically planned production to satisfy social needs.

> [Society] will have to arrange its plan of production in accordance with its means of production, which include in particular its labour-power. The useful effects of the various articles of

consumption, compared with one another and with the quantities of labour required for their production, will in the end determine the plan (Engels, *Anti-Duhring*, p. 37).

It is clear that these relations of production can only correspond to highly developed productive forces which make it possible to overcome the anarchy of production based on a multiplicity of independent units.[16]

Primitive communism on the other hand is characterised by a very limited development of productive forces and a limited division of labour. If there are no classes there is no surplus-product sufficient to maintain a class of non-labourers, together with their unproductive functionaries. The slogan 'From each according to his abilities, to each according to his needs' is impossible to apply. Nor is there any proportionality of labour to reward. Elders may receive more than cadets and men may receive more than women. Appropriation is collective by temporary or semi-permanent co-operative groups or by ideological unities into which the collective is divided, households, kinship groups, etc. The distribution of the product follows ideological criteria.

Our problem is not merely to show that primitive communism is indeed different from advanced communism. Rather it concerns the establishment of the conceptual basis for this distinction through the elaborated concept of the primitive communist mode of production. In the absence of such an elaborated concept we are left with little but a vague descriptive term designating whatever precedes class society, and with no rational grounds for asserting that primitive communism refers to a single mode of production in any strict sense. We shall see that the failure to work within an elaborated concept of primitive communism has led to serious errors of analysis on the part of Marxist anthropologists.

In the remainder of this chapter we establish that there is indeed a single primitive communist mode of production. The economic level is governed by a mode of appropriation of surplus-labour quite distinct from that of advanced communism which we shall call appropriation through the mechanism of the redistribution of the product. This mechanism, in its two major variants, simple and complex redistribution, governs the forms of the corresponding productive forces in this mode of production. We shall see, in particular, that the greatest development of productive forces necessarily involves the predominance of the second variant form, and that it is therefore tied to the growth of the gentile organisation. In this way we shall establish, as Engels in fact fails to do, the conditions of existence of the gentile constitution in the structure of the economic level of the primitive communist mode of production. The implications of this result with regard to contemporary anthropological theories of kinship will have to be briefly considered in a concluding section.

a THE RELATIONS OF PRODUCTION

The relations of production in this mode of production are constituted on the basis of ideological social relations between individuals. The product of any given labour process is distributed among the producers and others through the intervention of determinate social relations between the individuals involved. These forms of distribution of the product constitute the mechanism of appropriation of surplus-labour within primitive communism. We shall call this mechanism appropriation through the redistribution of the product. The mechanism of redistribution ensures both the reproduction of the labourer and the reproduction of the economy. To say that the relationships through which redistribution is effected are *ideological* is to say that they are constituted as the product of determinate ideological practices. They are not *economic* in the sense of being derived from the purchase of labour-power or of labourers, and they are not politico-juridical relations dependent on the intervention of the state. The relationships may be temporary or semi-permanent existing only for the duration of the hunt or of the growing season or for a number of such periods in succession. In these cases the distribution of the product of labour takes place through the variant of simple redistribution. Alternatively the relationships may be established on a permanent basis through the location of individuals at determinate points in a more or less extended network of kinship and marriage relations. Whether the structure of the network corresponds to genealogical relations or depends on purely notional kinship categories is of no significance here. What is important is that a system of kinship and marriage categories together with the real or imaginary ancestries that demarcate distinct marriage classes allow the definition of precise relationships between any two members of the collectivity. In this sense kinship provides the basis for redistribution of the product through a network of individuals far beyond the limits of those engaged in a determinate labour process. We shall argue below that kinship relations of one kind or another provide the only possible basis for a network of complex redistribution within primitive communism.

In both simple and complex redistribution the criteria governing the division of the product can only be ideological. The product is distributed in this precise way and no other because of these precise relationships between individuals. This collective mechanism of redistribution of the product is therefore quite distinct from the social planning mechanism of advanced communism. In the latter the product is distributed to individuals and to units of production not on the basis of determinate relations between one individual and another but on the basis of the scientific calculation of social needs. The two variants of simple and complex redistribution are both governed by the intervention of ideological social relations in the economic level. They differ in the character of the network through which redistribution takes place. One is restricted in scope and impermanent, the other is extended and relatively stable. In both variants it is clear that the ideological must be the dominant level in the social formation. Some examples will clarify these points. We shall see that these differences between the two variants are of the greatest importance for the analysis of so-called primitive societies.

(i) *Simple redistribution*

Here we are concerned with the redistribution of the product by means of a network of relations established on a temporary or semi-permanent basis. In the following passage from his *Anthropologie économique des Gouro de Côte d'Ivoire* Meillassoux compares the division of the respective products of hunting and agriculture.

> Whilst the hunt provides nourishment of quality but contributes only a fraction of the food supply, agricultural products are varied and proportionately abundant and constitute its daily base. Hunting is an intermittent activity with an instantaneous product. Agricultural production is the opposite, resulting from the completion of multiple and complex operations. The first requires the discontinuous and provisional cooperation of an effective minimum of men assembled to carry out a single task. The second demands regular cooperation sustained by individuals of both sexes to an extent which varies according to the nature of the work. For this reason, the collective hunt is associated with a large but structurally diffuse territorial group:

> the village; whereas agriculture is the continuous activity of social cells which are more restricted but more compact: the family communities and their social extensions. Finally, the product of hunting is the object of sharing, in its raw state, between the participants; the products of agriculture are treated and cooked and consumed in the course of a communal meal by the individuals or groups which have cooperated in the agricultural or domestic labours (p. 123).

Agriculture is discussed under the heading of complex redistribution. Hunting involves the complex co-ordination of a large number of men on an intermittent basis. Hunting with nets involves all the men in the village. Trapping of large animals involves a smaller number.

> Here again the enterprise could be undertaken on the initiative of a leader. After locating the beast, the hunter would assemble a team of 10 to 12 men to position a trap on the animals' anticipated path; the trap would be made of a heavy hunting spear suspended from the branches and the elephant would cause it to fall in its path. The sharing would be done on a collective basis much wider even than in the case of hunting with nets. The hunter would receive the tusks and certain parts of the animal, sometimes the trunk and the feet, sometimes the heart and the liver. He would reserve certain choice morsels for the elders of his village; the rest would be left for quarry in which not only the inhabitants of the hunter's village would participate but also those of the tribe and eventually of the neighbouring tribes which were in the vicinity (*ibid.*, pp. 98–9).

In this case the distribution of the product goes far beyond the circle of immediate producers. This point will be taken up later. Notice that while the product of the hunt does not provide the staple diet of the Gouro it is shared on the basis of simple redistribution with complex redistribution intervening in the case of the product of trapping of large animals. Thus hunting appears to provide an example of a complex labour process involving relatively large numbers on the basis of simple redistribution. However, this complex form of co-operation depends on the formation of work groups out of members of a village community who depend for their subsistence primarily on agriculture organised on the basis of complex redistribution. Among the Gouro complex redistribution is dominant and it is only this dominance that allows these complex forms of co-operation in hunting to develop.

What happens in communities where simple redistribution predominates? Consider the following description:

> There is no social structure more fragile, or shorter-lived than the Nambikwara band. If the chief is too exacting, if he allots himself too large a share of the women, or if he cannot find enough food for his subjects during the dry season, discontentment follows immediately. Individuals, or whole families, will break away from the group and go off to join a band with a better reputation. This other band may be better fed, thanks to the discovery of better places for hunting and scavenging; or it may have a larger store of ornaments, thanks to favourable exchanges with neighbour bands; or it may even have become more powerful as a result of a victorious campaign. One day the leader will find himself at the head of a group too small either to cope with the difficulties of everyday life or to protect its women from the designs of outsiders. When that happens he will just have to give up his position and ally himself and his few supporters with some more fortunate group (Lévi-Strauss, *Tristes Tropiques*, p. 300).

Lévi-Strauss appears to find the paucity of their natural resources a sufficient explanation for the division of the Nambikwara into bands. However, the availability of resources can only affect the size of viable bands. It cannot govern the formation of bands itself. Lévi-Strauss's description fits the characteristic forms of social life of hunting and gathering peoples in which, as we shall argue, simple redistribution must tend to predominate. In these cases, except in habitats unusually rich in edible plant and animal life, the complex co-operation characteristic of the Gouro hunt is unattainable. While complex co-operation within the more or less extensive band is still possible it cannot be relied on as a source of sustenance precisely because of the instability of the band itself. For this reason the, temporarily, larger bands tend not to develop the complex forms of hunting achieved by the Gouro. It should be clear that this argument does not concern the skills of hunting that may be developed by individuals or groups but rather the possibility or otherwise of hunting on the basis of the complex co-operation of large numbers of men. The productivity of labour under the domination of simple redistribution must therefore tend to be relatively low.

(ii) *Complex redistribution*

Here we are concerned with the distribution of the product throughout a stable and permanent network of relationships that is established in advance of any particular labour process or any temporary formation of groups. Again we take the Gouro as our example. The village community consists of one or more lineages or branches of a lineage each with an elder at its head. Other individuals have various statuses according to whether they are adult, married, the head of a family, and so on. The community divides into a number of work teams of various sizes for particular agricultural tasks:[17]

> The agricultural tasks of each [work team] are not the same but are hierarchised according to the nature of the work and the degree of cooperation it requires, with the result that the teams are not only added to but also fitted into each other. The smallest teams are composed of one or more monogamous or polygamous households (*ménages*) and correspond to the domestic groups formed according to the feminine plan (i.e. according to the distribution of women); they carry out mainly the tasks of crop maintenance such as binding yams, fencing rice fields, weeding grasses, day to day harvesting. The *gone* (male adult) may have assistance in these labours from kinsmen or friends within the framework of the *klala* (an association of a territorial kind in which the members are linked by relations of kinship and neighbourhood). A community consists of several teams which collect together to undertake the more exacting labours or those needing to be done in a short time: clearing undergrowth, earthing up, harvesting, etc. At this level, the elder of a community can call on a wider cooperative institution, the *bo* (an occasional form of collective labour organisation bringing together teams which are not regularly constituted) assembling kinsmen or neighbours (Meillassoux, *op. cit.*, p. 172).

The distribution of the agricultural product takes place as follows:

> The circulation of valued food crops (rice especially) begins the moment when, as the fruit of communal labour, it takes on a finished form, that is, after the harvest. The harvest will be accumulated in the community's storehouses and placed under the direct or indirect control of the elder. The second brother or the first wife will often have the management of it. The

> product will be used in the first place to feed the members of the community, occasionally a passing visitor, some kinsmen from neighbouring villages or the participants of a *bo*. A generally insubstantial fraction will now and then be exchanged or sold.
>
> The elder (*doyen*) of the community is the pole of the system of circulation. The production of the group makes movement towards him then returns for the greater part, if not in its totality, towards the members of the community (*ibid.*, p. 188).

In addition when a man achieves a certain adult status, e.g. married with children, he obtains partial control over the distribution of the product of his labour and that of his household: one part goes to the community, the other is retained. Finally, in the daily collective meal the food is distributed into groupings on the basis of age, status and sex, that is, not on the basis of work teams or families:

> By means of this fairly involved mechanism, the food products are redistributed to all the members of the community, and in this way the collective meal turns out to be the culmination of a process of agricultural co-operation: each person's indistinct labour reappears in a communal product. All mixed their labour and all participate in the product of the labour of all the others (*ibid.*, pp. 124–5).

The labour of each individual is 'indistinct' in the sense that there is no form of calculation which can assess the relative contributions of different individuals towards the final product. In this case it is clear that the social product itself depends upon a pre-existing system of relationships between members of the community. Otherwise, in a band collective for example, the co-ordinated labour of several work teams could not be achieved on any regular basis. The distribution of the product within the village community and beyond it is effected through this same system of pre-given relationships. Each individual receives his portion of the product on the basis of the position he occupies in the network and not on the basis of any temporary relationship he may have established with other individuals. The concrete operation of the distribution of the product through a system of complex redistribution is, of course, modified by disputes within the lineage, by punishment, and so on. Thus temporary interpersonal relationships may intervene in the functioning of the system but they do not define it.

(iii) *Comments*

These remarks have described and illustrated the two variant forms of the mechanism of appropriation of surplus-labour by means of the redistribution of the product. In making this distinction between variants it must be emphasised that we are not concerned with the multiplicity of different concrete lineage formations or with the numerous organisational forms taken by band collectives. Differences at that level have a definite effectivity with respect to the economy but they do not concern the structural properties of the mechanism of collective appropriation of surplus-labour. Simple and complex redistribution have distinct structural properties as mechanisms of collective appropriation which are independent of the concrete set of relations in which the mechanism may be realised. The concepts of the mechanism and of its variant forms are *economic* concepts. Each variant form requires as its condition of existence a system of ideological social relations with determinate properties since it is constituted by the intervention of these relations in the economy. To establish a principle of variation at the level of the economy is not to deny the existence or the effectivity of variation at the ideological level. On the contrary it is the structure of the mechanism of extraction of surplus-labour in the primitive communist mode of production that establishes the conditions of intervention of the ideological level in the economic.

In the primitive communist mode of production the extraction of surplus-labour is governed by some combination of the variant forms of the mechanism of appropriation. The mode of real appropriation corresponding to that mechanism and to its variant forms will be examined below. As for the distribution of the means of production, land and simple tools, it is clear that the appropriation of surplus-labour by means of the redistribution of the product requires that property be vested in the productive community, in the lineage or in the band collective. Possession in the sense of the effective capacity to set the means of production to work may reside at various levels within the community. Among the Gouro we find, for example, that wooden tools, mortars, pestles, canoes can 'be described as goods for collective use which are very freely borrowed and lent' (*ibid.*, p. 191) while possession of iron tools (machetes) remains at the level of the elder. Land is subject to overlapping proprietary rights at the level of the lineage, the village and the tribe.

b THE PRODUCTIVE FORCES

We have now to establish that the primitive communist mode of appropriation of surplus-labour corresponds to a determinate set of productive forces. To begin with, it is clear that collective appropriation through the redistribution of the product allows for the development of relatively complex forms of co-operation but that it absolutely precludes the complex division of labour characteristic of capitalist manufacture and industry or of advanced communism. In the absence of social planning relations the co-ordination of production must be left to the labourers themselves and to the possibilities of supervision and co-ordination given in the network of individual relations. For example, elders and adults of various statuses may supervise and co-ordinate the labour of those ranked below them in the lineage. Division of labour within the unit of production is limited by the available social mechanisms of supervision and co-ordination.

At the same time the growth of a technical division of labour within the community as a whole is effectively precluded by the mechanisms of appropriation and distribution of the product. The development of specialised labour processes necessarily involves the exchange of products between units of production. This exchange may be effected on the basis of commodity production and commercial exchange or of planning. But neither of these forms of exchange of products can develop to any great extent under primitive communist relations of production. Commodity production itself is not entirely precluded but under conditions of collective appropriation it cannot form the primary means of distribution of products *within* the community. It follows that commodity relations can only develop within primitive communism through the exchange of products between communities.

Thus the relations of production effectively limit the division of labour both at the level of the unit of production and at the level of the community as a whole. While these conditions do not entirely preclude specialist forms of production, for example, metal working, pottery or salt production, only a small minority can be engaged in such work. For the bulk of the population subsistence food production is the order of the day.

(i) *Simple redistribution*

So far we have examined the effects of collective appropriation through the redistribution of the product without considering the two variant forms of the mechanism of appropriation. Consider first the form taken by the productive forces under conditions of the dominance of simple redistribution. Here kinship relations are very elementary and do not form the basis of any durable social relations. The predominant form of the community is the band collective characterised by an extreme instability of membership. It consists of a small number of adults and their children and individuals or family groups may leave the band at any time.

This instability of band membership has serious effects on the forms of co-operative labour process that may develop. Division of labour, as Engels puts it, 'was a pure and simple outgrowth of nature: it existed only between the sexes' (*The Origin* . . . , p. 577). The reason for this is clear. The instability of size and membership of the band means that the division between the sexes is the only possible basis for a permanent specialisation of labour tasks. The band always contains some men and some women and usually a number of children, but the numbers of each are extremely variable. It follows that while the men or women of the band may co-operate in collective labour they cannot develop a system of co-operation based on the co-ordination of discrete individual tasks. Not only does this inhibit complex co-operation, in which individuals perform different tasks as part of the same labour process, it also severely limits the extended simple co-operation which depends on several individuals performing the same task in sequence. Thus temporary and intermittent forms of co-operation and division of labour may develop but no permanent organisation of labour in terms of a number of discrete statuses can arise. Division of labour in terms of age statuses is also precluded, except between adults, young children, and possibly the aged, because the conditions of maintenance of a system of age statuses do not exist.

So far then we have division of labour between the sexes and relatively simple forms of co-operation. But the effects of the dominance of simple redistribution go even further. Settled agricultural production requires a certain level of stability and continuity in the producing community. In this respect it matters little whether agriculture takes the form of the raising of plant crops or the raising and herding of animals. Here we shall take the former as our example. At least until the end of the growing period it is necessary that the land be cleared and worked in a systematic fashion. Under given conditions clearing and preparation of land, weeding and harvesting, all require a determinate number of labourers for a given area of land. At any given time the labourers depend on the product of the last completed cycle for food and for seed with which to begin the next cycle of production. When the size and membership of the collective is unstable agriculture, if conducted at all, can only be on the basis of small individual plots of land that are quite unable to furnish the main source of subsistence from one year to the next. Thus Lévi-Strauss reports that

> the Nambikwara year is divided into two distinct parts. During the rainy season, from October to March, each group . . . builds for itself rough and ready huts with branches and palm-leaves. In a burnt-out clearing in the forest gallery which fills the damp lower part of each valley they plant and till their gardens. . . . From these gardens they get enough food to keep them going *during part of their sedentary period*. . . . At the beginning of the dry season they abandon their village and split up into small roving bands. *For seven months these nomadic groups wander across the savannah in search of game* (our emphasis) (*Tristes Tropiques*, pp. 265–6).

The domination of simple redistribution therefore involves an extremely limited development of productive forces, a rudimentary division of labour between sexes, and a mode of subsistence based on hunting and gathering together, perhaps, with extremely limited and primitive forms of gardening.

(ii) *Complex redistribution*

With the dominance of complex redistribution the productive forces remain subject to the limitations determined by the general structure of the collective appropriation of surplus-labour through the redistribution of the product. Nevertheless considerable developments are possible within these general limits which are precluded under the dominance of simple redistribution. In the first place all of the forms of labour process, co-operation and division of labour developed under conditions of simple redistribution are possible also under the dominance of complex redistribution. In addition the greater stability in size and membership of the collective under this second form makes possible a systematic division of labour between individuals and the development of forms involving co-operation between work teams.

We have given an example of what can be achieved in this way in

Meillassoux's description of the Gouro system of agricultural production. Here production involves a whole series of overlapping and co-operating work teams. Some tasks require the labour of the whole village community and may even involve more extensive groupings. Other agricultural tasks are performed by lineages and portions of lineages, by the men or the women of particular groups, and so on. Agricultural production, then, involves a number of separate work teams each of which depends on the labour performed by other teams. While individual work teams are organised on the basis of simple co-operation it is clear that agricultural production among the Gouro involves the complex co-operation of the village community as a whole.

It is necessary to insist on this last point since Terray in the second part of his *Marxism and 'Primitive' Societies*, a commentary on Meillassoux's work, and Meillassoux himself to some extent contrast the *complex* co-operation of the collective hunt to the *simple* co-operation of agriculture as defining two distinct modes of production. In fact, as we shall argue later, it is impossible to use such essentially technical criteria as the basis for differentiating between modes of production.[18] The contrast between agriculture and hunting is, in any event, somewhat misleading. It is true that the collective hunt involves two distinct tasks, hunting and beating, which must be co-ordinated. To that extent the product of the hunt is the result of complex co-operation. Agriculture, however, also involves a number of discrete and interdependent tasks which must be performed at different times. Thus the difference between the hunt and agricultural production among the Gouro concerns not so much the complexity of co-operation but the length of the necessary production time. Terray interprets Meillassoux's findings as showing that Gouro society consists of two modes of production in combination: a tribal–village mode based on complex co-operation (hunting) and a lineage mode based on simple co-operation (agriculture). The latter is said to be dominant over the former. This interpretation, later supported by Meillassoux ('From reproduction to production', p. 98), is completely without foundation. Such a difference at the level of technique is hardly sufficient to demarcate between modes of production. We shall return to the theoretical errors of Meillassoux and Terray in a later section of this chapter.

As for the collective hunt itself we have seen that it involves the temporary and intermittent complex co-operation of relatively large numbers of men. Among the Gouro it seems that the distribution of the product of the hunt is governed by simple redistribution alone or in combination with complex redistribution. Nevertheless, if this form of production is to take place a certain necessary number of men must be readily available. We have seen that the requisite numbers cannot be provided by collectives governed by the dominance of simple redistribution. Meillassoux is therefore mistaken in suggesting that the collective hunt is the major integrating factor in the community.

> None of the forms of co-operation linked to other activities, even agriculture, is so extensive. Collective hunting with nets is an activity associated with the whole village and never with any smaller unit. It contributes to the making of cohesion between lineages often of distant origin (*Anthropologie* . . . , p. 99).

On the contrary the very possibility of the Gouro collective hunt requires the existence of a community already 'integrated' by other mechanisms. Meillassoux clearly interprets the collective hunt as performing the function of a collective ritual serving to reinforce collective sentiments. Such positions may have a place within a Durkheimian problematic of the forms of ritual and social cohesion but it has nothing whatever to do with Marxism.[19]

It has been argued, then, that the dominance of appropriation of surplus-labour by complex redistribution makes possible the formation of production communities that are larger and more stable than the band collectives characterised by the domination of simple redistribution. Within these larger communities the rudimentary sexual division of labour can be refined and more complex forms of co-operative labour process may be developed in connection with horticulture, herding, and even with the hunting and gathering practised by the band. In these respects the second variant of the primitive communist mechanism of appropriation of surplus-labour leads to a great increase in the productivity of labour within the primitive community.

Thus the primitive community in which the mechanism of complex redistribution is dominant tends to be characterised, first, by a greater productivity of labour, and second, by a greater number of labourers as compared with the band collective. These two characteristics involve an absolute increase in the volume of surplus-labour appropriated by the community. This fact is of the greatest importance in the history of primitive communism for two distinct reasons.

First, the improvements in both the volume of food production per head and the total number of heads make it possible for the community to support specialist producers who do not engage exclusively in food production and who may not produce food at all. The traditional Gouro community, according to Meillassoux, contains a number of specialist artisans engaged in metalwork, weaving, basket-making, and so on.

> The artisan is always integrated into a social unit built around agricultural activities . . . objects are made for the benefit of the elder or of the community as a whole and the only return the artisan receives for his labour is the food he shares with his group just as if he had been engaged in agricultural work (*ibid.*, pp. 189–90).

Among the Gouro these specialists are also agricultural labourers but a greater level of specialised production is clearly possible within such communities. This specialisation in turn leads to increases in the level of food production through the improvement of agricultural implements, hunting weapons, and the means of food preparation and storage. It is clear that this degree of specialisation cannot be sustained under the domination of simple redistribution.

Second, the community is in a position to support an increase in the unproductive population, in the number of the young, the old and infirm on the one hand, and in adults engaged, wholly or in part, in unproductive activities on the other. We shall take these points separately. The instability of the band collective and the low productivity of its labour impose severe limits on the size of families.

> The Nambikwara have few children; childless couples are not uncommon, though one or two children constitute the norm, and it is quite exceptional for there to be more than three in one family. Sexual relations between parents are forbidden while the child remains unweaned: often, that is to say, until it is three years old . . . the women do not hesitate to resort to abortion of one kind or another – medicinal plants, or some mechanical device – in case of need (*Tristes Tropiques*, p. 273).

There are no such severe limits on family size with the level of productivity that may be achieved under the dominance of complex redistribution. Communities therefore tend to reach a larger size than could be attained by the band collective and are in a position to introduce a systematic division of labour on the basis of age statuses.

For the same reason lineages that are depleted by disease or warfare are in a better position to replace lost members through natural growth than the band collective.

The possibility of sustaining unproductive labourers among the adult population has a different significance. In the first place the relatively high level of productivity achieved by the community depends on the sustaining of a systematic division of labour and a complex co-operation over long periods of time. These require not only a system of complex redistribution but also a certain necessary-labour of supervision and co-ordination. This socially necessary but unproductive labour develops alongside and together with the increase in the productivity of labour. Each is a condition of existence of the other.

In addition the increased productivity of labour allows the development of ceremonial and other activities not directly connected with immediate production. Particularly important here is the establishing and maintaining of relations between different lineages within a village, between villages within a tribe, and even between tribes. In this respect the dominance of complex redistribution provides the economic conditions of existence of a wider network of relationships. It must be recognised, of course, that systematic relations between villages or between tribes are not a function of the desires or feelings of the participants. They involve a determinate system of social relationships which must be sustained by determinate social practices, for example, ceremonials, exchanges of gifts or of individuals in marriage. Our argument on this point has concerned the economic conditions necessary to sustain such practices.

It follows that substantially larger populations can be sustained and united under conditions of primitive communism under the dominance of the variant of complex redistribution over appropriation by simple redistribution. The development of such relatively large and more or less integrated populations provides further opportunities for the emergence of specialist labourers and for the growth of exchanges between tribes on the basis of their specialist products. Iron bars for metal-working or agricultural implements themselves may be exchanged for other products over long distances through the inter-tribal exchanges made possible by the productivity of food-producing labour. If commodity relations are to emerge within primitive communism then they can do so in the first instance only under conditions of the dominance of the complex variant of the primitive communist mechanism of appropriation of surplus-labour.

Morgan's proposal for the periodisation of the history of stateless societies is summarised by Engels as follows:

> Savagery – the period in which the appropriation of natural products, ready for use, predominated; the things produced by man were, in the main, instruments that facilitated this appropriation. Barbarism – the period in which knowledge of cattle breeding and land cultivation was acquired, in which methods of increasing the productivity of nature through human activity were learnt (*The Origin . . .*, pp. 472–3).

We can now see that these two periods may be distinguished by the predominance of one or other of the variants of the primitive communist mechanism of appropriation of surplus-labour. Each of these variants has its conditions of existence in determinate types of ideological social relations: in the impermanent and fluctuating relationships of the band collective in the one case and in the more or less elaborated network of kinship relations on the other. The development of the arts of subsistence and, in particular, the transition from savagery to barbarism is necessarily tied to the formation and growth of the gentile constitution. Morgan's successive stages of integration in the archaic period, 'the gens, the phratry, the tribe and the confederacy of tribes, which constituted a people or nation' (*Ancient Society*, p. 6), have their economic conditions of existence in the appropriation of surplus-labour within the community through the dominance of the variant of complex redistribution. This correlation is an effect of the structure of the economic level of the primitive communist mode of production.

Engels, who follows Morgan in this respect, tends to favour an additional explanation of the advantages of the gentile constitution over more primitive forms in terms of the effects of natural selection in improving the human stock.

> In this ever widening exclusion of blood relatives from marriage [by the gentile system], natural selection also continues to have its effect . . . Tribes constituted according to gentes were bound, therefore, to gain the upper hand over the more backward ones (*The Origin . . .*, p. 488).

Here marriage forms are interpreted as *social relations of production of human beings.* Engels refers to 'the production of human beings themselves' (*ibid.*, p. 455). The gentile system produces a physiologically superior product. This astonishing position involves an impudent and fanciful play on the term *production*. We have shown that the tremendous improvements in the productivity of labour made possible by the gentile order are effects of the action of the variant form of the mode of appropriation of surplus-labour on the productive forces. These effects do not depend on any real or supposed improvements in the capacities of the skull and brain (cf. *Ancient Society*, p. 468).

C THE ARTICULATION OF THE RELATIONS OF PRODUCTION AND THE PRODUCTIVE FORCES

The concept of the primitive communist mode of production has been presented in terms of the articulation of a determinate mode of appropriation of surplus-labour, in two variant forms, with the corresponding set of productive forces. In this combination the mode of appropriation of surplus-labour is the dominant element in that it defines the limits and possible forms of development of the productive forces within primitive communism. If this articulated combination is to satisfy the theoretical requirements of the concept of a mode or production it is necessary to establish that the conditions of reproduction of this combination are satisfied. This task will be left to a later section. For the present it is necessary to consider the positions of those Marxist anthropologists, notably Meillassoux and Terray, who effectively reject the concept of the mode of production as a structure in dominance with the relations of production as dominant over the productive forces.

We have argued that the predominance of one or other of the variants of the primitive communist mechanism of appropriation of surplus-labour has consequences that are crucial for the level of development of the productive forces. In particular we have argued that the advance of the productive forces beyond the level of a hunting and gathering economy presupposes the predominance of the extraction of surplus-labour through the mechanism of complex redistribution. In Meillassoux's conception, on the contrary, the productive forces, in particular the mode of exploitation of the land, are dominant in the structure of the economy. Land may function primarily as a *subject* of labour or as an *instrument* of labour. In the first case the labour process consists in the extraction of the necessities of life from the land through hunting and gathering and of the production of the simple tools necessary for this extraction. In the second case human labour is invested in the land itself, for example, in the clearing of the land in preparation for planting, in weeding, and in other forms of agricultural labour. This difference allows Meillassoux to define two modes of production.[20] In both cases the forces of production, i.e. the mode of exploitation of the land, are dominant.

> the use of land as a *subject of labour* fosters a type of 'instantaneous' production whose output is immediately available, allowing a process of *sharing* which takes place at the end of each enterprise. The hunters, once they share the common product, are free from any further reciprocal obligations or allegiance. The process gives no ground for the emergence of a social hierarchy or of a centralised power, or even the extended family organisation. The basic unit is an equalitarian but unstable band with little concern for biological or social reproduction ('From reproduction to production', p. 99).

The survival, i.e. the reproduction of humanity before the discovery of agriculture, seems therefore nothing short of miraculous.

The use of land as an instrument of labour involves radical changes in

> the entire social, political and ideological structures. . . . Unlike the hunting band, the agricultural team is linked together, at least until the time of cropping, in order for every member to benefit from their joint labour. Furthermore, the vital problem of feeding the cultivator during the non-productive period of labour – between clearing the ground and harvest time – cannot be solved unless enough of the previous crop is available for this purpose. The members of one agricultural party are consequently linked not only to one another during the non-productive period of work, but also to the working party that produced the food during the previous cycle. . . . One can easily find here the material and temporal basis of the emergence of the '*family*' as a productive and cohesive unit and of '*kinship*' as an ideology: priority of the relations between people over the relations to things; lifetime duration of personalised social bonds; concern for reproduction; notions of seniority and of anteriority; respect for age; cult of the ancestors; fecundity cult, etc. All these features find their roots in the social conditions of agricultural production and underlying this, in the use of land as an instrument of labour (*ibid.*, pp. 99–100).

Relations of production are dominated by the productive forces.

Terray's position is in many respects more sophisticated and has the very great merit of insisting on the necessary complexity of the concept of the mode of production as an articulated hierarchy of instances. Nevertheless Terray's position has some theoretical effects that are equivalent to those of Meillassoux since it conceives of a unitary correspondence between relations of production and the productive forces. One thing corresponds to another thing.[21] This has the consequence that a mode of production can be identified by means of its productive forces

> bearing in mind the nature of the instruments of labour used in 'primitive' socio-economic formations, forms of co-operation are the keypoint at which the two systems are articulated. The number of different forms of co-operation found within any one such formation indicates the combined 'presence' of as many distinct modes of production (Terray, *Marxism and Primitive Societies*, p. 175).

Both authors, in effect, reduce the economic to the dominance of technique. Where one refers to the mode of exploitation of the land the other deals in the forms of co-operation. Both would therefore distinguish two Gouro modes of production: one in agriculture (simple co-operation, land as an instrument of labour) and the other in hunting (complex co-operation, land as subject of labour).

It is well known, of course, that the Marxist concept of the economic level of the social formation always refers to a necessary combination of the labour process and the mechanism of extraction of surplus-labour. Meillassoux and Terray give this necessity a purely formal character since their concept of mode of production is dominated by technique and the means of organisation of labour.

What are the consequences of this technicist conception of the structure of the economic level?[22] The labour process is defined by the combination of labourers, means of production, object of labour, and non-labourers. Every labour process involves a means of combining direct labour, the application of material instruments to the object of labour, and the presence or otherwise in a directing role of a non-labourer. The study of the labour process in isolation from or advance of the relations of production necessarily involves a conception of the labour process as a technical process. The relations between labourer and non-labourer must then be conceptualised in terms of a variety of technical possibilities: 'The elder plays the same part in matrimonial exchange as he does in material production: in both cases his power is simply a function of his office' (*ibid.*, p. 175). There is a determinate function for the labourer and a determinate function for the non-labourer but the conditions of the variation of these functions according to a determinate social division of labour must remain unknown. If we start from the primacy of the labour process we can never derive the relations of production on which it depends.

Meillassoux certainly appears to derive certain relations of production from the mode of exploitation of the land: kinship relations are derived as an effect of the use of land as an instrument of labour. In fact we have shown that the use of land as an instrument of labour itself requires a determinate structure of relations of production as its condition of existence. It cannot be responsible for generating these relations. Thus, given the primacy of the productive forces, any variation at the level of the relations of production must appear quite accidental.[23]

> Through historical accidents, usually due to contacts with foreign formations, a group takes for all its members the quality of 'senior' in relation to other groups considered collectively as minor. All the economic and social prerogatives of the elder are transferred to the dominant class, usually an aristocratic lineage. Prestations due to the elder become tributes due to the lord who may also gain control over the matrimonial policy of the community, and eventually over the means of production – land (Meillassoux, 'From reproduction to production', p. 101).

In this conception the land as an instrument of labour may combine with classless relations of production organised on the basis of kinship or with a social division of labour between classes. The difference is a matter of historical accident. In this example it is clear that the analysis of the labour process in isolation from the relations of production precludes the concept of the mode of production as a determinate articulated combination of relations and forces of production, with the result that there can be no theoretical definition of the variants of a mode of production. Hence there is a tendency to collapse into an empiricism in which modes of production are multiplied according to empirically given conditions. Forces of production and relations of production are given independently of the concept of their combination in the mode of production. Thus the concept of mode of production is effectively displaced from its position as a basic concept of historical materialism. We return to this point in the following section.

d THE CONDITIONS OF REPRODUCTION OF THE ECONOMY

We have seen that the conditions of reproduction of the economy and of the totality of social relations that constitute its conditions of existence are never reducible to those of the reproduction of the individual labourer. The reproduction of the labourer under conditions of primitive communism is a function of his membership of a redistributive system. This is clear enough with the relatively advanced productive forces developed under the dominance of complex redistribution. Here the process of production consists of the articulation of several discrete labour processes in a complex system of co-operation. The dependence of each labourer on the labour of the collective is apparent.

At more primitive levels where hunting and gathering and, perhaps, rudimentary gardening are the dominant forms of production the reproduction of the labourer is no less dependent on his position within the collective. The labour process itself involves no necessary co-operation since individual hunting and gathering are both possible and frequently practised. However, the low productivity and unreliable character of this labour make it almost impossible for an individual to survive by himself for any length of time. In the band collective men and women have different technical specialisms. They are employed in the production of different foodstuffs and each depends on the other to sustain a complete and more or less regular food supply. Under these conditions the position of the unmarried adult is precarious in the extreme.

> Denied food after bad hunting or fishing expeditions when the fruits of the women's collecting and gathering, and sometimes their gardening, provide the only meal there is, the wretched bachelor is a characteristic sight in native society. But the actual victim is not the only person involved in this scarcely tolerable situation. The relatives or friends on whom he depends in such cases for his subsistence are testy in suffering his mute anxiety, for, from the combined efforts of both husband and wife, a family often barely derives enough to avoid death by starvation (Lévi-Strauss, *The Elementary Structures of Kinship*, p. 39).

So much for the individual labourer. We must now consider the reproduction of the relations and forces of production. First, consider the position under the dominance of the appropriation of surplus-labour by the variant mechanism of simple redistribution. The social formation consists, at any given moment, of a number of band collectives of varying sizes which are unstable with regard to size and membership. Production is organised at the level of the band on the basis of a technical division of labour between the sexes and simple or complex co-operation. The internal organisation of the band around specific marriage and sexual relations may vary. The band may consist, for example, of a number of married couples together with their offspring or there may be a tendency towards polygamy on the part of the leader of the band. Variations at this level govern the precise character of the distribution of the product within the band since that is an effect of the intervention of ideological social relations. The possibility of such variation in the structure of the ideological relations intervening in the economy is an effect of the structure of the variant mechanism of simple redistribution.

The instability and the intermittent dissolution and formation of bands ensures a network of genealogical relations cutting across the distribution of the population into bands. Thus the continued reproduction of the economy establishes the conditions of the possibility of a kinship organisation in the society. The emphasis on possibility here is essential. The mere existence of genealogical relationships can no more ensure the presence of corresponding social relationships in so-called primitive societies than it can, say, in modern Britain. If such social relationships are to exist they must be generated and sustained by determinate ideological social practices, by ritual and ceremony, and by the social practices of reciprocal acknowledgment of relationship. The fact that genealogy extends beyond the band does not mean that the social relations of kinship must do so. This point cannot be made too strongly in view of the fetishistic treatment of kinship systems by contemporary idealist anthropology. We return to this question below.

The formation of a system of kinship relations is a possibility but not a necessity of primitive communism under conditions of the dominance of simple redistribution. The maintenance of ideological social relations between members of different bands is possible once the productive capacity of the bands is able to achieve more than a certain minimum of subsistence. To say that the development of kinship relations is possible but not necessary once the productive forces have reached a certain level of productivity is to say that there is no necessary tendency in the concept of primitive communism towards the dominance of complex redistribution. The formation of kinship relations requires a transformation of the structure of the ideological level which has its economic preconditions but is not the product of any economic necessity. The emergence of kinship relations is a necessary condition of transition to the dominance of complex redistribution. However, to effect the transition it is necessary not only that kinship relations exist but also that they intervene in the structure of the economy. Thus under conditions of simple redistribution kinship relations may or may not exist. Their reproduction is not essential to the reproduction of the economy.

This situation is completely transformed with the advance of productive forces induced by the dominance of the extraction of surplus-labour by means of the mechanism of complex redistribution. In this case the reproduction of the economy requires the reproduction of a determinate system of kinship relations. The example of the Gouro has shown how agricultural production requires a complex division of labour and the co-ordination of overlapping and interdependent work teams. It makes little difference to the necessity of this co-ordination whether the main form of food production is horticulture or herding. In all cases co-ordination is achieved by means of hierarchical relations within the household or the lineage, between elder and cadet, and so on, and by means of relations between lineages within a village community and between villages within a tribe. These relations allow for a direction of labour by adults and elders of various statuses in, for example, the assignment of land to a household or work team. Here we are concerned not simply with kinship relations but with their intervention in the economy as a double mechanism of extraction of surplus-labour on the one hand and of the co-ordination of the community's labour on the other.

In this case the reproduction of the economy necessarily involves the reproduction of a determinate system of relationships within and between lineages. This result has a number of important consequences. In the first place the existence of a system of kinship social relations necessarily involves some regulation of marriage exchanges if it is to be preserved from one generation to the next. Regulation requires a social mechanism of regulation. Thus, in addition to their function in the co-ordination of labour, the elders must also regulate marriage exchanges.

Secondly, the co-ordination of labour and the regulation of marriages involves the existence of forms of coercion. The application of the slogan 'if he does not labour, neither shall he eat' is one possibility. Another is the form of slavery practised throughout West Africa.[24] If the elder is not free to reduce cadets to slavery at whim the threat and possibility of such a reduction nevertheless has a certain effectivity. This does not involve a slave mode of production since the slaves or their descendants are normally integrated into lineages after a generation or two. The slave himself appears as a low status cadet. In this way a form of 'kinship' is created which does not reproduce any real genealogical relation.

This disjunction between kinship and genealogy brings us to our third consequence. The matrimonial policy of the elders cannot function as the sole mechanism of reproduction of the structure of the production community. Differential fecundity, accidents of birth and death, must prevent the community from maintaining the balance between sexes and ages, elders and cadets, required for a given organisation of work teams by lineage and segment of lineage. 'Kinship, therefore, cannot rely on "blood" ' (Meillassoux, 'From reproduction to production', p. 101).

> The agricultural community is fashioned on the model of the lineage or of a segment of a lineage. The genealogical relations are the ceaselessly modified and ceaselessly renewed terrain on which the relations of production are built. The relations of kinship which were revealed to us are the product of this alteration. The link of consanguinity is transformed under our very eyes into a social filiation. The oldest kinship relations, those of the first generations, no longer register any but this social kinship, whether or not it coincides with real filiation. In the place of the biological family, which is incapable of remaining within its strictly genealogical limits, there are thus substituted functional families whose members are associated more by economic obligations than by relations of consanguinity. In such a dynamic it is necessary for the bonds of kinship to be sufficiently flexible to adapt to these shifts: the terms of classificatory kinship anticipate the relations which can be established between individuals in the event of the death of the kinsman who links them together (Meillassoux, *Anthropologie . . .*, pp. 168–9).

These comments describe the situation within a lineage. In other cases, where several distinct lineages combine to form a village, the restructuring may produce lineages and fragments of lineages with no genealogical foundation whatever. Here again we find a lack of correspondence between the social relations of kinship and genealogy. The intervention of kinship relations in the economy which constitutes the complex redistribution variant of the mechanism of extraction of surplus-labour must therefore transform the conditions in which kinship relations themselves are reproduced.

In this brief examination of the conditions of reproduction of the economic level of the social formation dominated by the primitive communist mode of production we have argued that the structure of the relations of production assigns various co-ordinating functions to the elders and the adults of various statuses within the system of kinship relations. The control by the elders over the conditions of labour and over certain of the conditions of reproduction of the productive community is a necessary effect of the dominance of the complex redistribution variant of the primitive communist mechanism of appropriation of surplus-labour. Thus even if the elders in a lineage society perform little or no productive labour they do not necessarily constitute a class. Exploitation, in the sense of the appropriation of surplus-labour by a class, cannot be deduced from the co-ordinating and regulating position of the elders. This result follows directly from our analysis of the articulation of the relations of production and the productive forces. It does not depend in any way on Meillassoux's and Terray's technicist conception of the mode of production.

These conclusions concerning the position of the elders would be disputed by the Marxist anthropologists Dupré and Rey. These authors propose the following definition of exploitation: 'exploitation exists when the use of the surplus product by a group (or an aggregate) which has not contributed the corresponding surplus of labour reproduces the conditions of a new extortion of surplus-labour from the producers' ('Reflections . . . ', p. 152). There is therefore exploitation of cadets by the elders who control the process of reproduction. It is important to notice what theoretical position this conclusion is based on. Dupré and Rey make no distinction between the technical and the social division of labour. Exploitation appears whenever non-labourers perform functions that are necessary to the reproduction of the conditions of production. It therefore vanishes only when there is no surplus-labour or when the social mechanism of extraction of surplus-labour does not depend on the activities of non-labourers. We have seen that where there is no surplus-labour there can be no social formation. We are therefore left with the second alternative. This must preclude all mechanisms of extraction of surplus-labour more complex than simple redistribution. In particular, advanced communism with its mechanism of social planning and the complex redistribution variant of primitive communism must both appear to be exploitative in this conception.

In fact Dupré and Rey commit an error similar to that of Meillassoux and Terray. The latter, it will be recalled, analyse the forms of labour process without reference to the relations of production which determine the conditions of variation of these forms. They therefore lapse into an empiricist conception of mode of production in which forces of production and relations of production are given independently of the theoretical concept of their combination. Dupré and Rey on the other hand are forced to regard the elders as a given social category which can be identified without reference to the specific relations of production which govern the distribution of the population into various economic functions. It then appears that the question of exploitation may be settled in advance of the concept of the mode of production concerned.

Where one position leads to the denial of exploitation in lineage societies the other leads to its discovery. Both are the product of similar errors. These authors all work with what appears to be Marxist concepts, relations of production, forces of production, labour process, exploitation, mode of production, and so on. Where they differ from the problematic of Marxism is not so much in the presence of such terms but rather in their particular hierarchical relations as concepts. Mode of production is a fundamental concept of historical materialism in which the economic level is defined by the articulation of a mode of appropriation of surplus-labour (relations of production) and a mode of real appropriation (forces of production). The concept of the economic level is the concept of a determinate articulated combination of relations and forces of production. These latter concepts cannot be defined independently of the concept of the mode of production in which they are combined. In the present chapter, for example, in order to show that the concept of the redistribution of the product defines a set of relations of production we have had to establish that a determinate set of productive forces corresponds to that set of relations of production. Where, on the contrary, no set of corresponding productive forces can be deduced from a proposed mode of appropriation of surplus-labour this latter does not belong to any mode of production and cannot define a set of relations of production. In chapter 4, on the supposed 'Asiatic' mode of production, it is shown that the concept of appropriation of surplus-labour by the mechanism of tax/rent cannot define a set of relations of production since it belongs to no possible concept of mode of production.

Relations of production and forces of production cannot be defined independently of the concept of their combination and any attempt to identify the forces of production or the relations of production in a given society in the absence of an elaborated concept of mode of production must be doomed to empiricism. Both Dupré and Rey and Terray and Meillassoux fall into precisely this error. In both cases their empiricism is a necessary result of the attempt to study a given social formation in the absence of concepts defined at the appropriate theoretical level. With no elaborated concept of the primitive communist mode of production these authors rely on concepts of a lower theoretical level, forces of production, labour process, reproduction, all defined without reference to the structure of the mode of production to which they should belong. In these cases the Marxist concept of mode of production is surreptitiously replaced by a concept of a very different kind in which elements of the structure of the economic level appear to be defined independently of the concept of the structure itself. In spite of their different conclusions on the question of exploitation these authors are the victims of equivalent theoretical errors.

e KINSHIP AND THE THEORY OF THE GENTILE CONSTITUTION

In this chapter we have constructed the concept of the primitive communist mode of production as consisting of an economic and an ideological level. The structure of the economic level of all modes of production is defined by the articulated combination of a mechanism of appropriation of surplus-labour and forms of organisation of the labour process in which the former is dominant. In the case of primitive communism surplus-labour is appropriated by the mechanism of the redistribution of the product. This mechanism has two variant forms, simple redistribution and complex redistribution. In both cases a condition of existence of the mechanism, and therefore of the economic level, is the intervention of ideological social relations in the economic level in the form of a simple or complex network of social relations through which the product is distributed. Thus it is the structure of the economic level of primitive communism that establishes the conditions of intervention of the ideological in the economic. In particular we have argued that the structure of the complex redistribution variant of the mechanism of extraction of surplus-labour establishes that social relations of kinship of one kind or another are dominant within the social formation.

This argument raises a number of questions in relation first to the anthropological approach to the analysis of so-called primitive societies and of kinship systems, and secondly to Morgan's and Engels's theory of the gentile constitution as a non-political form of the social organisation of societies in the epoch of barbarism. While no attempt at a systematic examination of these questions can be made here a few comments on each are certainly in order.

(i) *The object of anthropology*[25]

The distinction between the problematics of Marxism and of anthropology may be briefly indicated in connection first with their conception of the structure of the social whole and secondly with their conception of the place and function of kinship relations. First, the object of anthropological discourse is the 'primitive' society. This is conceived as an expressive totality which is reducible to an inner essence of which the elements of the totality are then no more than its phenomenal expression.[26] In the functionalist anthropology of Malinowski, for example, the unifying inner essence of the totality consists of the organic needs of the human individual. 'Every cultural achievement that implies the use of artifacts and symbolism is an instrumental enhancement of human anatomy, and refers directly or indirectly to the satisfaction of a bodily need' (*A Scientific Theory of Culture and Other Essays*, p. 171).

Other anthropologists offer different candidates for the post of inner essence while retaining the expressive character of the structure of the whole. Lévi-Strauss, to take another example, clearly recognises the existence of distinct levels of social organisation but these are thought to be related in a system of transformations from one level to another in such a way that, in any given society, the transformations all belong to the same type. It is therefore possible in his view:

> to characterize different types of societies in terms of the types of transformations which occur within them. These types of

> transformations amount to formulas showing the . . . order of the convolutions that must be unravelled, so to speak, in order to uncover (logically, not normatively) an ideal homologous relationship between the different levels (*Structural Anthropology*, p. 334).

The different levels, then, are conceived as so many different forms of the same essence which is the mode of structuration peculiar to that society. Here the parts of the social whole are related in the mode of expression, not in that of effectivity.

There is therefore a clear disjunction between the theoretical objects of anthropology and of historical materialism. For one the social formation is an expressive totality, for the other it consists of a number of distinct structural levels whose articulation in dominance and forms of intervention are governed by the specific structural conditions of existence of a determinate economic level. These levels neither reflect nor generate each other; they are articulated in the mode of effectivity. In this chapter we have shown how the structure of the economic level of the primitive communist mode of production governs the conditions of intervention of the ideological level within the economy.

(ii) *The anthropological conception of kinship*

In the case of kinship, anthropology operates a working distinction between 'primitive' societies in which kinship is dominant and complex societies which are dominated by political and economic structures. Once again the example of Lévi-Strauss is instructive. We are presented with an account of kinship and marriage relations on two levels. In the first place the rules of kinship are presented as the basic mechanism ensuring the integration of *biological* families into *social* groups.

> If our proposed interpretation is correct, the rules of kinship and marriage are not made necessary by the social state. They are the social state itself, reshaping biological relationships and natural sentiments, forcing them into structures implying them as well as others, and compelling them to rise above their original characteristics (*The Elementary Structures of Kinship*, p. 490).

At this level there is no fundamental distinction to be made between 'primitive' and other societies. In another text Lévi-Strauss tells us

> The family connexions due to inter-marriage may result in the formation of broad links between a few groups, or of narrow links between a great number of groups; whether they are broad or narrow, however, it is those links which maintain the whole social structure and to which it owes its flexibility (*Race and History*, p. 27).

In both cases 'the ties of marriage represent the very warp and weft of society, while *other social institutions are simply embroideries on that background*' (*ibid.* – our emphasis). If the ties of marriage are the basic conditions of existence of society this fact alone cannot enable us to differentiate between distinct types of society. The distinction suggested above between elementary and complex structures of kinship, that is, between 'broad links between a few groups', and 'narrow links between a great number of groups', appears to correlate with another distinction that is of fundamental importance to Lévi-Strauss's conception of the object of anthropology. We refer, of course, to the distinction between 'hot' (modern) and 'cold' (primitive) societies, between 'stationary' and 'cumulative' histories, or between societies that are governed by 'blood ties' and those that are governed by economic relationships.[27] This last formulation is the most significant for our present purposes. In a reply to his critics Lévi-Strauss assimilates his own distinction between 'hot' and 'cold' societies to what he supposes to be the position of Marx and Engels on the character of so-called primitive societies. In particular he insists that the theoretical category of 'mode of production', while it may be appropriate enough for class societies, cannot be applied to the analysis of primitive society.

> It remained for Marcel Mauss, in *Essai sur le Don* to justify and develop Engels' hypothesis that there is a striking parallelism between certain Germanic and Celtic institutions and those societies having the potlatch. *He did this with no concern about uncovering the 'specific conditions of a mode of production', which, as Engels already understood, would be useless* (*Structural Anthropology*, p. 339).

Here the traditional anthropological conception of the primitive society as a unique socio-cultural entity which must be investigated by the peculiar concepts and method, called 'fieldwork', appropriate to this unique object is reproduced in a supposedly Marxist form. In fact Lévi-Strauss's position is no more than a variant of the traditional idealist problematic of anthropology.

The 'Marxism' of his conception of primitive societies may be simply exposed. If there are societies governed by the structure of kinship relations and others governed by the 'specific conditions of a mode of production' what determines that a society shall be of one type or the other? It cannot be the structure of the mode of production, since that concept is pertinent only to the latter type of society. The attempt to analyse the specific conditions of a mode of production in primitive societies must therefore be useless. If, for Lévi-Strauss, there is any set of concepts pertinent to the analysis of all possible societies it is the set of concepts of the elementary structures of kinship that are elaborated in his first major work. These general concepts are intended to cover all possible forms of integration of biological families into social groups. If his analyses have not been carried forward into the study of complex structures of kinship or the intermediate types of the Crow-Omaha systems this is only because 'their analysis raises tremendous difficulties which are the province, not of the social anthropologist, but of the mathematician' (*The Elementary Structures . . .*, Preface to the 2nd French edition, p. xxxvi).

Here the uniqueness of primitive societies is reduced to an effect of the relative simplicity of its mathematical structure. There can be no mistaking the theoretical ambition of Lévi-Strauss's conception, nor the fundamental character of his opposition to Marxism.

(iii) *The place of kinship in the theory of primitive communism*

This chapter has attempted to establish the concept of primitive communism within the Marxist theory of modes of production. We have argued in particular that what might loosely be called the dominance of kinship relations is itself an effect of the structure of the economic level of the primitive communist mode of production in one of its variants. The 'dominance of kinship relations' does not imply that there is any distinct 'kinship' level of the social formation peculiar to primitive societies. Nor does it imply, as Terray would seem to suggest, that 'kinship' is an element peculiar to certain 'primitive' economies (*Marxism and 'Primitive' Societies*, pp. 144f). Kinship social relations are ideological social relations which may or may not correspond to the structure of certain genealogical relations between individual human animals. Under conditions of the primitive communist mode of production a network of kinship relations is a condition of existence of the complex redistribution variant of the mechanism of extraction of surplus labour. Since this mechanism requires the dominance of the ideological level in the social formation we may speak loosely of the dominance of kinship relations in some, but not all, primitive communist social formations.

We have said that the structure of the primitive communist mechanism of extraction of surplus-labour in its complex redistribution variant has the dominance of some system of kinship relations as its condition of existence. This must not be taken to mean that the economy itself generates the necessary kinship relations or that kinship merely reflects the structure of the economic level. The economic and the ideological are distinct structural levels articulated in determinate relations of reciprocal effectivity. If the conditions of this articulation are determined by the structure of the economic level the precise structure of their ideological level itself is not.

The conditions of reproduction of the economic level under the dominance of the variant of simple redistribution ensures both the instability of the membership of individual band collectives and the formation of restricted 'kinship' relations within each band between adults and children. There is, of course, no necessity for these 'kinship' relations to correspond to genealogical relations between determinate adults and determinate children. All that is required for the reproduction of the economic level is some system of social relations in which children are reared by adults. These two conditions, the existence of kinship relations within the band and the continual splitting and reformation of bands, establish the possibility of the formation of a network of kinship relations involving individuals in different bands. We have seen that such a network of relations can exist only if it is maintained and generated by determinate ideological practices, by determinate rituals and ceremonies. If it is not an effect of genealogy alone, neither is it simply a continuation of relations existing within the band. If relations between individuals in different bands are not sustained by their own determinate ideological social practices they must cease to exist.

Thus the achievement of a certain minimum level of productivity within primitive communism establishes the economic conditions of the possible transformation of the ideological level which results in the integration of several band collectives into one social formation by means of a more or less extended network of kinship. The existence of such a network is necessary if kinship is to intervene in the structure of the economic level. Thus the ideological conditions of the transition to the dominance of complex redistribution may be formed under the dominance of simple redistribution. While, therefore, the development of productive forces within primitive communism is necessarily articulated on the growth of social relations of kinship the precise structure of these kinship relations is relatively autonomous with respect to the economy. If the structure of the variant mechanism of complex redistribution requires the intervention of kinship relations it cannot determine the precise structure of these relations. It follows, then, that primitive communism cannot be reduced to any single determinate structure of ideological social relations. The structure of the economic level in the variant of complex redistribution defines a field of possible variation with regard to the ideological social relations of kinship.

(iv) *The theory of the gentile constitution*

Finally it is necessary to comment briefly on the theory of the gentile constitution first advanced by Morgan and substantially accepted by Engels as giving 'the fundamental features of the social constitution of primitive times – before the introduction of the *state*' (*The Origin* . . . , p. 518). In spite of Engels's recommendation this theory is effectively ignored in the work of the Marxist anthropologists examined in this chapter. Their neglect in this case merely reproduces with regard to the level of ideological social relations the effects of their failure to work with an elaborated theory of the primitive communist mode of production.[28]

In Morgan's view the gentile organisation

> runs through the entire ancient world upon all the continents, and it was brought down to the historical period by such tribes as attained civilization. Nor is this all. *Gentile society wherever found is the same in structural organization and principle of action*; but changing from lower to higher forms with the progressive advancement of the people (*Ancient Society*, p. 62 – our emphasis).

The gentile constitution refers to the organisation of society in the following series.

> first, the gens, a body of consanguinei having a common gentile name; second, the phratry, an assemblage of related gentes united in a higher association for certain common objects; third, the tribe, an assemblage of gentes, usually organised in

> phratries, all the members of which speak the same dialect; and fourth, a confederacy of tribes, the members of which respectively spoke dialects of the same stock language. It resulted in a gentile society (*societas*) as distinguished from a political society or state (*civitas*) (*ibid.*, p. 65).

A detailed presentation of Morgan's theory of the gentile organisation of society cannot be attempted here. The reader may refer to Morgan's own text or to the concise summary given by Engels.[29] It will be apparent that, while using a different terminology, this chapter has reached a similar conclusion regarding the necessity of the gentile form of social organisation in the more advanced variant of primitive communism. We have argued, in effect, that the gentile organisation of society is a condition of existence of the complex redistribution variant of the primitive communist mechanism of extraction of surplus-labour. The conditions of the formation of the gentile constitution are to be found in the organisation of society into band collectives under the dominance of the variant of simple redistribution. Nevertheless it should be emphasised that the above account of the conditions of the formation of the gentile constitution in no way relies on Morgan's erroneous conception of the first 'organised form of society' (p. 427) preceding the gentile order in terms of the consanguineous family and group marriage.[30]

The structure of the mechanism of complex redistribution involves the organisation of the social formation into groups structured internally by kinship relations, for example, between elder and cadet, and combined into larger units, villages, tribes, etc., through a wider network of marriage exchanges. Kinship relations within these groups may correspond more or less closely to genealogical relations but they are never reducible to the effects of genealogy. The common ancestor is more likely than not a purely notional entity and, as we have seen, differential fertility and other demographic factors involve the chronic dissolution and reformation of lineages or gentes with scant regard to the niceties of genealogy. The wider network of marriage exchanges is organised on the basis of the social relations of kinship not the genetic relations of genealogy. Thus, as Morgan has insisted, systems of marriage in primitive society do not unite biological families, as in Lévi-Strauss's conception, but social gentes or lineages.

There remains the question of the democratic character of the gentile constitution. We have shown how the organisation of production on the basis of common possession of the means of production by the lineage, village or tribe, locates certain functions of co-ordination and supervision in the hands of elders and chiefs. The conditions of co-ordination and supervision involve the existence of forms of coercion ranging from the simple but undoubtedly effective application of the slogan 'If he does not labour neither shall he eat' to the forms of slavery practised by some West African lineage societies or even to more drastic measures.

In Morgan's view the democratic character of gentile society 'manifested itself in the retention by the gentiles of the right to elect their sachems and chiefs, in the safeguards thrown around the office to prevent usurpation, and in the check upon the election held by the remaining gentes' (*ibid.*, p. 72). It is well known that the principle of election is by no means universal in gentile societies. This is recognised by Morgan himself who notes that in parts of Africa the office of chief passes by inheritance from brother to brother or from uncle to nephew. He adds that 'the hereditary feature requires further explanation' (p. 383). In such cases, then, the social means of coercion are in the hands of a non-elective body of elders and chiefs. Does this not justify Dupré and Rey's treatment of the elders as a class, or at least as a class-like social category (*op. cit.*, pp. 142–3), which controls the reproduction of the economy?

In fact Morgan's difficulty over the inheritance of the office of chief in patently gentile societies stems primarily from his usage of the term 'democratic' to refer both to certain political forms and to the absence of a political organisation of society. The difficulty is compounded in this case by the fact that certain organisational features, viz. the holding of elections, are found in some forms of state and in some forms of gentile society. Thus, 'democratic' refers to certain forms of state and to the absence of a state. As far as the position of the leaders is concerned the crucial question is not whether they are elected but whether their position is maintained by means of a state apparatus. The intermittent exercise of coercion in lineage societies does not necessarily imply the presence of a *state* coercive apparatus which enables the elders as a class (or class-like category) to exploit their cadets. The coercion exercised by the elder is strictly limited in scope. He may punish an intractable cadet by delaying the moment when a wife is found for him, or in extreme cases, by putting him into slavery. On the other hand, elders may lose their office simply because their cadets depart and join other groups. Consider, for example, the following description of Gouro society:

> The payment of the dowry concludes the cycle of reproduction of the social structure. But if the general principle of ancestral authority is preserved and renewed by this means, it is at the price of the progressive dissolution of the individual authority of the elders. Each dowry payment, each marriage, loosens their grip on a part of their dependence group in giving this same part the means of independence. Although on each occasion he relaxes the bonds which join him directly with his cadets, and although it might be a permanent temptation to him to utilize his wealth to increase the number of his own wives rather than to marry his dependents, the elder cannot escape this imperative without the risk of seeing his community dying out or dispersing (Meillassoux, *Anthropologie . . .*, p. 223).

Meillassoux presents a voluntaristic explanation of this reasonableness of the elders with regard to the marriage of cadets. On the one hand they desire to appropriate wives for themselves, on the other they wish to extend and perpetuate their authority. If they give way to the first desire they lose all hope of satisfying the second. Here the system of marriage exchanges is reduced to an effect of the subjective balances achieved in the minds of the elders. This naïve egocentric mode of analysis is clearly inadequate; social relations cannot be explained by the feelings of participants. The very possibility of these conflicting desires on the part of the elder are an effect of the system of marriage exchanges and could not arise in the absence of that system. The system itself cannot be the product of a contingent balance of forces between these desires.

The apparent limit to the authority of the elders has quite another significance. If the cadets cannot be prevented from deposing their elder by the simple device of voting with their feet, that is possible only because there is no state apparatus to intervene on behalf of the elders. The coercion of individual cadets is not exercised by a state apparatus in the interests of a class of elders; rather it is exercised by the individual elders as representatives of the gentile community. The absence of the right to elect the elder or chief does not therefore signify the end of the gentile community.

Two

The ancient mode of production

> This much, however, is clear, that the middle ages could not live on Catholicism, nor the ancient world on politics. On the contrary, it is the mode in which they gained a livelihood that explains why here politics, and there Catholicism, played the chief part. For the rest, it requires but a slight acquaintance with the history of the Roman republic, for example, to be aware that its secret history is the history of its landed property (*Capital*, I, p. 82).[1]

It is a commonplace that politics is dominant in the ancient world. More precisely, it is dominant in the states of classical antiquity, Rome, Greece, the Hellenistic world, but not in the empires of the East. In the latter political life in the classical sense is absent, for example, in Persia which the Greeks saw as the seat of a despotism characterised by the absence of citizenship and therefore of freedom. In the ancient world freedom is always primarily the freedom of citizens. This chapter shows why and by means of what mechanisms politics reigns supreme in the ancient world. It does so by establishing the concept of the ancient mode of production which governed the social formations of classical antiquity but not those of the Eastern despotisms.[2] It is the essential structure of this mode of production and, in particular, its specific mode of appropriation of surplus-labour that determines the necessary dominance of the political level and which governs the forms of effectivity of politics with respect to the other levels of the social formation. We shall be particularly concerned with the forms of intervention of politics in the economic and of the economic in politics. The specific articulation of politics and economics in this mode of production governs the possible forms of development and effectivity of subordinate economic forms and relations, trade and commodity production, slavery, relations of personal dependence (i.e. 'feudal' relations). While the ancient mode of production is dominant in the social formations of classical antiquity this chapter takes its examples largely from the history of the later Roman Republic. If 'its secret history is the history of its landed property' this, as we shall see, is an effect of the conditions of articulation of politics and economics in this social formation.

> The community – as a state – is, on the one hand, the relationship of these free and equal private proprietors to each other, their combination against the outside world – and at the same time their safeguard. . . . The precondition for the continued existence of the community is the maintenance of equality among its free self-sustaining peasants, and their individual labour as the condition of the continued existence of their property. Their relation to the natural conditions of labour are those of proprietors; but personal labour must continuously establish these conditions as real conditions and objective elements of the personality of the individual, of his personal labour. On the other hand the tendency of this small and warlike community drives it beyond these limits, etc. (*Pre-Capitalist Economic Formations*, pp. 72–3).

In this and other passages Marx describes the ancient community as constituted by the body of independent peasant producers or citizens. At the level of the labour process, that is, as producers, they are independent. They co-operate as citizens. 'The member of the community reproduces himself not through cooperation in wealth-producing labour, but in cooperation in labour for the (real or imaginary) communal interests aimed at sustaining the union against external and internal stress' (*ibid.*, p. 74). The reproduction of such a community produces its disintegration with the development of slavery, the concentration of landed property, a monetary economy, wars of conquest, etc. 'Thus the preservation of the ancient community implies the destruction of the conditions upon which it rests, and turns into its opposite' (*ibid.*, p. 93).

Of course there can be no question of taking these passages from notes that Marx wrote 'for my own clarification' (quoted in Hobsbawm's Introduction, *ibid.*, p. 10) as a theoretical account of the structure of the ancient mode of production. In the questions that it poses this text clearly has a very different object, namely a genealogy of certain elements of the capitalist mode of production on the one hand and the ideological problem of the determination of the appearance of a given society by its structure on the other.[3] Neither here nor elsewhere in his work does Marx present the elaborated concept of the ancient mode of production or of its determinant element, the 'ancient' mode of appropriation of surplus-labour. Nor do his remarks account for the formation of classes and the conditions of class conflict in the ancient world. In particular they cannot be made to support the untenable position that the ancient world was dominated by a slave-owning mode of production.[4] Nevertheless they do provide an indication of one of the essential structural features of the ancient mode of production, namely, the necessary articulation of the conditions of citizenship on the conditions of production, and also of the tendency towards the disruption of the political and economic basis of any ancient form of state. This last point should not be misunderstood. Marx's formulations are too easily interpreted as supporting, for example, Hobsbawm's reading that 'the breakdown of the ancient mode is therefore implicit in its socio-economic character' (*ibid.*, p. 41). Hobsbawm's conclusion rests on the identification of the continued existence of a certain form of ancient community with that of the ancient mode of production itself, an identification that is possible only in the absence of the elaborated concept of the ancient mode of production. In fact the tendency towards the disintegration of any given ancient political community is itself an effect of the specific form of articulation of politics and the economy in this mode. This tendency therefore describes a pattern of internal development that is peculiar to the ancient mode of production. It does not describe the movement from one mode of production to another.[5]

If we are to avoid the errors of identifying a mode of production with features of a given social formation or else of mistaking the concept of a mode of production for Marx's working notes in the *Grundrisse* and his incidental remarks elsewhere it is necessary that we proceed from a systematic elaboration of the concept of the mode of production in question. Our proposal for the concept of the ancient mode is outlined below and is followed by a discussion of the theoretical effects of this definition and, in particular, of the possible forms of variation defined by the essential structure of this mode of production.

We begin by considering the mode of appropriation of surplus-labour which constitutes the dominant articulation of the structure of the economic level. In the ancient world we appear to be confronted by states which, whatever their different forms of political organisation, are all constituted primarily as the unity of a body of citizens who, individually and collectively, are the possessors of the state. This shared political form, however, appears to be based on a multiplicity of the most diverse economic forms, slavery, tax-farming, tribute, debt-bondage, helotry, clientage, booty, and so on. At first sight then it might seem that the unity of the ancient world is to be defined not at the economic level on the basis of such economic relationships but rather at the level of the political organisation of the city state and its derived forms. This appearance is deceptive. We shall see that the structure of the ancient mode of appropriation of surplus-labour encompasses the diversity of economic relationships as so many derived forms and also governs the necessary structure of the ancient form of state.

1 The concept of the ancient mode of production

The ancient mode of appropriation of surplus-labour, the dominant social relation of production in the ancient world, may be defined as appropriation by *right of citizenship*. This means that the extraction of surplus-labour by citizens and the distribution of productive property (especially land) take place by means of mechanisms articulated on the political and legal apparatuses of the state. These operate primarily through communal extraction by the state and subsequent distribution among the citizenry by the state apparatuses, for example, the distribution of tribute and booty, the provision of state doles of corn, bread, oil, etc., but also the distribution of taxes, liturgies, and other appropriations levied by the state on the citizens themselves. Particularly significant in the history of Rome are mechanisms which work through the direct or indirect access to the profits of government in payment or compensation for state service, for example to state magistrates and pro-magistrates on the one hand or to publicans (tax-farmers) and other 'private enterprise' state contractors on the other.

The existence of the state as a proprietor is obviously crucial here. If the citizens are to have rights that are legally defined and politically determined in the distribution of state appropriations then state property must exist as a category that is juridically distinct from that of the citizens. The existence of state property and of the determination of rights in respect of it by the political institutions of the body of citizens defines the field of political class conflict among the citizens of the ancient state. It is for this reason that state property, especially in land, figures so prominently in the history of the ancient world. Where commerce is poorly developed and the ancient community is overwhelmingly agricultural the *ager publicus* (public land) is the predominant form of state property and its possession or distribution is a prominent source of conflict within the body of citizens.

It is this necessity of state property that constitutes the crucial difference between the ancient mode of production and the Germanic form discussed in the *Grundrisse*. In the latter the 'community has no existence as a state' (*ibid.*, p. 78) and communal property is not that of a distinct juridical entity. 'It is genuinely the common property of the individual owners, and not of the union of owners, possessing an existence of its own in the city, distinct from that of the individual members' (p. 80). The Germanic form is therefore a variant of primitive communism in which the appropriation and distribution of surplus-labour is effected by ideological mechanisms of kinship and religion. It should be clear that the presence or absence of the city as a place where the homes of citizens are concentrated together is quite beside the point here. It is not the city as a location but the city as a *state* that is crucial to the ancient mode of production.

In addition, appropriation by right of citizenship in the ancient mode of production operates through the intervention of the state as a body of citizens in the determination or guarantee of contractual and other legal or customary relations between one citizen and another or between citizens and other legal subjects such as corporations, religious bodies, other communities, freedmen and sometimes even slaves. Examples of such relations include debt-bondage and certain forms of patron–client relation. The state also determines the legal statuses of helotry, slavery, and other forms of personal subordination of non-citizens.

Thus in the ancient mode of production citizens extract surplus-labour by virtue of their rights as citizens with respect to the operation of the political, legal and ideological (customary and religious) apparatuses of the state. The ancient mode does not depend on any separation of the direct producer from his means of production or on the development of a labour process based on more or less complex forms of co-operation. The reproduction of ancient relations of production consists in the reproduction of the conditions of citizenship on the one hand and of the legal and political mechanisms of surbordination on the other. We shall see below how these conditions define the limits to the development of productive forces under the dominance of the ancient mode of production. For the present it is sufficient to note that the predominant form of the labour process remains that of the individual peasant or artisan producer under a variety of more or less oppressive external conditions. More complex forms of the labour process, complex co-operation and division of labour, even the limited use of machinery, develop only in certain specialised sectors which are maintained through the more or less direct intervention of the state. Thus the scope for the development of productive forces within ancient society is extremely limited and the highest developments in slave-worked latifundia and manufactories[6] cannot affect the conditions of the labour of the mass of direct producers.

The ancient mode of production may therefore be specified as follows:

(1) a social division of labour between a class of direct producers and a class of non-labourers;

(2) appropriation of surplus-labour by *right of citizenship*. This ensures an articulation of the levels of ancient social formations in which politics occupies the dominant place;

(3) limited development of productive forces. The predominant form of labour process is that of the independent peasant producer but the intervention of the ancient state may provide for the limited development of more complex forms of co-operative labour process under conditions of slavery and even of wage-labour.

A first theoretical effect of this definition concerns the necessary intervention and effectivity of politics with respect to the structure of the ancient economy. We have seen that the appropriation of surplus-labour by right of citizenship involves a complex intervention of politics and of law: in the determination of the level and form of surplus extraction in the case of communal appropriation in the form of tribute, booty, tax, etc.; in the determination of the conditions of individual appropriation by legal subjects in the case of slavery and other forms of bondage; in the determination of the conditions of distribution and private possession of state property. The population is therefore distributed into a number of legally defined orders or estates with differential political rights and obligations and in differing forms of subjection: masters, slaves and freemen, citizens and non-citizens, different grades of citizen, etc. Thus the direct producers are exploited by mechanisms involving *first*, a system of differential rights in the determination of the level and form of surplus-labour extraction and to the possession of state property (revenues, booty, land, etc.) and *second*, the determination of the specific content of these differential rights by decision of the political institutions of the body of citizens. These conditions assign to politics its specific place of dominance in the social formation and govern the specific form of articulation of the instances of the social formation.

The second condition is especially important. In the ancient mode, relations between classes are realised at the political level in a system of legally defined statuses. However, the conditions of intervention of law and of politics are quite different from those of the feudal mode of production. Feudal ground-rent, the dominant feudal relation of production, is articulated on the politically and legally determined monopoly of the lords over the principal means of production, namely, the land. This monopoly which constitutes the basis of the division of society into classes and defines the limits of political intervention in the economy is an invariant of the feudal mode of production. In ancient society on the other hand, the distribution of land and formation of orders, estates or statuses is governed by the articulation of rights of citizenship on the political and ideological levels. This articulation may take various forms and may involve the development of landlord–tenant relations analogous to the lord–serf relations of certain variants of feudalism. The limits to this development of 'feudal' relations within the ancient form of state are discussed below. What particularly distinguishes the ancient mode of production here is the fact of citizenship and the mode of intervention of politics in the structure of the economy. The ancient state is constituted as the union of the body of citizens while the feudal state is constituted primarily as the legal and political condition of the maintenance of monopoly control of the land by the ruling class. Such a monopoly may or may not exist in the ancient world; it is not essential to the ancient mode of production. The specific mode of dominance of politics in the ancient mode of production means that variants of this mode of production appear primarily as variant political forms, especially variant forms of state, and that the limits to this variation are essentially political, that is, they are defined by the political conditions necessary to the existence of the state as the union of a body of citizens.

If the ancient form of state as the organised body of citizens is an invariant condition of existence of the ancient mode of production, this fact in no way precludes the exploitation of citizens. The body of citizens may or may not constitute an exploiting class ruling over a subject population. The possibility, but not the necessity, of the exploitation of citizens is inscribed in the concept of the extraction of surplus-labour by right of citizenship. Thus the ancient mode of production is dominant in societies as different as, for example, Sparta on the one hand and Athens or Rome on the other. In Sparta[7] citizens are not direct producers and direct producers cannot be citizens. The body of citizens constitute an exclusive estate ruling over a subject population of helots (direct producers) and over subject communities (*perioeci*). The latter possessed local self-government and local rights of citizenship but were allowed no part in the government of the state as a whole or in the determination of foreign policy. They were obliged to render military and other services to the Spartan state. The helots on the other hand were subjects of the state with no political community of their own. The Spartan *homoios* or 'peer' devoted himself to the noble profession of arms. In order that he might be able to pursue this career he was granted a certain amount of land by the state, a *cleros*. A number of helots would be tied to this land and obliged to cultivate it and to provide the *homoios* to whom they were assigned a certain fixed amount of the products of the land, sufficient to maintain him and his family and to cover his contributions to the *syssition* to which he belonged. This land and its proceeds were his by right of citizenship; it was assigned to him from the public land. The citizen was not the legal owner of his *cleros* and he was not free to dispose of it by sale or by will, at least until the law of Epitadeus was passed. Although he could not be dispossessed of his *cleros* while remaining a citizen he could mortgage it so that the entire income or more might be alienated. The helots were bound to the land and were obliged to supply a fixed quantity of the products of the land. They had no political rights and no freedom of movement but they were not slaves nor were they serfs in the feudal sense. Individual Spartans had no rights of possession in them. So long as they remained quiescent and paid their annual dues they were left alone.

Sparta then, at least in the period before the Peloponnesian war, gives an example of a variant of the ancient mode of production that is not articulated on the state as a body of independent peasant proprietors. Surplus-labour is extracted by a class of non-labourers by means of the coercive political apparatus of the state. In this variant mortgages and other contractual relations between citizens may function as relations of distribution of the surplus-labour extracted from the direct producers but they are not themselves means of appropriation of surplus-labour. In Rome and in Athens on the other hand, we have examples of ancient social formations in which the body of citizens is first and foremost a body of individual private landowners with collective property in public land. Initially the citizens are independent peasant proprietors and larger landowners. In these cases the exploitation of citizens takes place both through collective appropriation by the state and through contractual and customary obligations. Patron–client relations and debt-bondage provide examples of the latter. Appropriation by the state takes the form of taxes, direct appropriation, liturgies and forced labour. These last are particularly important in the Roman Empire.[8]

The importance of these forms of appropriation in generating acute political and economic conflict within the body of citizens in the history of Athens or in the Roman Republic is well known. Small peasant proprietors were constantly falling into debt. In Rome according to the law of the Twelve Tables the debtor who would not or could not pay was liable to be sold into slavery abroad. No actual cases of such enslavement are recorded, but a form of debt-bondage, the *nexum*, was abolished in the fourth century and popular agitation for the remission of debts and the distribution of public land recurred throughout the history of the Republic. The annalists of the Roman Republic also record a number of secessions or mass strikes against military service. For example in 494 B.C. a large body of the plebs sat down *en masse* outside Rome and refused to serve in the army. As a result the patricians were forced to concede the tribunate of the plebs in which ten tribunes, originally plebeians, were elected annually by tribal assemblies. A further secession was provoked in 287 B.C. as a result of the development of other forms of debt-bondage. Once again the secession produced political concessions from the patricians and an increase in the formally democratic character of the representative institutions of the state.

These examples illustrate the significance of the mode of domination of politics in the ancient world. The predominant form of class struggle between citizens is political. The objective of the plebeian struggle is a distribution of public land or a change in the law, that is, *inter alia*, in the conditions of direct individual appropriation of surplus-labour (e.g. remission of debts, change in the law of contract, legal limitation on the level of interest chargeable) or in the political constitution (e.g. the instituting of the tribunate of the plebs, the establishment of the legislative competence of the tribal assembly). The form of the struggle may be legal or illegal but the objectives are directly political. Even apparently economic objectives, remission of debts for example or the distribution of public land, can be realised only by means of legislative enactment. The situation of non-citizens, for example, slaves or subject communities, with respect to forms of the class struggle is quite different.

Before returning to the complex forms of political conflict generated by the mode of articulation of politics and economy in the ancient world it is necessary to consider further the significance of warfare for the ancient state with a peasant citizenry. It is clear that warfare provides the conditions of extraction of tribute or booty from subject and foreign communities, a major mechanism of appropriation of surplus-labour in the ancient mode of production. Warfare therefore assumes a contradictory significance for the peasant citizens. On the one hand the peasantry are constantly falling into debt through the vagaries of the harvest, disease, or economic fluctuations and this together with the effects of inheritance tends to generate a body of poverty-stricken and landless peasants. Apart from leading to agitation for the remission of debts or the distribution of public land it is clear that this condition may also generate a pressure for wars of aggression with the hope of booty and fresh land on the part of the poorer citizens. The history of the Roman Republic contains many instances in which the plebs force Rome into war against the wishes of the Senate. Nevertheless this tendency towards war and territorial expansion is an effect of quite specific political and economic conditions. It is not an invariant of the ancient mode of production. Sparta, ruled by a military caste of citizens, tended to limit itself to defensive wars, so did the Roman Empire after an initial phase of consolidation. Towards the end of the Roman Republic military expansion is an effect of quite different political conditions; the profits of military adventure are necessary to finance the political career of ambitious nobles. If war is not an invariant of the ancient mode of production it nevertheless provides one of the predominant mechanisms of appropriation of surplus-labour. Some states, for example the Aetolian league and the Cretan cities, specialised in conducting wars of robbery on land and sea and many others relied in part on such mechanisms.

On the other hand, the effect of extensive military service on a largely peasant citizenry is the ruination of small landed property and an intensification of the growth of a landless stratum among the citizens. This imposes a pressure towards payment for military service and the development of a professional citizen or mercenary army. In Rome the property qualification for military service had periodically to be reduced. In the case of the early Republic Marx notes that while warfare and conquest 'is an essential part of the community itself, it breaks the real bond on which the community rests' (*Pre-Capitalist Economic Formations*, p. 83). The destruction of the independent peasantry, the influx of slaves and booty, the concentration of landed property and the extension of the *ager publicus*, together effect the destruction of the original form of community.

> In the last instance the community and the property resting upon it can be reduced to a specific stage in the development of the forces of production of the labouring subjects – to which correspond specific relations of these subjects with each other and with nature. Up to a certain point, reproduction. Thereafter, it turns into dissolution (*ibid.*, p. 95).

This result implies no tendency towards the dissolution of the ancient mode of production as such. On the contrary, it describes a tendency that is internal to the ancient mode of production just as, for example, the tendency of the rate of profit to fall is internal to the capitalist mode of production without in any way implying its destruction.[9] In both cases, the tendency in question is a necessary effect of the structure and conditions of existence of the economy. The same is true of countervailing tendencies. These tendencies are not empirical generalisations and they do not describe factual movements. Rather, they are rigorously necessary effects of the structure of the economy in question. In a concrete social formation the predominance of one or another tendency must depend on the precise conditions prevailing at the time.

In the present case we are concerned with a tendency that exists in any given ancient form of state: the tendency to the destruction of the economic basis of the existing political constitution in the direction of a concentration of political power. Given the articulation of politics and the economy in the ancient world this is equivalent to a tendency towards economic concentration without, however, there being any necessary concentration at the level of the technical organisation of the labour process.

It is clear that this tendency operates in the community of independent peasant proprietors. In the ancient world usury has a revolutionary political effect through its transformation of the economic conditions of citizenship.

> Usury has a revolutionary effect in all pre-capitalist modes of production only in so far as it destroys and dissolves those forms of property on whose solid foundation and continual reproduction in the same form the political organisation is based (*Capital*, III, p. 597).

Marx also notes that 'as soon as the usury of the Roman patricians had completely ruined the Roman plebeians, the small peasants, this form of exploitation came to an end and a pure slave economy replaced the small peasant economy' (p. 595). This does not refer to a change in the dominant mode of production, for example, to a slave-owning mode of production, but only to a change in the specific mechanisms through which the ancient relations of production are realised in the Roman countryside. Appropriation by right of citizenship remains and only its institutional support in concrete social relations has changed.

However, this tendency is not restricted to the community of peasants. More generally it is an effect of the form of articulation of law and politics within the economy in the ancient world. It follows, in particular, from the political determination of the conditions of collective appropriation by the state and from differential access to the possession of state property through a system of property qualifications with respect to entry upon political and military careers, through the purchase price of state contracts, or through bribery. This means that the larger proprietors have privileged access to the distribution of booty and tribute and to the other profits of government. An effect of this tendency is that the more politically privileged categories of the population, for example, the higher census classes in Rome, tend to become a smaller proportion of the total population. In Rome the growth of the state, first in Italy and then throughout the Mediterranean and Europe, could only accentuate this tendency by increasing the costs and rewards of a political career. In addition, since tax collection and many other state functions were let out to private organisations of contractors or publicans on the basis of specific guarantees in the form of landed or other property, any increase in the territories of the state tends to increase the costs of access to the profits of government through 'private enterprise'.[10] In the late Republic enormous sums of money pass through the hands of the publicans. Nevertheless, returns obtainable through political and military careers were considerably larger.

Two significant countervailing tendencies may be noted. The first and most obvious is a further effect of the political and legal character of the determination of the conditions of appropriation. Popular and democratic agitation and political rebellion may produce concessions in the form of changes in the law or the democratisation of the constitution through the wider formal distribution of political rights. However, such changes hardly alter the effective differentiation of political rights either through the existence of formal property qualifications or through the *de facto* differentiation affected by the costs of political activity or of litigation. Secondly, there are the consequences of the conditions of existence of commodity production in the ancient world. This is discussed in a later part of the chapter. Here we should notice that the possibility of the appropriation or realisation of surplus-labour in monetary form depends on the existence of a substantial level of commodity production. We shall see that the concentration of political power beyond a certain point leads to the inhibiting of commodity production. This in turn increases the costs and reduces the effectiveness of the mechanisms of appropriation. In effecting a relative expansion of 'natural economy', that is, of production for use rather than for sale, the tendency to political concentration tends also to reduce the productive forces to a more primitive level. For this reason the flowering of commodity production upon the establishing of ancient empires is always followed, in the Hellenistic states of the East as well as in the Roman Empire, by a reversion to more primitive economic forms and by the necessity of state intervention to ensure the movement of goods.

2 Social conflict in the ancient world

It is well known that the ancient world was the site of acute social and political conflict both between and within states. Here we consider the characteristic forms of social conflict generated by the ancient form of state and by the specific articulation of politics and the economy in the ancient mode of production. For purposes of illustration, we will refer to the last century or so of the Roman Republic and consider how the great expansion of the empire in the east and in the west and the consequent influx of booty and rapid growth of the profits of government generated the series of civil wars that culminated in the overthrow of the republican form of government. In this section we are concerned with the political effects of the multiplicity of political and legal relations through which the appropriation of surplus-labour by right of citizenship is realised, ranging from custom and contract through various forms of subjection to the looting of formally independent communities.

While *de facto* differentiation of the legal and political status of the population is a condition of existence of the ancient mode of production it is not necessary that this differentiation should take any specific form. The population of the ancient state may be divided into citizens, members of subject communities, slaves and others who are personally unfree, freedmen who may or may not enjoy certain of the rights of citizens, and so on. Or again, as in large areas of the later

Roman Empire, the population may consist almost entirely of citizens with considerable internal differentiation into grades. The exploitation of non-citizen subjects by means of tribute and booty is not a necessary or invariant feature of the ancient mode of production.

Nevertheless the international warfare endemic to a system of ancient states promotes the growth of large and extremely complex political formations in which the formal institutional structure is transformed or superseded. By the beginning of the first century B.C., for example, Rome had effectively united the previously independent states of peninsular Italy and Cisalpine Gaul on the basis of a variety of political forms. Some communities were established on Roman territory and endowed with Latin rights, that is, their magistrates would be granted Roman citizenship and, subject to certain conditions, any Latin could obtain Roman citizenship merely by migrating to Rome. Other communities were bound to Rome by formal treaty or in many cases by informal and customary ties of subordination. In addition great tracts of land throughout Italy had been added to the *ager publicus* of the Roman people so that the economic life of 'allied', i.e. subject, communities depended on possession of what was legally Roman land. The Italian communities were bound to Rome in perpetual alliances. They retained a measure of local self-government and while they paid no tribute to Rome they were required to supply contingents for Rome's armies at their own cost and to fight in Rome's wars. Between half and two-thirds of Rome's armies in the second century had consisted of Latins and other allies.

By a variety of treaties and other legal or customary forms the Italian communities were integrated into a single state under the domination of Rome. It is quite misleading to describe this as a federation of states. The Italian communities had local autonomy only and they had no institutional representation in the government of Rome or in the determination of foreign policy. They were subjects of the Roman state, and were subjected to arbitrary interferences from Rome and had none of the legal protection accorded to Roman citizens, for example, against the actions of Roman magistrates or military commanders. In the absence of formal political mechanisms these communities achieved representation in the state through the patronage of Roman politicians. In this way the patron–client relation of Roman custom formed an essential part of the institutional apparatus of the Roman state.[11]

The effective political integration of Italy into the Roman state through the institutional mechanisms of the perpetual treaty and of patronage must transform and subvert the functioning of the formal political institutions of the Roman city state. It is the intervention of patronage on a massive scale, in other words, that enables the governmental institutions of the city of Rome to function as the government of the peculiarly complex state of Italy. What must appear from the standpoint of the representative institutions of the city of Rome as a corruption is an integral part of the institutional apparatus of a new form of state. It is often assumed that the Italians took no part in Roman political life before they were granted the citizenship (Sherwin-White, *The Roman Citizenship*, p. 126f) and that 'the structure of the city-state was maintained almost intact, with only some slight modifications' (Rostovtzeff, *Social and Economic History of the Roman Empire*, p. 35) during this period. These positions rest on a fundamental error which has grave consequences for the analysis of the political history of the Republic. It results from the failure to distinguish the concept of political representation, that is, the necessary representation of the class struggle and of class interests at the political level of the social formation, from particular institutional mechanisms of representation: citizens are thought to be represented, others are not. The fact that representation always takes place by means of determinate mechanisms with determinate institutional supports (parties, state apparatuses) means that it cannot be conceived in the form of a simple *expression* of interests or desires.[12] In the present case failure to recognise the institutional character of patron–client relations as mechanisms of representation induces a fundamental misrecognition of the character of the Roman state and the nature of Roman politics.[13]

The integration of the extra-Italian provinces and semi-autonomous domains into the political unity of the empire during the last century of the Republic in part by similar mechanisms raises the political significance of the institution of patronage to a considerably higher level. The sheer scale of the economic resources entering into the political representation of the non-citizen territories transforms the political and financial position of those able to function as patrons. It therefore multiplies the costs of maintaining an effective political career, increases still further the aristocratic and oligarchic tendencies in Roman politics and leads eventually to the disastrous civil wars that finally shatter the institutional forms of the Republic.

Before considering these conflicts we must return for a moment to the position of the population of Italy at the beginning of the first century. Apart from the various categories of Roman citizens and the partial citizenship of the Latins a substantial proportion of the Italian population have no formal citizenship rights in Rome while retaining various rights in respect of their own communities. They contribute substantially to the costs of Roman imperialism but receive little of its returns. Italian troops participate in the distribution of booty, but receive less than their Roman allies, and Italian traders may be allowed to trade throughout the empire. However, the really substantial profits of empire, through the government of provinces, participation in companies of publicans and state contractors, and the massive legal and illegal appropriation of booty, are denied to the Italians. This means that while the forces leading to the destruction of small landed property operate throughout Italy those leading to the formation of large estates tend to favour the Romans. Similar disparities arise with regard to money-lending and the various contractual devices whereby citizens in the ancient world are able to exploit their fellows.

To these disparities we must add the absence of effective political and legal rights in respect of the government of Rome and the behaviour of Roman magistrates and commanders, except indirectly through the mechanisms of patronage with all the risks and costs that it involves. Finally, recall that much of the land of the Italian communities, up to a third in many cases, belongs to the *ager publicus* of the Roman people. In a predominantly agrarian population this means that effective landed property, large and small, is subjected to the vagaries of the internal politics of the people of the city of Rome. In particular it is continually at risk from popular agitation for the distribution of public land, from the distribution of allotments to army veterans, from attempts by the Gracchi and others to recreate the small peasant basis for the citizen army. In these conditions the rejection of demands that Roman citizenship be extended to Italians created an explosive situation leading to the outbreak of the Social War (the war against the *socii* or allies) in 91 B.C.

There is some dispute among specialists about the aims of the Italians in the war. Sherwin-White maintains, for example, that the allies had little interest in the specifically political rights of citizenship, the vote in particular, that their main concern was 'their improper subjection to the undivided and unchecked *imperium* of Roman magistrates, and the exploitation of themselves by the power for which they had won the empire' (*The Roman Citizenship*, p. 127).[14] In fact there is no inconsistency between these demands. It is clear, for example, that the political rights of citizenship play an essential part in the maintenance of equality of legal status and of equal participation in the exploitation of the extra-Italian empire. In any event, the granting of citizenship to Italians as a result of war has two consequences of the greatest importance for the future of Rome. In the first place the Italians were incorporated into the body of citizens as communities which became self-governing *municipia*. The Roman citizen was then no longer primarily a resident in the city of Rome but a member of a sovereign state on the one hand and of his municipal patria on the other. This first step in the overthrow of the city-state form of government began the process of municipalisation that was to form the basis of the political organisation of the empire in the Imperial period. Secondly, while the body of citizens were no longer primarily inhabitants of Rome the Senate and the various assemblies were still held in Rome itself. This geographical expansion of the citizenship increased the disparity in the effective political rights of the different categories of citizens. The centuriate and tribal assemblies were dominated by the wealthy from all over Italy, who could afford to travel to Rome, and the proletariat of the city of Rome and its neighbourhood. In Rostovtzeff's view, 'the popular assembly of Rome, which consisted after the Social War of a ridiculously small minority of the Roman citizens, ceased to be a true representative of the aspirations of the Roman citizens and became a tool in the hands of clever politicians' (*op. cit.*, p. 25).

The Social War is followed by a series of civil wars which devastate large areas of Italy and produce massive transfers of land as the victors reward their followers and expropriate their opponents or neutrals in order to do so, which consume the wealth of the provinces through the massive appropriations by various armies and which finally overthrow the institutions of the Roman city-state and annihilate large sections of the old senatorial nobility. Rostovtzeff describes this period as dominated by the struggle between a senatorial and equestrian oligarchy supported by a municipal bourgeoisie on the one hand and the masses of the poor, the landless proletarians and the representatives of small landed property, on the other, 'between rich and poor, "oppressors" and "oppressed". The struggle between these two classes once begun could not be ended' (p. 24). In a predominantly agrarian world it is inevitable that the main issue of the struggle was the distribution of land. On the other hand the main political task facing Rome in this period 'was the adaptation of the city-state system to the needs of a world-state, its transformation into a new form of polity capable of governing the vast territories which now formed the Roman Empire' (pp. 25–6).[15] Others, on the basis of the detailed analysis of the shifting composition of political factions, have analysed the conflicts of this period primarily in terms of the struggle for power between a small number of powerful families and their allies or clients.[16]

These opposed conceptions of the fundamental character of Roman political conflict are partial and incomplete. In the absence of an elaborated theoretical analysis of the structure of the political level, in particular of the mechanisms of political representation of classes and class-fractions, and their institutional supports, and of the functioning of state apparatuses, they are quite irreconcilable. Yet they are both clearly inadequate. While we may quarrel with Rostovtzeff's conception of the formation of classes in the ancient world, he clearly recognises the importance of the land question in the history of the Republic and the effects of war, debt, and illegal expropriations by the powerful in the formation of a landless or near-landless stratum of the citizens. Nevertheless his analysis in terms of the struggle over land between rich and poor entirely fails to account for the form of political conflict in the late Republic. How, for example, can the conflicts Rostovtzeff describes take the form of factional conflicts among a small number of noble families and their allies in which popular demands appear to be taken up or dropped in a totally cynical fashion? On the other hand, if the struggle is primarily between a small number of noble families how are we to account for the political and economic conditions of existence of their power or for the devastating effects of the forces they appear to mobilise?

A concrete analysis of the political conjunctures leading up to the collapse of the Republic cannot be attempted here. In the present text it is possible to give only the briefest indication of the necessary complexity of the forces involved. The significance of the patron–client relation as the institutional support of mechanisms of political representation has been shown above. Even after the enfranchisement of Italy the location of representative assemblies in Rome ensures that such mechanisms continue to operate – the ability of the young Pompey to raise an army from his Italian clients is evidence enough of this – under rather different conditions. The position of the extra-Italian provinces with respect to the mechanisms of political representation remain unchanged by the results of the Social War. The existence of a large overseas empire and the representation of overseas communities by means of patronage effectively subverts what remains of the formal political institutions of the city-state by ensuring that vast resources are available to the small number of noble families that have been able to establish suitable relationships.

In addition the exploitation of the provinces of the empire provides a major source of income from the profits of government either directly through the proceeds of political administration or indirectly through 'private enterprise' in the service of the state. In the first case while the governors of the provinces receive no salary the expenses are quite substantial and there are numerous opportunities for extortion of provincials. Cicero, who is reputed to have been scrupulously honest, was able to save 550,000 *denarii* during two years as governor of Cilicia. Access to these positions was restricted to magistrates and ex-magistrates, that is, effectively to the senatorial class. On the other hand the provinces were exploited by companies of publicans, that is, of tax collectors who might also branch out into banking, money-lending and other subsidiary activities.[17] Since these companies had to supply substantial guarantees in the form of property sufficient to cover the tax they were contracted to collect, participation in their profits is again effectively governed by the possession of property. Thus in the Republic, and to a lesser extent in the Principate and Empire, we find the appropriation of surplus-labour from the provinces is articulated in two quite distinct forms within the political and economic structure. While the development of these two forms of appropriation generates a certain level of conflict within the ruling class it is clear that appropriation through formal political position predominates over appropriation through private enterprise. By the first century senators were able to participate indirectly in the profits of publicans so it is quite misleading to represent the conflict of governor and publican in the provinces as generating conflict between a class of equites and a class of nobles.

These consequences of empire must exacerbate the oligarchic tendencies of the political forms of the Roman Republic. The costs and potential rewards of a successful political career are enormously increased. The accumulation of vast financial resources in the hands of a small number of noble families and state contractors leads to the growth of large landed estates and intensifies the pressure on small landed property. Thus the creation of a debt-ridden landless proletariat and a near-landless peasantry develops together with the effective disenfranchisement of these sections of the citizenry. The army offers a chance of land in the allocation of allotments to veterans and military command is one of the major vehicles of political advancement among the upper classes. In these circumstances, as Rostovtzeff has observed, the army functions both as an instrument in the hands of political leaders and as a mechanism of political representation of the Italian lower classes. The army was to perform a similar function of political representation in the later Empire. In both cases the mechanism of representation is such that a direct polarisation of classes cannot appear. Instead, the class struggle takes the form of military interventions in the factional conflict of the ruling class. The loyalty of the troops to their noble leaders is a function of their ability to furnish the spoils of victory. Since political representation cannot be conceived as an *expression*, for example, of the hopes and desires of the masses, but is always an effect of determinate practices under determinate conditions, the fact that military service was generally unpopular does not contradict the representational character of the army. In the political structure of the Republic the conditions which exacerbate the conflict between classes must also intensify the internal conflict within the ruling class for factional control of patronage and the profits of government.

Thus it is the articulation of the class struggle within the Roman citizenry and the transformation and displacement of the representative institutions of the city-state with the political integrating of the empire that governs the conditions in which such destructive forces are mobilised behind the faction fighting of the nobility. The new form of state that emerges in the Principate of Augustus finally eliminates these conditions by centralising the institution of patronage in respect of provincial communities in the hands of the First Citizen and his functionaries and by removing the control of access to the profits of government from the arena of open factional conflict. This state leaves no place for the 'freedom' enjoyed by the old nobility, namely, the freedom to squabble among themselves over the spoils of empire.[18] The new forms of political integration of the provinces open the way to municipalisation and the gradual spread of Roman citizenship throughout the Empire while the new institutional structure of the state transforms the conditions of realisation of the surplus-labour appropriated by right of citizenship.[19]

3 Trade and commodity production in the ancient world

The concept of the ancient mode of a production has been represented above as one in which the predominant form of labour process is that of the individual peasant family, perhaps supplemented by a few slaves, under conditions of simple co-operation and natural economy. In all districts but those situated near to navigable rivers or the coast the tremendous costs of land transport compelled a large measure of local self-sufficiency and prevented any extensive development of commodity production. In the late Roman Empire, for example, it was cheaper to ship grain from one end of the Mediterranean to the other than to cart it 75 miles (Jones, *The Later Roman Empire*, II, p. 841f). In the absence of water transport, production is dominated by the peasants, more or less oppressed, more or less debt-ridden, and by the scatter of larger estates of the wealthy worked by slaves or by the labour of the free peasants. Luxuries apart, the development of trade and commodity production is confined to a more or less narrow coastal strip and to the valleys of the navigable rivers. In the towns and countryside of these areas more complex economic forms may develop and individual peasant production may no longer predominate. The question of slavery and of the conditions of slave production are discussed in chapter 3. Here we shall consider how the dominant relations of appropriation of surplus-labour define the possibilities and limits to the development of trade and commodity production and, incidentally, of wage-labour and of tenancy relations based on ties of personal dependence. We shall see that these last develop under conditions which preclude the establishment of capitalist or of feudal relations of production.

No one disputes that the ancient world saw extensive physical movements of slaves, grain, wine, oil, and pottery, or that at least some of these movements took the form of commodity circulation. The extent and the precise economic character of these movements have been and remain a matter of dispute. A concise account of the debate is given in Pearson's paper 'The Secular Debate on Economic Primitivism'. Bucher, for example, maintains that complex economic life in the form of an extensive exchange of goods and services on a national scale is no older than the modern state (*Industrial Evolution*, p. 88). Thus he denies the significance of trade and money in the ancient world and emphasises instead the self-sufficient *oikos* as the basic unit of the ancient economy. Rostovtzeff on the other hand maintains that the commercial capitalism of the Greek and Roman worlds brought them 'very near to the stage of industrial capitalism that characterises the economic history of Europe in the nineteenth and twentieth centuries' (*op. cit.*, p. 3). These economies were characterised by large internal markets, the mass production of goods for an indefinite market and the employment in industry and agriculture of 'the methods of pure capitalistic economy based on slave-labour' (*ibid.*).

An immediate difficulty appears in Rostovtzeff's conception of the structure of the ancient economy. In the Hellenistic monarchies we find that 'very soon the sound economic development described above was first stunted and then gradually atrophied by many and various causes' (p. 4). The same development had appeared in the city-states of Greece and was to appear again in the Roman Empire. Rostovtzeff locates the major cause of this development in the endemic warfare of the ancient world and in the consequent prodigious military expenditures which result in state intervention in the production and exchange of essential goods and in the progressive impoverishment of the mass of the population. This explanation is not so much false as inadequate. The endemic warfare and level of military preparedness of the ancient world cannot be considered as independent of the structure of the ancient economy and in this respect, as in others, the place and function of commodity relations in the structure of the economy of the ancient world are hardly comparable to those of nineteenth- and twentieth-century Europe.

Pearson observes that the confused and inconclusive character of this debate follows from the fact that both sides 'were unable to conceive of an elaborate economy with trade, money, and market places being organised in any manner other than that of the market system' (*op. cit.*, p. 10). Unfortunately while the authors of *Trade and Market in the Early Empires* demonstrate the necessity of the theoretical construction of types of economy quite distinct from the market system, i.e. from capitalism, their own attempts in this direction are less than successful.[20]

Pearson finds at least the outlines of a new approach in the following passage from Weber's *General Economic History*:[21]

> Taken in its entirety [the foregoing argument leads to the conclusion that] the city democracy of antiquity is a political guild. [It is true that it had distinctive industrial interests and also that these were monopolized; but they were subordinate to military interests]. Tribute, booty, and payments of confederate cities, were merely distributed among the citizens. . . . The monopoly of the political guild included cleruchy, the distributing of conquered land among the citizens, and the distribution of the spoils of war; and at the last the city paid out of the proceeds of its political activity theater admissions,

> allotments of grain, and payments for jury service and for participation in religious rites (pp. 244–5, quoted by Pearson, *op. cit.*, p. 9).

Here, far from offering a new approach, Weber merely reproduces the traditional and misleading doctrine that the Greeks and Romans lived by sharing the proceeds of plunder amongst themselves: 'war made the city rich, while a long period of peace meant ruin for the citizenship' (*op. cit.*, p. 245). Pearson, it appears, finds in the sharing out of the plunder an example of *redistribution*, one of the three or four basic patterns of economic integration identified by Polanyi.[22] The problem of the conditions necessary for a people to live by plunder is not ever posed within this position. Marx exposes this weakness with regard to an even more extreme version of the plunder thesis as follows.

> Truly comical is M. Bastiat, who imagines that the ancient Greeks and Romans lived by plunder alone. But when people plunder for centuries, there must always be something at hand for them to seize, the objects of plunder must be continually reproduced. It would thus appear that even the Greeks and Romans had some process of production, consequently an economy, which just as much constituted the material basis of their world as bourgeois economy constitutes that of our modern world (*Capital*, I, pp. 81–2n).

In proposing to discriminate between types of economy in terms of a small number of mechanisms of distribution of goods and persons, that is, at the level of circulation, these authors preclude the analysis of the determination and significance of circulation in the reproduction of the economy as a whole. As a result they mistake the essential significance of the circulation of commodities within capitalism (the market system in their terms) and, since they define other types of economy by contrast with the market system, must also misrecognise the essential structure of these other systems.

If generalised commodity exchange, the market system of Polanyi *et al.*, is an invariant of the capitalist mode of production this is because the capitalist mode of appropriation of surplus-labour through the production of surplus-value and its realisation for a capitalist class, works through the mechanism of the exchange of equivalents between capitalists and labourers of the two departments of production (department I produces means of production, department II produces means of consumption). Here the difference of necessary-labour and surplus-labour is realised in the difference between the value of a commodity, labour-power, and the value that is created by its productive use. The appropriation of surplus-labour under capitalism takes place through a system of commodity exchange involving the production of commodities by means of commodities, since labour-power and means of production must first be purchased by the capitalist. Thus commodity relations occupy the place of a central and invariant element in the capitalist mode of production while in all other modes of production they are assigned a subordinate place, neither essential nor invariant, with regard to the operation of non-commodity mechanisms of appropriation of surplus-labour.

We can now return to the problem of commodity relations in the ancient world. The essential point concerns the mechanism of the appropriation of surplus-labour by a class. In capitalism the mechanism of appropriation of surplus-labour works through commodity relations and involves the dominance of the economic level. In the ancient mode of production it is constituted by the intervention of political and legal relations which determine, for example, certain rights of possession of land, the position of the tax-farmer, etc. The revenues of the capitalist are devoted to personal consumption on the one hand and to the reproduction and expansion of the economic conditions of his continued exploitation of his labourers, that is, in the purchase of means of production and labour-power to replace those consumed in the production process. The structure of the capitalist mode of production imposes a tendency towards the increase in the rate of exploitation through the growth in the proportion of constant capital (i.e. means of production) to variable capital (i.e. labour-power). The conditions of a general increase in the level of capitalist exploitation therefore require an increase in the productive power of labour and in the general level of commodity production (not necessarily in the production of articles of individual consumption).

In the ancient mode of production commodity relations are articulated on the conditions of exploitation in an entirely different fashion. The revenues of members of the ruling class are devoted to the reproduction of the political and legal conditions of their continued appropriation of surplus-labour. Only to a limited extent do these conditions generate investment in production, the purchase of land and slaves or the means of production necessary to the running of slave-worked latifundia or manufactories. For the rest, individual expenditures among the ruling class are overwhelmingly directed at the maintenance or improvement of their political and social position among the body of citizens. Far from transforming their surplus product into *capital* the ancients invest it in unproductive expenditures on art, public and religious works, litigation and all kinds of social and political junketings.[23] This accounts for the very limited character of the development of productive forces in the ancient world and also, therefore, for the often catastrophic effects of temporary devastations of war. The rapid replacement of the means and conditions of production is often beyond the productive capacities of ancient communities.

Commodity relations are an essential element in the mechanism of appropriation of surplus-labour under capitalism and the market for commodity production is provided primarily by the productive expenditures of the capitalist class and by the reproduction of labour-power through the personal consumption of the working class. In the ancient world, and also under feudalism, the market for commodities depends primarily on the unproductive consumption of the ruling class and their functionaries on the one hand and state expenditures on the other. Clearly, it is not necessary to the ancient mode of production that either of these consumptions be met by means of commodities. While its needs may be met by purchase from state contractors the state may also supply its military materials or state doles of corn, oil, wine, directly from its own estates or manufactories. Similarly, the consumption needs of the ruling class may be met by purchase, directly from their own estates, in payments in kind from clients or debtors, and so on. To the extent that these consumptions do provide a market for commodity production it is clear that a secondary market for means of production or the consumption of direct producers may develop.

Under these conditions forms of free wage-labour may develop in agriculture and in urban artisan production and manufacture. Where this emerges in conjunction with the growth of a propertyless body of citizens, for example, the Roman proletariat, why should it not lead to the development of capitalist production? Two obvious answers suggest themselves. First, the conditions which lead to the massive alienation of peasant producers from the land, essentially the direct and indirect effects of war, also tend to produce masses of slaves and booty. Hence the development of slave-worked latifundia and manufactories may coincide with the growth of a propertyless stratum of the citizens. Where a ready supply of slaves is not available there are attempts, legal or illegal, to tie the impoverished peasants to the land.

Second, the propertyless citizenry in Rome, and to some extent in other cities, are not necessarily compelled to the regular and repeated sale of their labour-power in order to eat. They may rely also on state doles or the army, or they may sell their fists and votes to the political factions in the Senate. However, the fundamental obstacle to the development of the capitalist mode of production is precisely the articulation of commodity relations *within the ancient mode* of production. While 'capitalist' relations, i.e. commodity production on the basis of free wage-labour, may appear at the level of individual units of production they cannot be integrated within a system of capitalist exchange relations, at the level of the reproduction of the economy as a whole. Thus the structure and conditions of existence of commodity relations in the ancient world preclude the production and realisation of surplus-labour for a capitalist class by means of the circulation of commodities between the departments of production.

We have now reached a point of the greatest importance for the understanding of the place and function of trade and commodity production in the ancient world. The development of commodity relations is governed by the level of surplus appropriation which takes place through the intervention of politics by means which do not necessarily involve commodity relations, and by the conditions which govern the distribution of the surplus product within the ruling class and its agencies. It is not merely the level of surplus-labour appropriation but also the distribution of the surplus product among a more or less substantial body of citizens that provides the conditions for extensive commodity production. These conditions were satisfied in the cities and municipalities of the ancient world to a greater or lesser extent. We shall see the significance of this variation in a moment.

One consequence of commodity production is that the extraction of a certain portion of surplus-labour can be realised in the form of money. Hence commodity production plays a significant part in the appropriation of surplus-labour throughout the extensive empires of the Hellenistic monarchies and of the late Roman Republic and Empire. The existence of provincial cities allows for a substantial portion of the local surplus to be consumed by the local ruling classes and for the development of a certain level of commodity production on the basis of their consumption and that of army garrisons. Under these conditions a large proportion of the surplus appropriated by the imperial state can be extracted from the provinces in the form of money.

The advantages for the state of appropriation in money rather than in produce are obvious. Money is relatively compact, it is easier to transport under ancient conditions, and it does not rot or decay. In addition, the development of a banking system facilitates long-distance payments by reducing the need for physical transfers of goods or money. Thus the establishment of colonies and provincial municipalities becomes one of the dominant forms of imperial administration under this mode of production. This tendency towards the municipalisation of empires leads to the rapid growth of commodity production and of interprovincial trade within the limits imposed by transport costs.

However, this growth of commodity production and of local and long-distance commerce is essentially fragile and countervailing mechanisms can easily come into play. We have seen that the level of commodity production in the cities and municipalities depends essentially on the presence of a more or less substantial municipal 'middle class' and therefore on the volume of the locally retained surplus. In other words it depends on a certain type of distribution of the surplus-labour appropriated within the imperial system. Once these conditions are disturbed – for example, through the growth in imperial taxation of provincial cities beyond a certain point, through increased exactions by the large magnates, through indebtedness of the municipalities to money-lenders – the local commodity market must be reduced and the level of commodity production curtailed. This immediately reduces the amount of tax that may be extracted in the form of money and though this reduction may be staved off temporarily through the activities of money-lenders this merely redoubles the growing impoverishment of the municipalities. There is therefore a tendency to increase taxation in the form of produce and labour. Furthermore, because of the greatly increased costs of administering this latter form of taxation a general increase in tax levels is necessary if the earlier total is to be retained by the imperial authorities. This, of course, depresses the level of commodity production and inter-regional trade still further.

It is clear that the progressive impoverishment of the provincial cities after an initial flowering of commodity production may be brought about through the taxation needed to meet the costs of warfare and military defence. However, the warfare endemic in the ancient world gives only a partial explanation of this impoverishment. At a more general level this progressive impoverishment is an effect of the tendency discussed above towards political and economic concentration in ancient societies. The economic conditions of the municipal middle classes are maintained by virtue of their political and legal position with respect to the state political and military apparatuses and the larger magnates. If it does not require a war to effect a deterioration in these conditions the costs of maintaining a large standing army can only exacerbate the deterioration.

Finally, it may be observed that the progressive collapse of the money economy induced by the effects of war and by essentially political changes in the conditions of distribution of the surplus product must lead to further transformations of the political and legal structure of the state, and to the dominance of new institutional forms of realisation of ancient relations of production. On the one hand the necessity of increasing state exactions in the form of produce, liturgies and forced labour further decreases the extent to which commercial relations can be relied upon to furnish the movements of goods and services necessary to the existence of a large and complex state. In the late Roman Empire and in some at least of the Hellenistic states there appears what Rostovtzeff describes as 'the nationalisation of both production and exchange' (*op. cit.*, p. 4). The state is forced to take over control of more and more branches of economic activity. The Roman Empire set up state-controlled guilds in shipping, the distribution of grain, the production and sale of meat and bread, and in many other branches of production. More and more citizens were effectively bound to their occupations and membership of these guilds and of the governing bodies of the municipia became hereditary. The peasantry were subjected to forced labour and to forced military appropriations.[24]

These developments entail a vast increase in the bureaucratic apparatus and, because of the growing reliance on payments in kind, a catastrophic decline in the levels of efficiency and of centralised accountability of this apparatus. There follows an effective decentralisation of administration and an expansion in the forms of patronage that may be exercised by officials and powerful magnates, notably protection from more or less arbitrary requisitions and forced labour or from unpaid public service. Legally free citizens are effectively transformed into the subjects of an oppressive despotism. Townspeople flee the towns and peasants seek the protection of the powerful landowners.

The transformation of the state apparatus therefore produces conditions in which economic relations based on ties of personal dependence develop between the politically powerful and direct producers which are analogous in certain respects to the lord–serf relations characteristic of some variants of feudalism. Notables retired to their estates which were farmed by tenants owing labour service or rent-in-kind or by *de facto* tenants whose landed property is held only by virtue of the notable's protection. Artisan production tends to concentrate in these estates for similar reasons, thus the notables receive their income in kind and in labour and the state tends to receive a growing proportion of its taxes in the same way. In the late Empire large numbers of tenants, *coloni*, were legally bound to the land and to compulsory labour service for their landlord.

With the decline in commodity production, then, we find a reversion to natural economy, the localisation of production and the growing 'feudalisation' of the Empire. It must be emphasised, however, that this 'feudalisation' is nevertheless limited and subordinated by the structure of the ancient mode of production. The conditions of existence of the form of patronage that generates these 'feudal' relations is that the patron occupies a certain type of political position within the ancient form of state. This condition defines the limits to the 'feudalisation' of relations within ancient society. It is not based on monopoly of the land. For all the localisation of power and the natural economy of the late Empire, especially in the West, we are still dealing with the ancient mode of production and the ancient mode of appropriation by right of citizenship. In this case, of course, that great mass of the citizens are themselves the exploited but, as we have seen, the exploitation of citizens is in no way incompatible with the ancient mode of production. There is no natural or inevitable growth of feudalism within the ancient mode of production and the ancient mode does not naturally evolve through the development of clientage and the colonate, into the feudal mode of production. The transition of feudalism from the ancient mode in the West no more grows out of neo-feudal relations of clientage than the transition to capitalism grew out of the earlier development of wage-labour and commodity production. What is required for the transition to feudalism under the conditions of the late Empire is the destruction of the ancient form of state and, in particular, the destruction of a form of state based on the political and legal conditions of citizenship and of the conditions of existence of private property in land.

It is clear, then, that the structure of the ancient mode of production itself establishes the conditions which limit the development of commodity production and of productive forces in general in the ancient world. The predominant form of labour process is that of the individual peasant producer under a variety of more or less oppressive external conditions. More complex forms of labour process develop only in sectors of production which depend on the level of exploitation of the mass of direct producers. Thus the scope for the development of productive forces is extremely limited within the ancient world and the highest developments, in slave-worked latifundia and manufactories, hardly affect the productivity or conditions of labour of the mass of direct producers.

Three

Slavery

This chapter will not be confined to the analysis of slavery as a system of social production. Slave production presupposes the existence of slavery as an *institution* – slavery is always first and foremost a legal or customary *status*. Slaves and the institution of slavery can exist where slave labour is not the basis of the system of social production. In the first section of this chapter we will examine the legal form of slavery. No question is subject to more humanist mythologising than slavery – slavery is the most extreme form of denial of the human essence, the most important attribute of which is freedom. For the humanist slavery is a form of human subjection or domination – an impossible form, doomed to ruin and failure by the revolt of the slaves, and the degeneration and demoralisation of their captors. In the second part of this chapter we will question these humanist assumptions about slavery as a form of domination. In the third section we will pose the question: Is there a slave mode of production? We will attempt to develop a concept of a mode of production in which slave labour is the basis of social production. In the fourth and final section the effects of the analysis of slave systems of production in terms of humanist and subjectivist concepts will be examined and criticised – Eugène Genovese and John Cairnes will be taken as examples.

1 The nature of slavery as an institution

The forms of bondage of human beings are extremely varied, varying from serfdom, debt-bondage and contract-bondage, to the various forms and degress of slavery. It is for this reason that it is necessary to define the institution of slavery most exactly. To adopt a very general notion like 'mastership and bondage' without clearly specifying the institutional forms involved is to be led into a maze of quite different legal statuses and social situations: from peonage in contemporary Latin America to indentured labour in seventeenth-century North America. The effect of such notions is to suppress the legal/customary *form* in favour of inter-subjective relations which are essential and invariable. But legal forms do have a definite effectivity, as we shall see below.

In consequence our analysis will be centred upon *chattel slavery*; a form of bondage in which human beings are a form of *property* and in which the owner has all of the rights of property over the slave. We will concentrate upon this form of legal subordination because it has been the foundation of all significant slave systems, and because, as we shall see below, it represents the necessary legal form of slavery in the slave mode of production.

CHATTEL SLAVERY IN LAW

All forms of bondage entail a legally or customarily unequal and subordinate status for those subjected to them – bondage is a form of legally-sanctioned unfreedom. It is because of this that the features differentiating slavery from other forms of bondage and the salient features which all forms of slavery have in common are most readily understood through the laws pertaining to it.

The developed form of chattel slavery is that in which the slave is a particular variant of private property and in which there is a system of exchange corresponding to this type of property. Developed chattel slavery presupposes the existence of private property as a general institution and the repressive-legal apparatus corresponding to it, the state. Systems of slave law therefore only appear at a relatively high stage of development of the institution of slavery. But in order to understand the essential features of the institution of slavery it is not necessary to follow this long evolution, for the essence is to be found in the legal definition.[1] In recognising the slave as a *chattel* the law defines the essence of the slave's condition: whatever the variations of custom and practice which may grant the slave a larger measure of freedom, the law still makes it possible that the slave *may* be sold, punished or abused in contradiction of these customs and practices.

Roman private law reflects chattel slavery in the clearest and most developed legal form.[2] This law differentiates two classes of phenomena which it treats of, *things* (*res*) and *persons*.[3] These categories are fundamental to the law and are logically prior to all particular laws, they serve to establish the nature of the objects on which the laws operate.[4] We will consider here the nature of things and persons. The Roman conception of the legal personality does not refer to the characteristics of the human subject but to the attributes of the legal subject.[5] The legal personality is an entity which is legally free, legally responsible and which can appear as an autonomous party in legal actions and disputes. The legal personality is the support or carrier of the legal process; it is the subject which makes that process possible and necessary.[6] Personality is a *status*, it does not apply to human subjects as such, but only to certain human subjects in so far as they have a certain legal position and legal capacity. A thing, on the other hand, appears in law only as the property, the alienable attribute, of subjects and as the object of dispute between subjects. A thing can never be a legal subject.

The Roman concept of the legal person, which does not include within it all adult human beings, corresponds to a society in which many men were legally unfree or subordinate to others as dependants or clients. Political and legal freedom were attached to a definite social position. Citizenship was a status which entailed certain *political* rights and duties (at least in the period of the Republic) and legal freedom a status which entailed the right to social autonomy, in particular, the right to make contracts. Not all legally free men were citizens and there were also many conditions in which formally free men were not legally autonomous. It was possible for the law to recognise 'persons' who did not have all the rights and attributes of legal subjects, that is, who were recognised as being dependent on another person. The simplest case is when custody is especially given by the law to one person over another, for example, guardianship over a minor. However, the Roman head of household enjoyed the right of custodianship over his *familia*, consisting not only of his immediate family but also of his dependants, servants and slaves. In respect of this type of subordinate status (with the exception of the slaves) while legal responsibility and autonomy were vested in another the legal *personality* of the subordinate is recognised and limits are set to the jurisdiction and actions of the custodian which follow from the personality of the subordinate: examples are, the limit of the age of majority in the case of a minor, or, the limitation of the authority of the master to the period of service of the servant.

Slaves were not the only people in Rome whose freedom was bound by legal limits. In this legal system and this society, in which the concept of person admitted of several conditions of unfreedom, the position of the slave was not a mere extension or development of these unfreedoms but an entirely different status. The nature of this status depends upon the opposition person/thing. In Roman law the slave is unquestionably the *property* of his owner who may treat him as he would any other item of property; in particular, he is alienable. In the case of chattel slavery the law defines a human subject as a legal *non-subject* – a being who may be treated by its owner as a thing and who therefore may be treated as a non-subject in practice. Slavery reduces a human being to the status of a thing, an alienable attribute of persons.

The chattel slave is a contradictory being, a human subject and a legal non-subject, *a man-thing*.[7] The slave produces endless confusion because he is assimilable completely to neither of the legal categories.[8]

He cannot be counted a person for he would cease to be a slave, but he cannot be reduced to property pure and simple. A legal non-subject, the slave's value *as property* depends upon the fact that he has the attributes of a human subject, that is, the capacity to act on instruction, the faculty of judgment, etc. Hence the Roman division of forms of property into *instrumentum mutum*, *instrumentum semi vocale* and *instrumentum vocale*.

The criminal law holds the slave responsible for his actions; it must deal with him when he murders his master or commits some criminal offence against a third party. It thereby and contradictorily, recognises the slave as a *subject*; one does not try wardrobes for falling on their owners or dogs for biting their masters. In Rome, and elsewhere, *pure* chattel slavery never existed in fact, for the law recognised elements of personality in the slave and corresponding limitations on his master's rights.[9] In order to mitigate the harsh and barbarous treatment of slaves and its often disruptive social consequences legal systems have been led to support inconsistency in their definitions and their practice. These meliorations of the slave's legal condition on the part of enlightened Roman jurists, or, later, in the Anglo-Saxon Americas the laws to prevent the grotesque abuse of human chattels, reveal all the more clearly the nature of the slave's legal status and the social position following from it – the fact that laws *were needed* to prevent slaves from being callously killed or cruelly tortured by their owners.[10] Whatever the contradictions and inconsistencies it was predominantly as property and not as a man that the slave was regarded in law and in fact.

The law defines the status of the slave both formally and substantively, but this single and relatively constant legal status has existed in many different systems of economic, political and social relations. The study of the law pertaining to slavery although it is a necessary point of departure is not a *sufficient* basis for the understanding of slavery – to understand fully its political and social consequences one must also study the workings of the slave systems.

2 Is slavery a form of political domination?

Our analysis of the legal form of slavery has been a necessary preface to this section – it enables us to see the contradiction in the very terms of this question. From the foregoing section it will be evident that *slavery is a legal or customary institution, which necessarily implies its subordination as a partial form to a larger structure of socio-political relations.* Slavery is a legal form of property which gives to an owner certain rights over the person of a human subject. But this form and these rights only exist *within* a distinct form of state or community. Slavery always exists within a wider political and social system, it is never an exclusive form of domination or state in and of itself; a regime composed of masters and slaves as rulers and ruled. The masters are not absolute sovereigns each lording it over his kingdom of slaves; the masters are citizens or the subjects of a state, bound by its laws and customs and subordinate to its political control. The master enjoys the ability to exploit his human chattels from law and custom and the ability to control them from the existence of the repressive apparatus of the state. The mastership of the owner over the slave is a *proprietal* one and not a political one – it implies the pre-existence of laws and a political order which makes this possession of human subjects as chattels possible.[11] The slave is neither a subject nor a subordinate, he is a form of property; the master is not his *lord*, he is his *owner*.

Slavery is not a distinct form of political domination, but this is a recent and not unquestioned view. Slavery has played a very important role in Western political theory.

Certain natural law theorists, such as Grotius, saw slavery as harmonious with natural justice and argued that any denial of the rights of the master would weaken the authority of the magistrate, undermine the foundation of the laws, and challenge the right of princes to obedience. Certain political theorists of the absolutist form of state, such as Hobbes, have seen slavery as the essence or foundation of all forms of political sovereignty.[12] Hobbes did so in the sense that he modelled political obligation on the subordination of the vanquished who gives his obedience to the victor in exchange for his life: in the same way, he argued, do the subjects of the state give themselves unconditionally to the sovereign in exchange for the security of their own lives. This is not so much an *explanation* of political domination as it is a *rationale* for obedience, and a justification for the state's absolute power *vis-à-vis* its subjects.

Hegel's text on 'Lord and Bondsman' in *The Phenomenology of Mind* has been recognised (in certain readings) as giving a unique dialectic to slavery in that it is the slave who becomes the essential one of the relation, it is through him and in him that the master lives.[13] The consciousness of the lord and the consciousness of the bondsman are both partial, but it is in that of the bondsman that the truth of the relation is to be found and it is the bondsman who in the relation finds true self-consciousness. Hegel's passage is justly famous but it has nothing to do with slavery and establishes no special relation of domination between master and slave. Hegel's object is the genesis of self-consciousness not the dynamics of slave systems. For Hegel the relation has nothing whatever to do with slavery; it concerns the abstract subordination of one self to another, a subordination which may be one of willing and voluntary service. For Hegel the social status of the occupants of these places is inconsequential, and the status of these places in *The Phenomenology of Mind* is a function of its own object and its own logic.

Democratic and liberal political theory and ideology have also seen a unique political character in slavery, but it is the inverse of the absolutist's conception. For the democrats slavery is the most evil and oppressive form of domination of man by man. Despite his legal status as property the slave cannot be equated with a wardrobe and forgotten as in no way a problem of political control. Whatever the status of the wider political context men are still actually held in subjection by others. Democratic and liberal political thinkers have seen in slavery the absolute negation of freedom and in slave systems a source of corruption of any political order with pretensions to freedom. An example of the view that slavery is a negation of freedom and a violation of the human essence is the following passage of Jean-Jacques Rousseau:

> Besides, the right of property being only a convention of human institution, men may dispose of what they possess as they please; but this is not the case with the essential gifts of nature, such as life and liberty, which every man is permitted to enjoy. . . . As then to establish slavery it was necessary to do violence to nature, so in order to perpetuate such a right, nature would have to be changed. Jurists who have gravely determined that

the child of a slave comes into the world a slave, have decided in other words, that man shall come into the world not a man (*A Discourse on the Origin of Inequality Among Men*, pp. 211–212).

J. S. Mill stressed the corrupting influence of slavery on the wider political system:

A civilised people have other means for imparting civilisation to those under their influence;[14] and slavery is, in all its details, so repugnant to that government of law . . . and so corrupting to the master class when they have once come under civilised influences, that its adoption under any circumstances whatever in modern society is a relapse into worse than barbarism (*Representative Government*, p. 198).

The democratic case, despite the fact that it is no less ideological than that of the absolutists, is a serious one because it poses the possibility that slavery may only be compatible with certain forms of political system and that it may distort others to the authoritarian forms which are compatible with it. Despite our deductions from the status of slavery as an institution, that it is not a special form of domination, the democratic case still has to be answered by an analysis of slave systems. It is necessary to pose the following questions in order to settle with the democratic-liberal conception of slavery:

(1) Is slavery connected with distinct forms of state and systems of domination, that is, can only certain types of polity sustain the burden of unfreedom and repression entailed in slavery?

(2) Does any definite set of political and social consequences follow from the fact of the master–slave relationship?

In essence these questions amount to the following, does the institution of slavery pose problems for and require special changes in the wider social and political context in which it exists? The answer to these questions must be in the negative.

Slave systems have existed in, and persisted for a long time in, without radically changing or overturning, many different types of polity – in the Ancient World, in Despotisms (Syracuse), in 'democratic' City States (Athens), and in Ancient Empires (Rome); in the modern world, in the colonies of absolutist and constitutional monarchies (the islands of France and England in the West Indies) and in modern democratic republics (the USA). In each of these cases the pattern of relations between master and slave, the effect of these relations on, and their conditioning by, the wider social structure has varied very greatly and has been determined in its character by facts other than the master–slave relationship itself. The character of a slave system is dominated by the social structure in which it exists and not vice versa. In Ancient Athens, for example, slavery had a double character and these dual aspects corresponded to different elements of the Athenian economy. In Athens slavery was at once benign and at the same time savage. Its benign aspect is represented by the large number of slave artisans working and living independently and merely giving regular money payments to their masters, by the slave functionaries, such as the 'bank manager' Pasion, who controlled the administration and running of the enterprise and were sometimes freed and even bequeathed the enterprise on their master's death, and by the slaves who were allowed to work off their manumission as a matter of policy of the owner. This side of slavery gave the bondsman great freedom and independence, often making him in every way the equal of his master.[15] Its savage aspect is represented by the conditions of the slaves who worked for the contractors who operated the state's silver mines at Laurium[16] – here the slave was treated as a capital investment and systematically worked to death in order to extract the maximum value from him.

Liberal and democratic thinkers certainly think slavery ought to have certain effects because it is a negation of freedom and of human autonomy – there is no evidence that it does have these effects or that there is such a thing as a human nature which can be outraged by slavery. Do the remarks of the ex-slave Frederick Douglass demonstrate the realities of a human nature whose essence is freedom or the social malleability and variability of human subjects?

> Beat and cuff your slave, keep him hungry and spiritless, and he will follow the chain of his master like a dog; but feed and clothe him well – work him moderately – surround him with physical comfort, – and dreams of freedom intrude. Give him a *bad* master and he aspires to a *good* master; give him a good master, and he wishes to become his *own* master (Douglass, *My Bondage and My Freedom* (1855), p. 263).

The social psychology of plantation slavery

The modern social sciences reject the ideological, evaluative and justificatory character of classical political theory and aspire to a strictly objective account of social phenomena even when they be as abhorrent as slavery. These aspirations are far from being met, not because modern social science is distracted from its goal of objectivity by extraneous values and political prejudices, but because it rests upon anthropological assumptions of the very type that are at the root of classical political philosophy. Whereas classical democratic theory in the shape of Rousseau saw in man a being whose natural essence is freedom and insisted that this inherent species-nature could be *directly* represented in political and social life, modern sociology and social psychology recognise the human subject as a being whose *social* character is variable and malleable, but this recognition is combined with anthropological assumptions of a similar scientific status (although with a rather different concrete content) to those of Rousseau about the nature and attributes of the being upon whom these social relations work. Thus the debates in the modern social sciences (including social scientifically informed history) which touch on the question of whether slavery is a particular form of domination have tended to stress the effect of the slave 'role' and the social relations of slavery on the human subject. Does slavery make man docile or rebellious? Do different slave regimes produce different patterns of master–slave relations, and also different patterns of race relations? Such sociological discussions of slavery concentrate upon the immediate pattern and circumstances of social interaction between slaves and others – the wider social structure and political system is of relevance only in so far as they affect the conditions and nature of the slave's role and his 'role set'. The general character and working of the slave systems, and the consequences of them for the wider social and political structure, are either ignored or deduced from the effects of the social personalities of master and slave. Such work could justly be called the social psychology of the master–slave relation and in such work definite social and political consequences are seen to follow from the nature of this relation.

The best example of this approach is the work of Stanley M. Elkins, *Slavery: A Problem in American Institutional and Intellectual Life*.[17] Elkins is concerned to give a social-scientific foundation to the 'sambo' myth, the conception of the Negro as an irresponsible, child-like and incompetent being. Elkins sees the North American plantation as producing a servile personality, a being compatible with the conditions of its bondage. Elkins puts this construction of the slave personality in the context of the Atlantic slave trade, plantation slavery under conditions of unrestrained capitalism and profit-seeking,[18] and a legal-religious tradition which gave no sanction to the regarding of the slave as a person or a brother. Elkins compares the North-American slave plantation as a system of domination and subordination to a Nazi concentration camp. The slave is stripped of his socially acquired self-conception by the 'middle passage '– the voyage in the slave ships to America. It is in the plantation that the slave acquires a degraded and infantilised social personality – the reality which is the foundation of and gives validity to the 'sambo' stereotype. This is because the slave was denied personal autonomy, family-life and stable role models of mature-adult personalities; because he was led to seek gratification through and to identify with the authority of the master.

Elkins sees the slave plantation as – in Erving Goffman's terms[19] – a 'total institution', that is, a social institution in which the members are stripped of outside social roles and required to live their whole daily life within it and who are subordinated to its logic. Goffman's notion of 'total institution' amounts to little more than the application of the reactionary political theorists' notion of *totalitarianism* to the institutional level. The lamentable effects of total institutions and totalitarian societies stem from an identical cause, the subjection of every aspect of the individual's life to control and scrutiny. 'Sambo' is therefore a variant of the reactions of the inmates to such institutions, but with a significant difference from Goffman's conception of the inmates' reactions and adaptations. For Goffman the long-sentence prisoner or asylum inmate has various strategies before him and in particular the possibility of 'role-distance' – the inmate can 'play the system' minimising its effects by producing patterns of behaviour which conform to certain of his keeper's expectations and in so doing being able to exploit what avenues of melioration there are. For Elkins no such 'role-distance' is possible for Sambo – he *is* the stereotype his masters recognise in him.

Elkins's thesis rests upon an explicit conception of the mature-adult personality and the social conditions under which it is acquired. This personality and these conditions amount to no more than the conception of the human subject in liberal social-political theory. Liberalism (and Elkins) considers the 'autonomous' individual the *norm* of human nature; other forms are pathological. For the development of this 'individual' it is necessary that he be exposed to several complex and differentiated roles which give him the capacity for freedom and autonomy. The function of these distinct roles in the development of the personality is identical to the function of secondary associations in the maintenance of a free polity. In this correspondence, modern social 'science' is revealed as nothing more than the continuation of classical liberalism by other means.

The opposite of these conditions, the conditions of infantilisation, suppose the social structure of the concentration-camp/total institution to exist in the slave plantation. This notion was already at question when Elkins created it. Its existence supposes a refutation of the argument and evidence in Kenneth Stampp's *The Peculiar Institution.*[20] Stampp argues that the plantation Negro was far from being a 'sambo', that he often did have a stable family life (subject to tragic disruption when the 'human chattels' were sold) and that the slave plantation was a far more complex and varied situation (the slaves often having extensive contact with the outside world and other slave plantations) than Elkins's concentration-camp analogy can afford to admit. If some 'house Negroes' did play the 'sambo' they were correspondingly isolated from and held in some contempt by the society of the field hands in their slave cabins. The Negroes had their own separate society, pattern of social relations and standards of conduct. For Stampp 'sambo' was *a* form of role-playing before whites, who were regarded in general by the Negroes with some fear and reserve as best kept away from. Many field hands in no way played 'sambo', adopting an attitude of indifference, cynicism and even open hostility before their masters. The Negroes were never reconciled to slavery nor were they reduced to a sub-'normal' status by it (except, of course, for the brutalities and tragedies of slave life which produced its crop of victims).

Elkins clearly recognises that the analysis in Stampp's book completely contradicts his own, but rather than answering it point by point he discredits it. He discusses Stampp's work as a liberal riposte to the pro-Southern and racist positions of Ulrich B. Phillips (Elkins tends to prefer Phillips's stereotyped conception of the Negro slave since it fits his thesis). Elkins's criticisms of Stampp are largely confined to trying to show he is a politically biased and moralistic historian (Elkins posing as an objective social scientist), but an example of his 'empirical' criticism is that he argues that Stampp depends heavily on the 'scientific' work of Myrdal on the race question when in fact Myrdal's work has a strongly evaluative element to it. However, Stampp never gives a central role in his text to this work and rests upon the simple humanist assumptions that have been with us since the beginnings of abolitionism, that the Negro is a man like any other and in no important way is he different. Stampp clearly does operate with a certain conception of 'human nature' – for him the Negro slave is like any other human being trying to make the best of a difficult and degrading situation. This does not, however, *destroy* Stampp's analysis or his evidence concerning the society of Negroes and their response to whites under slavery. Without Elkins's equally questionable assumptions about the nature of the 'normal' mature personality and mature personality and the social means by which it is constructed the argument in his thesis is dislocated and loses its central pivot.[21]

Elkins's conception of the slave as the servile product of slavery is based upon a sociological analysis of the conditions of social interaction on the slave plantation and its effects on the socialisation of slaves. It is a paradigm case of the sociological reduction of social relations to inter-personal relations.

SLAVE REBELLIONS

Whereas for Elkins the essence of the North-American plantation slave is docile subordination[22] for some other modern writers the essential feature of the American slaves' condition are the facts of rebellion and resistance. The American Marxist writer Herbert Aptheker attempts to present an American Negro past based upon rebellion and resistance in his book *American Negro Slave Revolts*. His task is a difficult one since Stampp shows that there was much *resistance*, in the sense of restrictive labour practices, crime, occasional assaults, etc., and also considerable accommodation and acquiescence, but that there was precious little in the way of *revolt*; the Nat Turner rebellion in 1831 being the only really significant uprising and the Denmark Vesey conspiracy the only other thing that got anywhere close to it. Indeed, for the supporters of the notion that man's reaction to slavery is resistance and rebellion the history of slave systems outside the USA offers little more comfort. Slave revolts on any sort of scale have been few and infrequent compared with the duration of the various slave systems and the number of human beings who have suffered under them: the most notable are the First Sicilian Slave War 135–131 B.C., the Spartacus Uprising 73–71 B.C., the revolt of the Zanj under the Abbāssid Caliphate and the revolution led by Toussaint L'Ouverture in Haiti.[23] Eunus, Spartacus and Toussaint were clearly not 'sambos', but their rebellions prove nothing about the general tendency of slave systems. It is true, however, that most slave revolts have been based upon plantation slave systems or upon similar semi-custodial institutions (e.g. the Spartacus revolt began at the gladiators' school at Capua), but in itself this demonstrates very little. It is necessary to examine the conditions which produce such revolts in more detail, it will be seen that they are relatively contingent to the forms of plantation slavery and to the status of the slave in general.

THE FIRST SICILIAN SLAVE WAR

The example we will take here is that of the revolt of Eunus which is relatively well documented (whereas the revolts of Spartacus and the Zanj are not) and not so well known as that of Toussaint. Our account is based upon the excellent paper of Peter Green 'The First Sicilian Slave War' (1961).

In Sicily and South Italy in the last two centures B.C. a slave-worked system of large estates, cattle ranches and wheat farms developed – in which the conditions of the field gangs were similar to those of modern plantation slavery. Slave workers were plentiful and very cheap because of the series of wars and systematic piracy – this low price made it economical and possible to work the latifundia with unskilled labour groups. The produce of these estates was intended for the commodity market and the slaves who worked them were treated strictly as a capital investment, exploited as thoroughly as possible and written off in a relatively short period. There was little hope of manumission and the slave could only look forward to a short life of hard-driven labour. Among the slaves were many educated and often previously free men netted in through the kidnapping of pirates and also large numbers of men of the same nationality and religion. In the period prior to the revolt the machinery of repression in Sicily was very weak, Roman first-line troops being absent, and the regimes of the estates, while harsh, depended on very few overseers. Moreover, this was the period of the Gracchan agitation; the struggle for the popular programme in the Roman state.

The revolt was led by Eunus, a slave of Syrian origin who claimed the power of prophecy and to be in contact with the Gods. It was particularly successful; the slaves occupied large parts of the island and it took several years and large military forces to suppress them. In the areas controlled by the rebels a state was established and Eunus adopted the forms of Seleucid kingship – Eunus, now King Antiochus, was an absolute ruler and adopted the theocratic forms of the Syrian state. It is probable that the initial core of the rebels (apart from bandits and fugitives) came from a clandestine religious society practising the Syrian religion of sun-worship. In no sense could the revolt of Eunus be described as a revolt against slavery or a social movement based upon a popular programme.[24] Green establishes its status succinctly:

> The First Sicilian Slave war, then, was not an Urkommunist revolution against slavery, or, indeed, any kind of socialist or left-wing economic revolt. It was sparked off by the presence on the *latifundia* of intelligent Syrians and Cilicians – often free men by birth – who . . . had nothing against slavery as an institution; but objected violently to being enslaved themselves. No one suggests that Antiochus' kingdom, while it lasted, was classless or non-servile in its constitution: the reverse seems to have been true (Green (1961), p. 24).

The same appears to have been the case in respect of the later revolt of Spartacus – there being no evidence to support the notion that the revolt was sustained by a primitive form of communist ideology. Similarly, the masses of poor Roman freemen, at this moment engaged in their own struggle (conducted and led by an aristocratic faction), had no sympathy for the slaves.

The conditions which produced these uprisings had no precedent and were not repeated in the ancient world. The large slave-worked estate operating under these conditions was the product of an unusual and contingent conjuncture of factors – a conjuncture many elements of which were reproduced in eighteenth-century Saint Domingue. As slave prices rose with the restriction of supply the use of slaves for gang labour was no longer possible or economic – most agricultural slaves in the latter period being skilled workers (such as vinedressers, etc.). In Greece, apart, for example, from the attempts of Athens to incite the helots[25] of Sparta, and Sparta the slaves of Athens in an entirely opportunistic fashion to gain military advantage, there were few slave disturbances, let alone revolts. In Athens, for example, this was undoubtedly due to the fact that most slaves were domestics or artisans working in small workshops or independently for a master who often worked alongside them, to the large numbers of slaves with a high degree of freedom, to the relative ease of manumission and to the general acceptance of slaves as, if not equals, then at least as something other than sub-men.

Slave revolts, therefore, presuppose specific and unusual conditions.

Plantation or gang-slavery is obviously an essential precondition for slave revolts since it makes possible conspiracy and mass actions, but it is not a sufficient condition. Under other conditions, particularly those of relaxed and paternalistic plantation regimes, slaves *en masse* have been relatively reconciled to their lot and given the means to construct a society which admitted of a measure of satisfactions and rewards.[26] In this respect the remarks of Douglass cited earlier are less than accurate and we have no need to suppose such places to be peopled by the dependent 'sambos' of Elkins's invention. Like the unsung 'Village Hampden' such regimes might well have a 'Plantation Eunus', a man whose energies are directed into the avenues available in the plantation regime; the preachers, chief hands and Negro doctors of the South were not all 'house niggers'. Plantation slaves are neither rebellious nor docile – they are the complex products of the wide range of regimes possible within the institutional form of plantation slavery.

SLAVES IN POWER

The decisive argument against all conceptions of a definite form of domination being entailed in or emerging from the fact of chattel slavery or the master–slave relation are those cases where slaves have played a crucial role in manning the administrative and repressive machinery of the state. We will consider two main examples.

(i) *Greece and Rome*

In Athens the civil administration, such as it was, was in the hands of slaves and freedmen, while the police force of the city guarding it against sudden civil disturbance or a *coup d'état* was composed of slaves. This police force was a corps of specially recruited barbarians, Scythian archers, who were slaves owned by the state.[27]

In Rome as in Athens slaves and freedmen performed the main administrative duties in the Emperor's household staff, in effect the Imperial civil service, in the first and second centuries A.D. In Athens and Rome such work was considered beneath the dignity, and corrupting to the independence, of free citizens with full political rights. In the Roman fleet the captains of ships were imperial slaves and the admirals of fleets and flotillas, freedmen. The fleets were charged with the suppression of piracy and their most important task was to secure the corn supply of Rome.

(ii) *The Muslim Middle Ages*

In medieval Egypt and Syria slaves formed the basis of the state's military power and also the means of dynastic succession.[28] The military slaves, mamelukes, were recruited particularly from the Caucasus and Asia Minor as children and were owned by the Sultan and his emirs. These slave-soldiers were the basis of the state's domination – the indigenous populations being largely disarmed and having a minor part in state affairs. When a slave rose to the rank of officer (emir) he was emancipated and given a military 'fief' or share of the tax-revenue of a particular district.[29] Senior officers owned their own retinue of mameluke slaves. Succession to the throne was through the agency of nominating such a freedman who was favourite or most trusted subordinate of the current ruler, or through the deposition of the existing ruler in favour of a candidate of a faction of the freedman aristocracy. Later the Ottoman Turks adopted a similar system; the corps of janizaries which formed the élite of the army were slaves of the Sultan of Constantinople, recruited largely from children levied as a tax on Christian families and raised as Muslims. Both the mamelukes and janizaries became the decisive force in determining Egyptian and Ottoman state policy, dictating to, making and unmaking rulers. Yet even when in *de facto* control of state power, the mass of them remained slaves. Free mercenary troops have equally controlled or attempted to seize state power.[30] The power position of the mamelukes was not a specific consequence of their slave status but of their position within the state; the Sultan depended upon the mamelukes for the basis of his power and there were no other indigenous social forces which could form a counter-acting base of political power and support. Without the continuing recruitment of unfree infants and youths the mameluke military system could not have been sustained, and without that system the basis of political succession in the state would have vanished.

As an *institution*, slavery has no specific political consequences. Certain slave systems do have political consequences; however, these consequences are intelligible not in terms of the general legal status of slavery but in terms of the nature of the social and political structures of which these slave systems are a part. Domination cannot exist independently of a structure of relations of domination. The notion of the master–slave relation as a relation of domination between two subjects, as a *personal* duel of mastership and bondage, is a product of the age-old humanist myth that all social relations are in essence relations between human subjects. It is this myth that we have attempted to challenge in posing the question of the political effects of the legal status of slavery.

3 Is there a 'slave mode of production'?

The answer to this question is not to be found in the existence of given forms of production based upon slave labour, the latifundia of the ancient world or the slave plantations of the Americas. An enumeration or description of given slave systems settles nothing in respect of this question of the 'slave' mode of production; such systems may or may not be forms of this mode, but in the absence of the *concept* of this mode there is no means of knowing and no basis of proof. The question posed here is a strictly theoretical one. It is posed in a definite problematic, that of the theory of modes of production, and it is subject to the methods of resolution and the modes of proof of that problematic. The question, therefore, must be posed in the following form: is it possible to construct the concept of a distinct mode of production based upon slavery? In order to answer this question it is necessary to recall the constituent elements of the concept mode of production: mode of production = an articulated combination of a specific mode of appropriation of the social product and a specific mode of appropriation of nature. A mode of production is a complex unity of relations and forces of production: the mode of appropriation of the product is determined by the relations of production, that is, by the social distribution of the means of production, and by the distribution of the agents to definite positions (labourers, non-labourers) as a function of the former distribution.

It is only possible to answer the question posed by the construction of a concept of the slave mode of production which corresponds to the general definition of mode of production – a concept which yields a distinct complex unity of relations and forces of production. To anticipate, we may say that there is a slave mode of production (hereafter SMP) in that such an articulated combination of relations and forces of production is formable and that it is a combination distinct from that of any other mode of production. The demonstration of this anticipated conclusion will now follow.

THE CONCEPT OF THE SLAVE MODE OF PRODUCTION

(i) *The relations of production*

The relations of production in this mode are constituted by three distinct levels, the form of property/legal definition of the agents, the distribution of the means of production and the mode of appropriation of the surplus-product.

(a) *Property form/legal characterisation of the agents* Slavery is a mode of production characterised by a social division of labour into non-labourers and labourers and by private property relations. The labourers (direct producers) are the *legal property* of the non-labourers. As chattels they have no legal or social existence independent of their master and they are dependent on him for their maintenance.

COMMENTS

This point of articulation with the political/legal superstructure is a central precondition of this mode: the legal form of slave property defines the agents in this mode (freeman/slave, owner/chattel) and makes possible the particular mode of appropriation of the surplus-product. This legal articulation is as important to the slave mode as the *wage-form* is to the capitalist mode; it is a condition of its existence, without it the formation of its structure is impossible. However, it should be noted that the legal form of slave property is not peculiar to the SMP – it exists wherever slavery as an *institution* exists. It is when we reach the next level (the distribution of the means of production) that we pass the boundary between slavery as an *institution* – which remains at the level of a form of property – and slavery as a *mode of production*. It is the structure of slave production which subsumes the slave as the effective possession of his owner – the legal title of slave property is a precondition of slave production.

(b) *Distribution of the means of production* Slaves may be items of consumption, household servants, or labourers with a subordinate function in modes of production not based on slavery (for example, the Attic peasant who bought a slave to supplement his own labour). In the SMP, where slave labour forms the basis of production, the mere possession of a legal title to slave property does not give the owner effective possession of the slave as a productive labourer. The *effective possession* of slave property, where the labour process is based on slavery, depends on the capacity of the owner to set the means of production in motion. Thus the effective possession of slaves presupposes the possibility of the application of their labour power to some definite activity of labouring. The non-labourers must own not merely slaves but the instruments of production, raw materials and means of subsistence for the slaves. In the SMP the entire set of elements necessary to constitute the process of production are the property of the non-labourers. Slaves are separated from the means of production and they are unable to set the means of production in motion (and therefore reproduce themselves except through the agency of the non-labourers). It is this separation of the labourer from the means of reproduction of his labour-power which is the mode of subsumption of the slave labourer as the possession of the owner of the means of production.

COMMENTS

(i) The category freeman is not necessarily exclusive to non-labourers: free functionaries, servants, producers of items of luxury consumption, etc., are all possible; equally these positions may be taken by slaves who are not direct producers. Nor does the category freeman/non-labourer necessarily mean slave master: freeman may be state servants, rentiers, etc.

(ii) The slaveowner may only own slaves, he may then *rent* the means of production or obtain them on credit, equally he may rent his slaves to an owner of means of production. However, slaves *cannot* own the means of production (or possess them) – ownership is confined to freemen/non-labourers. In this case landowners, owners of instruments of production, etc., are equally dependent on the labour of slaves and in practice are members of the slave-owning class. The important difference between the SMP and the feudal mode is that slaves are separated by the property form and the organisation of the labour process from effective possession of the means of production in a different way from the feudal direct producers – it is this real difference between the relations of production that accounts for the difference in the conditions of slave and serf, not the legal distinction between slavery and bondage.[31]

(c) *The mode of appropriation of the surplus-product* The *whole product* of the direct producers (slaves) goes to the non-labourers (slaveowners). The master owns the product of the slave's labour just as he owns the slave – the capacity of the slave to labour is an attribute or use-value of this form of property. The slave receives the means of subsistence. In the SMP the reproduction of labour-power is assimilated to the renewal of the stock of fixed capital: there is no distinction between constant and variable capital, the slave is no different from any other form of capital investment in machines, animals, etc. The value of the slave is subject to depreciation as his labour-power is exhausted and the body of the slave engenders the costs of maintenance: a portion of the value produced by the slave reproduces the value of the capital invested in him (just as machines are written off in a certain time and a special depreciation fund created from the values produced over that time) and another portion reproduces the costs of his maintenance (just as with the cost of oil, fuel, repairs, etc., with machines). Hence there is no division apparent within the mode between necessary-labour and surplus-labour: the reproduction of labour-power appearing as a 'cost of production'. Marx illustrates this identity of the slave labourer with other forms of fixed capital in the following passage.

> In the slave system, the money-capital invested in the purchase of labour-power plays the role of the money-form of fixed capital, which is gradually replaced as the active period of the slave's life expires. Among the Athenians, therefore, the gain realised by the slaveowner directly through the industrial employment of his slave, or indirectly by hiring him out to other industrial employers (e.g. for mining) was regarded merely as interest (plus depreciation allowance) on the advanced money capital (*Capital*, II, pp. 478–9).

To the slaveowner the surplus-product is represented as a form of interest on the capital advanced and it appears as a natural capacity and result of the form of capital, interest/profit being an *attribute* of capital. The slave's capacity to labour is equated with the ox's capacity to haul carts, ploughs, etc.

If we compare the slave and the capitalist modes it is clear that one of the greatest differences between them is that in the SMP the reproduction of the labourer is subsumed under the reproduction of the stock of fixed capital. In capitalism, however, wage-labour is sold to the capitalist as a commodity and therefore the wage bill is represented to the capitalist as a distinct cost of production with a distinct magnitude. The reproduction of labour-power takes place *outside* of the orbit of capital, its reproduction is not subsumed within capital and is not a necessary function and calculation of the capitalist. The reproduction of labour-power is secured in the sphere of circulation: the labourer *sells* his labour-power, he appears under the guise of the seller of a commodity and the wage-form represents the wage-labour contract as an exchange of equivalents, and the labourer *buys* the means of subsistence, he purchases the means of his reproduction on the market with the money obtained from the sale of his commodity, labour-power.

Hence in the SMP the mode of appropriation of the surplus-product is a function of the slave being the *property* of his owner. The three levels of the relations of production form a unity: the separation of the labourer from the means of production and his subsumption within capital make the product of the labourer the property of his owner. The form of property, chattel *slavery*, its effective guarantee by the state, and the effective separation of the slave from the means of production are necessary for this mode of appropriation of the surplus-product to be constituted.

(ii) *Forces of production/labour process*

The relations of production are the principal determinant of the structure of a mode of production. The distribution of the means of production, the division of the agents into distinct functions which follows from this (labourers, non-labourers, etc.) and the consequent form of division of the product between agents of production, structure the labour process and the relation of the direct producer to nature. The relations of production impose a definite form and a set of limits on the forces of production. This dominance of the relations of production is particularly clear in the case of the SMP.

The specific characteristics of the forces of production in the slave mode are constituted by the contradictory status of the slave as a form of property and as a labourer. This is not an essentialist contradiction between the human essence of the slave (labour as human self-creation) and its alienation in the slave's reification into a chattel (which makes his essence and his product another's). It is a contradiction between two distinct economic forms, forms not reducible to the human subject but specific to the mode of production, the form of property and the labour process. It is a contradiction between the slave as a form of property (with a value in circulation) and the slave as direct producer (as the producer of value in some definite activity of labouring). *This contradiction, unlike the essentialist/humanist contradiction, only emerges when slavery is the basis of a particular mode of production, it is not a contradiction of the institution of slavery in general.*

This contradiction has a decisive effect on the forces of production of the SMP because it displaces the relation surplus-labour/necessary-labour and it renders the relation of the labourer to the process of production problematical. We shall develop a thorough account of this contradiction and its effects below.

Where slave production prevails the price of the slave represents the anticipated surplus-value to be obtained by the exploitation of his labour-power, but, as we have seen, in order to *realise* this value the slave must be set to some definite activity of labouring (and this entails the expenditure of additional capital on instruments of production, raw materials, etc.):

> The price paid for a slave is nothing but the anticipated and capitalised surplus-value to be wrung out of the slave. But the capital paid for the purchase of the slave does not belong to the capital by means of which profit, surplus-labour, is extracted from him. On the contrary. It is capital which the slave-holder has parted with, it is a deduction from the capital which he has available for actual production. It has ceased to exist for him, just as capital invested in the purchasing of land has ceased to exist for agriculture. The best proof of this is that it does not reappear for the slave-holder or for the landowner except when he, in turn, sells the slaves or land. But then the same situation prevails for the buyer. The fact that he has bought the slave does not enable him to exploit the slave without further ado. He is only able to do so when he invests some additional capital in the slave economy itself (*Capital*, III, pp. 788–9).

In the capitalist mode the commodity labour-power when purchased has a finite and perishable use value (the capacity of the worker to labour for the hour, day, week, etc.). The purchase of labour-power is for a special form of consumption – productive consumption – at the end of the period, even if no labour has actually been carried out, the commodity has no value to the purchaser (other than that generated by consuming it in the process of production) and it cannot be re-sold. The same is not true of the slave.[32] Unlike the wage-labourer the slave has a property form similar to that of fixed capital. *The slave retains his value whether he labours or not.* Whilst he retains the *capacity* to labour he retains his value, that is, he retains a value realisable through exchange, and while he *exists* the slave retains some value – although a sick old man will be worth little by comparison with a fit young labourer, just as a ravaged and barren hill farm will sell for far less than a well-tended fertile estate.

As Marx demonstrates, the value of the slave is realisable in circulation; the purchase price of the slave is not irrecoverably lost if the slave is not set to labour, it can be recovered when he is sold. We may add to this that the market in slaves is not merely and necessarily a market in labour-power, the use-values of slaves are varied, and hence the possibilities of the sale of slaves are widened beyond the sphere in which it would be limited by the demands of production for labourers.

Not only does the slave retain a value whether he labours or not, his destruction is a direct loss to his owner not only of the stock of values he is capable of producing but also of the capital invested in him, a direct and calculable money loss: 'The slaveowner buys his labourer as he buys his horse. If he loses his slave, he loses capital that can only be restored by a new outlay in the slave mart' (*Capital*, I, p. 266). *The slave must be provided with the means of subsistence to retain his value as capital.*

Here we will recapitulate the points made above:

(i) The price of the slave represents the capitalised surplus-value to be obtained from his labour-power and this can only be realised if he is set to work in some definite activity of labouring. *In himself* the slave cannot add to value.

(ii) The slave *retains* his value as a form of capital whether he labours or not – this value can be realised in circulation.

(iii) For the value of the slave to be preserved the body of the slave must be maintained.

Necessary-labour is equivalent to the time necessary to produce the means of reproduction of the labourer. Clearly, the slave labourer performs necessary-labour and surplus-labour, his own labour reproduces slave labour-power. However, this distinction is *displaced* in the SMP as an effect of the property form of labour-power. Unlike the wage-labourer under capitalism who is separated from the means of production and forced to sell his labour-power in order to live, the slave while separated from the means of production in the sense that he cannot set them in motion independently (he does not *possess* them) is assimilated to them in the fact that he is a form of fixed capital. As a form of property the slave is not *forced* to expend his labour-power in order to reproduce himself. The slave's maintenance is necessary independent of his labour – it is necessary to maintain him as a *chattel* whether he labours or not. The slave receives the necessities of life through his owner, whether or not he undertakes productive labour, whether he is a field hand or flunkey, he is provided for from his owner's storehouse or household budget. The slave because he is a chattel and because he is separated from the means of production is under no systematic compulsion to labour and to reproduce himself, unlike the wage-labourer or the free peasant proprietor. For the slave all labour is surplus-labour.

COMMENTS

This absence of a compulsion for the direct producers to reproduce themselves internal to the structure of the mode, the absence of any necessity to work for another and the absence of the *means* to work for oneself, generates the problematicity of the relation of the labourer to the process of production we outlined above. Here is a structural space, the space of a contradiction between the property form of labour-power and the labour process, which necessitates an ideological articulation of the mode of production. The specific forms of this articulation and, therefore, the forms of representation of the labour process to the labourer are not given by the structure. Thus a specific set of ideological *practices* which have the effect of resolving in one form or another the problematicity of the labourer's relation to the labour process is a necessary condition of existence of this mode.

The nature of the agent's relation to the labour process is constituted by the ideological instance – it is this instance which forms the agents as subjects. This means that the nature of the slave as a subject is not given. The slave may work through Christian religious duty, to serve God loyally in his station, etc. The slave need not work reluctantly nor is force necessary to make him work. Here we see the contradiction with essentialist and humanist conceptions of slavery most clearly. We have argued that there is no systematic mechanism which forces the slave to work and no means by which he can set the process of production in motion independently of his master. *This does not mean that the slave realises he does not have to work, that he will be fed however idle he is.* There is no essential slave subject to *see* this, to draw this conclusion. The reliance on such a conception of the human subject solves the question of the slave's relation to the forces of production very easily. J. E. Cairnes, for example, deduces the reluctance of the slave to work from his utilitarian principles, that men seek pleasure and avoid pain.[33] No material incentive is offered the slave to labour, therefore, idleness maximises his pleasure. Fear and coercion must be applied to alter the slave's 'felicific calculus' in the direction of seeing work as the lesser evil.

To introduce such a conception as Cairnes's would be absolutely impermissible. It would be to use an essentialist conception of the subject to overcome problems in Marxist theory – inserting *homo economicus* or *l'homme révolté* into this structural space to fill it without problems. To argue that the slave *sees* he is under no compulsion but force to work involves the generation of 'appearances' from structural relations, it entails introduction of the humanist/empiricist notion of the human subject endowed with the given faculties of perception, experience, consciousness, etc. However, the human subject of Locke and Descartes has no place within the Marxist problematic.

To introduce the human subject to articulate a *social* structure through its experience supposes a given pre-social effectivity of the subject, a human essence and a human nature. The effects of this essential subject cannot be confined to the point of its insertion, it becomes a necessary limitation of the effectivity of and a prior determination of the social totality itself. The error in this case is to treat the economic structure as a system of social relations, but to reduce the political/legal superstructure to *Man*, to the experience and consciousness of the human subject who recognises the appearances given off by the structure. This asymmetry is a function of the entry of humanist theory. All the levels of the social formation are effects of its structure, they are structures with a specific effectivity within it – the political/legal superstructure is as much a system of relations irreducible to any subject as the economic structure. It is therefore necessary to theorise the space of political/ideological articulations of the economic structure in different modes of production and to show that the forms of articulation are themselves complex social structures and not the ideological 'obviousness' of human 'consciousness'.

As a chattel set to labour the slave has a specific relation to the labour process. As we have seen, the slave is separated from the means of production which, like him, are the property of the slaveowner and under his control. The slave's relation to labour is through his form as *capital*, he works at the direction of his owner as part of a process controlled by his owner. The slave has no more independent a relation to production than a machine – he is not the agency by which the process is set in motion. Unlike the feudal mode, in which the direct producer could have effective possession of the means of production and could reproduce himself independently of the feudal landlord, there is no separation of the production and the appropriation of the surplus product in the SMP. The slave cannot 'work for himself' – unlike the serf there is no possibility of his calculating necessary-labour and surplus-labour by comparing the product he has produced with the portion of it he is forced to surrender, or the time spent on his own land with the time spent on the lord's demesne. Like the capitalist the slaveowner is a necessary agent of the process of production – his function is that of control and co-ordination.

From the foregoing we may derive three effects of the structure of the relations of production which determine the relation of the slave to the labour process and set a definite character on the forces of production:

Effect I – there is no structural compulsion for the slave to labour to reproduce himself;

Effect II – the slave is separated from the means of production and unable to set them in motion except at the direction of his owner;

Effect III – the function of the slaveowner is as the constitutive and co-ordinating agency of the labour process.

These effects of the relations of production – the existence of the slave as a form of capital and his non-possession of the means of production – engender a labour process with the following structure: co-ordination/supervision by non-labourers is necessary to it and it takes the form of simple co-operation.

Co-ordination/supervision The following passage from *Capital* indicates clearly the two different forms of the supervising function and their distinct sources:

> The labour of supervision and management is naturally required wherever the direct process of production assumes the form of a combined social process, and not the isolated labour of independent producers. However, it has a double nature.
>
> On the one hand, all labour in which many individuals co-operate necessarily requires a commanding will to co-ordinate and unify the process, and functions which apply not to partial operations but to the total activity of the workshop, much as that of an orchestra conductor. This is a productive job, which must be performed in every combined mode of production.
>
> On the other hand – quite apart from any commercial department – this supervision work arises in all modes of production based on the antithesis between the labourer, as the

> direct producer and the owner of the means of production. The greater this antagonism, the greater the role played by supervision. Hence it reaches its peak in the slave system (*Capital*, III, p. 376).

The first form of supervision has its source in the *technical division of labour*, it is necessary to co-ordinate the distinct labourers to a common end, to harmonise the divided tasks. The second form of supervision has its source in the *social division of labour*, it arises because of the division of the agents into non-labourers/owners of the means of production, labourers/direct producers. It should not be thought that the second form emerges solely in the form of the foreman or supervisor whose task is to see the workers really do work – co-ordination is a function which arises from the necessity of *combining* the labourer with the means of production.

In the slave mode the necessity of co-ordination/supervision arises from this separation of the labourer, (i) from the means of production, and (ii) from his subsumption within capital.

(i) The slaveowner must organise the process of production, amass the instruments of production, raw materials, etc., instruct his slaves and apply them to specific tasks – he must combine these elements into a process. The slave cannot work except as a result of this work of co-ordination and only under the conditions set by it.[34]

(ii) The slave as a form of capital is not compelled to work. To extract surplus-value from the slave he must not only be set to work in some constituted process he must be compelled to work, whether it be by ideological means, by incentives in money and/or kind, or by direct physical coercion. This is not an effect of the slave's 'human nature', but of the structure of the mode. No limits are set by the mode to the level of exploitation – this is a matter of custom and calculation. The direct supervision of the labourers is a necessary function because, as a consequence of the separation of the labourer from the means of production, the labourer and the form of organisation of labour do not coincide.[35]

Slave production requires both the management of the process of production as a whole and the detailed supervision of the workers within it. Both forms are necessary effects of the social division of labour. The combined working of labourers, the technical division of labour, is an effect of the conditions of labour imposed by the social division. This is another form of registering the dominance of the relations of production over the productive forces.

COMMENTS

Level of exploitation Custom and calculation can vary between relatively 'patriarchal' forms and forms where there is a direct stimulus to maximise exploitation. Supervision will be more or less intense according to the level of exploitation: this level depends on the degree of development of the credit system and commodity markets, in forms which approximate to capitalist production (Southern USA/West Indies) exploitation and supervision are most intense. For the owner the slave is equivalent to fixed capital and subject to depreciation. Hence under conditions where slaves are bought on credit, where a capitalist form of calculation obtains, where there is a buoyant market in the commodity produced by the slaves, etc., the tendency will be to 'burn up' the slave's labour-power in a short period of intense exploitation. The slaveowner calculates to maximise the slave's productivity in the shortest possible time and thereby minimise the costs of maintenance. The slave is literally 'worked to death'. This form of calculation is no different from the capitalist's calculation of the life of fixed capital and, therefore, of the rate of depreciation. Marx gives a succinct illustration of this point:[36]

> Hence the negro labour in the Southern States of the American Union preserved something of a patriarchal character, so long as production was chiefly directed toward immediate local consumption. But in proportion, as the export of cotton became of vital interest to these states, the over-working of the negro and sometimes the using up of his life in seven years of labour became a factor in a calculated and calculating system. It was no longer a question of obtaining from him a certain quantity of useful products. It was now a question of the production of surplus-labour itself (*Capital*, I, p. 236).

Supervision and coercion are particularly necessary to achieve this sort of exploitation. The labour of supervision is a direct cost of production; a form of functionally necessary labour which in itself produces no value. The maximisation of exploitation which reduces the duration of supervision per unit of value reduces the cost of production (cf. *Capital*, I, p. 332).

Co-operation Co-ordination/supervision is a necessary consequence of the relations of production of the SMP and a condition of existence of its labour process. Slave production takes a co-operative form. This form will tend to be that of *simple co-operation*: the application of several labourers to a single task, the simple combination of individuals engaged in similar activities of labouring. Slave production *inhibits the division of labour* within the process of production, that is, the application of labourers to distinct tasks in combination or distinct portions of the same task. This is because (i) the organisation of production and the work of labouring do not coincide, and (ii) there is an antagonistic* separation between the labourer and the owner of the means of production – as we have seen this makes supervision necessary. Simple co-operation makes the costs of the labour of supervision tolerable since it enables the minimum number of supervisors to control the labourers.[37] Except under conditions where the labourers can be concentrated in a small space the division of labour causes the costs of supervision to rise. The more intense the exploitation of the slave, the more antagonistic the relation of labourer and owner of the means of production, the more the division of labour is inhibited.

The units of production characteristic of the slave mode are, *in agriculture*, the *estate*, which is either a landholding large enough to be worked by several labourers in a gang (latifundium/plantation), or a farm employing several labourers which is large enough to permit a division of labour and small enough to permit close supervision (the ideal of the advocates of 'scientific' farming in Antiquity), and *in industry*, the *workshop*, the combination of several labourers under a single roof. Both of these forms make co-operation possible and minimise the labour of supervision. The form of simple co-operation enables units of a size and a scale of production which are impossible on the basis of production by isolated individuals – the single artisan or the peasant farm. Thus relative to peasant farming or artisan production the SMP represents an increase in the

* By 'antagonistic' we do not mean that there is necessarily an open conflict between slave and master, any more than the antagonism in the capitalist mode implies workers and capitalists are necessarily politically and ideologically opposed. Antagonism here means that there is an unbridgeable separation or gulf between the two elements, there is no simple unity or identity as in the case of peasant proprietorship. These elements must be brought together – as the labourer cannot set the means of production in motion independently, as he does not direct and control the process he must be directed and controlled in it. This supervision must be continuous. Supervision, it should be noted, also *maintains* the separation of the labourer from the means of production – the absence of supervision and the continuation of the process will in practice tend to reduce the control of the owner of the means of production over these means.

complexity, scale and volume of production – slavery is relative to these forms a more complex form of the forces of production.

COMMENTS I

The slave mode cannot have for its basis either the independent labour of artisans or independent peasant proprietors. It is true that slaves have worked as independent artisans, especially in Athens. Slavery here is a *legal institution* but not a definite form of *labour process*. The slave allowed to work independently is legally unfree, saleable, etc., but he is an independent producer, the master relates to him as a rentier, who advances him the instruments of production, etc., and to whom he pays *a rent for the right to use his own labour-power*. The slave has effective possession of (and may *own* under certain conditions[38]) the means of production but he does not own his labour-power. Likewise the slave peasant stands in relation to his master as a legally unfree sharecropper or tenant. In both these cases there appears a definite form of division between necessary-labour and surplus-labour – the slave reproduces himself and surrenders a portion of his product to his master.

COMMENTS II

Slavery is not the most efficient system of augmentation of the labour-power of a peasant farm. The chattel slave is a capital investment and must be maintained, although the farm's demand for labour-power is uneven. Casual wage-labour is a more satisfactory form of augmentation of the farm's labour-power when it is needed. The purchase of slaves by peasant farmers occurs only under conditions of absence of monopoly in land (and here contract bondage or indentured labour is an alternative form) or where social prestige attaches to slaveholding.

(iii) *Classes*

It is clear from the foregoing that there are three distinct classes determined by the structure of the relations and forces of production:

(i) Freemen, non-labourers, owners of the means of production; slaveowners, landlords, etc. – collectively the slaveholding class.

(ii) A class of functionaries engendered by the necessity of supervision: these functionaries may be slaves or freemen.

(iii) The direct producers who are slaves.

In addition to this there are state functionaries, unproductive labourers such as doctors, household servants, etc., who may or may not be freemen, and the possibility of a distinct stratum of artisan free labourers catering for the luxury demands of the slaveholding class, farm repairs, etc.

Thus far we have been concerned to develop the form of the relations and forces of production in the slave mode. It has been shown that these relations and forces form an articulated *combination*: a combination characterised by a specific form of dominance of the structure of the relations over the structure of the forces of production. It has been shown that this combination is a distinct one by means of comparisons with crucial elements of the capitalist and feudal modes (the primitive communist, Asiatic, socialist, etc., modes have little or no elements of correspondence with the SMP beyond the general structure of all modes of production; the relation of slave production to the Ancient mode remains to be discussed below).

(iv) *The economic forms the slave mode presupposes as its conditions of existence*

We have seen that the legal form of slave property and an ideological articulation of the relation of the labourer to the labour process are the *ideological/political* conditions of existence of the SMP. This articulated combination of relations and forces of production also has certain definite *economic* conditions of existence, it presupposes certain economic forms just as capitalism presupposes the separation of the labourer from the means of production, the wage-form and money.[39]

Slavery as a mode of production presupposes the existence of the developed form of private property, that is, private property and private property exchange in the means of production. In our presentation of the relations of production of the SMP we saw that the legal title to property in slaves is essential for this mode,[40] but legal titles are only one aspect of private property, property rights are a form of representation of real property relations, and it is developed private property as a system of real relations which is presupposed by the slave mode.[41]

In the absence of developed private property in the means of production the separation of the slave from the means of production, his subsumption within capital, is impossible. This renders the specific form of articulation of the relations and forces of production characteristic of the SMP impossible. Unless the slave can be separated from the means of production slavery will be no more than a *legal status*. A mode of production without such property relations and in which the direct producers have the status of 'slaves' will differ from the slave mode. In it politics will be dominant and the dominance of politics structures a different set of relations of production. Under these relations the conditions of appropriation of the surplus-product will be separated from the labour process.

The absence of private property in the means of production means that relations of production other than those of the slave mode must pertain, even though there is a form of slave status which subordinates all or some of the direct producers. Here are some examples of possible forms of slavery without developed private property in the means of production:

(a) In 'autosubsistence' societies, without fully developed class relations or a state, slaves (usually captives in war) are a mere augmentation of the labour-power of the commune/clan; slaves supplement the existing free labourers within the existing labour process, their addition to these forms of production does not change their nature. Slaves are ideologically subordinate, they become inferior members of the group and they are subject to the coercive power of the collective.

(b) In social forms where the state distributes 'slaves' and land in combination to members of the ruling class the slaves are tied to the land, they may produce their own instruments of production, they will certainly have effective possession of them and they control the process of production. Here the 'slave' is in effect not an alienable *chattel* but a legally unfree *bondsman* tied to the land. Such 'slaves' would correspond closely to the Spartan *helots*.[42]

(c) Where the state assigns captives to individual citizens who are free peasants (or such peasants subordinate others independently) the labour of the slaves merely supplements the existing labour-power of the peasant farm and enters into the existing labour process (that of small peasant proprietorship). These slaves are equivalent in economic function to bond servants or wage-labourers. The suggestion here is that there is not in the case of this form of peasant production fully developed private property in the means of production because, either the free peasant cannot readily alienate his land for example, because monopoly possession of the land does not yet exist – the

Teutonic mode where land is open to colonisation[43] – or because the peasant is given state support (e.g. the cancellation of debts and creation of new peasant landholdings for citizens in early Republican Rome) and/or forbidden to alienate his land.

In each of these examples no labour process specific to slavery is constituted. All that can be said of the slave in examples (a) and (c) is that he is a legally/ideologically inferior subject who is added to an existing set of social relations. In example (b) the distribution of the means of production is politically determined, the mode of appropriation of the surplus-product correspondingly depends on the intervention of the political instance, and the appropriation of the surplus-product is separate from the labour process. These examples are not intended as proofs, they are merely illustrative. Their effectiveness rests on the logical fact *that no labour process specific to slavery can be constituted on any other basis than private property in the means of production.*

Two points follow logically from the above condition: A mode of production based on slavery presupposes private property in land and slaves, and a form of commodity exchange corresponding to both.

(i) *Private property in land* Without alienable private property in land (or effective private possession/transfer of land) the unit of production characteristic of agriculture in the SMP, the *estate*, cannot be constituted. In the absence of such private property in land the combination *slaves + land* is impossible without the intervention of the political instance, thus other modes of distribution of the means of production must prevail (e.g. the Spartan).

(ii) *The slave market* Three distinct questions are involved in the necessity of a market in slaves as a commodity:

(a) There must be no effective legal prohibition of the alienation of or the trade in slaves. If this does exist then slave labour has no value as a commodity, slave labour is not renewable on the commodity market, and the mode of calculation engendered by the slave as a form of capital investment ceases to have any foundation. If the slave has no value in circulation then the central contradiction which is constitutive of the forces of production in the SMP will not exist.[44]

(b) In the SMP the distribution of labour-power to the units of production takes place by means of the commodity market – it is within the sphere of 'civil society' and is not determined by the state. Thus even if the state appropriates freemen such as captives in war, criminals, tax-defaulters, etc., as slaves they are sold to free subjects of the state in a commodity transaction between buyer and seller. That is, the state enters the commodity market as an agent with the same status as any other. Likewise, if the state owns slaves and uses them for production, or whatever, they are the private property of the state, property held like that of any free subject, and the state's slave production is that of one private unit(s) of production among others. The state's production is not the basis of social production. *This is yet another indication of the fact that politics is not the dominant instance in the slave mode.*

(c) Slaves are seldom *produced* as commodities, that is, by breeding them for sale, rather, slaves originate as captured or condemned free-men. Marx calls this the element of 'natural economy' in slave systems:

> But the slave system too – so long as it is the dominant form of productive labour in agriculture, manufacture, navigation, etc., as it is in the advanced states of Greece and Rome – preserves an element of natural economy. The slave market maintains its supply of the commodity labour-power by war, piracy, etc., and this regime is not promoted by the process of circulation, but by the actual appropriation of the labour power of others by direct physical compulsion. Even in the United States after the conversion of the buffer territory between the wage-labour states of the North and the slavery states in the South into a slave breeding region for the South, where the slave thrown on the market thus became himself an element of the annual reproduction, this did not suffice for a long time, so that the African slave trade was continued as long as possible to satisfy the market (*Capital*, II, p. 479).

In Capitalism the labourer *sells* his labour-power, the slave's labour-power exists in that form as the result of an extra-circulatory compulsion. The slave system *as a whole* appropriates labour-power whereas the capitalist system *buys* it. However, *within* the slave system labour-power is distributed to the units of production through the medium of the commodity market. The existence of slave production therefore creates the slave trade.

The slave trade creates specific forms of merchants' capital: merchants' capital, whose essence is to monopolise the market in any commodity not produced within a given region or which is scarce, actively develops and promotes the slave trade. In promoting this trade it promotes the system of slave production.

COMMENTS I

Slave labour-power tends to be reproduced by seizure of hitherto free men for the following reasons:

(i) Reproduction by breeding raises the price of slaves, this is because of the cost of maintenance during their unproductive period and the cost of maintaining women who do not contribute to production. Thus in Rome and the USA the price of slaves increased dramatically when the major external sources of supply were cut off.

(ii) Where the rate of consumption of the slave's labour-power is particularly intense, that is, where the slave's labour-power is exhausted in less than a generation, breeding becomes impossible as the major source of supply – production cannot keep up with wastage. The collapse of the external slave trade therefore will tend to curb the level of exploitation of slaves and lead to attempts to conserve their labour-power.[45]

COMMENTS II

The existence of a commodity *market* in slaves will tend to promote slavery as a system of commodity *production*. Marx argues that since merchants' capital exists entirely within the sphere of circulation its conditions of existence can be met in relative independence of the mode of production, it can therefore operate in respect of very diverse modes of production, its effects will vary from mode to mode but in general it will stimulate the production of goods as commodities:

> The extent to which products enter trade and go through the merchants' hands depends on the mode of production, and it reaches its maximum in the ultimate development of the capitalist production, where the product is produced solely as a commodity, and not as a direct means of subsistence. On the other hand, on the basis of every mode of production, trade facilitates the production of surplus products destined for exchange, in order to increase the enjoyments, or the wealth of the producers (here meant as the owners of the products). Hence commerce imparts to production a character directed more and more towards exchange-value (*Capital*, III, p. 320).

Merchants' capital makes trade possible and stimulates commodity production to obtain the means of exchange for luxuries, scarce products, etc., in non-capitalist modes of production. But in the SMP the consequence of the slave-market, of labour-power as a commodity, is more far reaching: *the purchase of labour-power as a commodity supposes its use for the production of commodities.* Unless, that is, it is purchased for unproductive consumption, but is impossible on a general scale since it supposes another source of income and, therefore, another mode of production.

(v) *Can the slave mode exist independently of other modes of production?*

This question does not raise the possibility of the existence of the SMP in simple 'empirical isolation', it does not even entail the SMP *ever having existed*, under whatever conditions. The question is a strictly theoretical one, it means: can the conditions of existence of the SMP be secured independently of its combination with other modes of production, does its *concept* presuppose the existence of other modes of production? Is it possible for the slave mode to reproduce itself within its own limits, or does it suppose its articulation with other modes as the conditions of its reproduction?

These questions are posed by the existence of two problems which arise in connection with slave labour-power as a commodity and the production of commodities by means of slaves:

Problem I – Given the difficulties of breeding slaves as a means of reproduction of labour-power, how in the absence of other modes of production can free labour be appropriated? To 'live on plunder' presupposes a means of production of the plundered?

Problem II – the SMP cannot exist in the absence of certain elements of commodity production and exchange, the form of constitution of the unit of production (slaves + land) supposes commodity exchange and this in turn supposes elements of commodity production. Slavery cannot exist on the basis of a 'natural economy' as a mode of production. Can it, however, exist on the basis of generalised commodity production without articulation with another mode of production?

In respect of the first problem two tendencies may be noted which result from the absence of an external supply of slaves: first, the price of slaves rises – this will tend to encourage breeding; second, the labour-power of the slave is conserved. These tendencies create a labour supply and reduce the rate of consumption and wastage. Howerer, the expansion of slave production is limited by the supply of labour-power – attempts may be made to develop the forces of production by labour-saving techniques, instruments of production and the introduction of incentives. Further, the internal redistribution of slave labour takes place, this will tend to be from the least efficient branches/units with a lower profitability to the most efficient units/branches, e.g. from farms with less productive soils, from unproductive occupations (domestic service, transport, etc.) to productive ones. The effect of this is a tendency toward the obliteration of subsistence production, to concentrate labour in the most profitable branches of production, and to produce severe imbalances between branches. While the absence of external sources of labour-power will tend to develop the forces of production to the limits possible within the slave mode this development is necessarily checked by the relations of production. We should recall that the work of labouring and the organisation of labour do not coincide, that slavery inhibits the division of labour, and that the more complex the process the greater the costs of superintendence. Compared to the slave system which consumes labour recklessly from foreign reserves the system forced to reproduce itself in this respect will be more developed in its forces of production.

In this example we have supposed that for various reasons and difficulties labour supply does not keep pace with demand. If this is not the case then the problems outlined above do not develop. However, even if they did develop in a serious form we can see that they would only create certain internal unbalances between branches and a tendency for the forces of production to develop to their limits. A slave mode *could*, therefore, exist without external supplies of labour. It should be noted here that an external supply of labour-power depends on the relation of the SMP to another mode at a *lower* level of technical and social development and unable to resist the depredations of its slave traders.

We have noted that to suppose the absence of external labour supplies tends to produce generalised commodity production. This relates to our second problem. The production of commodities by slaves as the dominant form of production within a social formation (and supposing that this production is not primarily for export) is conceivable and it generates certain interesting problems of the development and reproduction of this system of production. Let us note to begin with:

(a) the slaves are not (primarily – although they may be given wages as an incentive or 'pocket money') commodity purchasers;

(b) that the relations/forces of production do not suppose any large class of functionally necessary freemen;

(c) that there is between the units of production an anarchic separation similar to that of capitalism;

(d) that the law of value (= form of distribution of labour to different branches of production) operates to distribute labour toward the most profitable sectors.

Let us also note what the problem is *not*; it is not a problem of *under-consumption*. Although it is true that there are finite limits to the demand for commodities these do not stem from the forcing down of the slave's subsistence to a biological minimum or from the predominance of 'natural economy' (subsistence production) – it is possible to conceive of a variant of the SMP in which all items of consumption are commodities, there is no subsistence production, and the slaves have a high standard of living. The limits of *consumption* stem from the limits of slave *production* (that is, the effect of the relations of production is to prevent the revolutionisation of the forces of production and to reproduce the existing level of forces of production) and so a certain proportionality is enforced by production itself between production and consumption.

The problems stem from a disproportion between branches of the slave economy rather than a disproportion between production and consumption. The effects of the inhibition of the transformation of the forces of production are as follows:

(a) Unlike capitalism the surplus-product is not accumulated in an accelerating investment in the instruments of production, simple co-operation in agriculture and manufacture remains a labour-intensive system.

(b) Hence the branches of production specialising in producer's goods (Dept I) are weakly developed and those branches specialising in the production of items of consumption (Dept II) are dominant.

(c) Agricultural production is the dominant form of production. It is based on a labour-intensive system and the mass of workers cannot be separated from the soil. There is a limited market in industrial crops which corresponds to the limited development of manufacture. The production of items of consumption, principally food, is dominant in agriculture.

(d) Expansion of production takes the form of combining slaves and land (or adding more slaves to the workshop – the effect is the same); thus the general form of expanded reproduction in the SMP is by *geographical* expansion, that is, the linear addition of units of production rather than a qualitative change in the productivity of existing units, thus

Unit 1 *Land* = Product 1 + *Unit* 2 *Land* = Product 1 +
Labour-power Labour-power
. . . etc.

Observe that the predominant commodity exchanges here are the sale of items of consumption for the purchase of items of consumption. The value of food produced will preponderate over all other commodities (there are more labourers on the land and there is no reason to suppose that manufacture entails the expenditure of more labour). The consumption of manufactures is limited to the demands of agriculture and to a portion of the surplus-product of the slave-owning class. In certain other modes (e.g. feudalism) where agriculture is dominant, commodity exchange takes place on the basis of a *surplus* over subsistence production, here the whole social product takes the form of commodities. Thus we find food producers selling to and buying from food producers. Now, either this means there is trade between different regions and their specialist products (pomegranates – potatoes), or there is a 'needless' recourse to circulation in the case of a portion of the product (C-M-C = wheat –M –wheat), a recourse that entails all the risks and costs of circulation. The object of bringing this point out is not to argue that such a situation is *impossible*, we have no intention of supposing a 'rationality', nor do we wish to argue that the imbalance between the sectors in any sense makes the existence of such a mode untenable. All that is demonstrated by this example is that generalised commodity production and exchange on the basis of a pre-capitalist system will produce such imbalances between sectors and that this is an index that the system of circulation does not correspond to the system of production. In this mode, as in all pre-capitalist modes, the forces of production limit the development of the social division of labour and, therefore, the foundation of generalised commodity exchange.

The above discussion does illustrate that the SMP is particularly suited to the production of agricultural commodities in combination with another mode. The problems outlined above derived from the supposition that this was not so. Slavery *can* exist as a mode of production in the absence of articulation with other modes – its *concept* does not suppose other modes as necessary to its existence. However, the principal forms of slave production which have existed have existed under conditions of combination with another mode. The two major examples are:

(i) slave production appears as the most developed form of production in agriculture and manufacture in the ancient mode;

(ii) slave production in the Americas appeared as a specialist agrarian region subordinate to the capitalist mode of production and the capitalist world market. In both these cases elements of the slave mode appear as developed or subordinate forms within another mode.

4 The concept of the slave mode of production and the analysis of slave systems

In this chapter we have been concerned to challenge, and to avoid in our own analysis, the humanist reduction of social relations to effects of consciousness or will considered as natural attributes of human subjects. In the concept of the SMP each of the elements and levels is part of a structure of social relations. The effects of the SMP are those of a specific structure of social production, they are not consequences of the institution of slavery as such. In this section we will try to show the importance of a rigorous concept of SMP in the analysis of social formations in which slave labour forms the basis of social production. We will consider two analyses of the system of slave production in the USA, both of which attempt to rise above the level of simple empiricism and both of which attempt to analyse the South's economy as a whole. The first is John Cairnes's *The Slave Power*, the theoretical basis of which is the utilitarian political economy of Bentham, James Mill and John Stuart Mill. The second is Eugène Genovese's *The Political Economy of Slavery* and *The World the Slaveholders Made*, the theoretical basis of which is an idealist/historicist variant of Marxism strongly influenced by Gramsci. It is the logic of both of these theories to reduce the explanation of the social relations of slavery to the experience, consciousness and motivation of human subjects. Despite the apparent diversity of these theoretical positions the reductions in question are strikingly similar: thus Cairnes deduces the economic evils of slavery from the absence of an incentive to labour on the part of the slave, and Genovese, although more cautiously, lays the burden of low productivity and soil exhaustion on the slave's unfree status and unwillingness to work. Genovese seeks to explain the dynamics of this slave system, the slaveholders' rebellion and their defeat in the Civil War in terms of the unique ideology and social psychology of the master class. Cairnes gives some considerable place to the effect of the authoritarian outlook and habits of the master class, acquired in the domination of their slaves, in his explanation of the political conflicts between North and South.

Cairnes and Genovese have not been selected because they are especially weak and open to criticism. The works of these two authors are the most serious attempt to analyse the slave system of the South and the origins of the Civil War. Cairnes and Genovese are a necessary starting point in any attempt to understand the South's economy, its dynamic and its consequences.

The object of both Cairnes and Genovese is to explain why the Civil War occurred, to show that in essence it was a conflict between two distinct and incompatible social and economic systems and that it was an unavoidable conflict. Both analyses of the Southern slave system are therefore directed toward isolating those of its elements which must lead to competition and conflict with the North. In substance their basic theses are very similar, although Genovese seeks to qualify and correct Cairnes's basic arguments in the light of subsequent historical research.[46] Both writers analyse the slave system of the South by means of a comparison with their own conceptions of capitalism and find in those features which differ from capitalism the essence of the conflict with the North. Their common theses may be outlined as follows:

(i) The Southern economy because it was tied to slave labour and the production of agricultural commodities for export could not compete with the North in economic development and industrialisation. The inefficiency of slave labour (Cairnes), the concentration of income and wealth in the hands of the small planter class, the sparseness and general poverty of the free white population, all these factors retard home demand, restrict the market for manufacturers, encourage dependence on imports, and inhibit both the rate of reinvestment and investment in non-slave production.

(ii) In banking, credit, commerce, the carrying trade and manufactured goods the South was heavily dependent on the North.

(iii) That slave labour led to low productivity, a backward regime of cultivation and monoculture, soil exhaustion and a constant need to expand the territory available to slave cultivation. This dynamic of expansion based on soil exhaustion led to a conflict with Northern free farmers and certain elements of Northern capital, a conflict for control of the western territories between the slave and the free-labour systems.

(iv) Both Cairnes and Genovese argue that the slave system was neither dying out of its own accord nor were its basic characteristics capable of reform. Cairnes shows that the states which suffered most from soil exhaustion, far from ceasing to be slave states, survived by slave breeding and selling their surplus slaves to states further to the west. Genovese shows that the reform and renovation of agriculture in these earliest slave states, continuing to use slave labour, was dependent on the export of slaves to the western territories.[47] It is in the conflict for the unsettled western territories, an expansionist dynamic imported to slavery by soil exhaustion, that both writers see the economic foundation of the Civil War crisis. We will consider these explanations separately, beginning with Genovese.

(a) GENOVESE – 'THE POLITICAL ECONOMY OF SLAVERY'

Genovese poses the problem of the nature of the South's economic relations by asking the question – was the South capitalist or not? He is forced to tackle this question in order to answer those historians who have argued that the South was a capitalist society, that slavery was not a crucial economic problem and that there was no irreconcilable conflict between the interests of these two essentially capitalist regions. These historians have argued that the Southern economy was capitalistic because of its integration into the world market, because of its use of developed banking, financial and commercial institutions, and because the planters invested for profit and calculated with a capitalistic rationality. In opposition to this, Genovese argues emphatically that the South was not a capitalist society and that its non-capitalist features led it into conflict with the capitalist North.

Genovese argues that elements of commerce, money exchange and a bourgeois class are not sufficient to constitute capitalism:

> Capitalism has absorbed and even encouraged many kinds of pre-capitalist social systems: serfdom, slavery, Oriental state enterprises and others. It has introduced credit, finance, banking and similar institutions where they did not previously exist. It is pointless to suggest that therefore nineteenth century India and twentieth century Saudi Arabia should be classified as capitalist countries (p. 19).

He then goes on to argue that commerce credit and the existence of a merchant class are not necessarily capitalist forms and that: 'their fortunes are bound up with those of the dominant producers' (p. 20). In the South, commercial, banking and industrial capital were subordinate to the conditions imposed by slavery. He catalogues the limitations to the development of demand and the growth of the market which follow from slavery. Slavery as a system of production limits the development of commodity production and the development of new branches of production. It does so through its effects on *demand*: the extreme concentration of wealth and land in the hands of the planter class limits the home market. Slaves and poor whites generate little demand, and it is cheaper to import goods than to buy them from indigenous industries limited in their level of development and efficiency by the home market. The lack of industrial development and the limited growth of cities restricts the growth of commodity production in agriculture other than that specialising in export staples. Country and town retard one another.[48]

This is the extent of Genovese's attempt to settle the question of capitalism or non-capitalism. In effect he argues that the South is non-capitalist because it is not characterised by generalised commodity production and exchange. He traces this absence to the restriction of demand and this restriction in turn to slave production. Slave production is consigned to the general category 'pre-capitalist', the method of assignment being its difference from certain essential features of capitalism. No *concept* of a slave economy or a slave mode of production is produced. The characteristics of slave production are derived from an empirical description of conditions in the South. What is different between India, Saudi Arabia and the South? In all of them there is the same absence of generalised commodity production and exchange. *Slavery* is the distinctive feature of the South, and the various concrete conditions of the Southern economy are ascribed to it. This is the classic procedure of speculative empiricism and the comparative method.

The question of the presence or absence of capitalist social relations is not posed in terms of whether the conditions of existence of the CMP are or are not met in the southern USA. Genovese has *no concept* of mode of production. Capitalism is defined by the presence or absence of a characteristic which is given to observation, commodity production and exchange. Capitalism for him is a more or less coherent unity of empirically given 'features'.

> If for a moment we accept the designation of the planters as capitalists and the slave system as a form of capitalism, we are

> then confronted by a capitalist society that impeded the development of every *normal* feature of capitalism (p. 23) (our emphasis).

The slave system is different from the features capitalist societies *normally* exhibit – the notion of a *norm* supposes that 'capitalism' is a generalisation which results from observation. These 'features' are empirically given facts and their presence permits the recognition and classification of such relations as 'capitalist'. Non-capitalist social relations are equally unities of such features. *No concept* of such relations is required. They are known through an empirical description which isolates their distinctive features, this description suitably generalised will then serve as a model by means of which slave systems can be identified in other cases. Genovese uses certain criteria (presence/absence of given 'features') to argue that the South is non-capitalist. It does not match the normal features of capitalism. Placed as it is outside the model of capitalism the designation of the non-capitalist characteristics of slave production is a matter of empirical research.

For Genovese industrialisation, commercial-financial autonomy and a capitalist class characterised by a high rate of reinvestment of profits are such normal features of capitalism. England and the North exhibit such features. This norm is absent in the South, hence capitalism is absent. The closest Genovese gets to a conceptual analysis of the slave economy is his use of Max Weber's argument that slavery is 'irrational' because it does not use the most efficient means to the end of maximising profits.[49] This inefficiency is because slave labour is expensive, inflexible in response to fluctuations in the demand for labour, it entails a greater capital outlay, and the dominance of the planter class creates the possibility of irrational political influence of the market. In capitalism competition and 'the bourgeois spirit of accumulation'[50] force a high rate of reinvestment and of qualitative change in methods of production. In the South the planters, forced as they are by the pressures of the world market to reinvest, merely produce a quantitative expansion in slave production. This is because slavery in limiting internal production channels investment into the existing branches of production and because there are systematic limitations on the raising of the productivity of slave labour.

This comparison of slave and capitalist production is in and of itself valueless. Weber's notion of 'irrationality' is only possible by comparing slave production and capitalism as alternatives, as means to an end. This is pointless since we are not concerned with means but with systems of social production. If slave production is non-capitalist production then its 'irrationality' relative to capitalism is irrelevant so long as the conditions of existence of slave production are secured. Genovese does not raise the question of the reproduction of the slave system of production. He does not argue that capitalism necessarily breaks down the conditions of existence of slave production and supersedes it. The relation of capitalism and slavery is not one of modes of production articulated in antagonistic combination, it is the parallel development of the distinct systems. For Genovese the contradictions of slave production are all contradictions *relative* to capitalism; such 'contradictions' are a falling behind of slavery in the sphere of economic 'development'.

Genovese sees the South as suffering from economic backwardness. The notion of 'backwardness' can only have meaning relative to a *norm*. The South is like Baran's conception of an 'underdeveloped' country; it has obstacles to industrialisation and it lacks economic national autonomy. In this case, however, backwardness is not due to imperialist exploitation but to a primitive and retarding system of production. The South's weaknesses were that it was not being industrialised, and that it was dependent on the North for its commerce, its financial and credit system and its manufacturers. This concentration on the failure to '*keep up*' with capitalism reveals the National Economy[51] standpoint that lies behind Genovese's positions. He reproduces the position of Southern ideologues like De Bow, who regarded the South as *already a nation* and were concerned to argue the need for economic autarchy and industrial production to counter the powerful rival in the North.[52] This position presupposes the conflict *that is to be*: industrialisation, autarchy, etc., can have value only as part of a nationalist policy, they are only important relative to conflict, blockade and war between the two systems.

It is only in this context that these notions like 'backwardness' can have any meaning. In fact, the *development* of the slave power (which we will assume for the moment to be governed by the laws of the SMP), the expanded reproduction of its economy could not but lead to a path quite different from the North. Development of the slave economy is the expansion of slave production, of estates-plantations producing largely agricultural commodities for sale outside the region. Expanded reproduction would therefore accentuate those features of the economy which Genovese sees as backward or underdeveloped. The limits to the development of the South's economy have nothing to do with economic competition from the North. Those limits are: (i) the demand for the commodities produced in the capitalist world market, (ii) the supply and price of slave labour-power, and, (iii) political limits to the expansion of the slave system. None of these limitations was operative in the period up to the 1850s and there is no reason to suppose that the expansion of slave production would have been checked given that existing economic and political conditions continued. Despite cyclic fluctuations, world demand for cotton, sugar, tobacco, etc., was rising rapidly. The supply of labour, although limited and relatively inflexible, was by no means exhausted nor incapable of internal reproduction.

Political limits did not exist in the 1850s, there was no chance of slavery being abolished, and as a result of its aggressive policy, the Slave Power had all the land it needed for economic development for some time to come. Thus there were no immediate checks to the expanded reproduction of the plantation economy, and no systematic mechanisms inhibiting the expansion of slave production. There was no crisis of the South's economy in the 1850s and certainly no crisis stemming from the failure of the South to keep pace in a race toward some norm of 'development'. *The economic development of the South meant the development of slave production.*

The contradiction between slavery and capitalism Genovese seeks is not to be found at the economic level. Even the competition for western land was not immediate or fatal, and it was not a conflict with capitalist production as such, but with the independent farmer settlers. The origin of the Civil War is not to be found in some failure of the South in economic competition with the North. In a sense, Genovese accepts this. He does not conceive the 'crisis' which led to the Civil War as an *economic* crisis, but as a *general* crisis in which political, ideological and cultural elements are dominant.[53] The essence of the South's situation *does* lie in the economic competition of the North and South, but only in so far as it is *reflected and created* in the experience, consciousness and ideology of the planter class.

Genovese argues that the economic weakness of slavery relative to capitalism would ultimately lead to the political defeat of the planter class, the loss of its hegemony:

> The slow pace of their economic progress, in contrast to the long strides of their rivals to the North, threatened to undermine their political parity and result in a Southern defeat on all the major issues of the day (p. 17).

And again:

> The political, economic and ideological barriers to capital accumulation, to the development of the home market, and to the rise and consolidation of independent middle classes effectively prevented the South from keeping pace with Northern material development. The attendant sapping of Southern political power in the Union threatened to sap slaveholder hegemony in the South (p. 285).

This thesis supposes what it must prove. Nothing made the threat of a government opposed to slavery expansion a reality but the actions of the Southern party itself. The South's political representatives were dominant in the American state and the Southern interest was only defeated electorally *after* its representatives were split with their Democratic allies in the North. There was no necessity in the Republican victory in 1860 and no necessity for a political programme for the extirpation of slavery. Contrary to the position he apparently takes, Genovese does not in fact suppose that the Civil War crisis was the product of any mechanism generated by the economic conflict of the two systems. It is not an economic crisis in the normal sense, but it is 'economic' in that this competition of the two systems is made real and turned into a 'crisis' in the consciousness of the planter class. It is an economic crisis in the sphere of consciousness. This ideological/experiential mediation and actualisation of the economic is in fact decisive in Genovese's explanation, it is the decisive cause of the Civil War. The crisis is an ideological and spiritual crisis for the planter class. Its essence is the consciousness of the slaveholder threatened and isolated in a world more and more hostile to slavery. The Civil War was the result of a gamble on the part of the planter class to risk losing all rather than to be gradually and ignominiously extinguished. The planter class is considered as a historical actor or subject. That this is the general tendency of Genovese's work can be seen most clearly in his study of George Fitzhugh, 'The Logical Outcome of the Slaveholder's Philosophy'.[54]

This unique class subject has its origin in the master–slave relationship:

> The planters were not mere capitalists; they were pre-capitalist, quasi-aristocratic landowners who had to adjust their economy and ways of thinking to the capitalist world market. Their society, in its spirit and fundamental direction, represented the

> antithesis of capitalism, however many compromises it had to make. The fact of slave ownership is central to our problem. This seemingly formal question of whether the owners of the means of production command labour or purchase the labour power of free workers contains in itself the content of Southern life. The essential features of Southern particularity, as well as Southern backwardness, can be traced to the relationship of master to slave (*The Political Economy of Slavery*, p. 23).

Here we have it! The planter class as a historical actor is formed in the confrontation of superior subject and subordinate subject in the master–slave relation. The experience of the master forms his consciousness, and his consciousness his actions. Slaveholding is the essence of the master class, it is no mere economic relation but the foundation of its social being. For the master class, the crisis, the threat from the North, is the challenge to their existence as slaveholders, to the essence of their social being. Genovese's 'crisis' shifts from the economy to consciousness, and in consciousness it concerns not debit and credit but a way of life. The slaveholders gamble all not because of economic 'backwardness' as such, but to secure the foundations of a society based on slaveholding.

The whole question of slavery is reduced to this essential relation of master and slave, it is the essence of the totality of the South and the key to the Civil War. Genovese reproduces exactly and brilliantly the structure of the essentialist totality – all particular phenomena, all apparently conjunctural forms, from soil exhaustion to the attack on Fort Sumter, can be traced to the relation of the master to the slave and to the consciousness of the master class.

(b) THE NATURE OF THE SOUTH'S ECONOMY

We have seen that Genovese is unable to develop any *concept* of slave production and that he is unable to give a satisfactory analysis of the relation of the South's economy to northern capitalism and to the world capitalist system. This is a limitation internal to and necessary to the historicist problematic which dominates his investigations. Whatever the limitations of Genovese's work, it represents a serious attempt to explain the Southern system and the causes of the Civil War, in criticising this attempt it is necessary to offer some alternative explanation, however provisional and partial. We will attempt to characterise the system of slave production in the South and its relation to the capitalist system. Our starting point in doing so is to pose the question, under what conditions and by what necessity did this system of production come into existence?

Slave production in North America and the West Indies developed in three main phases. Each of these phases has a distinct character and distinct and separate conditions of existence. There is no evolution here, no necessary progression from the origin, but a series of distinct and conjunctural systems of production using slave labour. These phases are:

Phase I the use of slaves, convicts and indentured labourers to cultivate farms and estates in colonies in which production is primarily for subsistence and where only a small portion of the product is fitfully sold for trade. Such conditions existed in the seventeenth and for much of the eighteenth centuries on the northern American mainland and in the early part of the seventeenth century in the West Indies. This phase is dominated by non-capitalist settlement; slaves often supplementing the labour of the settlers.

Phase II the large-scale production of crops such as sugar as commodities for sale in European markets, production being by means of plantations worked by slaves and the slave labour being purchased as a commodity. Such conditions existed in the late seventeenth and in the eighteenth centuries on the islands in the West Indies. Here slave production is an effect of commerce: merchants' capital dominates the export of agricultural commodities as items of domestic consumption to Europe and promotes the trade in African slaves to supply the plantations with labour-power.[55]

Phase III the production of cotton as a commodity to supply the demands of capitalist industrial production in Europe for raw materials. Such slave production came into existence in the South from the late eighteenth century onwards. This phase is dominated by the constant expansion of capitalist industrial production and by the world market created by capitalist industry.[56]

The slave-worked estates of the West Indies and the South came into existence as the units of production of a specialist agrarian commodity-producing region. This region appears as a function of the demand for items of industrial and domestic consumption by the most-developed capitalist regions. These plantations are an effect of the international division of labour created by the needs of capitalist industry and the growth of the world market. In the latter part of the nineteenth century and in the early twentieth century, in Argentina, Australia, Canada and Malaya other such specialist agrarian commodity-producing regions came into existence on the basis of free peasant proprietorship or capitalist farming using free wage-labour or indentured labour.[57]

Slave production is therefore not a necessary form of production for such specialist agrarian regions. Why did slave labour form the basis of the system of production in the West Indies and the South in the period of the seventeenth to the nineteenth centuries? Firstly, why *slave* labour? There are four conjunctural reasons:

(i) the African slave trade and slavery as a legal institution pre-existed the development of large-scale production in the region;

(ii) merchants' capital promoted slaves as a commodity and the African slave trade was capable of more or less indefinite expansion, hence there were no limitations to the supply of slave labour-power;

(iii) convicts and indentured labourers from Europe could not be made available in sufficient numbers to meet the demand for labour-power and to fill the gaps in the ranks caused by the high mortality;

(iv) there were by and large no indigenous peoples suitable for conversion into subordinate producers.

This explains why slaves *could* be supplied and why they were employed *instead of another unfree labour system.* But slaves had no necessity – sugar, cotton, tobacco, rice, etc., are now produced in these same regions by free white and black labourers. Why did capitalist agrarian production based on free labour or production based on free peasant proprietorship not develop? There are two main reasons:

(i) Capitalist farming could not be imported to these regions because capitalist relations of production could not be exported to them. The separation of the worker from the means of production on the basis of the wage form is not possible in the absence of the monopoly ownership of land by non-labourers and the existence of land free for cultivation. Under such conditions free labourers would tend to become independent proprietors and artisans. Marx tells the story of a Mr Peel, an English capitalist, who attempted to establish large-scale capitalist production at Swan River in Australia, taking with him capital to the value of £50,000 and 3,000 working-class men, women and children. On arrival he was deserted and 'left without a servant to make his bed or fetch him water from the river'.[58] Marx drily remarks: 'Unhappy Mr. Peel who provided for everything except the export of English modes of production to Swan River!' (*Capital*, I, p. 766).

Marx goes on to argue:

> the expropriation of the mass of the people from the soil forms the basis of the capitalist mode of production. The essence of a free colony, on the contrary, consists in this – that the bulk of the soil is still public property, and every settler on it can therefore turn part of it into his private property and individual means of production without hindering later settlers in the same operation (p. 768).

In the seventeenth and eighteenth centuries these regions of the Americas were virgin and unsettled territory. Free labour could not be imported without greatly raising its wages and its cost relative to countries where the worker is separated from the means of production and by providing better conditions of work than obtain for unfree labour. The absence of a monopoly ownership of land does not by any means absolutely prohibit the use of free labour but it does greatly increase its cost to the employer and reduce the level of its exploitation.[59] In all probability free labour would have been more expensive than slave labour, given the highly developed African slave trade, and the supply of freemen wishing to work in such places as the West Indies for any length of time rather than becoming free proprietors must be a matter of uncertainty and conjecture.

(ii) To a considerable extent this explains why slave labour predominated instead of free wage labour; however, it does not explain the absence of large-scale competition from free peasant settlers. Cairnes produces an interesting argument to explain this.[60] He argues that the greatest limitation of independent peasant production is that it sets severe limits to forms of co-operation and division of labour, and therefore limits the size of the unit of production. Slave labour, however, 'admits of the most complete organisation, that is to say it may be combined on an extensive scale, and directed by a controlling mind to a single end . . . ' (Cairnes, *The Slave Power*, p. 44). Cairnes notes that the Slave States correspond to those areas where the soil and climate are particularly suited to the production of tobacco, rice, cotton and sugar, and the Free States to those areas where the conditions favour cereal crops. The cultivation of cotton in particular requires large investments of labour and the combined working of several labourers. In the case of cereals they can be raised efficiently by free peasant proprietors and the acreage workable with family labour (plus supplementary wage-labour) is sufficient to make a satisfactory living. In the case of cotton the acreage workable by family labour is too low to support a prosperous existence for the peasant. Cotton, sugar, etc., permit the efficient working of labourers in combination, cereals do not. Thus Cairnes argues:

> We thus find that cotton, and the class of crops of which cotton may be taken as the type, favour the employment of slaves in the competition with peasant proprietors in two leading ways: first, they need extensive combination and organisation of labour – requirements which slavery is eminently calculated to supply, but in respect of which the labour of peasant proprietors is defective; and secondly, they allow of labour being concentrated, and thus minimise the cardinal evil of slave labour, the reluctance with which it is yielded (p. 51).

Various labour systems can form the basis of the production of agricultural commodities – free labour, indentured labour, slave labour, etc., and slave labour is but one possible system among others. It developed as the basis of commodity production in the plantations of the Americas for a variety of conjunctural reasons, which have been outlined above, and it has been replaced by free labour. It should not be thought, however, that slave labour is no different from, or a mere substitute for, wage-labour. The introduction of slave labour had a distinct and definite effect on the system of production. Slave production entailed the introduction of a distinct labour process and a distinct mode of appropriation of the surplus product. If we examine the plantation systems of the West Indies and the Americas from Phase II onwards, we find the following conditions:

(a) slave labour forms the basis of social production, it is not supplementary to any other labour system;

(b) the slaves work in gangs on estates/plantations, they are separated from the means of production and are not merely legally unfree direct producers;

(c) slave labour-power is a commodity and the slave is a form of capital;

(d) the product of slave labour is sold as a commodity.

These conditions mean that the basic elements which constitute the relations and forces of production of the SMP are present. If such a combination, relations/forces, exists, then in some form, the SMP is present in the social formation. Slave labour under these conditions cannot be a mere substitute for wage-labour. The system of production in question exists within the limits set by the forces of production of the SMP.

In what form is the SMP present? It is present in the following form: it is a mode of production subordinated to the capitalist mode of production within the international division of labour and the world market created by capitalism. The conditions of reproduction of the SMP under these circumstances depend upon the capitalist system; upon world demand for the commodities it produces, competing regions and methods of production, alternative sources of investment, etc. To say that a mode of production is *subordinate* in a combination is to say that it depends for its conditions of existence on the mode or modes with which it is combined.

The SMP in the South was not merely dependent on world capitalism, but also upon American capitalism – American capital provided both the apparatus and the means of circulation. Slave production in the South depended on the same forms of commerce, credit, banking, etc., as the capitalist mode (the West Indies similarly using the financial and commercial institutions of England and New England). Money capital from various sources within the capitalist mode (profits derived from surplus-value, merchants' capitalist profits, etc.) can be invested in slave production (either directly or through the advance of credit). The surplus-product of slave production can be converted into capitalist profit in exactly the same way as the surplus-value derived from wage-labour. Capitalist calculation therefore enters into the investment in slaves and profits are expected from the use of slave labour. Slaves are reckoned as a form of fixed capital. This intersection with capitalist relations of circulation provides slave production with an advanced commercial and financial apparatus and ties it into the capitalist system. It should be noted that it also ties sections of commercial and financial capital to slave production. The South might depend on New York and Baltimore, but the dependence was mutual, and it was in such centres that support for the Southern interest was strongest.

Slave production is tied to the capitalist market, to the demands of capitalist industry, to the cycle of boom and slump and to changing demands in the sphere of domestic production. The fortunes of cotton producers were settled in Manchester.[61] Like any other specialist agrarian region the South was not and could not be independent of the effects of capitalism on a world scale.

There is no antagonism between the capitalist system in general and slavery – slave production appears under specific conditions as a subordinate form to the CMP. Later on we will enter into the question of whether or not the specific forms of capitalist development in the North and the opening of the West by free labour were antagonistic to slavery. Before we tackle that question, we must first settle another: the tendency of the slave system to expand as a consequence of soil exhaustion.

(c) SLAVERY, SOIL EXHAUSTION AND EXPANSION

Cairnes deduces the destructive effects of slave cultivation from the slaves' lack of incentive and unwillingness to labour. The slave's lack of incentive stems from the fact that he has no prospect of material reward and the harder he works the more effort he expends for nothing. Cairnes quotes the following passage from Bentham:

> Fear leads the labourer to hide his powers, rather than to show them; to remain below rather than to surpass himself. . . . By displaying superior capacity the slave would only raise the measure of his ordinary duties; by a work of supererogation he would only prepare punishment for himself (p. 45).

The slave in seeking pleasure and avoiding pain attempts to reduce his labour to the absolute minimum. The absurdity of utilitarianism as a theory in political economy, psychology and ethics has been demonstrated time and again by authors as diverse as F. H. Bradley and Marx.[62] We need not bother to repeat these criticisms in detail here; utilitarianism is nullified by its simple-minded circularity.

Cairnes argues that slave labour has three main defects: '. . . it is given reluctantly; it is unskilled; it is wanting in versatility' (*ibid.*, p. 44). Slaves are reluctant, inflexible and unskilful workers because it is not in their interest to be otherwise and because the slaveowner fears to educate the slave. Slave agriculture is condemned to a regime of monoculture with the toughest and most clumsy tools, with the most primitive cultivation methods, on the most fertile soils which make up in their natural productivity for the defects in the means of labour. The effect of monoculture is soil exhaustion and the exhaustion of the most fertile soils in a given region. Soil exhaustion leads to a constant tendency of the slave system to expand:

> Slave cultivation, whenever it has been tried in the New World has issued in the same results. Precluding the conditions of rotation of crops or skilful management, it tends inevitably to exhaust the land of a country, and consequently requires for its permanent success not merely a fertile soil but a practically unlimited extent of it (*ibid.*, p. 62).

Soil exhaustion and the constant need for new territory is the 'fundamental principle in [the] political economy' of slave societies. It results in expansionist and monopolistic tendencies, backed by aggressive political policies:

> The aggressive character of a social system deriving its strength from slavery – that is to say of a slave power – proceeds primarily from the well-known economic fact . . . the necessary limitation of slave culture to soils of more than average richness, combined with its tendency to exhaust them (*ibid.*, p. 180).

Slave societies cannot develop within a limited area, they must expand or perish. Further, slavery is an exclusive social system, it cannot tolerate effective competition from free institutions within its borders. The sparse population which is an effect of the system of slave plantations produces a restricted demand for goods and services, barriers to the development of cultural life and institutions, and to the development of a generalised commodity exchange economy. Slavery therefore excludes by its moral and political atmosphere, and by its economy, free institutions and forms of production based on free labour. Cairnes spells out clearly his conception of the essence of the political and economic contradiction between North and South. It is a contradiction very different from that of Genovese's argument, although it has a similar foundation. Cairnes, a contemporary observer and democratic anti-slavery propagandist, saw in the South an aggressive Slave Power led by a cohesive and authoritarian planter class which was a threat to the free institutions and the free labour system of the North.

Cairnes arguing from his utilitarian principles maintains that slavery is an inefficient labour system based as it is on reluctant, unskilled and inflexible labourers. This must be a general and necessary feature of all slave labour systems since one slave's felicific calculus can be little different from another's. And soil exhaustion must be a universal feature of all slave production. Many who do not share Cairnes's utilitarianism also suppose that slavery is an inefficient labour system. It is a truism in orthodox Marxist literature that slavery limited the development of technique and knowledge in the ancient world because it made labour a curse and separated thought and action. L. Leontyev, in a recent Soviet textbook on political economy, puts this point of view most clearly:

> Slave labour was unproductive. A slave was not interested in the results of his labour. His position remained hopeless and

> oppression did not become less hard to bear no matter how hard he worked. The slave owners were not particularly interested in raising labour productivity; they commanded an enormous unfree labour force.... The slave-owning system educated a deep contempt for labour.... Physical labour came to be considered the lot of slaves, an occupation unworthy of free people. Contempt for productive labour became an obstacle to social development (1968, pp. 32–4).

George Thomson, although more cautious and subtle in his arguments, maintains a similar thesis, in particular that in Greece slave labour inhibited the development of the free labour system:

> As the supply of slave labour increased, the demand for free labour declined, with the result that the free labourer was either unable to find employment or else compelled to work in conditions which reduced him to the economic level of a slave (*Aeschylus and Athens*, p. 326).

What truth is there in these arguments? We consider there to be none at all. In the Ancient World the slave-worked estate and manufacturing workshop were the most developed forms of the forces of production. Slavery stood in comparison with the other current forms of production, with free peasant proprietorship, with sharecropping tenancy, with independent handicraft workers, as a more productive and efficient labour system. In agriculture the textbooks on 'scientific' farming presupposed the medium-sized slave-worked estate.[63] On such estates a division of labour, the development of specialised skills, and the freedom of the owner or his functionary for planning and co-ordination made possible the most advanced and productive forms of agriculture in the ancient world. This type of estate produced crops like olive oil or wine; quality crops requiring skilled and attentive care. On such estates the slaves were, by and large, the *skilled* workers, involved in such trades as vinedressing. Free tenants and bondsmen, cultivating the less suitable lands, were used as *unskilled* labour to supplement that of the slaves, particularly at peak periods. The great estates producing corn for the market and worked by unskilled slave labour gangs were far from being typical. The latifundia of Sicily and southern Italy were a product of the peculiar conditions of the late Roman Republic. These estates could only exist because of the vast numbers of slaves generated by the civil strife and the wars of conquest of this period. When the supply of slaves was severely curtailed and their price rose dramatically, such estates were converted from slave cultivation to client sharecropper or free tenant regimes.[64]

Why was slave labour the basis of the most developed forms of production in the ancient world? The answer is to be found in the limitations of the dominant forms of free labour in the ancient world, independent peasant production and independent handicraft production. Far from conferring the benefits of enterprise and innovation which are ascribed to them by utilitarians and orthodox Marxists alike, these forms of free labour were the real brake on the ancient economy. Slave production overcame these limitations. Slave labour supplemented but never supplanted these free labour systems. Peasant and artisan production remained the dominant forms of social production and it was these forms which set definite limits to the development of the ancient economy.

It is the *inefficiency* of free labour in contrast with slave labour which is the most striking and the most neglected feature of the economies of Classical Antiquity. What are the sources of this relative inefficiency? Small peasant proprietorship and artisan handicraft production limit the possibilities for even simple co-operation and a rudimentary division of labour. Co-operation and division of labour are possible only *within* the peasant or artisan household or, by express agreement in respect of a specific task, between otherwise independent households. Such forms of production require regular and unstinting application to the task of labouring by the peasant or artisan and his family. In general the peasant or artisan lacks the time, general culture and the capital to develop new techniques of working and new instruments of production. The unit of production is too small to support certain developments in the instruments of production or method of working. Add to these general limitations in such forms of production the particular limitations imposed by the conditions of the ancient world, the burden of military service, taxes, debts and harsh laws against debtors, etc., and the difficulties of the peasant or artisan are correspondingly magnified.

The slave-worked estate is characterised by none of these limitations:

(i) the owner has the time and the cultural means to acquire relevant knowledge, to plan and to supervise;

(ii) labourers can be set to work in combination, tasks can be divided, specific skills differentiated and cultivated – the unit of production can be large enough to permit this;

(iii) the slave can be trained and instructed, he is not compelled like the peasant to labour ceaselessly to reproduce himself;

(iv) slaves are not subject to military service, the well-to-do were less heavily taxed, and they were not dependent like the peasant upon loans to tide them over a bad harvest. The textbooks of scientific agriculture of the period suppose such an estate and such means, it is not supposed that such techniques could be applicable to peasant cultivation. The development and extension of slave production was limited by the predominantly political and parasitic forms of accumulation of capital, by the necessity that such accumulation be confined to a small class of wealthy notables, and by the fact that the bulk of the population was not separated from the land, thereby limiting the level of commodity production. Wealth acquired through political means was 'squandered' in luxury consumption, in politics and patronage. The dominance of independent peasant production, however harassed and oppressed the peasantry might be, confined slave production to a definite sector. The same conditions that limited the further extension of slave production *also limited free wage-labour*. It too must have been limited, even if slavery had not existed, by the forms of concentration of wealth and the dominance of peasant production. It is therefore quite incorrect to argue that slavery inhibited the growth of wage-labour relations in the ancient world.

Slavery was the basis of the most developed forms of production in the ancient world and such slave labour was in the main skilled labour. Cairnes in fact recognises that there is a real difference between ancient and modern slavery. Cairnes knows that the agriculture of the ancient world was not characterised by this dynamic of expansion based on soil exhaustion. He produces the remarkable argument that because the whole of the culture of the ancient world rested on slave labour the slaveowner's progress, culture and standard of living was directly dependent on the level of skill and application of his slaves. The owner, therefore, had a definite incentive to promote the welfare of his slaves:

> He was, therefore, naturally led to cultivate the faculties of his slaves and by consequence promote generally the improvement of their condition. *His* progress in the enjoyment of the material advantages of civilisation depended directly upon *their* progress in knowledge and social consideration (Cairnes, *op. cit.*, p. 113).

Hence we have the mutually beneficial linking of the felicific calculus of the master with that of the slave. The better the one is treated and cultivated the better the other lives. A happy arrangement!

This argument by which Cairnes attempts to explain away the productivity, skill and application of slave labour in Antiquity rests on a fallacy. Whether the slave is treated well or not, cultivated or not, his capacity as a labourer does not depend on his response to, or his experience of, his condition. The slave's labour takes a definite social form irrespective of his experience, a form constituted by the forces and relations of production. The productivity of factory labour is not dependent on the experience of the labourer. However tired, bolshie, 'alienated', suffering from an excess of lunch, or smitten by hay fever the labourer may be, this *form* of labour is still of a level of productivity altogether different from the labour of manufacture or handicraft production. This is not merely because the factory worker's pace and level of production is set by the machine. Labour has a social form which determines its character and the character of the labourers who perform it.[65] A slave vinedresser, however well or ill disposed he is to work, has a determinate skill to perform in a determinate labour process. This skill and this process are conferred on him by the system of social production and not by his 'motivation'. This skill is performed in combination with other workers and to a plan – the nature of his labour is prescribed by the nature of the labour process/process of production in which he is involved. The advantages of slave production over peasant production are those of management, co-operation and division of labour. These advantages remain with it independent of the 'motivation' of the slaves, just as the limitations of independent peasant production remain with it no matter how hard-working or lazy the peasant is.

Cairnes subjectivises the forms of social productivity, he makes the differences between them differences of motivation on the part of the workers who experience them. This is nowhere clearer than in the case of slavery and factory industry. Cairnes argues that slaves cannot be used in industrial production or in combination with machines because slave labour is unskilled, unintelligent and unable to take an initiative. Cairnes sings the praises of free labour. It is intelligent, creative and active by nature. 'Free' labourers are, however, free only in the sense that they are free to sell their labour-power on the market. They appear to be free agents at the level of the process of circulation. Once the labourer has sold his labour-power the picture changes.

Once the labourer enters the process of production, his labour-power is the *property* of the capitalist and the labourer is subject to discipline and supervision. Cairnes the capitalist-apologist cannot see that in factory production, (i) the concentration and supervision of the labourers is greatly facilitated, and, (ii) that the labourer's operations and pace are dictated by the enterprise as a working unity, either directly through his subsumption to the pace of the machine or through his place in the division of labour. Factory production in no way excludes the use of slaves, it makes supervision easier and it sets an inescapable pace of labour. While the SMP does not and cannot develop the forces of production beyond certain limits imposed by the relations of production, this does not mean that slave production cannot make use of advanced techniques developed under other conditions or that slave labour cannot be inserted into forms of production developed within the capitalist mode of production.

Cairnes is led by his subjectivist position to argue: 'Slavery, therefore, excluded by these causes from the field of manufactures and commerce, finds its natural career in agriculture' (*op. cit.*, p. 73). This is nothing but nonsense. This career is *natural* because Cairnes in the guise of a Utilitarian philistine[66] sees it as lacking the 'initiative' and 'motivation' he conceives to be the attributes of free labour. Slave labour is not reluctant, unskilled and inflexible by *nature* – soil exhaustion cannot be ascribed to slavery *as such*. We must look for the causes of soil exhaustion in the system of production and not in the supposed attributes of the slave's nature as a subject.

There can be no doubt that the South *did* suffer from serious soil erosion. We have no need to rely on the reports and opinions of contemporaries, the effects are still manifest in the South: 41 per cent of the costs of farm operations in the South were represented by fertilisers in the 1930s against 5 per cent in the rest of the country, and the South in 1930 accounted for two-thirds of the tonnage of fertilisers consumed in the USA, but represented only one-sixth of the nation's crop land.[67] Contemporaries often spoke of ravaged and abandoned fields, but this provides no clear notion of soil exhaustion or its effects. As Genovese argues, soil exhaustion is not an agronomic absolute, it is an *economic* margin zone. Economic conditions determine the 'exhaustion' of the soil. Thus exhaustion for primitive slash-and-burn subsistence cultivators is not the same as it is for commodity-production agriculture which is subject to capitalist calculation. We may define soil exhaustion relative to conditions of commodity production and capitalist calculation as follows:

soil exhaustion = *a significant fall in the productivity of the land irrecoverable within existing cost levels and requiring the expenditure of additional labour time, technique and raw materials to restore the level of productivity.*

Soil exhaustion raises the cost of production.

Let us consider the nature of the system of agriculture in the South in order to determine the causes of soil exhaustion and of the tendencies toward 'geographical' expansion.

Soil exhaustion in the South, in the West Indies, and so on, is not simply a function of the labour system involved. Soil exhaustion is primarily an effect of the planter's relation to the land and to the process of production. This relation is conditioned by the fact that there is no monopoly possession of land. Land values and rents on property to which there is a title are, therefore, low. The relation of the planter to the land is similar to that of the capitalist farmer or industrialist. Land has no value in itself, it is merely a necessary means of production of commodities. Land enters into capitalist calculation in a similar way to raw materials and constant capital, it is consumed in the process of production and must eventually be renewed. The capitalist works the land to the full, calculating how to get the maximum production from it, and then when yields fall off to move and to purchase, rent or settle on new land. Land is cheap – the planter's primary investment is in labour-power and the conservation of the land merely wastes the slaves' labour-power. The object of the planter is to minimise costs of production. The application of fertiliser, commodity crops lost in crop rotation and fallowing, the labour-power expended in hoeing, the increased costs of supervision involved as the slave's tasks become more diverse, all of these things raise the costs of production.

These conditions and this relation of the commodity-producing capitalist to the land are not specific to slave production; they occur wherever there is commodity production for the world market on a large scale in conditions where there is ample surplus land. Wage-labour entails a similar rise in costs if conservation techniques are used. This pattern of soil exhaustion and 'nomadic' cultivation is typical of the specialist agrarian commodity-producing regions where these conditions pertain. A similar problem of ruthless exploitation of the land and nomadic enterprises to that in the South can be seen in the Brazilian coffee plantations in the early part of this century – these plantations were worked by free labour.

Only when the possession of the land is effectively monopolised does soil conservation become a necessity. Here the costs of maintaining the productivity of the soil must be set against higher land values and rents. Conservation techniques are in the interest of the landlord because if they are used the land retains a higher rentable value. Such techniques become *necessary* to agricultural production – they become necessary to the tenant or purchaser to maintain a level of production commensurate with the rent or price he is forced to pay for the land.[68]

It is the specific conditions of commodity production and capitalist calculation in the absence of monopoly possession of the land which produce these tendencies toward soil exhaustion and expansion, and not slavery. As we have seen, slave production in agriculture in the ancient world made possible a form of 'scientific farming' which both raised the level of production and represented a higher form of cultivation. The use of slave labour did not lead to soil exhaustion, rather to the reverse. Cairnes's 'fundamental principle of [the] . . . political economy of slave societies' is nothing more than one of the side effects of exploitative capitalist agriculture. It is true that this form of capitalist agriculture combined with the particular form of expanded reproduction of the SMP (that is, the linear addition of units of production) would tend to produce both a high rate of land wastage and a tendency toward geographical expansion. This wastage and this expansion are, however, due to causes quite different from those Cairnes and Genovese suggest.

(d) EXPANSIONISM AND CONFLICT

Although Cairnes and Genovese are wrong in attributing a necessary dynamic of expansion based upon soil exhaustion to the Southern slave system, it would not be true to say that the expansion of the slave system is no different from any other form of capitalist agriculture or that expansion in the USA was as neutral in its consequences as expansion in Brazil. The difference between the expansion of slave production to new territories and forms of production based on free labour is that the institution of slavery must be politically/legally guaranteed in the new territory. The state in the region concerned must not be actively hostile to slavery and must preserve its title as legal property. The difference between the expansion of slave production and its legal guarantee westwards in the USA and the expansion of the coffee plantations further into the interior of the Brazilian plateau is that in the latter case there were no effective competitors for the land and in the former the slaveholders came into direct conflict with land-hungry settlers.

In explaining certain of the conditions of the Civil War we will place considerable stress on the difference between the political and legal conditions of existence of slavery and those of free labour, and we shall also stress the role of the free settler. That only *certain* of the conditions of the Civil War are explained here must be insisted upon; the Civil War is the product of a complex conjuncture and to explain it properly requires much more knowledge of American political forms and events than is available to the authors of this book. Our object must be limited to attempting to explain why there was a political crisis in the 1850s and why this crisis threatened the political dominance of the Slave Power.

The conflict between North and South was not a general conflict of social systems, of capitalism and slavery. It was a conflict in which the South started with more Northern allies than foes. In 1850 there were more social forces prepared to support slavery or indifferent to it than there were actively hostile to the institution. The plantation economy of the South was closely allied with important sections of Northern banking, commercial and industrial capital. Much of the credit system, the commerce and the carrying trade of the USA was dependent on or heavily involved in the Southern plantations economy. The working classes of New York, Baltimore, and many lesser Eastern ports and manufacturing centres were dependent for their livelihood on Southern commerce and the export of manufactures to the South. Racism and pro-slavery sentiment were widespread among the workers and petite bourgeoisie of such cities as New York, as Frederick Douglass testified.[69] The established farmers of the Eastern seaboard faced no threat from slave labour or slave production. No direct economic contradiction between slave production and capitalist industry and agriculture of the Northeast can be found. Far from the economic interests of capitalists, petite bourgeoisie and workers being threatened by slavery, there were in so many cases the strong economic foundations of a pro-slavery sentiment. The conflict between North and South was in the first place a struggle between the slaveowning class and the free settlers of the Western states and territories. It was a conflict over the dominance of slave property right or bourgeois property right in the as yet unoccupied Western lands, a conflict between land-hungry free settlers and a planter oligarchy seeking to monopolise these land reserves.

This struggle created a political crisis and a complex transformation of American politics. It is a complex political, legal and economic struggle. It is economic not in the sense that the forces involved were competing in some race for 'development', but because one class sought to exclude another from the means of maintaining a livelihood as free and independent producers. Initially it is a class struggle between two classes, the politically dominant planter oligarchy and a section of the free peasantry and small capitalist farmers. It is a struggle which is generalised and made explosive at the political level. What is at stake in this battle is of wider significance because of the political conditions and forms in which it is fought. The struggle for the Western lands is also a struggle as to who shall rule the USA. The North as a whole is involved because the issue is not the *existence* of slavery but the *expansion* of slavery and on the outcome of that issue depends another, more important issue: will the USA be ruled by the representatives of the planter oligarchy or not?

What makes the conflict and the crisis inevitable is the determination of the political representatives of the planter class to obtain a land monopoly, aggressively to challenge and exclude the free farmers. This determination is not a function of some class psychology, but of the position of the Southern representatives in the American state and the political history of the land question. Far from being, as it is for Genovese, a conflict between social systems mediated and realised in the mind of a class subject, it is the struggle of real social forces and their political representatives, a battle of concrete programmes and policies. Cairnes, the radical democrat, is a far sounder guide to the topography of this conflict, if not to its causes. He correctly recognises the political dominance of the Slave Power – the planter class and its representatives – in the American state, its aggressive policy, and the centrality of the struggle with the free farmers for the Western lands. Cairnes recognises that the question of slavery emancipation is at best secondary, the object of the Republicans was not freedom for the blacks but the freedom of free men to till the soil. Cairnes recognises that the explosive issue in the conflict is, who shall rule? Will the slaveholders rule the free men of the rest of the nation or not?

Slave production presupposes the institution of slavery. For slaves to be a form of property and a commodity the state must guarantee and defend the legal title of slave property. For the guarantee to be secured, the slaveowning class must either be politically dominant or it must be allied with classes not opposed to slavery. Slavery requires the effective dominance not only of political representatives favourable to it or not hostile to it, but also the existence of state institutions and functionaries charged with its defence. These conditions are formal, they tell us nothing about the form of politics or the form of state involved. The USA was a bourgeois democratic republic. Such political conditions suppose that the slave party has an effective majority in the representative institutions of the state. However, this majority need not be a popular majority based on the votes of free citizens. In the USA the dominance of the Southern interest was made possible by the following two means:

(1) the existence of an upper chamber, the Senate, based not upon numbers of electors, but upon the fixed ratio of two Senators to each state – by keeping the number of slave *states* equal to or greater than the number of free states, the slave party could control the Senate;

(2) that representation proportional to population included slaves who were counted as three-fifths of a free man – the slave states were thereby guaranteed representation in the lower chamber far greater than was warranted by their free population.

Under a democratic form of state if slavery challenges the interests of a substantial section of the masses who have effective political representation they can be contained in three ways, through mechanisms to maintain a permanent majority, through political/electoral alliances, and through the institutions and apparatuses of the state. If the opponents of slavery have a majority then the interests of the slave party can only be preserved by extra-democratic means. In the USA the South secured its dominance through 'artificial' constitutional provisions, through electoral alliance with the Northern Democrats, and by controlling the apparatuses of the state. Given these methods of dominance and a policy of compromise with Northern interests, there was no real obstacle to the continuance of this system. In the USA radical democracy, egalitarianism and populism were opposed by the *Northern* bourgeoisie and the majority of the petite bourgeoisie – given the weakness of the popular democratic forces there was no real principled opposition to the dominance of the South in political life.

Slave property right and bourgeois property right are not in essence contradictory: under capitalist conditions slave property is a special variant of private property in general. Slave property does *formally* contradict the ideological basis of bourgeois right, formal legal equality and the proportionality of labour and rewards. However, given the specific institutional confinement of slavery to Negroes and the ideological support of Negro slavery provided by racism, there need be no substantive contradiction with the ideological forms of bourgeois right. Only a tiny minority of radicals opposed slavery in principle and in order to emancipate the slaves.

How then does the contradiction between the planters and the free farmers develop? We know that the property of the free farmers of New England was not threatened by the existence of slave property right. The contradiction has two main dimensions. First, it does not involve free farmers and slaveowners settled in different regions but competing to occupy the *same* region. The struggle concerns the unoccupied Western territories which are state property. The conflict is in the first place a political struggle for the right to occupy certain lands, a struggle to obtain state sanction for the importation of the legal form of slave property into these regions.

Second, given the right to import slaves to these regions the struggle becomes a matter of whether slave cultivation or free cultivation will predominate. That the two systems cannot co-exist under these conditions is a function of a political and an economic factor. The political factor is that if free settlers predominate, and the territory becomes a state with a majority of free settlers, then the institution of slavery may be threatened. This threat is not simply that the settlers may wish to outlaw slavery and abolish slave right, but that they will discriminate against slave production by laws and policies in favour of free independent cultivators. The economic factor is that slave production relies on large land reserves which are the effective monopoly of the planter class. This is not because the planters are slaveowners but because they are commodity producers and subject to capitalist calculation. The absence of such land reserves secured against free settlement raises the price or rent of land and raises the cost of production. The large capitalist graziers of the Western plains were, in a later period, equally opposed to settlement by small farmers.

Throughout the first half of the nineteenth century the political representatives of the planter class, dominant in the state, secured numerous concessions of territory to the slave system. These lands were then controlled by state legislatures dominated by the planter class or its nominees. A monopoly control of land reserves secured against free settlement was thereby created in those regions ceded to the Slave Power. Slave production could expand with the demands of the world market into regions reserved for slavery and in which land was cheap. Such territories were the lands of the Louisiana Purchase, the Florida peninsula subjugated for the slaveowners in the Seminole War,[70] and the Mexican province of Texas annexed by the USA. The Missouri Compromise of 1819 secured the region of slavery up to the parallel 36° 30′ North. In return for ceding territory to the free labour system (California) the slaveowners won the important legal concession of the Fugitive Slave Law which extended the legal rights of the slaveowner into the free states.

The admission of California as a free state upset the balance of political power. It threatened the balance of political representation and the dominance of the Slave Power through the medium of the representative institutions of the state:

> From the passing of the Missouri Compromise down to the year 1850 the balance between the Free and Slave States had been fairly preserved. The North had during that time acquired Michigan, Iowa and Wisconsin; the South, Arkansas, Florida and Texas; the natural expansion of the one section had been steadily counterpoised by the factitious annexations of the other. But the admission of California as a free state had disturbed this equilibrium. To restore it, there was need of a new slave state; and where could this be more conveniently placed than in the rich contiguous territory of Kansas? (Cairnes (1863), p. 224).

Kansas was a territory adjacent to slaveholding lands and open to settlement. It was denied to slavery by the terms of the Missouri Compromise. This agreement was abrogated through the agency of the Kansas and Nebraska Bill of 1854 introduced by the Northern Democratic allies of the Southern interest. Kansas was opened to settlement on a slave and free basis. There followed a class war between the planters and the free settlers, the planters acting as an organised conspiracy and using poor whites from slave states as their instrument. The election of a territorial delegate and a territorial legislature if won by representatives of the free settlers would threaten the right of slavery in Kansas. Consequently ballot-rigging, intimidation and armed force were used to suppress the free population. Those who resisted such violence were in no way aided by the representatives of the Federal government sent to 'oversee' affairs. The result was a political struggle of the free settlers against this extra-legal denial of their democratic rights.

The free settlers were forced to fight for their political rights which the Slave Power attempted to deny them in the interests of maintaining the political/legal conditions of existence of slave production. The most extreme political representatives of the planter class in seeking to preserve the dominance of that class threatened it by challenging the political and economic existence of an important section of the peasantry and petty-capital. In attempting to preserve by extra-democratic means the balance of power in the institutions of the Republic, the planter class created a political force opposed to the expansion of slavery in its own interests – the Republican Party. The aggression of the Slave Power gave the anti-slavery cause the basis that radical religious ideology, humanitarianism and egalitarianism could never have given it.

In the Republican Party the planter class faced for the first time a real threat to its political dominance in the Federal State. In attempting to meet this threat, the South's political representatives followed a policy that was at one and the same time aggressive and inept. They made the victory of a party opposed to the *extension* of slavery possible in splitting from their Democratic allies in the North.:

> Mr Douglas was, therefore, cast aside. The combined phalanx which had so long ruled the Union was broken in two, and the Slave Power stood alone. This position of affairs could only lead to one result – that which actually occurred – the triumph by a large majority of the Republican party (Cairnes (1863), pp. 254–5).

This split was over the issue of the Kansas and Nebraska Bill, for which the South had pressed, and for the repeal of which it campaigned after it had been worsted in Kansas. It was encouraged in this forward policy by the Dred Scott decision which in effect made the whole of the USA a single slaveholding domain – a slaveholder could now not merely pursue his fugitive slaves but reside in free territory with his slaves in bondage. This decision threatened Free States with slave laws, with the interference of the planter class. Northerners who were happy to let Negroes toil in bondage in the South did not want the slaveowners to have the power to meddle in their affairs. This, coupled with a move to the centre by the Party itself, gave a great advantage to the Republicans. In struggling for landed monopoly and political supremacy the South threatened to subordinate the whole of the Union to slave laws and the rule of the slaveowners. That it enjoyed a great measure of success in its attempts at control ultimately threatened its position far more than failure.

The origins of the Civil War are to be found in the political crisis surrounding the 1859 elections. That crisis was created by the South's own representatives. Having, in pursuit of political dominance and land monopoly, exhausted their privileged constitutional position, their electoral alliance with the Democrats, and their control of such state apparatuses as the Supreme Court, they were forced to resort to means outside the machinery of the state. Secession promised a state based exclusively on the planter class.

Four

The 'Asiatic' mode of production

1 Questions of method

The notion of an 'Asiatic' mode of production (hereafter AMP) has been the subject of much debate on the part of Marxist and bourgeois commentators alike. It is the most controversial and contested of all the possible modes of production outlined in the works of Marx and Engels.[1]

This debate has been dominated by empiricist problems – the question of the validity of the concept of AMP has been raised in terms of whether or not it corresponds to the reality of certain given societies. Historians have questioned the value of the notion of the AMP as an interpretation of the 'facts' of Indian or Chinese history; an example is the debate about the presence or absence of private property in land in certain periods of Chinese history. Both Marxist theorists and bourgeois scholars have disputed whether the social relations of China and India in the modern period should be characterised as 'Asiatic' or feudal.[2] Opponents of the Soviet Union, such as Karl Wittfogel, have contended that the political character of the Soviet state stems from the fact that it is a direct outgrowth of the 'semi-Asiatic' conditions of pre-revolutionary Russia, that this form of modern 'totalitarianism' has its roots in the despotism of the East. In all of these questions it is the correspondence or non-correspondence of an idea with the real which is decisive.

What is at stake in these disputes is not, however, the accuracy of one empirical description or another. In spite of the empiricist mode in which the questions have been posed, what is at stake in them has often been of crucial political and ideological importance. Clearly, it was of some consequence for the strategy of the revolutionary movements in China and Russia to settle the question of whether the supposedly static 'Asiatic' mode, characterised by the absence of private property in land, or the feudal mode prevailed in their countries. Marxism-Leninism has rejected the notion of an AMP on theoretical and political grounds, and in doing so it has come nearest to posing the problem of the AMP in a *theoretical* rather than an empiricist form. The AMP has also been used as an ideological weapon against Marxism-Leninism. The notion that Stalin's Russia was the outgrowth of essentially 'Asiatic' conditions reveals all too clearly the attempt to consign the Soviet form of socialism to a region different in essence from the West.

It is not our intention to enter and to reproduce the tortuous and ideological terrain of these controversies in this chapter. This is not because we consider the analysis of concrete social formation unimportant. It is, for example, of the first importance to the masses of India that a scientific analysis of their country and a strategy for its revolutionary transformation be produced. It is not because we wish to shun politics, to dismiss political and ideological struggles in the name of some ideology of 'pure' and 'disinterested' study. Our refusal to enter this terrain follows from the impossibility of settling the theoretical status, and assessing the validity of, the AMP on it. Rather than catalogue and reproduce the errors of empiricism we will attempt to solve this question of the AMP at the correct level. The AMP must be considered within the Marxist theory of modes of production, within the field of concepts which define what a mode of production is and what possible modes of production there are. This theory is a part of, a distinct theoretical region of, historical materialism. The question of the AMP will, therefore, be subjected to the modes of proof particular to the Marxist theory of modes of production.

In this chapter we shall be concerned with the problem of whether or not it is possible to construct a concept of the AMP, that is, a concept which corresponds to the general definition of mode of production in historical materialism and which is distinct from any other mode of production. Any such concept is general and abstract. It is the product of theoretical work: the work of application of the concepts of a problematic to a definite problem posed within it. Concepts are not produced by generalising from the description of any set of 'given', 'real' conditions – concepts are not derived from or confined to any particular set of observables. The limits of the construction of a concept are not whether a reality corresponding to it exists. The concept AMP can only be constructed if there is a space for it in the theory of modes of production, if it is a possible mode of production according to the concepts of that problematic. These are its conditions of existence as a concept. They are secured solely within the realms of knowledge, nothing which has happened or has existed, in Asia or elsewhere, can alter that.

It will be recalled that in the Introduction we outlined the difference between the concept of mode of production, the concept of social formation, and concrete social formations. The concepts of the various modes of production and the concept of social formation are the means of production of knowledge of concrete social formations – it is from these general concepts that the theoretical definitions and explanations of particular social formations are derived, it is these general concepts which provide the criteria of validation for those theories of particular social formations. The concept of a mode of production is not confined in its application to this or that social formation, and it is not a description of a particular set of social relations but a means of analysis of them. Concrete conditions do not validate concepts, it is the concept which makes possible and validates analyses of the concrete.

Therefore, the question of the existence or non-existence of the AMP cannot be settled by reference to concrete social formations, it is a strictly theoretical question. Asia, past or present, is not at issue in it because the concept is not limited in the way an empirical generalisation is limited to certain given conditions. If its concept can be formed then the AMP is a possible mode of production; whether forms of this mode have existed or not does not affect its validity as a concept. Nothing limits its application to Asia or requires that it exist in Asia rather than somewhere else – concepts can no more be 'Asiatic' than they can be green or feline. If a concept of a mode of production is formable which corresponds to any of the elements of the notion of an AMP, it cannot retain the ideological category of 'Asiaticness'. The very conception of an *Asiatic* mode of production is ideological in that it supposes a definite correspondence with certain real conditions which cannot be abstract and general.

It is for the above reasons that the Marxist classics on Asia, the writings of Marx, Engels, Lenin and Mao Tse-Tung, are not a necessary point of departure in the analysis of the possibility of a concept of the AMP. Because the concept AMP is a general one it is neither necessary to look for it in, nor is it necessarily to be found in, the Marxist writings on Asia. It could, indeed, be present in certain of those writings, but in that case its presence is an effect of theoretical work and not because the subject is Asia. If the concept of an AMP is formable it must be constructed on the basis of general Marxist concepts (forces and relations of production, etc.) and it must correspond to these concepts – it is, therefore, necessary to begin in those regions of Marxist theory which differentiate the modes of appropriation of the surplus-product, forms of property, forms of labour process, co-operation, division of labour, etc. It is to *Capital* rather than to the collections of journalism and letters on the East that we shall turn in our search for the *concept* of the AMP.

This method may at first appear surprising in relation to the way previous discussions of the AMP have proceeded. However, it is our contention that these discussions of the AMP have been stifled by their empiricist method. In order to illustrate the general epistemological argument we will cite some examples of this method. Western commentators like Lichtheim or Wittfogel see the question of the 'Asiatic' mode as a question of the nature of Marx's 'views' about the societies of Asia.[3] The criteria for discussing this collection of 'views' are doubly empiricist, empiricist in the method of reading which extracts these 'views' from the texts in which they are 'found', and empiricist in the relation they establish between a theory and its object.

The status of Marx's 'views' and writings is that they are all equivalent – they are all the thoughts, opinions, etc., of a particular human subject. Discourse has no structure and the texts have no status other than that of the record of the thought, experience and judgment of a subject. Thus both Lichtheim and Wittfogel happily piece together their 'histories' of the notion of the Asiatic mode and Asiatic society from journalism, letters, incidential or illustrative remarks in theoretical texts, etc., with no real concern for the theoretical status of the materials or their place in Marx's theoretical development. This method reflects the absence of any conception that texts are the product of a practice, that different practices (theoretical, ideological, etc.) produce texts of a distinct status and which are governed by specific conditions of reading, criticism and evaluation. Because these 'views', opinions, etc., are considered as emanations of a subject, the discourse in which they are inscribed is reduced to a mere medium, and these 'views', opinions, etc., are separated from any systematic relation to discourse.

In this humanist and author-centred conception what differentiates different texts, 'views', etc., are conditions external to the text, conditions which act on the experience of the subject. These external circumstances, the changing political interests of the subject, the changing real conditions, are the basis on which views and opinions may be differentiated and ranked. Thus Lichtheim argues that Marx's support for the progressive role of capitalism in 'breaking down all Chinese walls' became less enthusiastic in the latter part of the nineteenth century in response to the barbarities committed by Western imperialism, and that Marx began to look with greater interest at the potentialities of Eastern societies to change internally and to develop independently of Western capitalism. Just as discourse is reduced to the subject's consciousness and experience, so the measure of the validity of the 'views' and opinions of an author, which are derived from his experience, is their correspondence/non-correspondence with the real.

This method of producing a set of 'views' of an author and of establishing their consistency or change is quite arbitrary. This arbitrariness is the field of play of the ideological interests of the commentator. Thus Wittfogel's history of the 'rise and fall' of the concept of the Asiatic mode of production in Marxism is based on the following method: first, a notion of 'Asiatic society' is extracted from Marx's writings, in particular his *New York Daily Tribune* article of 10 June 1853, 'The British Rule in India'; this notion, it is argued, corresponds to the reality of hydraulic society and of the East (that is, to the conceptions entertained by Wittfogel himself) and, second, all difference from these positions on the part of Marx and Marxists is branded as a 'retreat from truth'.[4] Lenin and Stalin suppress the truth because of political necessity. Wittfogel makes no attempt to *argue* against the positions of Lenin and Stalin, the error is already given and their position is dismissed because it is discrepant from what is manifestly true. The Russian critics of the AMP rejected the notion 'that a functional bureaucracy could be the ruling class' (*Oriental Despotism*, p. 402), they opposed the managerialism and technological reductionism of a conception of the AMP like that of Wittfogel, and they considered that the notion of the AMP had a reactionary political effect.[5] Russian Marxist-Leninists preferred to characterise Asiatic countries like China and India as feudal or semi-feudal. Wittfogel's rejection of this interpretation is based on a conception of feudalism which limits it to the European Middle Ages and to Japan. The Soviet conception based on the concept of *feudal-rent* is applicable to a far wider range of social formations and does not suppose the specific political and legal institutions of medieval Europe. Wittfogel never entertains the notion that the Russians could be correct in rejecting the notion of the AMP – there can be no theoretical argument of this kind for the fate of the concepts is already settled by empiricist fiat, the notion of the AMP as presented by Wittfogel corresponds to the real conditions of Asia. Empiricism in relation to the text and in relation of theory to its object are systematically linked – the correspondence of the constructed set of 'views' with the real obviates any necessity for their justification as a reading or analysis of the texts concerned. Empiricism escapes argument by claiming the correspondence of its constructions with the order of the real.

These modes of discussing Marxist theory have nothing whatever to do with the mode of practice of Marxist theory. They render its questions untheoretical, incapable of solution and open to the endless rumination of ideological commentary. Marxist theoretical problems can only be solved by the use of the Marxist theoretical method.

2 The theory of rent

Our point of departure is within the problematic of historical materialism; to answer the question 'Is there an AMP?' it is necessary to begin by posing the question: what constitutes a mode of production? At the risk of repetition we will answer this latter question as follows: a mode of production = an articulated combination of a specific mode of appropriation of the product and a specific mode of appropriation of nature. A mode of production is a complex unity of *relations and forces of production*: the mode of appropriation of the product is determined by the relations of production, that is, by the distribution of the means of production and the relation this establishes between the labourer and the labour process. The relations of production are the dominant element of the combination forces/relations of production. The form in which the *surplus*-product is appropriated (which defines the distribution of the whole social product) is determined by the distribution of the means of production and by the control this confers over the process of production to certain agents. Hence the mode of appropriation of the surplus-product varies with the forms of distribution of the means of production in the different modes of production – it is an effect of the structure of the relations of production. A distinct mode of appropriation of the surplus-product supposes a distinct structure of relations of production. A distinct structure of relations of production supposes a set of forces of production which correspond to the conditions of the labour process it establishes. It is for these reasons that the mode of appropriation of the surplus-product can serve as an initial index of the existence or non-existence of a mode of production:

> The essential difference between the various economic forms of society, between, for instance, a society based on slave-labour

> and one based on wage-labour, lies only in the mode in which this surplus labour is in each case extracted from the actual producer, the labourer (*Capital*, I, p. 217).

In the first instance, therefore, the existence or non-existence of a mode of production may be examined in terms of the existence or non-existence of a mode of appropriation of the surplus-product.

Certain common and basic elements recur in all discussions of the AMP: first, that it is the state which extracts the surplus-product, there is no exploiting class independent of the state; second, that there is an absence of private property in land, the land is state property; and, third, that non-commodity production in agriculture is the dominant form of production. Is there a mode of appropriation of the surplus-product which corresponds to these conditions to appropriation by the state, to the absence of private property in land, and to non-commodity agricultural production? The answer to this question is to be found in the Marxist theory of *rent* (developed by Marx in *Capital*; III, section VI) – it is to be found there because (with the exception of slave production) rent is the mode of extraction of the surplus-product under conditions of pre-capitalist agricultural production. It is necessary to give a brief summary of this theory beginning with the most developed form of rent, capitalist ground-rent, and then proceeding to the pre-capitalist forms of rent.

CAPITALIST GROUND-RENT

'All ground-rent is surplus-value, the product of surplus-labour' (*Capital*, III, p. 619). However, capitalist ground-rent is a *surplus above profit*: it is 'the excess of surplus-value paid the landlord by capital invested in land in the form of rent, after the various capitals have shared in the total surplus-value produced by the social capital in all spheres of production in proportion to their relative size' (*Capital*, III, p. 763). *Capitalist ground-rent is not the surplus-product itself*; rent is not the mode in which surplus-labour is appropriated in the capitalist mode of production. To explain the conditions of the production of surplus-value in capitalism is not to explain rent – the landlord receives a portion of the surplus-value already produced in the process of capitalist production and appropriated by the capitalist.

In order to explain the origin of capitalist ground-rent we must first explain the form of agricultural production which is its condition of existence (in this summary we will consider only the rent of agricultural land). Capitalist rent supposes capitalist farming. Capitalist agriculture presupposes the following conditions:

(i) the separation of the direct producer from the means of production; in this case the separation of the peasant, serf, etc., from the land and his conversion into a wage-labourer;

(ii) a class of capitalist farmers who do not own the land, who own the means of production (other than land), hire wage-labourers (who do not own the means of production) and produce commodities;

(iii) the displacement of the bulk of the rural population from the land, the development of the forces of production in agriculture, and the increase in the productivity of agricultural labour;

(iv) a social division of labour into distinct branches of production, agriculture being one branch among others, and commodity exchange as the mode of distribution of the products between branches;

(v) capitalist investment in agriculture is equivalent to investment in any other branch of capitalist production, agricultural capital receives the same rate of return on capital or profit as all other capital. (It should be noted that these conditions are a combination of the necessary conditions of any capitalist agriculture (ii, iv, and v) and the conditions of transition from pre-capitalist to capitalist agriculture (i and iii).)

Capitalist agriculture is like capitalist industry: its conditions are the conditions of the production of surplus-value and its realisation in the sale of commodities. The profit of the capitalist farmer has the same source as that of the capitalist factory owner – in the surplus-labour concealed by the wage-form.

How is it that there can be rent if agricultural capital receives the same average rate of profit as other capitals? It could not receive less than the average rate or capital would desert this branch of production for other branches where the average rate prevailed. What is entailed here is that rent is the form in which the landlord class appropriates the *surplus-profit* in agriculture. *Where there is rent there is surplus-profit*. Surplus-profit in all branches of capitalist production implies a productivity greater than the average and a lower cost of production than the socially necessary cost. Surplus-profit in agriculture arises from the differential fertility of the soil (that is, from differences in productivity which are 'given' by nature under a certain regime of cultivation and with certain techniques).[6] Rent which has its source in surplus-profit is called *differential rent*.

Differential rent is highest where the discrepancy from the social cost of production is greatest and lowest where the discrepancy is least. The social cost of production in agriculture is determined by the cost of production on the worst soil (that is, the least fertile soil which is cultivable under the existing conditions of production) – the worst soil which produces no surplus-profit is either not in cultivation or there is no rent paid on it. Rents rise to the level of the surplus-profit because capitalist agriculture is competitive just like any other branch of capitalist production, the level of rent is, therefore, bid up to the level of the surplus-profit by agricultural capitalists seeking to enter or to expand production. Differential rent does not depend on the private ownership of land: it arises whether or not the land is privately owned; if the land is nationalised, then this rent goes to the state.

Lenin has given one of the ablest short accounts of the theory of differential rent in his text *The Agrarian Programme of Social Democracy in the First Russian Revolution*, 1905–1907:

> Marx's theory distinguishes two forms of rent: differential rent and absolute rent. The first springs from the limited nature of land, its occupation by capitalist economies, quite irrespective of whether private ownership of land exists, or what the form of landownership is. Between the individual farms there are inevitable differences arising out of differences in soil fertility, location in regard to markets, and the productivity of additional investments of capital in the land. Briefly, those differences may be summed up (without, however, forgetting that they spring from different causes) as the differences between better and worse soils. To proceed. The price of production of the agricultural product is determined by the conditions of production not on the average soil, but on the worst soil, because the produce from the best soil alone is insufficient to meet the demand. The difference between the individual price of production and the highest price of production is differential rent. (We remind the reader that by price of production Marx means the capital expended on the production of the product, plus average profit on capital.)
>
> Differential rent inevitably arises in capitalist agriculture even if the private ownership of land is completely abolished. Under the private ownership of land, this rent is appropriated by the landowner, for competition between capitals compels the tenant farmer to be satisfied with the average profit on capital. When

the private ownership of land is abolished, that rent will go to the state (*Collected Works*, 13, p. 297).

Differential rent arises from capitalist production; from the competition between agricultural capitals, and from the fact that the products of agriculture are commodities (and, therefore, the cost of production plays its regulating role). Differential rent is the *specifically* capitalist form of rent, but it is not the only form of rent possible under capitalism. *Absolute rent* arises out of the private ownership of land. It exists because of the monopoly created by the private ownership of land; land is of finite quantity – thus it is necessary for non-owners to pay for the right to use the land irrespective of its productivity. This absolute rent arises solely from monopoly possession, from the right to exclude others from the finite and necessary resource. As Lenin argues, far from being necessary to capitalism, the private ownership of land actually *inhibits* the development of capitalist production in agriculture by restricting the operation of competition and preventing the formation of an average profit on agricultural capital:

> Absolute rent arises from the private ownership of land. That rent contains an element of monopoly, an element of monopoly price. Private ownership of land hinders free competition, hinders the levelling of profit, the formation of average profit in agricultural and non-agricultural enterprises. And as agriculture is on a lower technical level than industry, as the composition of capital is marked by a larger proportion of variable capital than of constant capital, *the individual value* of the agricultural product is above the average. Hence, by hindering the free levelling of profits in agricultural enterprises on a par with non-agricultural enterprises, the private ownership of land makes it possible to sell the agricultural product not at the highest price of production, but at the still higher individual value of the product (for the price of production is determined by the average profit on capital, while absolute rent prevents the formation of this 'average' by monopolistically fixing the individual value at a level higher than the average).
>
> Thus, differential rent is inevitably an inherent feature of every form of capitalist agriculture. Absolute rent is not; it arises only under the private ownership of land, only under the historically created backwardness of agriculture, a backwardness that becomes fixed by monopoly (*Collected Works*, 13, p. 298).

As Kautsky argues in *The Agrarian Question*:

> [an important] distinction between differential rent and absolute rent is that the former is not a constituent part affecting the price of agricultural produce, whereas the latter is. The former arises from the price of production; the latter arises from the excess of market price over price of production. The former arises from the surplus, from the super-profit, that is created by the more productive labour on better soil, or on a better located plot. The latter does not arise from the additional income of certain forms of agricultural labour; it is possible only as a deduction from the available quantity of values for the benefit of the landowner, a deduction from the mass of surplus value – therefore, it implies either a reduction of profits or a deduction from wages. If the price of foodstuffs rises, and wages rise also, the profit on capital diminishes. If the price of foodstuffs rises without an increase in wages, then the workers suffer the loss. Finally, the following may happen – and this may be regarded as the general rule – the loss caused by absolute rent is borne jointly by the workers and the capitalists (*Die Agrarfrage*, pp. 79–80, cited by Lenin, *Collected Works*, 13, 299).

Landed monopoly creates absolute rent; this rent, unlike differential rent, does not derive from surplus-profit, *it is a deduction from profit* (reducing the rate of profit below the average) and a *deduction from wages* (in reducing the rate of profit, it forces the farmer to increase the level of exploitation of the labourer in order to maximise his returns).

In conclusion to this section, it should be recalled that differential rent is not a form of direct extraction of the surplus-product, it arises from conditions quite different from those of the production of surplus-value. The nature of the pre-capitalist forms of rent is very different from this as we shall see.

PRE-CAPITALIST FORMS OF RENT

Marx discusses these forms of rent in Ch. XLVII of *Capital*, 'The Genesis of Capitalist Ground Rent'. Differential rent is impossible under pre-capitalist forms of agricultural production:

> To be able to speak at all of a surplus over the average profit, this average profit itself must already be established as a standard and as a regulator of production in general, as is the

> case under capitalist production. For this reason there can be no talk of rent in the modern sense, a rent consisting of a surplus over the average profit . . . in social formations where it is not capital which performs the function of enforcing all surplus-labour and appropriating directly all surplus-value (III, p. 764).

The major difference between differential rent and the forms of pre-capitalist rent is that the former represents not surplus-value but surplus-profit, it does not arise directly from the condition of exploitation of labour but from conditions secondary and ancillary to this, the competition between capitals and the differential fertility of the soil, while the latter, the pre-capitalist forms of rent, are forms of appropriation of the surplus-product; they are the mode of exploitation of the direct labourer. Pre-capitalist rent is, therefore, directly comparable to surplus-value in the capitalist mode of production rather than to capitalist ground-rent.

Pre-capitalist forms of agricultural production (with the exception of slave production) suppose the non-separation of the labourer from the means of production. The non-separation of the labourer from the means of production under pre-capitalist conditions results from the limited development of forms of wage-labour and the retention by the labourer of a portion of the product, a low level of the division of social labour into different branches of production, the unity of handicrafts and agriculture in the local community, and the reproduction of the economic conditions of production within the unit of production. The direct producers have effective possession of the means of reproduction of their own labour-power.

Differential rent is impossible under pre-capitalist conditions. However, it would be wrong to conclude from this that all pre-capitalist forms of rent are nothing but variants of absolute rent. Absolute rent arises from monopoly possession of the land, but only under certain economic conditions. The mechanism whereby this form of rent is generated from private property in land presupposes a *market* for the commodity land-use rights and *competition* between buyers for the purchase of that commodity. It is these economic conditions which confer this power to landed property – its monopoly is effective because of the laws of competition.

Absolute rent *can* exist under pre-capitalist conditions, but only where economic relations create the conditions of private property in land, scarcity and commodity exchange. Absolute rent is not, however, the dominant form of pre-capitalist rent – this is because of the non-separation of the direct producers from the means of production.

Landed property in itself yields no value, it has no effect independently of definite relations of production: 'The mere legal ownership of land does not create any ground-rent for the owner' (*Capital*, I, p. 739). Pre-capitalist rent, therefore, cannot emerge simply from the ownership of land by non-labourers. It supposes a mechanism by which the surplus-product can be extracted from the direct producers – the direct producers are under no economic compulsion to render surplus-labour, since they have effective possession of the means of their own reproduction. Pre-capitalist rent presupposes the political/ideological subordination of the direct producers to the exploiting non-labourers. The surplus-product is extracted in the form of *rents* (payments for the right of use of the land) and by a non-economic mechanism: 'Under such conditions the surplus-labour for the nominal owner of the land can only be extorted from them (the direct producers) by other than economic pressure, whatever the form assumed may be' (*Capital*, III, p. 771).

The relations of production must exist in the first instance as relations of domination of the exploiting non-labourers over the direct producers:

> in all forms in which the direct labourer remains the 'possessor' of the means of production of his own means of subsistence, the property relationship must simultaneously appear as a direct relationship of lordship and servitude, so that the direct producer is not free; a lack of freedom which may be reduced from serfdom to a mere tributary relationship (*ibid.*, p. 771).

The direct producers must be held in a relationship of political/legal subordination: pre-capitalist forms of rent presuppose a form of state in which the direct producers are subject to the exploiters. In order for such a mode of extraction of the surplus-product to prevail, these political conditions must be secured. This means that an instance other than the economic, the political or the ideological, must be the dominant instance in the hierarchy of instances established by the structure of any mode of production in which pre-capitalist rent prevails.

There are three variant forms of payment of pre-capitalist rents: labour-rent, rent-in-kind and money-rent. All three forms are identical in that they are all forms of surplus-labour, but they differ in the conditions of extraction of this surplus-labour. *Labour-rent* supposes the direct separation of necessary and surplus labour-time: the direct producer reproduces his own labour-power by labouring in his own plot and produces a surplus-product by labouring on the landlord's land. This form separates the land which produces the surplus-product (landlord's land) and the land which produces the means of subsistence of the labourer (rented land) – for the right of use of which the labourer works on the landlord's land. Labour-rent is the foundation of what Lenin calls the 'corvée economy', and which he identifies with serfdom.[7] *Rent-in-kind* does not presuppose the separation of the land of the direct producer and the landlord. The surplus-product here takes the form not of unpaid labour but of a portion of the product. This need not be purely products of agricultural labour but also products of handicraft labour (just as labour service need not be purely in agricultural work). Labour-rent and rent-in-kind can clearly be combined – a portion of the rent in unpaid labour, a portion in kind. *Money-rent* is not capitalist ground-rent; it is merely the surplus-product in the form of money. Money-rent supposes that a portion of the product is converted into commodities and sold by the direct producers, this in turn supposes that there is a commodity market and the elements of a social division of labour between town and country. Money-rent cannot appear unless these conditions are met.

The basic form of pre-capitalist rent is *feudal rent*. The conditions of feudal rent are:

> 1 A special type of landed property which was directly linked with the exercise of lordship over the basic producers of society, the peasants; though, of course, with considerable variation in the degree to which that lordship might be exercised.
>
> 2 A special type of class of basic producers with a special connection with the land – which remained, however, the property of the ruling class of feudal lords (Kosminsky (1956), p. VI).

That is, a ruling class of landlords who hold the direct producers in a relation of political/legal subordination, and direct producers who own the means of reproduction of their labour-power, are legally unfree and are compelled to render surplus-labour to their political superiors. Feudal rent can take all three forms of pre-capitalist rent: labour-rent, rent-in-kind and money-rent. We shall consider feudal rent in some greater detail in chapter 5.

Feudal rent is not the only form of appropriation of the surplus-product in the form of rent discussed by Marx:

> Should the direct producers not be confronted by a private landowner, but rather, as in Asia, under the direct subordination of the state which stands over them as their landlord and simultaneously as sovereign, *then rent and taxes coincide, or rather, there exists no tax which differs from this form of ground rent*. Under such circumstances, there need exist no stronger political or economic pressure than that common to all subjection to the state. The state is then the supreme lord. Sovereignty here consists in the ownership of land concentrated on a national scale. But, on the other hand, no private ownership of land exists, although there is both private and common possession and use of land (*Capital*, III, pp. 771–2).

Here Marx defines a mode of appropriation of the surplus-produce which conforms to the following conditions: that the state extracts the surplus-product and that there is no private property in land. We shall call this mode of appropriation of the surplus-product the *tax/rent couple*: in it rent and taxes are indistinguishable. This couple is a function of the coupling of sovereignty and landed proprietorship in the state. In the absence of private property in land and the absence of any ruling class which is not subsumed within the state, it is the state which appropriates the surplus-product in the form of taxes which are simultaneously payments for the right of possession and use of the land, that is, rents.

The mode of appropriation of the surplus-product takes the *form* of taxation. It is no different in this respect from the taxes levied by any other type of state: taxes are a deduction from the total social product, the level of which is politically determined, and which is the means of maintenance of the state. The extraction of this deduction depends upon the state's possession of the means of coercion. It is the difference in the totality of social relations which explains the different nature of taxes in this case, from, say, taxes in social formations dominated by the capitalist mode of production. The major differences between this mode of appropriation of the surplus-product and that of feudal rent are:

(1) That there is no class of landlords *distinct* from the state, the state is sole landlord, and, therefore, there is no ruling class separate from the state machine;

(2) Feudal rent requires that the direct producers be politically and

legally bound subordinates of the landlords; in the case of the tax/rent couple no *special* mode of political domination is required to appropriate the surplus-product – the means used are identical to those used by all states to levy taxes, and the direct producers are subject to no special mode of political/legal subordination, unlike serfs or slaves – their subordination is identical to that of all subjects to that state.

3 Is there a mode of production which corresponds to the tax/rent couple?

We now have a rough and ready *index* of the presence of a mode of production; what *appears* to be a distinct mode of appropriation of the surplus-product. An index of the fact that we are not in a wholly ideological terrain is that we have broken with 'Asiaticness', the question 'is there an AMP?' has become the question, is there a mode of production which corresponds to the tax/rent couple?

In order to proceed with this question it is necessary to elaborate all the possible elements of the relations and forces of production which can be *deduced* from the tax/rent couple. Once this is done, the question of whether these elements form an articulated combination of relations/forces of production can be posed. We already know that the tax/rent couple supposes the following conditions:

(1) that the land is state property, that it is cultivated by state subjects, and that these subjects have effective possession of the means of production;

(2) that non-commodity production in agriculture is the dominant branch of production, that there is no developed social division of labour, that handicrafts and agriculture form a unity, and that the conditions of reproduction are secured within the units of production – these conditions follow logically from the fact that tax/rent is a form of rent corresponding to pre-capitalist agriculture.

From these two sets of conditions we can elaborate a series of deductions of the social relations supposed in them, that is, the social relations which correspond to or which are the conditions of existence of the tax/rent couple.

TAX/RENT COUPLE =

(1) This mode of appropriation of the surplus-product corresponds to a social division of labour into labourers and non-labourers and to the absence of private property in land.

(2) Property rights in land are held by the state which is the collective landlord.

(3) The surplus-product is appropriated in the form of tax. State taxes, whether levied directly through state officials, through tax farms, etc., are a form of rent in that they represent the condition of possession and use of the land by state subjects as well as providing the revenue of the state. The tax may be paid in labour (on state farms as public works, etc.) in kind, or (a portion of it) in money.

(4) The distribution of the means of production is politically determined; by the mode in which it grants tenure and controls taxation the state determines the variant forms of production and appropriation of the product. This political determination of the distribution of the means of production operates within the limits of the non-separation of the direct producers from the means of production. Thus the units of production may be: (a) independent peasant farmers; (b) collectives of direct producers organised into communities. In the latter case the community regulates the division of labour and the form of possession of the land – agricultural production may be undertaken with or without co-operation, but, even if within the community there is individual cultivation and possession, the conditions of reproduction are communally determined, for example, by the periodic or customary division of the land. These forms of unit of production correspond to forms of tax; the state can create or abolish individual possession of the land by the conditions of tax and tenure it enforces. In the case of independent peasants, they may pay taxes to the state directly or they may be bound into *unions* which are collectively responsible for the tax debt (and which may determine the level of taxation of their individual members). However, in the latter case the forms of *tenure* remain individual even though taxes are paid through the collective. In the case of communes where there is individual possession/cultivation of land, individuals may pay taxes separately but it is the commune which remains the unit of landholding and which is ultimately responsible for the tax debt.

(5) The division of labour between handicrafts and agriculture is realised within the units of production (or the local community in the case of some forms of independent peasant farming), each of which is, therefore, self-sufficient and self-reproducing. The units of production (individual farms/communes) are separated from each other, they are socially independent, united by no social division of labour and depending on no other unit for their conditions of reproduction. The units of production are also separated from the state which plays no

necessary role in production – state taxes are a simple deduction from an already produced stock of values.

(6) The division between direct producers (exploited)/non-labourers (exploiters) takes the form of a division between subject and the state. There is no independent exploiting or ruling class – the state machine and the ruling class are coterminous. The state's rulers control the distribution of the means of production and the appropriation of the surplus-product only through the mechanism of *state power*. It is the state which is the exploiter and the state machine which is the mechanism of exploitation – both rulers and functionaries are mere agents or supports of the state apparatus. The state's rulers and functionaries (who are non-labourers) live off the surplus product in the form of salaries, grants, etc. In this respect, however, they are no more members of an independent ruling class than any other type of state servant, parasites and agents of exploitation though they may be. Class relations are represented as relations between the state and the subject. The presence of other classes dependent on the state's tax fund (the surplus-product), for example, merchants, skilled craftsmen, servants/clients, scholars/priests, etc., merely adds to and complicates their basic class division, but does not change it. These classes are parasitic on the state's revenues, that is, the surplus-product extracted from the direct producers – even if they are taxed the state merely receives back a portion of the surplus-product which it has already extracted in the form of tax.

(7) The level of exploitation, the number and character of the exploiters are politically-ideologically determined – there are no limits given to the level of exploitation. The mode of consumption of the surplus-product/surplus-labour is likewise politically-ideologically determined: it may be consumed in luxurious living on the part of the state functionaries, or largely consumed as corvée labour in the construction of monuments by abstemious priest/rulers, etc.

(8) The internal character of the state, its complexity and the size of the state territory are variable – the sole condition is that the state be sole proprietor of a territory. The state may take many forms: a theocracy ruled by a God/King; a secular and 'despotic' monarchy; a collegium of priests; a confederacy of tribal warriors; a colonial administration; a commercial company (e.g. the English East India Company); these are all possible forms.

These elements of social relations are deducible from the tax/rent couple; they are entailed in it or it presupposes them. Do these elements enable us to set up an articulate combination of relations/

forces of production? If they did, then we would be able to answer the question of the existence of a mode of production corresponding to the tax/rent couple in the affirmative. This answer is, however, not to be.

This mode of appropriation of the surplus-product corresponds to at least two distinct sets of forces of production: the forces entailed in independent peasant cultivation and communal cultivation. The presence or absence of these forces is determined by the modality of the tax and tenure – it is a variance which is not only politically determined but also arbitrary. There can be no articulated combination of forces and relations of production here since the relation of the *relations and forces* is characterised by a necessary arbitrariness. The substitution of one set of forces for the other does not effect or transform the basic mode of appropriation of the surplus-product, the distribution of the means of production, the relation of labourers/non-labourers – in essence, the relations of production. This arbitrariness is a necessary one because both sets of forces of production are equally deducible from and compatible with the supposed relations of production of the tax/rent couple.

That these two sets of forces of production *are* distinct can be shown as follows. Communal forms of production facilitate co-operative working by the members of the commune and the division of labour within the commune – labour can be planned and co-ordinated by the collective agency. Thus the scale and forms of labour involved in communal production are quite different from independent holdings which necessarily inhibit co-operation, restrict the possible level of division of labour, and depend primarily on the labour of the peasant and his family. Communal production allows both for the regular undertaking of large-scale tasks (drainage, irrigation, etc.), which are only possible in the case of independent holdings on the basis of a *special agreement* among the independent peasants and the neglect of other work, and also for the specialisation of the members of the collective in particular skills in agriculture and handicrafts.

The problem of the tax/rent couple is not only that two quite distinct sets of forces of production can be derived from it but more important than this is the fact that neither of these sets of forces of production necessarily supposes relations of production which correspond to the tax/rent couple. Independent peasant production can be brought under it only on the condition of the absence of private property in land; this form of production does not presuppose this absence as a condition of its existence but it is compatible with it. Where this condition does not apply peasant production corresponds to quite different relations of production, those of the ancient mode, the 'Teutonic' mode, etc. Moreover, state property in land in the case of the tax/rent couple is a legal title imposed on the direct producers by state power – the existence of the state is its sole *raison d'être*. Communal production does presuppose the absence of private property in land, but it does not presuppose *state* property in land. In the case of communal production the mode of appropriation of the surplus-product and the distribution of the means of production can be by means of the institution of the collective itself.

No articulated combination of relations/forces of production is formable corresponding to the tax/rent couple: first, because it supposes two distinct and arbitrarily variant sets of forces of production; and, second, because these forces do not necessarily correspond to the relations of the tax/rent couple but to other, quite different, relations of production. The essence of the impossibility of deriving the structure of a mode of production from the tax/rent couple is signalled by the latter point. The reason for this impossibility is to be found in the nature of the tax/rent couple as a mode of appropriation of the surplus-product; that is, that it entails no *special* mode of appropriation different from the general form of all state taxation. The limits of the forms of forces of production which can be brought under this supposed set of relations of production are negative; that is, this subsumption is impossible only where another exploitative mode of appropriation of the surplus-product is supposed by the forces of production in question. Those forces of production which *can* be brought under the tax/rent couple *do not* suppose an exploitative mode of appropriation of the surplus-product, and are compatible with the absence of private property in land and a limited social division of labour. In themselves, neither communal production nor independent peasant production suppose exploitative relations of production and the existence of *classes*. It is for this reason that they are compatible with the tax/rent couple. In essence, the constitution of the tax/rent couple as an exploitative mode of appropriation of the surplus-product is possible only *if the state is superimposed on forms of production which do not suppose exploitation or classes*. The state has no necessity in this case, it appears suspended over society as a given without conditions of existence in society.

The tax/rent couple supposes a state but does not explain its conditions of existence. How can this form of state exist other than by arbitrary fiat? Let us remember that the Marxist theory of the state, outlined by Engels in *The Origin of the Family, Private Property and the State*, and by Lenin in *The State and Revolution*, explains that the division of society into classes and the existence of irreconcilable class antagonisms is the condition of existence of the state. *No classes, no state.* The development of classes creates an antagonistic division between the members of society which is not and cannot be represented in the Gentile constitution, its means of reconciliation of differences and its organisation of force. Classes cut across the divisions which are necessary to the working of this constitution, hence it cannot represent and regulate the divisions that arise from the existence of classes. The state and the political level comes into existence out of the Gentile constitution as a mechanism of *representation* and regulation of the class struggle. Far from being a mere tool of the dominant class, the state represents class society *as such* – it is a means of preservation of class domination in so far as it maintains the conditions of existence of class society. The state and the political level develop out of the contradiction between the economic structure and the ideological superstructure in the transition from classless to class society.

How can the state exist in the absence of classes, since in that case it represents *nothing*, and the Gentile constitution continues to provide the means of representation and perpetuation of the existing social relations? Two quite different answers have been suggested:

(i) that the state arises from functional necessity; for example the notion of an 'hydraulic' state (which will be discussed in greater detail later in this chapter) as the means of organisation and co-ordination of the large-scale systematic waterworks which are (supposed) to be necessary for agriculture under certain conditions;

(ii) that the state arises from conquest, from the super-imposition of one people over another (or others) whom they exploit through tribute.

Let us examine each of these answers in turn. The first answer, that of functional necessity, is teleological, and of no explanatory value in that the 'need' for something does not of necessity bring it into being – the action of other conditions must, therefore, explain its existence. The Marxist theory of the state *does* explain the existence of the state as the result of concrete conditions, the class struggle, and as developing out of a concrete institutional basis, the Gentile constitution. Furthermore, this functionalist explanation supposes something it must prove, that the necessity of an agency of co-ordination implies the state rather than some other form of organisation. It should be noted here that no technical conditions which make the state functionally necessary can be deduced from the concept of tax/rent; the state of the tax/rent couple does not suppose a complex and integrated irrigation agriculture.

The second answer is also of no use whatsoever to the present case because it does not explain the formation of the state *in general* and it does not explain the formation of a state corresponding to the tax/rent couple. Conquest does not *of itself* produce state domination. The conquering people are not phantoms, they existed prior to the conquest and they must have a social organisation and a mode of producing the means of subsistence. In the first instance, the conquerors' mode of production will be represented alongside that of the dominated people. The dominant people receive *tribute* which is redistributed according to their social institutions and relations of production. No state is formed by this relation, dominant people/subject people; the means of coercion to obtain tribute are provided by the Gentile constitution of the dominant people, and the subject people regulates its own affairs by its own institutions. The fact of conquest does not produce either class society or the state. The conditions of transition to class society, of the conversion of the conquerors into a non-labouring ruling class, are not *given* in conquest as such. If such a transition does take place then it is on the basis of class society and irreconcilable class antagonisms that the state is formed, not on the basis of conquest. Conquest only explains certain conditions under which the state *may* be formed, it does not explain the mechanism of the formation of the state. This failure of the conquest theory to explain the formation of the state shows that it cannot explain the formation of a state corresponding to the tax/rent couple. Nothing requires that if a state *is* formed out of the conditions created by the conquest that it will be a state independent of any ruling class which appropriates the surplus-product in the form of tax/rent. Everything supposes otherwise, since the creation of *class society* is the basis on which the domination of one people over another can be converted into the domination of one class over another maintained by the apparatus of the state.

Neither of these forms explains the existence of a state which corresponds to the mode of appropriation of the surplus-product tax/rent. The only condition that does explain tax/rent is the extension of the rule of already constituted states to previously stateless peoples. But these colonial and tributary relations, however frequent and important they have been in history, do not and cannot amount to the social relations of a mode of production. Tax/rent may be collected but its conditions of existence are other than those of a 'tax/rent mode of production'. It supposes another social formation, a state which already exists and the imposition of state rule on a hitherto stateless people.

No concept of a mode of production can be derived from the tax/rent couple, no articulated combination of relations/forces of production can be deduced, and no systematic conditions of existence for the mode of appropriation of the surplus-product, tax/rent, can be constituted. This is crucial in settling the question of the validity of the notion of the AMP in that there is no other possible mode of appropriation of the surplus-product corresponding to the absence of private property in land and the dominance of pre-capitalist forms of agricultural production. To suppose irrigation agriculture and a functionally necessary state based on the co-ordination of large-scale waterworks in no way resolves the difficulties which result when the attempt to derive the structure of a mode of production from the tax/rent couple is essayed. In addition to the criticisms made above, the notion of a functionally necessary 'hydraulic' state machine depends upon a technologistic conception of mode of production – upon the dominance of given technical conditions over the social relations of production. This notion will be criticised in greater detail at the end of this chapter when Wittfogel's *Oriental Despotism* is considered. Suffice it to say here that in *Pre-Capitalist Economic Formations* Marx conceives the essence of the AMP to be the absence of private property in land and the self-reproducing unity of handicrafts and agriculture in the commune – *not* the regulation of irrigation water by the state (this is also true of Marx's incidental remarks about Asian societies in *Capital*). No adequate concept of a mode of production corresponding in any way to the notion of the AMP can be developed.

It may be pertinent at this point to note that these elements of social relations which *are* deducible from the tax/rent couple in no way correspond to those forms which are widely considered by historians and others to be essential features of 'Asiatic' society. The concept of tax/rent does not necessarily suppose the commune, the 'Oriental' form of state or the regime of state-controlled irrigation agriculture.

4 The 'stasis' of the AMP—Asia has no history

Marx certainly accepted the notion that the basic social and economic structure of the East was static and unchanging. The turbulent 'history' of the Orient, its political conflicts and wars, the rise and fall of states, only served to conceal the fundamental absence of change or development in its economic structure. It was this unchanging basis that made these successive states, these essentially repetitive political events, possible. Marx explains the 'secret' of this eternal repetition at the political level and the essential continuity at the economic level, which he considers characteristic of the Orient, as follows:

> These small and extremely ancient Indian communities, some of which have continued down to this day, are based on the possession in common of the land, on the blending of agriculture and handicrafts, and on an unalterable division of labour. . . . Occupying areas from 100 up to several thousand acres, each forms a compact whole producing all it requires. The chief part of the products is destined for direct use by the community itself, and does not take the form of a commodity. . . . The simplicity of the organisation for production in these self-sufficing communities that constantly reproduce themselves in the same form, and when accidentally destroyed, spring up again on the spot and with the same name – this simplicity supplies the key to the secret of the unchangingness of Asiatic societies, an unchangeableness in such striking contrast with the constant dissolution and refounding of Asiatic States, and the never-ceasing changes of dynasty. The structure of the economic elements of society remains untouched by the storm clouds of the political sky (*Capital*, I, pp. 357–8).

Handicrafts and agriculture form a unity in each community, this makes it possible for the community to contain within it all the conditions of its reproduction. Each of the places in the community's division of labour is systematically reproduced: the individual cannot emancipate himself from the community or his predestined place in the division of labour. The absence of a division of labour *between* communities and the reproduction of a rigid division of labour *within* the communities systematically excludes the possibility of change or development; except for purely quantitative change within existing social relations, the growth of communities or the foundation of new communities. The unity of handicrafts and agriculture within the community and the social separation of communities one from another gives Asiatic society a cellular structure – each of the cells is unaffected by the presence or absence of the others, and the cells remain unaffected by the dissolution of any state which unites them at the political level. The community can survive the fall of states and serves as the material basis of their reformation. Hence the political repetition and economic continuity of Asiatic society.

There are two major problems with this explanation of the fundamentally static character or Oriental societies. The first is that the conditions supposed in this explanation – the combination of handicrafts and agriculture within the unit of production and the separation of the units from one another (i.e. the absence of a social division of labour between them) – are in no way confined to India or to the Orient as a whole: they are in no way circumscribed by the notion of the AMP. These conditions apply equally in the case of the feudal mode of production, in the case of independent peasant proprietorship, etc. There is nothing specifically 'Asiatic' about these conditions; they apply alike in the eleventh-century Ile de France and ancient Germany as they do in the eighteenth-century Deccan. These conditions could equally well explain the 'stasis' of feudal production as they do the persistence of the Indian village system. These conditions are common to several forms of pre-capitalist production. The second is that the systematic reproduction of a particular form of production should appear as a 'problem' requiring special explanation. Central to the concept of mode of production are the concepts of *reproduction* and *limit*. Entailed in the concept of reproduction is the persistence of the structure if its conditions of existence are secured – the concept of any mode of production must define the structure of that mode as one which makes a particular form of reproduction possible. The concept of *limit* specifies that the structure of a mode of production can only exist as a definite hierarchy of determinations, and that it exists as a totality only in so far as its structure in dominance and the form of action of that structure is preserved. Nothing in its concept prohibits the continued reproduction of a mode of production and nothing in its concept requires that a mode of production transgress its own limits, i.e. dissolve itself. It is because the concept of mode of production entails the concepts of reproduction and limit that the theory of transition is a theory limited to explaining the concrete conjunctures of transition between the dominance of one mode of production in a social formation and the dominance of another.[8]

To suppose that a mode of production of necessity ceases to reproduce itself and dissolves its limits is to suppose a teleological theory of history and to suppose that the mode of production is a stage or means of realisation of that teleology. The structure of a mode of production is then defined in such a way that it must give rise to another mode of production. This supposes that a mode of production is a form which is historically finite, that is, that its conditions of existence are necessarily entirely external to its structure. In any teleological history all finite portions of history, periods, modes of production, etc., are the *phenomena* of the action of a trans-historical cause. The conditions of existence of a mode of production are external to it; it is these conditions that transform this mode into another. Teleological theories inevitably conceive the concept of mode of production in a technicist or humanist mode: the essence of history and the conditions of existence of all particular modes of production is either, the evolution of technique/instruments of production, considered as an autonomous process, or the realisation of the nature or destiny of man, as freedom, the self-conscious control of his existence, etc. It is technique or humanity which is the trans-historical cause, the essential part of history and the meaning of its end. In such a conception the concept of mode of production is a *secondary* or partial concept, and in it there can be no dominance of the relations of production, for that dominance is possible only under a different kind of causality.

To suppose an essential duality in the history of the world and an essential duality in Marxist theoretical explanation between the West, the essence of which is teleological development toward freedom and the self-realisation of humanity through the mechanism of contradiction, and the East, the essence of which is a static repetition of the existing conditions of backwardness and despotism, is to impose a rigorously Hegelian philosophy of history upon Marxism. Marxism has a non-teleological theory of history; a theory in which history has no necessity other than that produced in the conjunctures of its actual and non-pre-given course. History is not a unity with an essential structure, it has no 'end' and in it there are no 'privileged' regions or peoples. Marx undoubtedly remained under the influence of Hegelian ideology, particularly in respect of the East and 'Asiatic' society. The text of *Capital* contains important Hegelian elements. However, the effect of Marx's theoretical work was to produce a decisive critique of Hegel and of all teleology, and a non-Hegelian and anti-teleological theory of history. It is this theoretical work which makes possible the scientific criticism, by means of Marxist concepts, of the ideological elements in the given texts of Marx.

Hegel's theory gives the difference of the East and the West as a rational and a necessary form. This geographical division of the world and its peoples is no accident, it is an essential division of World history. This difference of East and West is a difference of *Spirit*, a difference in the realm of the Idea realised on the ground of and in the form of nature. The Spirit of the East is essential to it – geography becomes a necessity because the essence of the Eastern spirit is unchanging.[9] The East is a partial form of realisation of the Spirit. The essence of Spirit is freedom. The East is a limited form which is superseded by the Western spirit, a higher and universal form of the realisation of freedom. The very nature of the Western spirit is change and development.

Geography becomes necessity – it is the necessary sphere of appearance of the world-historic peoples which represent the forms of realisation and development of Spirit on earth.

> Contrasted with the universality of the moral whole and with the unity of that individuality which is its active principle, the *natural* connection that helps to produce the Spirit of a People, appears an extrinsic element; but inasmuch as we must regard it as the ground on which that Spirit plays its part, it is an *essential* and *necessary* basis. We began with the assertion that, in the History of the World, the Idea of Spirit, appears in its actual embodiment as a series of external forms, each one of which declares itself as an actually existing people. This existence falls under the category of time as well as Space, in the way of natural existence; and the Special principle, which every world-historical people embodies, has this principle at the same time as a natural characteristic. Spirit, clothing itself in this form of nature, suffers its particular phases to assume separate existence; for mutual exclusion is the mode of existence proper to mere nature (Hegel, *The Philosophy of History*, p. 79).

The East, its separate and essential nature, its limitation and distinct geographical existence, is a necessary moment of a teleology – the *rationality* of this geographical division is a function of the Hegelian dialectic. It is only in this form, as a realisation of Spirit, that *geographical* division can have any necessity. If the East were not conceived teleologically, as the location of a moment in a process, then the differences between East and West would be contingent and variable and not systematic.

The essence of the Eastern spirit for Hegel is the following:

> The Oriental World has its inherent and distinctive principle the Substantial (the Prescriptive), in Morality. We have the first example of a subjugation of the mere arbitrary will, which is merged in this substantiality. Moral distinctions and requirements are expressed as Laws, but so that the subjective will is governed by these Laws as by an external force. Nothing subjective in the shape of disposition, Conscience, formal Freedom, is recognised. Justice is administered only on the basis of external morality, and Government exists only as the prerogative of compulsion.
>
> . . . Since Spirit has not yet attained subjectivity, it wears the appearance of spirituality still involved in the conditions of Nature. Since the external and the internal, Law and Moral Sense, are not yet distinguished – still form an undivided unity – so also do Religion and the State. The Constitution generally is a Theocracy, and the Kingdom of God is to the same extent also a secular Kingdom as the secular Kingdom is also divine. What we call God has not yet in the East been realised in consciousness, for our idea of God involves an elevation of the soul to the supersensual (*ibid.*, pp. 111–12).

This absence of the subjective and the dominance of the arbitrary and external will (expressed in the form of a supreme state) is a form of realisation of Spirit which is essentially static – its very nature, the non-subjective spirit precludes change, for the principle of change is the subject. It is in the West, the sphere of realisation of the Spirit in the form of the subject, that change and development are given in the essence. Stasis and repetition is the essential destiny of China and India:

> If we compare these kingdoms in the light of their various fates, we find the empire of the two Chinese rivers the only durable kingdom in the world. Conquests cannot affect such an empire. The world of the Ganges and the Indus has also been preserved. A state of things so destitute of . . . thought is likewise imperishable, but it is in its very nature destined to be mixed with other races to be conquered and subjugated (*ibid.*, p. 115).

Change can only come to the East from without by the effects of an antithetical form of Spirit, the West and its principle, the freedom of the subject realised in the rational laws of the state. It is in Hegel that we find what lies behind the 'duality' of history.

George Lichtheim, probably the most able and perceptive of the modern bourgeois commentators on this question, recognised the Hegelianism implicit in the notion of the AMP, and in the difference of the historical destinies of Asia and the West which is supposed in it:

> . . . we may, nevertheless, extract what comfort we can from Marx' belief that the inner principle of Western historical development has from the start been quite different from that of the East or of Graeco-Roman antiquity. For my own part I am inclined to think that in this as in most other matters he was right, and that we are entitled to look upon European history as an evolution propelled by a dialectic of its own, to which there is no parallel in Oriental history. Needless to say, this Hegelian-Marxist view is incompatible with the notion that European, or Western, society is subject to any general law of growth and decay . . . applicable to *all* major civilisations. On the contrary it insists upon the West's uniqueness; and to that extent the present writer has no hesitation in calling himself a Hegelian ('Marx and the "Asiatic Mode of Production" ', p. 112).

It is for this very reason that Marxists like Lenin rejected and fought against the notion of 'Asiatic' society. Hegel attempted to give a rational form to the notion that the West is historically privileged. In Hegel this attempt was part of a radical humanist ideology in which the realisation of the freedom of the subject was the end of history. This notion of the world-historic role of the West and of the necessity of subjecting the unfree and unchanging East to Western tutelage became in the era of European imperialism a reactionary ideology,[10] and in the era of the Russian and the Chinese revolutions an absurd delusion. As Lichtheim's embrace of Hegel indicates, the notion of the privileged nature of the West has become little more than a means of denegation of the *reality* of the East for the Western liberal intelligentsia. It is they who wish to return the East to its 'unchanging' past, to the mandarins, the Confucian sages, the Brahmins and the despots. Those who find it symptomatic that Marxists have largely abandoned the notion of the AMP might in their turn ponder the symptomaticity of its adoption by the Western intelligentsia.

5 Wittfogel and 'hydraulic' society

Earlier in this chapter we considered the possibility of a functionalist explanation of the development of a state corresponding to the *tax/rent couple*, a state made necessary by the peculiar conditions of large-scale irrigation agriculture. Such an explanation, if it were possible, would provide a mechanism for the formation of, and a social foundation for, a state without a ruling class. It would also make possible an argument for a distinct combination of relations and forces of production based upon irrigation agriculture, its regulation and control. The functionalist explanation links the form of the state and a particular form of production. This conception is vitiated by a double teleology: complex irrigation agriculture is supposed to require the state as its condition of existence, it cannot, therefore, provide the material conditions of existence of the state; while the state supposes irrigation agriculture as its foundation and *raison d'être*. Despite its logical flaws, the functionalist conception of the *AMP/'Asiatic society'* enjoys considerable prestige and popularity among both Marxist and non-Marxist social scientists. Karl Wittfogel's *Oriental Despotism* is the principal example of such a functionalist explanation of 'Asiatic society'. It is for this reason that we have included an examination and critique of this work as the concluding section of this chapter – a settling of accounts with the functionalist thesis in the shape of its leading exponent.

We will confine ourselves to a consideration of the validity of Wittfogel's thesis, that is, that a definite structure of social and political relations is consequent on the necessity of state supervision and control of complex systems of irrigation agriculture. We will not discuss in detail Wittfogel's account of the vicissitudes of the concept of AMP in the history of Marxism, nor will we discuss his attempt to relate Soviet 'totalitarianism' to its supposed pre-industrial agro-despotic foundation in Tsarist Russia. Both of these themes reflect Wittfogel's obsessive anti-communism and anti-Sovietism. Although these ideological interests shape his whole work, his importance and influence stands or falls on his thesis about the existence and nature of 'hydraulic' society. It is this that we will now consider.

It should be noted that Oriental despotism – hydraulic society is not a *concept*, in the sense that the AMP or any concept of a mode of production are (or are supposed to be) concepts. *Oriental Despotism* is an empirical generalisation/description, it is supposed to correspond to the reality of the Asiatic world. If Wittfogel's hydraulic despotisms do not exist in Asia they have no other validity, no other conditions of existence. It is by means of empirical evidence that we shall challenge this identification with, and disappearance into, the real; we shall attempt to use empiricist criteria to challenge Wittfogel's empiricist pretensions. We shall also attempt to show that Wittfogel's thesis is logically impossible and presupposes what it must prove in its explanation.

THE WITTFOGEL THESIS

Summary

Any short summary of Wittfogel's text will necessarily be partial and selective, both because of the length of the book and the author's tendency to qualify his more emphatic statements.

In essence Wittfogel's thesis is that there are pre-industrial forms of state system of a totalitarian character – a conception whose basic features Wittfogel claims are to be found in the Western notion of 'Oriental despotism' stemming from Locke and Montesquieu – and that these despotic state systems arise as a function of or as a result of the necessities of large-scale irrigation agriculture under certain cultural and social conditions – Wittfogel traces his conception of this despotism based upon the control of water resources to Marx.

Oriental/hydraulic despotism is a form of domination whose essence is *bureaucratic* and *managerial* control. The following conditions make such a bureaucratic-managerial form necessary in the pre-industrial world.

> Thus, too little or too much water does not necessarily lead to governmental water control; nor does governmental water control necessarily imply despotic methods of statecraft. It is only above the level of an extractive subsistence economy, beyond the influence of strong centres of rainfall agriculture, and below the level of a property-based industrial civilisation that man, reacting specifically to the water-deficient landscape, moves toward a specific hydraulic order of life (*Oriental Despotism*, p. 12).

These are the general socio-cultural conditions of hydraulic despotism; Wittfogel conceives it as an institutional adaptation to the challenge of aridity under the limitations of pre-capitalist and pre-industrial organisational and technical forms. A simple subsistence economy, an adequate rainfall regime, capitalism and industrialism prohibit or render unnecessary such an adaptation, but outside of these conditions Wittfogel considers hydraulic despotism to be the general social type; Wittfogel estimates (p. 19) that arid and semi-arid landscapes 'cover almost three-fifths of the globe's surface'.

Given the assumption of *full-aridity*, a widely-diffused surplus-producing agricultural system must depend on the organising and co-ordinating activities that only a complex 'bureaucratic' state system can provide:

> In a landscape characterised by full aridity permanent agriculture becomes possible only if and when co-ordinated human action transfers a plentiful and accessible water supply from its original location to a potentially fertile soil. When this is done, *government-led hydraulic enterprise is identical with the creation of agricultural life* (*ibid.*, p. 109, our emphasis).

Under these conditions large-scale irrigation works, the mobilisation and direction of labour, planning and co-ordinating are necessary *before* productive agriculture can begin – these activities can only be performed by a centralised administrative staff with executive power, the ability to calculate and record. Agriculture here presupposes bureaucracy.

Given the assumption of *semi-aridity* (areas with a limited rainfall regime) and an existing *hydro-agriculture* (decentralised system based on local irrigation) then the development of the segmented local units into a complex and controlled system also requires 'bureaucratic' administration – even if agriculture itself does not presuppose bureaucracy, the control of flooding, the storage of water to prevent drought, etc., require works and co-ordination on a scale far beyond the needs of agriculture proper. Further, in most semi-arid regions rainfall is irregular and intense – flood protection and water-storage are essential to agricultural life in most semi-arid regions, they are not an 'optional extra'.

Once in existence a complex irrigation and/or flood protection system, with extensive subsidiary works for the provision of drinking water, water and food storage, defence, etc., requires a centralised 'bureaucratic' apparatus to make it work. Localised and *ad hoc* administrative means are inadequate to perform the necessary tasks of calendar making to predict the seasons and, therefore, rainfall or flood; inadequate to control the distribution of irrigation water so that all areas receive an adequate supply; inadequate to calculate the need for and to organise corvée labour for the maintenance and extension of the works, for emergency mobilisation for flood control. Such a bureaucracy does not merely calculate and co-ordinate, it must *command*; the supply of water and corvée labour must be under its *control* not merely its supervision.

These large-scale hydraulic enterprises require a centralised control for their creation and maintenance. The power of the hydraulic higher authority is essentially *managerial*, rather than *proprietorial* or military. That is, it rests upon the indispensability of control and co-ordination for the working of the system and the livelihood of the masses. The ultimate sanction of hydraulic despotism is its *necessity* rather than its ownership of the land or its possession of military force. The power of the hydraulic state, its ability to command men and resources, stems from this fact: a hydraulically-based economy is an essential condition of this type of bureaucratic despotism: 'The formation of hydraulic society . . . depends on the presence of an hydraulic economy proper as an essential condition' (Wittfogel, *op. cit.*, p. 227). For Wittfogel bureaucratic despotism's necessity stems from both the conditions of existence and maintenance of hydraulic economy.

Hydraulic agriculture creates a distinct type of despotic power system: it is a totalitarian state stronger than any other combination of forces in the society. The state is above society and 'pulverises' it into its own likeness, destroying all forces for change, independence or deviance. The structure of this totalitarian system is as follows:

(i) the state control of the essential features of the production system, the irrigation and ancillary works – thus the state enjoys a decisive sanction against any individual or group of the agrarian population and production is impossible without the state's action;

(ii) a comprehensive network of political intelligence, spying, and the supervision of the populace, and an efficient state communications system (posts and roads, waterways, etc.);

(iii) a large standing army under centralised control and the absence of other centres of effective military power – the disarming of the people;

(iv) a system of corvée labour for the state, on irrigation works, monuments, public agricultural land, etc., and a comprehensive tax system with a heavy tax burden, the level of taxation being arbitrarily set by the will of the state authorities and reinforced by periodic confiscations and requisitions;

(v) 'weak property', the absence of economic centres independent of the state (i.e. of free trade and manufacture), the subordination and control of commerce and industry. Merchants and other property owners are at the mercy of the arbitrary whim of the state. The threat of persecution or confiscation inhibits productive investment in favour of the concealed horde of mobile wealth – thus no independent class of wealthy proprietors counterbalances the state and the possibility of the development of non-hydraulic economic relations (proto-capitalism) is crushed by the state's political supervision of the economy;

(vi) the state is a centralised despotism which legitimises itself through theocratic ideological forms, which identifies itself with the divine order and makes social and economic life appear as the product of its will and benevolence alone. Religion is a state-controlled activity. Heterodox sects and popular religious practices are subject to control and are suppressed if they threaten the state or its religion. The 'benevolence' of Oriental despotism is, Wittfogel claims, spurious because the great works which are its manifestations are frequently functionless glorifications of the state or, if functional, benefit only the state. Thus while the state represents itself as necessary to agricultural life it does singularly little for the people and extracts vast surpluses of products and labour from them;

(vii) the supervision of independent thought and action through a regime of terror, the isolation and subordination of individuals through spying and informing, and the suppression of genuine independence of officials and prominent men through the total insecurity of their positions and wealth in the face of the arbitrary will of the despot. Such freedoms as there are, are confined to matters which are unimportant to and do not threaten the state.

Such a social system is *totalitarian* and *managerial* for Wittfogel because: it is a highly centralised and arbitrary form of government; there is an absence of effective secondary associations and independent social groups which can limit and contract the power of the state – there is actual or potential government control of all key institutions and activities. This is a variant of liberal political/social theories which define totalitarianism by the absence of political and/or social pluralism. The bureaucracy and ruling class are closed, the bureaucracy monopolises access to the means of administration. In such a society monopoly control of the state apparatus means a monopoly of real social power (political, economic, ideological) – power does not stem from private property ownership (such property is mere '*revenue property*', its owner enjoys economic wealth but by virtue of it no political power) but from access to the bureaucratic means of control and appropriation. Thus hydraulic society is a system under the total (or as nearly total as pre-industrial conditions permit) control of a managerial staff. The ruling classes exist *because* of the state system rather than any socio-economic position they enjoyed prior to it or independently of it.

The *scope* of Wittfogel's thesis includes all non-basic subsistence, non-feudal and pre-capitalist societies. The generalisations about the nature of this type of pre-industrial despotic state extend to the systems of power in societies with *non-hydraulic* economies because Wittfogel argues that it is in the hydraulic areas proper that the agromanagerial despotic form of rule is *developed* and from there it is *diffused* to other non-hydraulic areas: 'Virtually all historically significant agrodespotisms that fulfil no hydraulic functions seem to have been derived from hydraulic societies' (*Oriental Despotism*, pp. 193–194).

This style of rule is diffused because it places immensely greater power in the hands of the ruler. The minimum organisational and structural condition of an agrarian despotism is the 'effective co-ordination of absolutist methods of organisation and acquisition' (p. 195) – that is, the systematic linkage of a centralised state apparatus with a tax system based upon corvée labour and arbitrary confiscation. The density of bureaucratic control of social relations is directly proportional to the density of the hydraulic agricultural system. Using this correspondence, societies are divided into core, marginal and sub-marginal hydraulic societies. By means of these latter qualifying concepts and of diffusionism from hydraulic to non-hydraulic systems Wittfogel is able to incorporate into the 'hydraulic' world: Ancient Egypt and Mesopotamia, Rome and Byzantium, the Arab Caliphates, Muslim Spain, the Ottoman Empire, India and China, the pre-conquest empires of Central and South America, the Pueblo Indians, the Chagga, pre-modern Hawaii, etc. For Wittfogel, Oriental despotism is the widest-diffused social type with the greatest influence prior to modern capitalism.

A CRITIQUE OF WITTFOGEL'S THESIS

It is our object to show that this very general social type does not exist outside of the pages of *Oriental Despotism*, and that it is in ideology rather than in the Orient itself that it has its conditions of existence.

Wittfogel's conception of the totalitarian power system of a hydraulic society is little more than a modernised version, in social-scientific jargon, of the concept of *despotism* in Western liberal political thought. This concept is a polemical not a scientific one and it has a very specific function in Western political theory. Despotism in Western thought is confined to the East; it is a specifically Oriental form of rule different in essence from the political systems of Europe. The nature and the function of this concept are very evident in the work of Montesquieu.[11]

The polemical character of the concept is evident in that it designates an impossible form of political system, where all institutions and forms of the exercise of power vanish before the necessity of the absolute power and absolute arbitrariness of the despot. Pure despotism is like the concept of a frictionless machine; it can have no social structure or institutional support. The function of this concept is to serve as a means of highlighting and accentuating the virtues of a well-ordered constitutional monarchy (previously it had served to differentiate absolutism as a *lawful* form of rule[12]); a monarchy in which the property and life of the subjects is free from arbitrary seizure or threat. Despotism is an ultimate or pure concept whose function is to make all forms of constitutional rule and rule within the law appear both reasonable and necessary. Like totalitarianism it derives its content and function from its character as a pure negation of freedom. Once the political system is recognised as being constrained by a social structure ('civil society'[13]) or the totally constraining grip of the political system upon the social structure is recognised as an impossibility, despotism and totalitarianism vanish – all societies become more or less 'pluralistic'. In all societies power is limited by the means of its exercise, and in all societies the power of the state is finite and there are more or less effective sources of opposition to its present controllers. Despotism and totalitarianism can only exist on the plane of polemical abstraction; as concepts they are valueless in the study of actual political systems.

Thus the realities of power in the pre-capitalist state are quite different from Wittfogel's conception of a monolithic state machine which 'pulverises' the social structure. Wittfogel's conception of Oriental despotism is a continuation of the Western misconception of the Orient (a misconception in which the West flattered itself; a device as misleading as its opposite, the self-criticism Montesquieu wrote through his Persians and Diderot through his Tahitians) and a projection into the pre-capitalist era of the modern concept of 'totalitarianism' (the modern variant of the concept in which the West recognises its own virtues in the absolute evil of another).

Wittfogel constantly *supposes* what he must *prove* if his argument about the conditions of existence of agromanagerial despotism is to have any validity.

He supposes that the irrigation works in question form a *system* and that the system requires *managerial* control. Leach[14] has argued that in the case of the 'hydraulic' Dry-Zone of Ceylon while there are still extant irrigation and other works of immense size and extent these do not indicate that the ancient state of Sinhala was a 'hydraulic despotism'. Leach presents evidence to show that at no time did the works form a unified whole or system, having been built at different times and never all being in use at the same time. Given quite modest yearly outlays of materials and labour these works were built up piecemeal and to no overall master plan; the 'system' took over 1,400 years to construct. Thus no massive mobilisation of labour was necessary, and the demands on the organising and planning capacity of the rulers' administrations were modest:

> In other words, although the Ceylon irrigation works and the associated palace and temple construction works do represent a gigantic accumulation of capital resulting from an enormous number of man-hours of labour, this fact does not *in itself* imply any massive control over labour resources by the 'bureaucratic' rulers (Leach, 'Hydraulic society in Ceylon', p. 14).

Similarly, the construction and working of the 'system' did not require a *managerial* type of control:

> The extremely high level of engineering skill displayed in the design and construction of these works does clearly imply the existence of professional engineers but the indications are that such men were members of Buddhist monastic institutions and not direct servants of the crown (*ibid.*, p. 14).

Wolfram Eberhard also questions Wittfogel's assertions and evidence about irrigation systems, in this case with respect to medieval China.[15] He contends that the evidence concerning ancient Chinese irrigation systems is inadequate and patchy, and that Wittfogel makes little use of what evidence there is. He argues that there was no 'Ministry of Public Works' in the sense in which Wittfogel conceives of it, namely as an agency of planning and control of a national irrigation network. Rather, the 'Ministry' was a department of the Imperial household's administration, and as such it was directly responsible only for the Imperial household and its supplies. Far from being built at the order of the central government most irrigation works were built by local administrations in response to local pressure (e.g. from farmers). Eberhard disputes the managerialist interpretation that irrigation systems were controlled by specialist government officials; he suggests that the water supply was regulated by 'elders' appointed by local farmers and not by state officials.

Wittfogel constantly assumes that all complex activities requiring co-ordination will require some form of managerial control; this assumption can be questioned. For example, complex tasks and relations can be handled by pre-literate peoples by means of 'operational' techniques[16] and without the existence of a specialised bureaucratic caste with a monopoly of administrative power. Eberhard, in addition to disputing the state control of water-distribution, argues that the prediction of the period in which the farmer should commence sowing does not depend on complex astronomical predictions, but upon the simple direct observation of certain constellations by the farmer. Court astronomers and the state were in no sense technically necessary for agriculture. Furthermore, in China the official astronomical system did not correspond at all well to the needs of the agricultural community.[17]

He supposes that definite social relations correspond to these systematic forms of 'hydraulic' agriculture. Leach questions this, he argues that irrigation agriculture is compatible with other systems of socio-economic relations than the one Wittfogel outlines. Thus he argues that the type of social relations accompanying hydraulic agricultural production in the seventeenth-century kingdom of Kandy (also in Ceylon) was a form of 'feudalism'. Leach quotes a contemporary observer Robert Knox:

> Many towns are in the King's hand, the inhabitants whereof are to tilland manure a quantity of land according to their ability, and lay up the corn for the king's use. These towns the king often bestows upon some of his nobles for their encouragement and maintenance, with all the fruits and benefits which before came to the king from them (Leach, *op. cit.*, p. 15).

The Kandian king was a 'despot', irrigation agriculture was a crucial element of the economy, but there was in Kandy no 'agromanagerial' bureaucracy or 'hydraulic' form of subordination of the people to the state.[18]

Wittfogel never advances any evidence on these questions – there is no detailed account of a single bureaucratically-administered irrigation system and its workings in the whole book and yet these agro-technical conditions are the crucial element in his argument as to the managerial and totalitarian nature of this type of society.

Wittfogel's assumption of *full-aridity* necessarily presupposes that the state machine and an adequate economic base are already in existence. The state enters the arid region and renders it cultivable; there is a necessary lapse of perhaps several years before the system produces food to support the direct producers and a surplus to support the state. The state plays the role of the *deus ex machina* here, and in a way that overturns Wittfogel's argument: for if the creation of agricultural production in an arid region presupposes the state, it also presupposes a non-arid agricultural base for this state. Thus the state and its features do not derive from the hydraulic agricultural base.

Semi-aridity also presupposes that the state and its characteristics exist prior to the construction of the large-scale flood protection works – it must organise and coerce the labour necessary for their creation.

Thus full- and semi-aridity explain (if we accept the rest of Wittfogel's assumptions) only the *need* for this type of state if agricultural life is to take the 'hydraulic' form. Wittfogel's causation is teleological in that either the need for such a state gives rise to it or that it arises as a pure act of will – a will which moulds a state whose end and destiny is the construction of a hydraulic agriculture not yet in being. Wittfogel does not and cannot prove that a totalitarian state emerges from the conditions of and necessities of hydraulic agriculture, rather the totalitarian state is already supposed and hydraulic agriculture is its foundation and support in the pre-industrial world. As Leach says: 'Wittfogel theorises about what he supposes would be the case' (p. 15) – Wittfogel seeks to ground the abstract and unrealisable notion of despotism/totalitarianism on a concrete social base.[19] This attempt is doomed to failure; Wittfogel's supposed conditions of existence of this state reveal its real conditions of existence – the ideological desire that needs it to exist.

'Despotic' forms of rule do not necessarily have a 'hydraulic' economic base – Wittfogel admits this and his explanations of the hydraulic 'connections' of the main non-hydraulic systems have a decidedly *ad hoc* character which indicate that he is trying to preserve his theories against the evidence by means of the device of diffusionism. If such 'despotic' systems *can* exist without a hydraulic agriculture then they do in fact prove that such an economic system is not their principal condition of existence. There is no good reason why 'despotic' systems cannot develop in non-hydraulic areas without the influence of hydraulic regions. Wittfogel's attempt to link the hydraulic and non-hydraulic despotisms by claims of 'influence' is logically valueless.

Wittfogel's contention that power in 'hydraulic' societies is *managerial*, that the state apparatus derives its power from the technical necessity of continuous administration and control of the waterworks, etc., is both an anachronistic application of the concept and an absurdity under the prevailing socio-economic conditions of the pre-capitalist world. Wittfogel's position explicitly contradicts that of Max Weber, probably the most systematic and rigorous exponent of the notion of bureaucratic domination or managerial rule. Whether this notion is of any value in itself does not concern us here, we merely wish to demonstrate that Wittfogel's use of 'managerialism' is incorrect and anachronistic *in managerialist terms*.

Pre-capitalist conditions do not permit of such necessities, for they make a continuous and regular 'managerial' administration impossible. Max Weber's conception of a rational bureaucracy, of an administrative machine which works through stored written documents according to a system of rational rules and which employs salaried career officials appointed on the basis of technical competence,[20] is the pre-condition of a *managerial* form of administration. Such a rational bureaucracy cannot exist without a rational legal system and a developed money economy – this presupposes modern capitalism and the modern state. In Weber's analysis centrifugal and localising tendencies are very powerful in all pre-capitalist bureaucracies: 'According to historical experience, without a money economy the bureaucratic structure can hardly avoid undergoing substantial internal changes, or indeed transformation into another structure' (*Economy and Society*, Vol. III, p. 964).

Given the political and economic vicissitudes to which all pre-capitalist systems are subject, no highly centralised administration could long avoid the tendencies to appropriation of office and its rewards. The only condition upon which such a 'managerial' system could exist is that of an irrigation system which presupposes centralised control, but this is what Wittfogel presumes rather than proves, and, even if it did exist, the limitations inherent in pre-capitalist administration would ensure its degeneration and with it the degeneration of agricultural life. In fact, there is every reason (as we have seen in the case of Ceylon) to believe that irrigation agriculture is essentially decentralised – in no other way can the stability and persistence of developed irrigation agriculture in China and India be explained; centralisation would have entailed its eventual disappearance.

Weber contended that the types of administration which could survive best in the pre-capitalist world were those which did not presuppose a highly centralised or 'managerial' form. Weber conceived the system of domination in China to be traditional-charismatic;[21] Chinese officialdom, far from being a modern bureaucracy, had a far greater likeness to the household staff of a prince (central administration) and to the rule of a gentry, aided by representatives of the central administration (local administration). For Weber, bureaucratic forms were the exception rather than the rule in the pre-capitalist world; for Wittfogel the situation is the reverse – 'managerial' oriental despotism is the most general social type.

Wittfogel claims that his work continues and develops the insights of Marx on Asiatic society. Wittfogel, however, distorts Marx's conception of the Asiatic mode of production in claiming its affinity with his own thesis. An index of the distortion is the stress Wittfogel places on Marx's article 'The British rule in India' and Marx's letter to Engels of 14 June 1853.[22] In both of these texts Marx lays considerable stress on the role of public works, but at no point does he adopt the technicist 'hydraulic society' thesis and base the nature of Asiatic society upon the governmental construction and control of large-scale waterworks. Wittfogel supposes he did subscribe to this thesis (Wittfogel's own) and brands Marx's later positions as a 'retreat from truth'.[23] It is Marx's refusal to reduce social relations to technique rather than his 'retreat from truth' which is clearly borne out in his later writings on Asia. This is particularly clear in the portion of the *Grundrisse*, *Pre-Capitalist Economic Formations*. From the foregoing sections of this chapter it will be obvious that we do not support or agree with Marx's position on the AMP. Nevertheless, it is impossible to accept Wittfogel's interpretation of Marx's position; *Oriental Despotism*, of necessity, reduces Marxism to vulgar Marxism.

The essence of Marx's conception in *Pre-Capitalist Economic Formations* is the absence of private property in land and the dominance of agricultural production based on the commune, which gives rise to the discrepancy between the communal forms of agricultural production/distribution and the 'higher unity' of the state. 'Asiatic' society has a *cellular* structure based upon the autonomy of the local communities – it is on this basis that more or less elaborate state structures rise and fall. Hence the political system of this mode of production oscillates between more or less extensive political dissolution and the rise of 'despotic' states alien to and over and above the serial totality of village communes. The village commune is a self-reproducing independent entity which can survive the absence of the state. This type of society is politically unstable, but structurally stable (new state systems are constantly reconstructed on the basis of the communes); it inhibits the development of commerce and manufacture, limiting the degree of their development to a function of the state's revenues and the state's power. As we have seen, it is in this concept that Marx reconciled the turbulent political history of such societies (to call it a 'history' is mistaken since nothing changes, it is better called a repetition) and the basic 'unchanging' stability of their social structures.

Marx's concept differentiates the mode on the basis of *social relations* not of *technique*, it does not matter if the specific technique is the rainfall farming of wheat or the irrigation cultivation of rice. In *Pre-Capitalist Economic Formations* Marx clearly does not conceive the Asiatic mode as specifically a 'hydraulic' mode or as a state-dominated, centrally planned and controlled 'agromanagerial' system. Marx would have regarded the former notion as a vulgar technicism and the latter as a fantasy of some Chinese Fourier. Marx locates the stability and uniqueness of the Asiatic mode (which is not confined to Asia) in the gulf between state and commune, not in hydraulic agriculture or bureaucratic dominance. Wittfogel is more than somewhat disingenuous in claiming himself the true successor of Marx.

Wittfogel distinguishes his method as: 'the use of big structural concepts for the purposes of identifying big patterns of societal structure and change' (*Oriental Despotism*, p. iii), and compares it to the method of Aristotle, Machiavelli and Adam Smith. We would prefer to call it empiricist speculation on a grand scale – the production of a generalised pseudo-description, in which empirical evidence features as exemplification and illustration, and where the generality described is an inexistent and ideological one. The Wittfogel thesis is without foundation. 'Hydraulic' societies are the product of a combination of vulgar technicism, conceptual anachronism and political ideology. Similarly, the notion of an 'Oriental' form of state is the product of Western political ideologies and Western attempts to give the East an essential and alien culture different in every respect from the West. The same concepts apply to the Orient and the Occident.

Five

The feudal mode of production

1 Feudal rent and the feudal mode of production

In the previous chapter we introduced the concept of feudal rent, in this chapter that concept will serve as the point of departure in the process of constructing a concept of the feudal mode of production (hereafter FMP). It may appear that our route in the construction of the concept of FMP is an easy one, that we may begin by assuming that feudal rent is the mode of appropriation of the surplus-product specific to the FMP and proceed by deducing the structure of that mode from the conditions of existence of this form of rent. Nothing could be further from the truth. The concept of feudal rent presented in the previous chapter is a limited one and if it is used as the starting point for a series of deductions the result can be nothing other than the inadequate conception of feudalism current in Marxist theory. It is by problematising the concept of feudal rent that its limitations, and the limitations of the current conception of feudalism, will become apparent.

Why is the concept of feudal rent presented in the previous chapter a limited one? Its function in that chapter was as one of a series of forms of rent which served to establish tax/rent as the mode of appropriation of surplus-labour corresponding to the nominal elements of the AMP derived from various of Marx's works. But the limitations of the concept of feudal rent are not reducible to its limited function in that chapter. The limitations of the concept stem from the fact that it was not developed as part of the process of construction of a concept of FMP. In chapter XLVII of *Capital* Marx elaborates certain pre-capitalist forms of rent in order to illustrate the distinct nature of capitalist ground-rent – to emphasise that rent is not the mode of appropriation of surplus-labour in capitalism. Developing the concept in this way and for this purpose Marx has no reason to pose the question of its adequacy as the concept of the mode of appropriation of surplus-labour in the FMP and certainly no reason to pose the question of the possibility of constructing a concept of FMP or of how this might be done. These questions are not relevant to the problems of *Capital*. They are neither asked nor answered in *Capital*. The object of *Capital* is to construct a theory of the capitalist mode of production, where pre-capitalist forms are discussed in the discourse of *Capital* it is to illustrate features of capitalism and not in order to construct a general theory of modes of production.

Marx is concerned in chapter XLVII, despite appearances, with the specificity of capitalist forms of rent to the capitalist mode of production, not with feudal rent and its relation to the feudal mode of production. Consequently, the concept of feudal rent as it is presented in *Capital* cannot be taken as a given and the structure of the FMP deduced from it.[1] The subsequent discussion of feudalism in Marxism has suffered from the failure to read *Capital* theoretically, to relate concepts like feudal rent to their discursive function, and to question their value when transposed to other discourses, to other questions.

Later Marxist writers, including those concerned specifically with the question of feudal rent, have made little advance on Marx's concept. The Russian historian E. A. Kosminsky is one of the most theoretically aware and sophisticated of recent Marxist writers on feudalism.[2] However, Kosminsky's definition of feudal rent rests upon Marx's, and Kosminsky, as a historian, is concerned above all with the correspondence of the concept with the conditions of the Middle Ages. Kosminsky is therefore led away from the problem of the theoretical value and status of the concept of feudal rent, and into the question of the validity of the concept with respect to given conditions. Kosminsky's highly formal definition of the feudal social relations which are the conditions of existence of feudal rent is an index of the domination of his conception of feudal rent by the historian's practice: the content of the 'special type of landed property' and the 'special type of class of basic producers with a special connection with the land' is not specified theoretically; the content of this nominal definition is to be provided by the real, by the concrete economic relations of the Middle Ages. Conceptual criticism and theoretical development are displaced in favour of the refinement of historical interpretation.

To return to the concept of feudal rent. From *Capital* and Kosminsky we know the following: that feudal rent supposes that landed property is in the possession of a ruling class who hold the direct producers in a relation of political subordination, that the direct producers have effective possession of the means of production and that, as a consequence, the surplus-product is appropriated on the basis of extra-economic coercion. Feudal rent may be in the form of labour-service, in kind or in the form of money. The political subordination of the direct producers to the exploiters, the possession by the direct producers of the means of production and the extra-economic mode of appropriation of the surplus-product are features common to the principal pre-capitalist forms of rent outlined by Marx.[3] The distinctive characteristics of feudal rent which separate it from the other pre-capitalist forms of rent appear to be the specific character of the landlord class and the specific status of the subordinate direct producers.

In order to demonstrate the limitations of and the difficulties involved in this conception of feudal rent the procedure adopted in the previous chapter will be reversed; there tax/rent and feudal rent were differentiated for the purposes of the exposition, here that differentiation will be problematised. In posing the question – is there any fundamental difference between feudal rent and tax/rent? – we hope to show why the concept of feudal rent as it is at present is inadequate, and why it cannot serve as the concept of the mode of appropriation of surplus-labour in the FMP.

FEUDAL RENT AND TAX/RENT

In the previous chapter the conditions in terms of which feudal rent and tax/rent were differentiated were: (i) that in the case of feudal rent the ruling class exists independently of the state machine, the ruling class is not reducible to the state functionaries, and, (ii) that in the case of feudal rent the direct producers are politically-legally bound to their exploiters, while in the case of tax/rent no subordination other than the general subordination of the subject to the state is involved in the appropriation of the surplus-product. The essence of the difference is the independence/non-independence of the ruling class and the private/state possession of the land. No other conditions of differentiation are given in the concepts of these two forms. In the absence of any structural mechanism explaining the independence of the ruling class or its possession of the land, of any mechanism specific to the FMP, we are forced to conclude that these features are accidents of political history. The tax/rent state is different because it has a different constitution and a different history. The distinguishing features of two 'modes of production', the AMP and the FMP, exist in the form of specific institutions and specific political *acts*, the granting of land rights by the state to a ruling class, and the subordination of the common people, or the formation of a state which is little more than a confederacy of militarily dominant landholders. *It appears that the constitution of the state is the key element differentiating feudal rent and tax/rent.*

The key difference between these two forms lies in the degree to which the ruling class is subsumed within the state machine – from this private property in land and the legally subordinate status of the direct producers can be derived. This autonomy/subordination is a simple given, a fact without apparent conditions of existence. It cannot be grounded in the social relations of production since in itself this difference, an autonomous ruling class, a ruling state, is the basis of differentiation between two forms of social relations of production. If this is the case then it appears that the constitutional and legal historians are fundamentally correct about the nature of feudalism – what is essential is the form of state constitution, and the political-legal relations of state, lords and subjects. What differentiates the feudal state from the state which levies tax/rent is the degree of centralisation of state power. In the one case the state is sole landlord, taxes and rents coincide. In the other the landlord represents state power, his rent depends upon his capacity to exert that power. In feudalism the lord stands in relation to serf as state to subject, seignorial power is state power writ small, and serfdom is the subjection of the serf to the state in the *person* of the lord. Serfdom is a legal status and it exists in so far as it is politically enforced – it is a form of political subordination which provides the basis for exploitation. The feudal lord extracts the surplus-product through political coercion; he holds the land because of his political position, and extracts the surplus through force. 'No land without a master' – a landlord is such because he is *seigneur*.

In both the tax/rent system and in the case of feudal rent exploitation depends on and is realised through political dominance. There is no difference in the modality of exploitation – in both cases the subject faces a politically enforced deduction from his total product, a deduction which goes to an exploiter who plays no part as an agent in the process of production. What then is the difference between tax/rent and feudal rent but the scale of the appropriating units and the legal status of the exploited subjects. From this it follows that there is no fundamental difference between tax/rent and feudal rent as forms of exploitation – *feudal rent is nothing more than the decentralised form of tax/rent.*

Paradoxically, if we suppose a centralised form of 'feudal' state the limited nature of the difference between tax/rent and feudal rent is no less evident. In a centralised state the feudal element is either reduced to the residual presence or persistence of the *seigneur*/serf relation, to an index of the limitations of centralisation, or, the elements of local power and the autonomy of the landlord class appear as creations of state *policy*. If feudal landlordship does not exist (or is abolished) feudal rent is reduced to mere 'tax feudalism'; to the allocation of the tax revenues from particular districts to definite state functionaries, functionaries whose revenue depends on their connection with the state and does not exist independently of service to the state. If we suppose the degeneration and decentralisation of a state with a tax feudalism system then a form of feudal landlordship is the possible result. In this way tax/rent and feudal rent may be generated one from the other.

It is correct that feudal rent in the senses outlined above is a possible mode of exploitation of surplus-labour, but so are banditry and extortion by political 'bosses'. Every seizure of the product of direct producers is not the mode of appropriation characteristic of a mode of production. It is the structure of a mode of production which creates a division of surplus-labour and necessary labour specific to it; without its being determined by a definite mode of production there can be no *surplus*-labour. In this sense feudal rent has exactly the same status as the tax/rent couple – it has doubtless existed as a method of exploitation where certain forms of state are imposed on hitherto existing direct producers, but it is not the mode of appropriation of the surplus-product characteristic of a mode of production. No specific set of productive forces is structured by these 'relations of production' – the conditions of the appropriation of surplus-labour do not transform the labour process, or the relation of the labourer to it. Political dominance is presupposed to explain these forms of exploitation, it is not explained by them. The state not only *creates* exploitation, it is its sole source and condition of existence. Tax/rent and feudal rent are imposed by a state machine on pre-existing forms of production – feudal rent arrives in the baggage train of William the Conqueror or the Teutonic Knights! These conditions enable us to state a thesis: *Feudal rent* (in the sense considered above) *does not suppose the FMP as its conditions of existence*. Feudal rent can exist without the FMP in so far as feudal rent is a variant form of tax/rent.

POSSESSION, EXPLOITATION AND FEUDAL RENT

In the previous chapter the possibility of pre-capitalist rent taking the forms of money rent, rent-in-kind and labour-rent was outlined, it was explained that the forms in which the surplus-product was appropriated (money, kind, labour) do not affect the basic nature of the mode of exploitation. If the *forms* are secondary, what is the nature of pre-capitalist rent, what is the basis of the appropriation of the surplus-product? We know that in the CMP the wage *form* is not accidental to the production of surplus-value, that the structure of the CMP acts through it to appropriate surplus-labour. Why the forms remain secondary, why the nature of the appropriation involved in pre-capitalist rent remains shadowy, without a definite mechanism, is because pre-capitalist rent is not in fact conceived as an economic relation at all, but as a relation of political domination.

Let us re-examine the discussion of the pre-capitalist forms of rent in *Capital*, chapter XLVII. We saw that pre-capitalist conditions of production prevent the separation of the labourer from the means of production and that 'in all forms in which the direct labourer remains the "possessor" of the means of production . . . the property relationship must simultaneously appear as a direct relation of lordship and servitude' (*Capital*, III, p. 771). The appearance is in fact the reality. Given the non-separation of the direct producer, property remains at the level of a political-legal relation, it does not take the form of the conversion of 'property' into effective possession, that is, the subsumption of the direct producer under exploitative relations of production. The pre-condition of the subsumption of the direct producer within relations of production which constitute the process of *production* as a process of exploitation is some form of separation of the direct producer from the means of production. Marx argues that when this separation does not exist, where there is no specific economic mechanism of exploitation, exploitation must be secured by non-economic means and that this exploitation has non-economic, political or ideological conditions of existence. Political or ideological forms predominate, they secure the conditions of exploitation that cannot be secured in a system of production where the direct producer is able to set the means of production in motion independently of the exploiter. Balibar elaborates this argument. Under such conditions the political or ideological *instance* is dominant. He attempts to develop the argument that although the political or ideological instance is dominant it occupies that place through the determination of the economy in the last instance. This dominance assigned by the determination of the economy in the last instance is supported by a quotation from Marx:

> According to these objections: 'in my view . . . that the mode of production of material life dominates the development of social, political and intellectual life generally . . . is very true for our own times, in which material interests predominate, but not for the middle ages, in which Catholicism, nor for Athens and Rome, where politics, reigned supreme. In the first place it strikes one as an odd thing for anyone to suppose that those well-worn phrases about the middle ages and the ancient world are unknown to anyone else. This much, however, is clear, that the middle ages could not live on Catholicism, nor the ancient on politics. *On the contrary, it is the economic conditions of the time that explain why here politics and there Catholicism played the chief part*' (*Capital*, I, 81n, modified – cited in Althusser and Balibar, *Reading Capital*, p. 217).

This 'determination in the last instance of the economy' remains enigmatic. It is a determination of the economy as technique and as an absence. As technique: 'the middle ages could not live on Catholicism.' Economic relations are reduced to the simple fact of material production. As an absence: it is the lack of relations of production as relations of exploitation which necessitates the existence of forms of domination as *mechanisms of exploitation*. Clearly, there is a silence here. Are these relations of domination, political-ideological mechanisms of exploitation imposed upon certain forms of material production, relations of production? This silence speaks volumes – it indicates a specific failure to think the character of the relation of the forces and relations of production in pre-capitalist modes of production.

In *Capital* Marx uses a relatively simple differentiation of capitalism/pre-capitalism, this is: (i) Capitalism = separation of the direct producer from the means of production, subsumption of the direct producer in a process of production structured by exploitative relations of production, dominance of the economic instance; (ii) pre-capitalist forms = non-separation of the direct producer, necessity of intervention of a non-economic form to secure and constitute the relations of exploitation, dominance of a non-economic instance. Marx can be satisfied with this because it is specific elements of the *capitalist* mode of production which are to be illustrated. But we cannot be satisfied with the comparison because it does not settle the question of the nature of pre-capitalist relations of production; it does not provide the *mechanism* by which exploitation takes place, and it provides no basis for differentiation between pre-capitalist modes of production. Indeed, this conception of pre-capitalist forms of exploitation tends to dissolve the specific modes of production into a generality, 'pre-capitalism'.

In order to go beyond Marx's conception it is necessary to develop the concept of exploitation and its connection with the relations of production. In Marx's discussion of pre-capitalist modes of production in chapter XLVII the problems stem from, on the one hand, a separation and, on the other hand, a conflation. First, Marx separates the mode of exploitation in capitalist and pre-capitalist modes of production; in the CMP exploitation takes place through an economic mechanism; in pre-capitalist modes exploitation exists through political or ideological coercion. Second, in the discussion of pre-capitalist forms of appropriation of the surplus-product two distinct levels are confused, the dominance of the political or ideological *instance*, and the political or ideological domination of *subject by subject*. The absence of a specific mechanism of exploitation, which is an effect of an articulated combination of forces and relations of production, conditions the reduction of political and ideological social relations to relations between subjects. Political or ideological domination is used to explain exploitation in the absence of a mechanism of exploitation deriving from the system of production, and this domination becomes the exploitation of man by man, a simple and direct relation between subjects. This is because it has no social conditions of existence. Definite political and ideological structures arise on the basis of the structure of the social relations of production, yet in this case political and ideological domination must be presupposed to constitute the social relations of production.

The dominance of the political instance is translated immediately into the political domination of exploiter over exploited; exploitation appears '*as a direct relation of lordship and servitude*'. Political dominance means that exploitation takes place by 'other than economic pressure'. The effect of the separation capitalism/pre-capitalism in *Capital* is that the capitalist economy becomes the measure of the economy *per se*, pre-capitalist forms of the *economy* are not discussed. The economic is consigned to the status of technique or of an absence which necessitates the presence of another instance. The dominance of, for example, the political is therefore not a dominance exercised *over* the economic instance and exercised *through* the structure of the economic instance, it is a direct relation of domination between *subjects*, between the political in the *person* of the exploiting superordinate and the economic in the *person* of the exploited subordinate direct producer. In the exchange where one subject compels another to obey him and to give to him a portion of the proceeds of his labour the entire problem of pre-capitalist forms of exploitation disappears.

It is here that the problem of the presupposition of the state which we have encountered in the case of tax/rent and feudal rent has its origin. The state not merely guarantees the title to property, or secures the class relations, it constitutes the titles, the classes, and it provides the condition for, and the means of, exploitation. The state appears as determinant and yet its role is undetermined and unexplained. Because the relation between *instances* is misrepresented as a relation between *persons*, political domination must take on a mystical character and the state must appear groundless, without conditions of existence. Because exploitation is conceived as domination, because relations of domination between subjects stand in the place of relations of production, the state becomes the sole condition of existence of exploitation. How is tax/rent extracted? Because the state has effective possession of the means of coercion. How is feudal rent extracted? Because the feudal lord as the personification of state power is able to compel the peasants to render labour-service, or to deliver a portion of their product or its money equivalent. The relations of production here are equivalent to the relations of the subject to the state, exploitation to taxation. The possibility of appropriating the surplus-product is determined by the level and the efficiency of the coercive means available: thus ideological means, in providing subordinate subjects with an extra-coercive rationale for compliance, is the most effective means of coercion. Such relations of exploitation can be superimposed upon various forms of production – since all they require is some form of material production. Politics creates the different forms of title, of subject and the methods of coercion. It is the particular features of the apparatus of political domination which differentiate the various pre-capitalist 'modes of exploitation of surplus-labour' and not the forms of production to which they are applied.

It should be clear that this conception of relations of production as relations of political domination, and this conception of the dominance of the political or ideological instance as the dominance of subject over subject entails a retreat from historical materialism. In particular, the 'direct relation of lordship and servitude' entails a retreat from structures of *social* relations to *inter-subjective* relations, a retreat toward Hegel. *Marx* does not go in that direction, he uses the pre-capitalist forms as illustrations and proceeds with the exposition in *Capital*. *But to take Marx at his word*, to take these positions as given and to attempt to elaborate pre-capitalist modes of production from them, cannot but lead in this direction.

The thesis that political relations are dominant under conditions of the non-separation of the labourer from the means of production has been problematised; however, the purpose of this problematisation is not to reject this thesis absolutely. In general the thesis is correct, but only on the condition that it be recognised as the site of a problem rather than its solution. The position that it is necessary to construct a concept of the economy for each mode of production that the economy is not a given, reducible to technique, certain human motives, etc., and that it is the relations of production which are the crucial element in any concept of the economic level, enables us to develop this problem. What is it that necessitates the 'dominance' of political or ideological relations in order that exploitation exist under conditions of the non-separation of the labourer from the means of production? This 'dominance' supposes that certain political structures provide certain conditions of existence of the relations of production; it does not suppose, however, that these relations of production are reducible to their conditions of existence. This *dominance* is not political *domination* in the simple humanist sense, the rule of subject over subject, but the domination of the political instance as part of a *structure in dominance*.

This dominance supposes the complex structure of a mode of production. The dominance of the political instance is exercised within this structure over and through the economic instance. In the absence of a distinct structure of the economic instance specific to a mode of production this dominance of the political is impossible, the political acts on and through the economic. The conditions of existence of the political instance are not mystical, the state is not groundless – in securing the conditions of existence of exploitative relations of production the political instance secures its own conditions of existence. The relations of production constitute an exploiting class, a class which provides the basis of the state. The political dominance provides the conditions of existence of exploitative relations of production *within the structure of the FMP*, these conditions must be secured at the political level if feudal relations of production are to exist. This is why the political instance is dominant; it is dominant *within* the structure of a mode of production. The political is not a 'first cause' which, once presupposed, enables us to explain domination and exploitation. If *its* conditions are not secured then the whole structure is threatened. As a structure of social relations it is quite unlike domination, a relation between subject and subject, whose conditions are not structural but rest on a trial of strength between inferior and superior.

This dominance of the political instance refers to the structure of a constituted mode of production – it is quite different from the political, legal and ideological *pre-conditions* of a mode of production's development. Capitalism presupposes certain political and legal conditions, 'primitive' accumulation, the wage form, etc., but in the CMP the relations of production are not dominated by the political as their condition of existence. Similarly, to argue that the political instance is dominant in the FMP in no way presupposes a certain set of pre-conditions or a certain *origin* of the FMP. It does not suppose that the FMP originates in conquest, in military/ideological subordination of the direct producers. The conception of feudal rent as a function of domination is driven in that direction, however; domination is presupposed as the condition of the rent, as its basis, force must exist as a prior condition.

We may contrast the two conceptions, domination and dominance, as follows: *domination*, exploitation merely provides the *material* foundation ('the Middle Ages could not live on Catholicism') for a political domination which is presupposed, the tribute extracted from direct producers who lack the capacity to resist a superior subject who plays no part as an agent in the process of production; *dominance* provides the conditions of existence of exploitative relations of production, which in turn provide the *social* foundation for the political instance by creating the division between exploiters and exploited – a division internal to the system of production, and thereby creating the ruling class.

The 'feudal' state arises because, within the structure of the FMP, the economic instance creates a division into classes of agents, exploiters and exploited, with a certain specific character. To understand what 'feudal' means we must forget all about the legal and constitutional history of the Middle Ages, 'feudal' will have a meaning in so far as we can give a determinate content to the phrase 'with a certain specific character'. In order to proceed in this direction let us return to the thesis of chapter XLVII; that the non-separation of the direct producer from the means of production involves the dominance of non-economic relations between exploiter and exploited if exploitation is to exist under pre-capitalist conditions. We have seen that the conception of this dominance as the forced exaction of a portion of the product is insupportable. It is true that if the direct producer were able to produce without the intervention or agency of the exploiter coercion would be needed to get him to part with a portion of his product. However, this supposes that the exploiter has a purely external relation to the process of production, that he intervenes only *after* this process has taken place. It is this *separation of the exploiter* from the means of production which is problematical. As it stands the thesis in chapter XLVII supposes that the direct producers are not and cannot be separatedfrom the means of production – hence the intervention of coercion as a mechanism of exploitation. This non-separation of the labourer/separation of the exploiter is not problematised in chapter XLVII. To give the thesis non-separation/dominance of the political a satisfactory form, this non-separation/separation must be problematised. We may reformulate the thesis thus: *the separation of the producer from the means of production, the condition of exploitative relations of production, depends upon political/ideological conditions of existence. The feudal economy supposes the intervention of another instance in order to make the conditions of feudal exploitation possible.* This thesis does not simply suppose the non-separation of the direct producer from the means of production, it concerns the mode in which he is separated from them, it indicates that separation is a *problem* (that its conditions are not like those of the CMP). The form in which the direct producers are separated from the means of production and subsumed within exploitative relations of production differentiates the distinct pre-capitalist modes of production (with, of course, the exception of primitive communism in which there is no system of exploitation and no classes). The mode in which this separation/subsumption/exploitation takes place determines the role of the political instance and the form of the state – Marx makes this point very clearly in the very chapter of *Capital* whose contents we have been criticising:

> The specific economic form in which unpaid surplus labour is pumped out of the direct producers, determines the relationship of rulers and ruled, as it grows directly out of production itself and, in turn, reacts upon it as a determining element (III, p. 772).

The feudal *economic instance* is the form which effects this separation/subsumption/exploitation, it is the structure which subordinates the direct producer. Without the subsumption of the direct producer under specifically *feudal* relations of production, and, therefore, the structuration of the labour process by those relations of production, it is impossible to have a mode of appropriation of the surplus-product specific to the FMP. This economic instance has political/ideological conditions of existence, *but it is through the structure of the feudal economy that exploitation takes place*. Exploitation in the feudal mode takes place at the level of the economy no less than in the CMP – it is the nature of the economy and its conditions of existence which are different, not the level at which exploitation takes place.

A 'feudal' mode of production exists if the direct producers are subsumed under specifically feudal relations of production – the FMP requires a *feudal* economic instance. We now have the basis on which to raise the question of the constitution of a concept of FMP. That basis is a question – can the existing concept of feudal rent be criticised and developed in order to yield a distinct form of separation of the labourer from the means of production and the subsumption of the labourer within exploitative relations of production? It should now be clear why it was impossible to begin with the question – can the concept of feudal rent be used to derive the mode of appropriation of surplus-labour specific to the FMP? In order to pose the question – feudal rent → feudal mode of production? – in the correct manner it has been necessary to problematise the conception of exploitation and the dominance of the political connected with the concept of feudal rent. Using these rectified concepts of exploitation and dominance we will now attempt to move from feudal rent to the feudal mode of production.

2 The concept of feudal mode of production

Our object in attempting to construct a concept of FMP is to establish an articulated combination of relations and forces of production, a combination structured by the dominance of the relations over the forces of production. This combination relations/forces is the feudal economic instance. The non-economic conditions of existence of this instance enable us to determine the specific content of political/ideological relations in the FMP. The minimum condition of this combination relations/forces, of the domination of the productive forces by the production relations, is that the relation of the labourer to the labour process is structured by the relations of production. That is, *the structure of the process of production is not independent of the conditions of appropriation of the surplus-product.*

In the case of tax/rent we have seen that the form of production carried on by the direct producers exists independently of and in a form unaltered by the extraction of tax/rent. Similarly, the existing concept of feudal rent supposes that the exploiter has no direct relation to the labour process, and that exploitation takes place externally to the process of production and after it has taken place. It would appear that feudal rent may be equated with tax/rent. However, does the existing concept of feudal rent provide any conditions for a mode of subsumption of the direct producers? Yes, it does, but only by default, as it were, through two elements which are given secondary significance in the existing concept. These elements are the concepts of *feudal landed property* and the *forms of payment* of the rent-in-kind, labour-service and money. The concept of feudal *rent* supposes a feudal landlord class, the ownership of the land by a specific class. The forms, as we have seen, are elaborated but are considered not to affect the basic nature of the rent.

Let us begin with the concept of feudal landed property (FLP). FLP remains an enigma while it is connected to the notion of feudalism as a relation of political domination between lord and serf. Landed property vanishes into the rule of the superordinate subject, the landlord into the *seigneur*. The fact that the lord has a *title* or right to the land is less important than the fact that the serf has a legally and politically subordinate status. If we ignore the element of personal domination the 'feudal' element in FLP may appear to have no foundation. Nothing could be further from the truth. All forms of landed property have specific political/legal conditions of existence, it is these conditions which give the term 'feudal' its content and these conditions are not reducible to the legal status of serfdom. For the moment we shall consider FLP nominally and abstractly as a politically sanctioned *title* to land. In and of itself the title means nothing more than the existence of certain legal rights in the land – as a *title* it has no necessary economic significance. For the purposes of our argument we shall suppose a *monopoly* of landownership – that is, that the land potentially available for productive use is the 'property' of the state, large landowners and free cultivators. We shall also suppose that the form of this politically sanctioned property is that the title to a large portion of the land is in the hands of few large landlords and that there are a substantial number of landless labourers. Having supposed these conditions we are interested in how the *title*, the political/legal property right, becomes *effective possession*, how the holder to a title comes to control the means of production and how definite mechanisms of exploitation are connected with the process of production.

How does FLP become effective possession? How are the direct producers subsumed under exploitative relations of production connected with FLP? In the case of the tax/rent couple we saw that the state as sole landlord stood in an external relation to the forms of production. In all cases of monopoly land ownership and land hunger titles may yield rents if they can be enforced. Feudal rent is not reducible to a payment for the right to use the land, not, that is, feudal rent as the mode of appropriation of surplus-labour in the FMP. FLP contains the possibility of a direct relation of the landlord to the process of production, this direct relation depends upon two elements: (i) the title to the land as a *right of exclusion*, and (ii) the forms of payment of the rent. The first provides a basis upon which the second operates – it is the forms of payment which are the primary element. All rent is based upon the title to the land as a right of exclusion; in this case the right to exclude the direct producers from the land is a necessary legal separation of the direct producers from the means of production upon which a real separation can be constituted. The *forms* of rent provide a means of control of the direct producers' relation to the means of production and the reproduction of the means of production. The political/legal form of *landlordship* makes possible the extraction of *rent*, but it is through the *forms* of rent that the conditions which make exploitation a necessary consequence of the system of production are created. Paradoxically, it is rent, a form of exploitation depending on landlordship, which makes possible rent as a form of exploitation based on the real economic subsumption of the direct producer. Rent in the first sense remains a politically/ideologically enforced deduction from the product; the labourer is not separated from the means of production – it is *feudal rent* as conceived in chapter XLVII (with an important exception, in this case it is not supposed that the tenant is a politically/legally subordinate subject). Rent in the second sense separates, and rests on the separation of, the direct producer from the means of production – it is both the form of exploitation and the condition of existence of that exploitation (like surplus-value in the CMP which is both the form in which the labourer is exploited and the condition of the continuing separation of the labourer from the means of production).

How does feudal rent in this second sense operate to produce its own necessity? *By controlling the size, the character and the reproduction of the units of production it makes the reproduction of the means of production simultaneously a reproduction of the exploitative production relations.* This is the mechanism which ensures the subsumption of the direct producer under feudal relations of production. This subsumption is not given (the direct producer is not automatically separated from his means of production); separation is a function of the intervention of the landlord. Separation/subsumption requires a definite policy and calculation on the part of the landlord. Subsumption is the object of a struggle between the landlord and the tenant/direct producer – the primary form of the class struggle in the FMP. It is only by means of the landlord's relative success in this struggle that the effective possession which characterises FLP in the FMP is maintained.

How do these two elements, the right of exclusion and the forms of rent, work to effect the separation/subsumption of the direct producer in concrete terms? Under pre-capitalist conditions of production, given the absence of generalised commodity production and the dominance of agricultural production, the labourer tends to have effective possession of the means of production. We have seen that title as a right of exclusion enables the landlord to exclude the direct producers from the use of the land if the legal and coercive means of state power are available to act on behalf of his title. The direct producers are therefore forced to pay rent for the right to use the land, to produce their own means of subsistence. Given the existence of rent in this sense the *forms* of rent can take effect. Through the *forms* of rent the landlord is able to control the direct producers by controlling: (i) the whole economy of the land to which he has title; (ii) crucial elements of the means of production and therefore of the access to subsistence of the direct producer; and (iii) the reproduction of the direct producers' means of production.

COMMENTS I

We have supposed, (i) that the whole of the land is governed by private property right and (ii) that the landlord owns and controls both the land on which the direct producers produce their own means of subsistence and that on which they produce the surplus-product. *Given these suppositions then there is no reason why the direct producer should be the legal subordinate and bondsman of the landlord.* The legally sanctioned unfreedom of the direct producer is not only not necessary, it is problematical; serfdom as a legal status has no more economic reality than has landed property as title. Serfdom as a formal legal status means nothing if the serf has effective possession of the means of production and if the landlord lacks the means to exploit the serf to more than a limited and customary degree – the serf is then equivalent to a tenant. However, the subsumption of the direct producer under exploitative relations of production, whether he is legally a free man or not, creates conditions of economic surbordination to and dependence on the exploiter. There is no need to suppose unfree *personal* status to arrive at the real relations of serfdom. There is no need to suppose the legal subordination of the individual. The dominance of the landlord class in the state or the preparedness of the state to sanction and enforce titles to the land is all that is required. FLP as title, as an enforced right of exclusion, is a sufficient means to bring free men under feudal exploitative relations. It should be noted that this conclusion, while it shatters certain myths about the FMP – derived from and illustrated by the 'history' of the European Middle Ages – is supported by the arguments of several medieval historians. Vinogradoff, in particular, argues that there were large numbers of free tenants and freemen holding in villainage throughout the eleventh and twelfth centuries, and that the widespread commutation of labour services and other obligations for money rents in the thirteenth century was in no sense a dissolution of feudalism.[4] Postan[5] shows that servile or villein legal status was in practice no bar to making contracts, owning property, buying and leasing land, and even to taking action in defence of property rights in the courts.

COMMENTS II

Given that separation/subsumption is possible, then it is not the case that under the FMP the direct producer has 'possession of the means of production' – this must be qualified. We may note here that the concepts possession of/separation from the means of production must be specified for different modes of production. In the CMP the worker is separated from the means of reproduction of his *labour-power*. This separation exists on two levels: (i) from the means of production as *property* – the labourer does not own the means of reproduction of his labour-power, hence he must sell his labour-power in order to subsist; (ii) from the capacity to set the means of production in motion – the worker has a specific function in the process of production, which is organised *as a process* by the capitalist. The worker is separated from the means of production through the wage form, he relates to them only through the sale of his labour-power and by that sale he places his concrete labour, as the use-value of that commodity and for the period of the wage contract, at the service and direction of another. In the FMP the direct producer is separated from the means of production in a different sense. In the absence of demesne production the labourer can set the means of production in motion; under demesne production the means of production by which he produces his subsistence are under his control. However, this capacity to organise and to use the means of producing his subsistence is a limited one, for the tenant/labourer does not control all the elements necessary to production in the feudal economy and he has this capacity only within the conditions and period of his tenure. Although he may *own* the instruments of production, have tenant-right to the land, and be able to organise the production of his subsistence, he does not control the *reproduction* of means and conditions of production. It is primarily through the control of the reproduction of the means of production that the landlord/exploiter separates the tenant/labourer from the means of production. It should be noted, nevertheless, that the control of the production of the *surplus-product* under demesne production, and the ownership and operation of certain important means of production (mills, dykes, etc.), are important means of control of the conditions of reproduction for the feudal landlord.

How do the forms of rent provide mechanisms of control and subsumption which enable the landlord to exploit the direct producer? These mechanisms are as follows:

(i) FLP entails the possibility of *labour-rent*. Labour-rent involves the division of the landlord's land into a portion which reproduces the labourer and a portion on which the surplus-product is produced. Labour-rent makes possible *demesne* production: the demesne is the land on which the rent for non-demesne land is rendered in the form of labour service. The existence of the demesne gives rise to a form of production under the control of the landlord: here the landlord functions as the agent of co-ordination of the process of production. Demesne production gives the landlord a direct and functional relation to the process of production. More important than this for our present concerns is the possibility of control of the whole manorial economy that demesne production provides. The proportion of demesne land to rented land and the level of labour service obligations determine the balance of necessary-labour and surplus-labour. The balances demesne land/rented land, necessary-labour/surplus-labour, control the whole organisation of the economy of the 'manor'.[6] These balances determine the conditions of production on the land rented by the direct producers – an extreme example would be where the proportion of demesne land is such that the rented plots of the direct producers are insufficient to produce the necessary means of subsistence, here the labour-rent of the tenant will be supplemented by wage-labour. We may illustrate this example by reference to the large proportion of *cottars* forced to sell their labour-power on many English feudal estates. This depressed class of sub-tenants provided the casual labour needs of well-to-do peasants and the regular demands of the demesne for wage-labour to supplement or to replace labour-service.[7]

It should be noted that demesne production does not presuppose that all rent is labour-rent or that the majority of tenants render their rents in the form of labour-service. The balance demesne land/rented land is a variable one.

(ii) The landlord can control the reproduction of the direct producers' own units of production through the size of the units let, the form of the tenancy and the level of the rent. (a) By controlling the size of the units let (even if there is no demesne) the landlord can ensure that *the units of tenancy do not correspond to the units of production*, that the units let cannot in and of themselves produce and support all the means of production that are necessary. The direct producer is thereby placed in a contradictory position if he rents the land for rent-in-kind or a money-rent. He is required to render a definite rent which can be expressed as a portion of his product – this supposes he has the means to produce this rent. Yet the very conditions of his tenancy place his capacity to render that rent under the control of the landlord – the tenant is not in fact an independent producer. An example would be where the plough teams necessary to cultivation can only be assembled by the combination of units of tenancy, each contributing one or two of the necessary draught animals. If it is the landlord who acts as the agency of combination of these units then through this function of combination he is able to dominate the organisation of production and coerce any individual direct producer who challenges him. Where the producers as a community control this combination then the landlord is unable to subsume the direct producers through this mechanism.[8] (b) By controlling the form of the tenancy, in particular the conditions of re-tenancy, by varying the size of the units let and re-let, the landlord can control the conditions of reproduction of individual direct producers. By using these measures the landlord can prevent the development of holdings large enough to contain all the necessary means of production, can prevent autonomous exchanges between tenants which redistribute the land, and can render void any attempts by the larger and more enterprising tenants to increase the size of their holdings and thereby attain a measure of autonomy. (c) The landlord may control other essential means of production other than land for cultivation; into this class come pasture land and water. By controlling the letting of pasture or determining the number of animals allowed to graze on common pasture the landlord can control a vital means of production. By controlling the numbers of livestock and charging for them the landlord can control the conditions of production of individual tenants, he can limit or promote their wealth, and they have no guarantee that their pasture-rights or livestock holdings are secure beyond an immediate period.

(iii) Given the landlord's receipt of surplus-product in the form of rent and the fact that the landlord is the only agent in the unit of landholding whose conditions of possession are reasonably secure, then he can amass and control certain means of production which are beyond the capacity of any tenant to produce or which it is not worthwhile for him to accumulate the resources to produce. These means of production may be vital elements in the process of production which it is necessary that every tenant have access to. Examples of such means of production are mills and large-scale drainage works. The ownership of such means enables the landlord to dominate the whole economy of his land (and perhaps that of free cultivators and lesser landlords) and to levy additional rents for the right to use or to have access to these means.

In examining the means of subsumption of the direct producers under exploitative relations of production we have started from these suppositions: (i) that under pre-capitalist conditions the separation of the labourer from the means of production is problematical; (ii) from the conception of landed property as monopoly possession of the land; and (iii) that the form of landed property differentiates between a landlord class and a class of landless direct producers. The political/legal instance is limited in its intervention to the determination and defence of property rights in land. The subsumption of the direct producer has been derived only in the first instance from the monopoly ownership of the land, from the *right of exclusion*. Subsumption rests on economic control. Legal title does not make a landlord, and landlordship does not guarantee subsumption. We have not derived subsumption from the political/legal subordination of the direct producers to the landlord – FLP and seignorial power are not equivalents.

The tenant holds under economic conditions which subordinate him to the landlord as an exploiter; these conditions are based upon the monopoly possession of the land. Feudal rent might in this case appear to be a pre-capitalist form of absolute rent, a form which also derives from the monopoly possession of the land. However, absolute rent supposes the mechanism of the market, a compulsion stemming from competition for a scarce resource. In the absence of the market and of competition, the mechanisms which generate absolute rent, this form of rent cannot exist. Under capitalism private ownership of land can generate rents which are *deductions* from profits and wages;[9] title to landed property (where it exists) is defended by the state as is all private property (from the factory to the workers' possessions). Titles in conditions other than these require other mechanisms for their conversion from *rights* into *facts*. How does the landlord prevent the appropriation of the land by the direct producers? This is particularly difficult if there are large reserves of land available for colonisation. Under such conditions to exact rent supposes not only a general title to property enforced by the state, but the political dominance of the landlord class, a state in which the landlord class is the dominant force represented. This dominance of the landlord class must, as we have seen, rest upon the economic subsumption of the direct producers. Feudal rent, unlike absolute rent, must therefore be the primary mode of appropriation of surplus-labour if it is to exist.

That the state effectively guarantees the right of exclusion and sanctions monopoly possession supposes that the direct producers are not the dominant class in the state, that their representatives do not exercise state power. It does not suppose the *personal* unfreedom of the direct producers; indeed, there is no reason in theory why they should not have equal legal rights and some form of political representation. Feudal relations of production do not suppose serfdom, nor do they suppose that the landlord has seignorial power. The landlord may have no political rights over his tenants and may be forced to proceed against them through state courts. The feudal state may be highly centralised and the landlord may have no guaranteed or privileged access to state power – such a state machine, while reducing the political independence of the members of the landlord class, may nevertheless represent that class's interests more effectively and guarantee feudal landed property.[10] The political dominance of the landlord *class* and of the *landlord* are quite different things. Equally, the forms in which that class predominates in the state can vary; thus French absolutism, while it subordinated the nobles politically, continued to depend on them as its social base and it continued to defend feudal exploitation.[11]

Political dominance provides the conditions of existence of feudal exploitation, but the form of that exploitation is necessarily economic. The feudal economy creates the objective conditions of existence of the feudal state, it creates and reproduces the division of the classes landlord/exploiter, tenant/labourer, which forms the social base of the feudal state. It is the economic subsumption of the direct producers on which the FMP rests.

What is 'feudal' about these relations of production and this form of state? In fact nothing is 'feudal' about them in so far as the word 'feudal' refers to the specific legal forms and political conditions of the European Middle Ages, to serfdom or seignorial power. We retain the term 'feudal' because of its currency in Marxist theoretical discourse, because this concept has been derived from Marx's concept. Feudal relations of production can exist wherever the conditions of FLP exist – serfdom, a baronial state, manorialism, etc., have nothing to do with 'feudalism' in this sense.

3 The relations of production and the forces of production

We have criticised at length the existing Marxist conception of the FMP and we have attempted to develop another and distinct concept, specifying in a very different way the nature of feudal relations of production. Having specified those relations it is necessary to show that they form an articulated combination with a specific set of forces of production – forces of production dominated by feudal relations of production.

Three elements of the feudal relations of production are particularly important in constituting this articulated combination. These elements are:

(i) that the subsumption of the tenant/labourer is not a given – the level of the landlord's control of the means of production and the ratio of surplus- to necessary-labour are not fixed, they are determined by a class struggle between landlord and labourer;

(ii) that the forms of feudal rent entail a particular relationship between necessary-labour and surplus-labour for the labourer;

(iii) demesne production, an effect of the labour-service forms of feudal rent, constitutes a differential and opposed relation of landlord and labourer to the labour process as a process of producing the surplus-product. These three elements of the relations of production structure the forces of production. The forms of distribution of the means of production and the forms of appropriation of the surplus-product determine the relation of the labourer to the labour process and assign a place to the exploiting non-labourer in the organisation of production.

Before analysing how the relations of production affect the relations of the agents to the process of production it is necessary to characterise those agents more carefully. In so doing we will be able to specify in more detail the forces of production peculiar to the FMP. So far the agents have been defined as the landlord and the tenant/labourer. It has been supposed that individual tenants (and their families) rent the land and that the units rented are worked as independent units of production. Why is the form of tenancy individual? Why is the land cultivated by independent tenants? These questions are pertinent because we have not yet logically and explicitly eliminated communal forms of tenure and cultivation. If communal production and independent tenant production were both possible then our analysis of the FMP would be subject to at least some of the criticisms levelled against the notion of an AMP in the previous chapter.

Why is tenancy not communal? Communal forms of land tenure necessarily involve the commune's control and organisation of production; the collective tenant creates a division of labour and distributes the labour of its members to distinct tasks. The commune controls the distribution of the product of necessary-labour among its members. It merely renders surplus-labour or the surplus-product to the landlord as nominal ground-rent after production has taken place. The landlord does not intervene as an agent in the process of production. The landlord is separated from effective possession of the means of production through the commune's control of its members' labour, and the landlord therefore has no means of subsuming the direct producers. The landlord does not deal with a tenant/labourer but with a collective tenant. Further, the commune, unlike an individual tenant, cannot be evicted without totally disrupting production.

The right of exclusion is only effective if the landlord is large enough to rent the land to several communes and if he has the coercive means to overcome communal resistance to eviction. Communal forms of tenure and production completely undercut the two bases of feudal relations of production, the control of the organisation of production and the right of exclusion. No feudal mode of production is possible with communal forms of tenure and production.

In the FMP the individual tenants may *co-operate* in certain tasks, and this co-operation may be affected either by the landlord's will or by agreement among the tenants; however, the organisation of production is not *communal.* Co-operation involves the uniting of *independent* units of production for specific tasks while in communal forms a *single* unit of production combines and co-ordinates the activities of labouring of its members.

COMMENTS

It is sometimes thought that the systems of production in medieval England and the forms of production and land tenure in pre-Emancipation Russia were communal. This is not the case. Tenure was *individual* in both England and Russia. In England the system of collective responsibility in the village community pertained to the maintenance and administration of the *common laws,* not to *production,* and included free cultivators as well as feudal tenants.[12] In Russia the elements of periodic redistribution of the units of land and collective tax responsibility did not amount to communal tenure; Blum (1961) argues that redistribution was imposed by the landlords. In England *fields* might be common but the *land* was not; strips within the fields were strictly differentiated.[13] Such elements of co-operation as did exist were based upon agreement between independent cultivators, and, particularly if there was demesne land, the landlord or his agent.

In addition to the landlord and the tenant/labourer there may be cottars or landless labourers. Both the landlord and the tenant may hire wage-labour; the landlord to supplement or to replace labour-service on demesne land, the labourer to *supplement* the labour-power of his family. If the tenant uses wage-labour not to supplement but to *replace* family labour then he becomes an exploiter who pays ground-rent rather than an exploited direct producer. When the tenant relies principally upon wage-labour he can no longer be considered as a feudal tenant but as a proto-capitalist or capitalist farmer. This would be the case even if he still retained the formal legal status of serf (if, that is, such legal relations exist in the given conditions). Feudal relations of production do not prohibit landlessness and wage-labour. In addition to providing necessary supplementary labour they actually re-enforce these relations. For the landlord they perform the function of the industrial reserve army, they stoke the fires of land hunger and give force to the right of exclusion.

The relation of the agents, landlord and tenant/labourer, to the labour process as a process of production and a process of exploitation will now be examined.*

LABOURER

All the forms of feudal rent, labour-service, rent-in-kind and money-rent create a specific form of division of necessary-labour and surplus-labour. In the case of labour-rent there is a direct physical separation between the labour which reproduces the labourer on land which he rents and the labour of producing the surplus-product (rent) for the landlord on demesne land. In the case of money-rent and rent-in-kind, surplus-labour is expressed as a calculable and measurable portion of the total product. The relation of surplus-labour to necessary-labour in feudal rent is a direct separation of different magnitudes (of hours of labour, bushels of corn, sums of money). Surplus-labour or the surplus-product appears as a *deduction* from the labour-time or the product available to the labourer – unlike the wage form in which the wage appears as a *compensation* for the labour expended.[14] The relation surplus-labour to necessary-labour is open to relatively simple calculation, unlike slave labour or wage-labour, in which the portions of the working day which produce SL and NL are not readily calculable. The relation SL/NL, the form in which production and exploitation are combined in the labour process, is important in its effect on the differential relation of the labourer to working for himself and for the exploiter, and on the forms of economic class struggle.

LANDLORD

In the case of labour-rent and demesne production the exploiting non-labourer has a specific function in the process of production,

* In order to simplify the exposition it will be assumed throughout that the tenant is primarily an agricultural producer and that the surplus-product takes the form of agricultural produce.

that of co-ordination and supervision. In demesne production the work of labouring and the task of the organisation of production do not coincide, hence the non-labourer is assigned the function of co-ordination. In demesne production all labour on the demesne is surplus-labour to the labourer, hence the necessity of supervision. From this it might appear that demesne production is equivalent to slave production, but this is not the case. There are two significant differences. The first is that, unlike the slave, the labourer does have a systematic compulsion to render surplus-labour. This compulsion is that surplus-labour is a *rent* for the land on which the labourer produces his means of subsistence and if he does not render that rent he can be compelled to quit. The second is that the labourer brings with him to demesne production the methods of working (and possibly the instruments of production) which he uses in the labour for his own reproduction. The labourer is therefore unlike the slave, who has to be given the instruments of production and instructed in the methods of their use. The fact that feudal labour brings with it determinate social skills is both an advantage to and a limitation on the landlord. The limitation is that if the landlord attempts to use instruments or methods other than those customary, then instruction becomes a necessity, supervision becomes more complex, and the costs of co-ordination and supervision rise. The development of the forces of production in the FMP is therefore limited to developing the productivity of the labour of the tenant *within the limits set by independent peasant production.* To go beyond these limits involves adopting another labour system and form of exploitation, wage-labour.

In the case of money-rent and rent-in-kind, given that the landlord controls the distribution of at least some of the means of production, he is able to affect the organisation of production and to compel the rendering of a level of surplus-labour above that possible in the case of a simple rent based on the sanctioned right of exclusion. The more effective the control of the means of production and the more effective the control of the organisation of production the higher the potential level of exploitation. Far from being confined in his intervention in the process of production to demesne production, the landlord can so control the direct producers that even when there is no demesne and all rent is rent-in-kind or money-rent they do not have effective possession of the means of production.

COMMENTS

Money-rent supposes a commodity production sector in the

economy and the sale of a portion of his product as a commodity by the direct producer. It does not, however, necessarily signify greater freedom and less exploitation for the labourer. The landlord may control the reproduction of the means of production, certain vital auxiliary means of production, and he may control the conditions of sale, acting as or through a merchant/money-lender. More important than this, however, is that money-rent, being dependent on the *sale* of commodities, is threatened by fluctuations in demand, bad harvests, and by the operations of merchants. This is particularly the case in that the commodity production associated with feudal rent consists of a *surplus* over subsistence production. In the case of rent-in-kind a bad harvest may reduce the level of receipts in a given year, but as the upper level of the crop is relatively fixed it cannot easily be recouped in succeeding years even if harvests are good, especially if the rate of exploitation is high. With money-rents the shortfall in rent due to fluctuations, bad harvest, etc., can be converted into a *debt* (and perhaps subjected to interest) which is paid off in successive years, however long it takes. Through such debts the landlord may tighten his grip over the tenant/labourer. He may convert the debt into labour service, seize means of production, etc. Hence the falsity of the conception of the commutation of labour services to money rents as a dissolution of feudal relations.[15] (It should be noted that while each of the forms of rent has been examined separately, and their logical features derived, they may be and are in fact combined.)

The relations of the labourer and the exploiting non-labourer to the labour process are complex and asymmetrical. The different forms of rent and the struggle for and against subsumption create different relations of the labourer and the non-labourer to the labour process as a process of production and a process of exploitation. These complex and opposed relations define the space of the economic class struggle in the FMP. It is the forms of the class struggle and their outcomes which determine the specific forms of the forces of production in the FMP and their variation. The relations of production produce a complex structure of antagonistic 'interests' on the part of the labourers and their exploiters.

COMMENTS

By 'interests' we mean objects pertinent to the agents imposed by the structure of the mode of production, for example, the object of the labourer *qua* agent is to resist subsumption. It is not supposed that these 'interests' are represented to human subjects through the mechanism of 'experience' – our strictures against this will be recalled from the chapter on slavery. Landlord and labourer are economic *categories* not concrete subjects. The ideologies by which representations are constituted for subjects are not given by the definition of the structure of the FMP or the characterisation of the agents. Such ideologies may produce effects which contradict these 'interests' – for example, believers who render extra and voluntary labour-service on the demesne of the religious foundation from which they rent land. It is the object of this text to constitute a *general* concept of FMP, not to analyse particular social formations in which feudal social relations are an element, and their ideological and political forms.

The basic form of the economic class struggle in the FMP is the struggle for and against subsumption. It is the *site* of this class struggle which is economic – the struggle for effective possession of the means of production. This struggle presupposes the landlord's legal property rights and tenancy as its conditions. The *means* of this struggle are not confined to the economic, they may be political/legal, and/or ideological. Thus peasant 'revolts' are not necessarily attempts to overthrow feudal social relations any more than workers' demonstrations, the election of workers' representatives, etc., are necessarily anything but a political defence of the conditions of trade-union struggle.[16] The struggle which takes place on the basis of feudal landed property is a struggle to make the *tenant* a *subordinate direct producer*. The object of the landlord is the economic subsumption of the tenants, the separation of the tenants from the means of production. The object of the tenant is autonomy as a producer and to pay no more than a limited rent for the right to use the land, that is, to control the conditions of his reproduction as an independent producer.

The forms of these antagonistic 'interests' and the means of struggle to attain them will now be outlined.

LABOURER

The general 'interests' of the labourer are effective possession of the means of production (land + instruments of production), to control the reproduction of these means, and to minimise the extraction of surplus-labour/surplus-product.

In the case of labour-service, apart from the compulsion to labour involved in renting land, the labourer gains nothing from rendering more than the acceptable minimum of labour-time, effort and skill. Moreover, if the labourer does not use his own instruments and accustomed methods of production the productivity of his labour and his care for the means of labour is dependent on the landlord's organisation and supervision. The labourer has no reason to develop, or to co-operate in developing, the forces of production involved in demesne production. The labourer has a differential relation to labour for his own reproduction and labour-service. Under other forms of rent the labourer may have an interest in developing the productivity of his labour, but only given certain conditions, as we shall see.

The means of realisation of the interests of the labourer are the following.

(i) *Political/ideological struggle*

This involves an attempt to undercut the political/ideological conditions of FLP and of tenancy. Such struggle may take two forms: political class struggle, and the use of the existing political/legal apparatus of the state. In the first case the tenants/labourers as a collectivity either attempt to overthrow the political dominance of the landlord class in the state, or attempt to solicit reforms or remissions within feudal social relations but outside of the existing political/legal framework. The revolutionary course supposes conditions of transition and an advanced ideological foundation for the labourers' political practice. An example of the 'reformist' course is the 'Peasants' Revolt' of 1381. This revolt was a protest against the attempt of the landlord class to impose villein status and servile tenure on tenants holding on non-servile customary terms.[17] In the second case collectivities of tenants or individual tenants use the legitimate political and legal means available to them to improve or to preserve their conditions of tenure. An illustration of this form of struggle is the frequent pleas of English feudal tenants to Royal courts for recognition of freeman status and release from servile obligations.[18] In both of these forms of struggle, the tenants attempt to prevent or to revise subsumption by attacking the political/legal conditions on which it rests, or changing the terms of these conditions.

(ii) *Improvements in productivity*

Under certain conditions the tenant/labourer has an 'interest' in developing the forces of production on the land which he rents. This is an effect of the relations of production since the primary object in raising the productivity of labour is to reduce exploitation. Increases in productivity can have this effect where the landlord's control of the means of production is relatively weak – the landlord cannot therefore simply raise the rate of exploitation. Rising productivity can lead to a reduction in the rate of exploitation because of the character of feudal rent and the relative fixity of the terms of the rent. In the FMP, unlike capitalist or slave production, in which increases in productivity go directly to the exploiter, the labourer can retain whatever portion of the product remains after the terms specified for the rent (surplus-product) are met. The surplus-product is specified in a certain number of days of labour-service, a portion of the product or a sum of money.

A larger total product, given that the rent is fixed as a definite amount of produce expressed in labour-time or money, means that the surplus-product is a smaller portion of the total. This larger product may be produced by increasing the productivity, intensity or duration of labour. Even if, as would usually be the case with rent-in-kind, the rent is fixed as a *proportion* of the crop the labourer in raising the total product raises his own standard of living. With labour-service it is only on the land which he rents that the labourer has an interest in raising the productivity of his labour or increasing the product. In raising the productivity of his labour on demesne land the labourer merely assists in increasing the landlord's surplus-product. In this respect demesne work is similar to slave production or wage-labour; all increases in productivity go to the exploiter.

Such developments challenge the control of the exploiter. The rent can only be altered upwards to meet these increases in productivity or in the size of the product if the landlord can find means to secure greater economic control over the tenants or if state support can be obtained to sanction increased exactions through increased oppression.

In order to raise the level of production and reduce the level of exploitation it is more effective to increase the *productivity* of labour rather than its *duration* or *intensity*. A lengthening of the working day, especially in agriculture, is not necessarily possible or effective: given the relatively low productivity of labour implied in pre-capitalist production that day is already long, the technical means to work at night in the open will not be available, and agricultural work is seasonal. Harder work, given existing instruments and methods, must mean a greater drain on labour-power, and, after a certain point, diminishing returns. Improvements in productivity involve such things as new methods of working, improvements in division of labour and co-operation, improvements in the instruments of production, augmentation of existing forms of labour-power (e.g. by wage-labour) and the development of new branches or production (e.g. handicraft work at night or in the slack season). Time saved in the production of staples may create time for other forms of work, on industrial or cash crops, on improving the instruments of production, etc.

Certain methods of improving productivity presuppose the co-operation of the direct producers, and also perhaps the landlord. Improvements in crop rotation with a common field system involve general co-operation, including the landlord if the demesne is included in the common fields. Co-operative ownership and operation of vital means of production, e.g. larger and heavier plough teams, formed from the combination of separately-owned draught animals, restrict the autonomy of individual tenants.[19] It is difficult to prevent such benefits of improvements in productivity as stem from such co-operative forms from being conferred on the landlord also, if there is demesne production. Rising social productivity of labour benefits the landlord.

It should be noted that it is not only in the interests of *reducing* the level of exploitation that labourers may develop the forces of production. Under conditions of land hunger, money-rents and tenant indebtedness the labourer may be racked to the utmost. He may be forced to increase the productivity, the intensity and the duration of his labour in order to meet rising rents. Productivity is increased not to reduce exploitation, or to raise the standard of living, but to pay for and to retain the means to produce a bare subsistence. Where a steady market for handicraft commodities, services, or seasonal labour exists, as is the case with large cities, merchants, capitalist trade, or the capitalist world market, the labourer may be forced to augment the productivity of his labour by night work, or handicraft or wage-labour in the slack season. Such intense exploitation and seasonal migratory labour were characteristic features of the feudal forms of tenancy and landholding in pre-revolutionary China.[20]

(iii) By renting or purchasing land *outside* of the control of the landlord. For example, buying or renting from a free cultivator. In this way the tenant may reduce the level of his dependence upon the landlord and reduce his acreage of rented land. Under conditions where the labourer is personally unfree or, more important, *holds in villeinage* (i.e. a freeman holds a tenure subject to servile obligations), this provides a toehold in the legal struggle for free status or a means of escaping a tenancy with servile conditions. By sub-letting among themselves the tenants can effect a distribution of land which corresponds to need, to demand, and which challenges the landlord's attempt to control the economy of the unit of landholding through the size of the units let. Thus large families which need more land and have the labour-power to cultivate it, or rich peasants seeking to expand, may obtain land without recourse to the landlord.[21]

(iv) By co-operation between tenant/labourers in the organisation of production and possession of the means of production. The tenants acting as a body may rent or own certain means of production, common pasture, mills, etc. By collective action they may obtain better terms from the landlord or control means of production too hazardous for the individual tenant to own under the landlord's policy of *divide et impera*.

LANDLORD

The general 'interests' of the landlord are the conversion of property right into the economic subsumption of the direct producers, which involves the control of the conditions of reproduction of the tenants' means of production, and the maximisation of exploitation. We have already discussed at some length the means available to the landlord to achieve these objects; here only those means which affect the form of or the level of development of the forces of production will be considered.

(i) Like the labourer the landlord, under certain conditions, has an 'interest' in the development of the forces of production. A landlord with a steady and expandable demand for the produce of the demesne (to support unproductive consumption of some kind), or who can sell the product of the demesne as a commodity (particularly in the case of production for capitalist markets), has an interest in raising the productivity of labour on demesne land. By increasing the productivity of surplus-labour the landlord increases the surplus-product. Improvements in the productivity of labour on demesne land are possible through increased supervision and raising the intensity of labour – although the cost of supervision must be set against the increase in productivity. Improvements are also possible through changing the organisation of production (for example, concentrating the fields of the demesne) and through developing the instruments of production. Such improvements augment the productivity of the process of production to which the labourer is accustomed rather than radically changing that process.

In addition to raising the productivity of surplus-labour, the level of surplus-labour and the ratio of demesne land to rented land may be increased. As we have seen, this presupposes the economic and political means to overcome the resistance of the tenants. Given that the duration of labour-service is relatively fixed, it is through increasing the productivity of surplus-labour that the landlord can most easily raise the level of exploitation. To do so the landlord requires time or personnel for supervision or co-ordination. The larger landlord who can support specialist functionaries for administration, calculation and supervision is most able to improve the productivity of demesne land. Indeed, the small landlord who is compelled to rely on his family to provide the means of supervision may find demesne production has few advantages and convert to another form of rent.

Examples of conditions favourable to the development of the productivity of surplus-labour, the increase in the level of labour services and the expansion of the demesne are:

(a) where the landlord can use the increased product to support and to expand political or ideological activities, and has the necessary administrative means – thus in England the religious foundations made extensive use of labour-rent and demesne production, they tended to persist with labour-services longer, to manage their estates more carefully and to supervise production more thoroughly, and to defend their rights to labour-service more tenaciously than any other type of feudal landlord;

(b) where the product of the demesne can be sold as a commodity – Kosminsky has shown the close correlation in thirteenth-century England between the existence of commodity markets and demesne production, and in Russia, as Blum (1961) argues, labour-service was developed and intensified with the development of a commodity market for wheat from the sixteenth century onwards.

(ii) Where the resistance of tenants to increased labour-service is strong, where commodity production is possible, and where there is a cottar class the landlord may substitute for labour-service, or supplement labour-service with wage-labour. The tenants may be prepared to pay a money-rent on the land they hold rather than perform labour-service. The landlord can, therefore, both develop commodity production and receive a steady (though smaller) income in rents. It should be noted that such practices on the part of landlords are not necessarily signs of a transition toward capitalism; the bulk of the labouring population is not separated from the land, generalised commodity production does not exist, and wage-labour produces only a *portion* of the surplus-product. Indeed, such a move may *strengthen* feudal social relations, re-enforcing the ties that bind the bulk of the labourers to the land. Wage-labour may *supplant* labour-service but it *supplements* feudal rent. Wage-labour is employed within the general system of feudal relations of production.

(iii) The small landlord without a demesne, under conditions of commodity production, has an interest in encouraging the development of the productivity of his tenants' labour. He receives a steady if relatively fixed income in money-rents and is relieved of the burden of supervision involved in labour-service. If peasant productivity rises then, given that he has some means of economic control, the tenants will be less resistant to rises in money-rents.

The basic form of the forces of production in the FMP is the labour of the individual tenant cultivator. This may be augmented by co-operation, intensified by supervision in the case of labour-service, and supplemented by wage-labour. None of these forms can supplant tenant production within the feudal relations of production: co-operation is a development of these forms, and communal production is antithetical to feudal relations of production; demesne production cannot supplant independent tenant cultivation because of the form of rent implied in labour-service – to replace rented land by demesne land it is necessary to convert the tenant/labourer into a *slave*; wage-labour cannot supplant tenant cultivation except in the process of transition to a capitalist agriculture. Independent tenant cultivation is dominant, the dominance of this form of the forces of production is an effect of feudal relations of production, it is an effect of the forms of feudal rent.

It will have been noted that the conception of the FMP developed here in no way excludes extensive sectors of commodity production, and a strong element of wage-labour relations. It differs from conventional notions of feudalism in that the feudal landlord intervenes as an agent in the process of production. Although we have devoted considerable space to the discussion of demesne production in this chapter this is in no way meant to imply that labour-rent is the primary form of feudal rent.

4 Variant forms of the FMP

From the preceding section it will be evident that the structure of the FMP includes within it a space of complex variation and that the forms of this variance are largely determined by the class struggle. Variant forms are not empirical givens *outside* of the concept of a mode of production, but are specified by the concept. It is not empirical difference but a theoretically defined and necessary variation which concerns us here. The general concept of FMP in defining the articulated combination of relations and forces of production designates the space of variation and all the variant forms possible within this space. Specific social formations necessarily exhibit only some of the variants and these variant forms are the mode of existence of the FMP in these conditions. *Variants*, specific variant forms, are a necessary effect of the structure of *variance*. Which variants predominate is determined by the class struggle. The structure of feudal social relations has been so defined that the dominance of certain variant forms is inevitable, all the variants cannot exist together. All the variants are internal to the structure of the FMP, the dominance of certain variants or of others does not change that structure but represents the modality of its existence.[22]

In this section we will consider variations in which one of the three forms of rent is dominant, in the level of subsumption of the direct producers, in the differential relation of the landlord and labourer to the forces of production, and in the forces of production themselves, which together form a complex unity. This complex unity of related variant forms which constitute a specific mode of existence of the FMP will be termed a *set*. These sets of variants define the characteristics of the FMP within a particular social formation – they are not simply co-present elements, but as a unity are the specific form of the structure of the FMP in these conditions. The variant elements which form a set exist in a hierarchy of dominance – certain of the forms are more important than others.

How are such sets constituted? By the specific forms and outcomes of the economic and political struggle between the classes, and by the conditions which affect the terms of the class struggle. Conditions which cannot be specified in the general concept of the mode, for example, the level of development of commodity markets, the intrusion of capitalist trade and capitalist production, the amount of land reserves suitable for colonisation, etc., affect the terms of the class struggle and the relative position of the parties. These conditions act through the structure of the mode in that they alter the terms of the class struggle but it is that struggle which determines the resultant forms.

The best way to explain what a set is in more detail is to give some illustrations. Two very different sets of variants will be contrasted below. It must be insisted on that these sets are illustrations. They do not exhaust all the possible variants or sets which may be generated from the structure of the FMP.

SET I

Here we will suppose extensive opportunities for commodity production.

(a) If we suppose in addition that the landlord class is supported by state power and that, in general, there is a high level of economic subsumption of the direct producers, then the following variant forms will exist and combine in a complex unity:

(i) the dominance of the form of rent labour-rent, the expansion of demesne production and increases in the level of exploitation;

(ii) the conversion of demesne production to wage-labour, the differentiation of the peasantry into a labourer or cottar class and independent tenants paying money-rents;

(iii) on smaller estates a tendency for the demesne to disappear and be replaced by money-rents;

(iv) increasing differentiation of the peasantry and the appearance of the rich peasant who hires wage-labour. These forms constitute a unity, which we will call a 'Junker' economy. Labour-rent and wage labour/money-rent can clearly co-exist in the same region, larger landlords may adopt either form according to the conditions specified in section 3 (above) of this chapter. The conversion of the demesne to wage-labour necessarily accelerates the differentiation of the peasantry.

(b) If we now suppose that the landlord class, in general, has a low level of economic control and the political means and economic conditions to do no more than enforce the right of exclusion exist then we will obtain a different set of variant elements. The elements of this combination are:

(i) the dominance of money-rents as ground-rents based on the right of exclusion (given a monopoly of landed property);

(ii) the relative freedom of sub-letting between tenants, and the competition between the more successful for more land;

(iii) the differentiation of the peasantry and the formation of a class of rich peasants who hire wage-labour. Under these conditions the differentiation of the peasantry will proceed more freely and rapidly. It should be noted that competition for more land, fluctuations in money earnings and indebtedness may provide an avenue for the landlord to control the means of production but only within the conditions set by the mechanism of differentiation. The rich peasant may avoid the landlord's attempts at control, acting as a money-lender and *de facto* landlord himself.

In these cases commodity production makes certain variant forms possible and transforms the role and position of others (labour-rent); however, it is the level of economic subsumption and the political conditions of FMP which determine the combination of the elements. It should be made clear that while the two types in Set I, (a) and (b), are differentiated for the purposes of exposition they may be combined in the same social formation in different regions (in certain regions the level of subsumption may be lower due to greater land reserves), elements of them may even vary between estates, or they may represent the alternative objectives of struggle of the two main classes.[23]

SET II

Here we will suppose at best limited opportunities for commodity production.

(a) If we suppose in addition that state power firmly supports the landlord class and that, in general, a high level of economic subsumption exists, then the following variant forms will predominate and combine:

(i) on estates with a steady and expandable demand for produce labour-rent and demesne production will predominate;

(ii) on other or smaller estates rent-in-kind may predominate (given the difficulties of supervision) or rent-in-kind combined with seasonal or non-agricultural labour-service;

(iii) money-rents, where they can be exacted, will be favoured but they must of necessity be a subordinate form;

(iv) the differentiation of the peasantry will be much less than in Set I given the low level of commodity production and it will result from rather different mechanisms (family size, supply of labour-power, etc.).

(b) Given a low level of economic subsumption of the direct producers then feudal rent will be a politically based exaction for the right to cultivate the land; its level will depend upon the coercive means available to the landlord class through the state. The FMP will here degenerate to the feudal form of tax/rent.

In addition to illustrating what a set is these examples have another value, they help to explain the conditions under which the transition to capitalism is possible. It should be clear that it is only under Set I that the possible conditions for the transformation of feudal social relations and the construction of capitalist relations can exist. Of course, the conditions specified in Set I in no way necessitate that the FMP be subject to transformation or constitute a transitional conjuncture. The social relations in Set I are *feudal* relations.

The variants in Set I can give rise to *three* distinct roads to the development of capitalist production in agriculture. Which of the roads in question predominates is settled by which class is victorious in the political/economic class struggle and under what conditions that struggle takes place. In *Capital*, I, pt VIII Marx outlined one road to the development of capitalist agriculture in which the landlord class separates the direct producers from the soil and replaces them (directly or by stages, e.g. *métayage*) with tenant farmers who hire wage-labour. This route may exist where the landlord class has the backing of state power in evicting the independent tenant producers over whom it has little economic control or where a Junker economy is converted into capitalist agriculture with tenant farmers. The other two roads are outlined by Lenin in his text *The Agrarian Programme of Social Democracy in the First Russian Revolution*:[24]

> But there may be two forms of that development. The survivals of serfdom may fall away either as a result of the transformation of landlord economy or as a result of the abolition of the landlord latifundia, i.e. either by reform or by revolution. Bourgeois development may proceed by having big landlord economies at the head, which will gradually become more and more bourgeois and gradually substitute bourgeois for feudal methods of exploitation. It may also proceed by having small peasant economies at the head, which in a revolutionary way, will remove the 'excrescence' of the feudal latifundia from the social organism and then freely develop without them along the path of capitalist economy.

> Those two paths of objectively possible bourgeois development we would call the Prussian path and the American path, respectively. In the first case feudal landlord economy slowly evolves into bourgeois Junker landlord economy, which condemns the peasants to decades of most harrowing expropriation and bondage, while at the same time a small minority of *Grossbauern* ('big peasants') arises. In the second case there is no landlord economy, or else it is broken up by revolution, which confiscates and splits up the feudal estates. In that case the peasant predominates, becomes the sole agent of agriculture, and evolves into a capitalist farmer. In the first case the main content of the evolution is transformation of feudal bondage into servitude and capitalist exploitation on the land of the feudal landlords – Junkers. In the second case the main background is transformation of the patriarchal peasant into a bourgeois farmer (*Collected Works*, 13, p. 239).

The 'Prussian' road is different from that outlined by Marx in that in this case the feudal Junker economy is transformed into capitalist production by the landlord acting as capitalist, without the intermediary function of the tenant farmer. Furthermore, the Junker landlord retains controls over the labourer which are different from and additional to those of the wage form (tied housing, allotments, etc.). The 'Prussian' road corresponds to the conditions given in Set I, (a), and the revolutionary path to conditions similar to those given in Set I, (b). While the two sub-sets may co-exist in different regions within the FMP, the two routes to capitalist agriculture are antagonistic. The second route, that in which independent peasant production predominates, requires that the landlord class be displaced from political dominance in the state and that the political/legal forms of feudal landed property be smashed and replaced by bourgeois private property right. The Prussian road requires the political subordination of the peasant class within the state and the maintenance of the legal forms of feudal landownership, favouring the great estates and their existing owners. Lenin emphasises that the question of which road predominates is settled by the class struggle, by the victory of the programme of the landlord class or of that of the advanced sections of the peasantry. No teleological process or evolutionary necessity is operative here – the road taken is determined by the outcome of a battle between classes, a result which cannot be pre-given.

Six

The transition from feudalism to capitalism

This chapter analyses the problem of transition from one mode of production to another with special reference to the transition from feudalism to capitalism. It is concerned in particular with the problem of how periods of transition must be conceived. We shall see that they cannot be conceived as linear or evolutionary developments, that they cannot be thought of in terms of transitional modes of production and that there can be no necessary evolutionary sequence of modes of production. There is nothing in the concepts of the feudal and of the capitalist modes of production that requires the first to evolve into the second. In discussing the transition from feudalism to capitalism we pay particular attention to the separation of the labourer from his means of production, to the transformation of feudal ground-rent and to the place and effectivity of trade and commodity production in the transition period. This last involves a short discussion of the significance of the absolutist state in the development of capitalism and of the so-called 'general economic crisis' of the seventeenth century.

Marxism conceives of the social formation as an articulated combination of distinct structural levels, economic, political and ideological, each with its own specific effectivity and modes of intervention with respect to the others. Periods of transition apart, the social formation is dominated by a determinate mode of production. The concepts of the different modes of production are constructed on the basis of the same set of general concepts, labourer and non-labourer, necessary- and surplus-labour, mode of appropriation of surplus-labour, and so on.[1] Marx has elaborated the theory of the capitalist mode of production and has made a number of more or less elaborated suggestions and indications for others. Some of the other possible modes of production have been examined in this book. Once the social formation is conceived in this way as an articulated combination of structural levels dominated by a determinate mode of production, then the transition from the domination of one mode of production to that of another necessarily involves the effective destruction of one articulated social whole and its replacement by another.

If, as we shall see, many Marxist theorists of the transition from feudalism to capitalism fail to respect this necessity it is because they effectively reduce the complex articulated totalities of the Marxist theory of history to the expressive totalities characteristic of the idealist philosophies of history in which, explicitly or implicitly, the end of history is already given in its beginning. An index of what is at stake can be given by considering first the consequences for a theory of transition of the widespread conception which effectively reduces capitalism to commodity production so that the expansion of commodity production is thought to be equivalent to the development of capitalism itself. We have met a position of this kind in Rostovtzeff's treatment of the Hellenistic and Roman empires as exhibiting a capitalism not too different from that of nineteenth- and twentieth-century Europe. A similar conception of capitalism underlies Postan's description of the large feudal estate of thirteenth-century England as 'capitalist concerns: federated grain factories producing largely for cash' ('Revisions in economic history: the 15th century', p. 162). These positions define a type of economy by reference to the circulation of products between economic agents. Capitalism equals commodity circulation; other types are then defined by contrast. Postan and many theorists of economic development work with the crude dichotomy, money economy/natural economy, with the result that the difference between feudalism and capitalism or between underdeveloped and developed is reduced to the predominance of one element over another. Others, for example, Polanyi and his associates, reject the crude dichotomy in favour of a more complex and sophisticated theory of types of economy. In the course of our discussion of the place and function of commodity production in classical antiquity we have shown that the reduction of capitalism to commodity circulation involves a serious misconception of the fundamental significance of the commodity form within capitalism and also, therefore, of the structure of all economic types that are defined by contrast with capitalism.

As far as transition is concerned such conceptions reduce the development of capitalism to the predominance of commodity production, the market system, the spirit of capitalism or some such equivalent, over other elements. In this respect they reproduce the characteristic structures of the idealist sociologies of, for example, Parsons or Tönnies, in which structural differences between societies are reduced to the expression of one or more simple dichotomies (*Gemeinschaft/Gesellschaft*, the pattern variables, etc.). Such positions are possible only on condition that all structural components are conceived as so many expressions of the same essential elements. The articulation of structural components is here thought of not in terms of effectivity and levels of determination but in the mode of expression. In 'The Economy as Instituted Process', Polanyi, to take just one example, elaborates his substantive view of the economy in terms of four distinct types of economic integration: exchange, reciprocity, redistribution and householding. To each type there corresponds a determinate set of social institutions as its conditions of existence. The economy must be instituted. In effect the economy and the corresponding institutions are both conceived as expressions of one and the same principle. Thus the market system and the market institutions embody the market principle. The result is that in his paper 'Aristotle Discovers the Economy' the development of the market system is thought of in terms of the irruption of the market principle into history (about the time of Aristotle), that is, of an essence which will grow of its own accord unless prevented by a more powerful opposing essence.[2] Weber sometimes presents the development of modern capitalism in precisely such terms.[3]

In Polanyi's case, then, a serious and sophisticated attempt to theorise the social structural conditions of existence of distinct types of economy is vitiated by a failure to conceive the structure of the social whole in terms of levels of determination and of effectivity. The result is a collapse into the idealist reduction of history to the development of essences. Here we can see that the structure of the theory of transition from one form of society to another is nothing but the effect of the manner in which these forms of society are themselves conceived. A theory of transition as a linear or evolutionary movement is the rigorous effect of an idealist conception of the structure of the social totality. Theories of transition advanced by Marxist authors are not always free of this tendency.[4]

1 Balibar's conception of manufacture as a transitional mode of production

If the social formation is a complex structured whole dominated by a determinate mode of production, how is the period of transition to be conceived? We have seen that the specific form of articulation of instances in each mode of production is determined by the structure of the economy and that, within the economy, the mode of appropriation of surplus-labour is dominant. For example, it is the conditions of existence of the feudal economy dominated by the extraction of feudal ground-rent that governs the articulated hierarchy of instances in any social formation dominated by feudalism. The capitalist mode of production, in which surplus-labour is appropriated by means of the production and realisation of surplus-value, has quite different structural conditions of existence. We return below to a detailed examination of these differences. For the present we should notice that the presence in a given social formation of the conditions of existence of one mode of production means that the conditions of existence of any other mode cannot be satisfied. Thus a social formation in which the conditions of existence of the feudal mode of production are present and continue to be reproduced cannot, at the same time, be responsible for producing the conditions of existence of the capitalist mode of production. Otherwise one and the same social formation would have to be characterised by two distinct articulated hierarchies of its economic, political and ideological instances. It follows that while certain elements of the capitalist mode of production may be present in feudal society the capitalist mode of production itself cannot. We have seen, for example, that it is possible for commodity production and wage-labour to develop within the feudal, ancient and slave modes of production under conditions which are entirely foreign to capitalism. This point merits particular attention in view of the place of commodity relations as a crucial and invariant element in the capitalist mode of production. Certain authors, Dobb and Sweezy for example,[5] regard trade as being in some sense external to feudalism and many others treat the expansion of trade as if not synonymous with, then at least a major cause of, the development of capitalism. The signficance of commodity relations in the transition to capitalism will be examined below.

Since the conditions of existence of the capitalist mode of production cannot be produced as effects of the reproduction of the feudal mode it follows that any determinate transition from one to the other must involve the transformation, i.e. the non-reproduction, of the political, ideological and economic conditions of existence of the feudal mode of production in the course of a transition period. Nevertheless the period of transition cannot be conceived as a moment of destructuration between two periods in which the social formation is governed by the structure, first of one mode of production, then of the other. It is not an irrational hiatus in which the social formation ceases to exist as a complex structured whole. In particular, the process of social production as a whole is not suspended while we wait for transition to take place.

> Every child knows that a nation which ceased to work, I will not say for a year, but even for a few weeks, would perish. Every child knows, too, that the masses of products corresponding to different needs require different and quantitatively determined masses of the total labour of society. That this *necessity* of the *distribution* of social labour cannot possibly be done away with by a *particular form* of social production but can only change the mode of its appearance, is self-evident (Marx to Kugelman, 11 July 1868).

Nor can this necessity be done away with for the duration of the transition period. It follows therefore that the general structure of social production, the distinction between necessary- and surplus-labour, the division of the product into means of production and means of consumption, and so on, is manifested also by the forms of transition from one mode of production to another. So far so good. Balibar goes further and uses this point to argue for the necessity of conceiving the social formation in transition as governed by a transitional mode of production (*Reading Capital*, p. 273f).

In effect this conception means that two types of mode of production are distinguished according to the type of complexity of the structure of the economy. In the first, relations of production and productive forces must *correspond* in the sense that their relationship takes the form of a reciprocal limitation of their effectivities. For this reason the process of social production as a whole takes the form of the reproduction of both the relations of production and the corresponding productive forces. In the second, transitional type relations of production and productive forces do not correspond; they are related in the mode of *non-correspondence*. This relationship takes the form of the transformation of one by the effect of the other. The reproduction of the relations of production induces a progressive transformation of the productive forces and a displacement of the instances of the social formation. Balibar takes his example of a transitional mode of production from Marx's analysis of manufacture and the industrial revolution

> in which the capitalist nature of the relations of production (the necessity of creating surplus-value in the form of relative surplus-value) determines and governs the transition of the

> productive forces to their specifically capitalist form (the industrial revolution arises as a method of formation of relative surplus-value beyond any predetermined quantitative limit). The 'reproduction' of this specific complexity is the reproduction of this effect of the one connexion on the other (p. 304).

We will return to this example. It seems, then, that modes of production may be structured either by the correspondence or by the non-correspondence of the relations of production and the productive forces. In the second case each moment of reproduction is also a moment of dissolution of the structure of the mode of production. The concept of a transitional mode of production is also the concept of its supersession. Manufacture, as a transitional mode of production, contains the seeds of its own destruction.

Balibar thus assigns to the transitional mode of production characteristics that many Marxist theorists of the transition from feudalism to capitalism would assign to all modes of production. Dobb, for example, conceives the decline of feudalism as a necessary effect of tendencies internal to the feudal mode of production.

> it was the inefficiency of feudalism as a system of production, coupled with the growing needs of the ruling class for revenue, that was primarily responsible for its decline; since this need for additional revenue promoted an increase in the pressure on the producer to a point where this pressure became literally unendurable (*Studies in the Development of Capitalism*, p. 42).

Here the very development of feudalism and the consequent intensification of its basic contradiction is thought to be responsible for its supersession.[6]

All such conceptions are open to serious objections which may be summarised under two headings: (i) the concept of mode of production precludes forms which are transitional in this sense; (ii) the dichotomy, correspondence/non-correspondence of the relations of production and productive forces, depends on a formalist and idealist conception of the structure of the economy which reduces it, Balibar's denial notwithstanding,[7] to an expressive structure.

(i) The concept of a determinate mode of production is that of a complex unity of relations and forces of production and it has determinate economic, political and ideological conditions of existence. If these conditions of existence are maintained, then the mode of production will continue to be reproduced. There is nothing in its *concept* that requires a mode of production to come to an end. The concept is not also the concept of its own supersession. This is not to say, of course, that the structure is reproduced without change, but rather that the articulated hierarchy of instances and their respective affectivities and also, therefore, the limits of the mode of production, are reproduced. To speak of a transitional mode of production is to speak of a structure which, like Dobb's concept of mode of production or the Spirits of Hegel's *Philosophy of History*, is time-bound in its very concept: it has a beginning and an end and a unilineal tendency to move from one to the other. This temporal necessity is conceivable only within a historicist problematic that is entirely foreign to historical materialism.

(ii) The use of the dichotomy, correspondence/non-correspondence, in connection with what Bettelheim has called 'the law of necessary correspondence or non-correspondence between the relations of production and the character of the productive forces' (*La Transition vers l'économie socialiste*, p. 48), implies a thesis of reciprocal determination and consistency. In the case of inconsistency where the productive forces do not correspond to the relations of production they are brought into correspondence by the action of the relations of production. It is this that ensures that the period of non-correspondence, whether it is conceived as a transitional mode of production or as a transitional form,[8] cannot be other than transitional. Reciprocal determination either maintains consistency or acts to bring it about. In such a conception of the necessity – if not now then in the future – of correspondence there is no place for any hierarchy of determination within the concept of the mode of production, in particular, no dominance of the relations of production over the productive forces. If there is to be a correspondence, then one element or component must correspond with another element or component. If one *thing*, relations of production, must correspond with another *thing*, productive forces, then each thing is an expression of the correspondence which unites them. This concept of mode of production has the characteristic structure of what Althusser has called an expressive totality. We return to this question in the following section.

A crucial consequence of this position is that it renders impossible the theoretical construction of the variants of a mode of production. For any given relations of production there will be one corresponding form of the productive forces. If there are variations, there cannot be a correspondence unless the theoretical effectivity of the variations is denied and the variations themselves conceptualised as external to theory. If there is to be unitary correspondence of the form of organisation of the labour process (the productive forces) with the mode of appropriation of surplus-labour (the relations of production), then the variable features of the labour process cannot be pertinent to the concept of the mode of production. Thus the variations will appear as *real*, empirically given, variations from an *ideal*, or theoretical model: the mode of production is then conceived as an ideal-type.[9]

In this conception, then, the identification of the pertinent features of the productive forces suffices for the identification of the mode of production – unless it is transitional. A mode of production may be identified by its characteristic form of organisation of the labour process and, in the last analysis, each theoretically distinctive form of the labour process corresponds to a distinct mode of production. Thus the effect of this position would be to restrict the feudal mode of production to manorial production, the ancient mode to slavery, and capitalism to the machine production of modern industry rather than the handicraft production of the manufactory.[10]

But the articulation of relations of production and productive forces cannot be reduced to this teleological correspondence. We have argued that the economic level of the mode of production must be conceived as a structure in dominance, as the articulation of labour process and mode of appropriation of surplus-labour under the dominance of the latter. It is this dominance that governs the forms of labour process that are possible within the mode of production and that determines their limits and their characteristic forms of development and transformation.

This last point is crucial. It appears to be contradicted in Balibar's analysis of manufacture as a transitional mode of production which suggests that it is precisely in the transitional modes that the labour process is transformed so as to correspond to the relations of production. His argument is based on an interpretation of the chapters of *Capital* that Marx devotes to the analysis of the formation of relative surplus-value. For the purposes of the present text it is sufficient to consider Balibar's commentary on the following passages from *Capital*:

> At first capital subordinates labour on the basis of the technical conditions given by historical development. It does not change immediately the mode of production. The production of

> surplus-value in the form considered by us – by means of a simple extension of the working day, proved, therefore, to be independent of any change in the mode of production (I, p. 310).

> The production of relative surplus-value revolutionises out and out the technical processes of labour, and the forms of social grouping. It therefore presupposes *a specific mode, the capitalist mode of production*, a mode which, along with its methods, means and conditions, arises and develops itself spontaneously on the basis provided by the formal subsumption of labour under capital. In the case of this development, the formal subsumption is replaced by *the real subsumption of labour under capital* (*ibid*., p. 510 – modified[11]).

In Balibar's commentary the difference between the formal subsumption of labour under capital and real subsumption appears as an index of a chronological dislocation in the formation of the different elements of the structure of the capitalist mode of production. Thus capital as a social relation, the capitalist ownership of the means of production, exists before and independently of real subsumption, the specifically capitalist form of the labour process. The necessity of this dislocation, in Balibar's view, is to be found in a theory of the forms of transition from one mode of production to another. Thus manufacture and modern industry are equally opposed to individual handicraft production through their formal subsumption to capital but that formal subsumption is not the real break that inaugurates the capitalist mode of production. Balibar's argument on this point depends precisely on the identification of the capitalist mode of production with the combination of capitalist relations of production, formal subsumption, and *corresponding* productive forces, real subsumption.

The quoted passages cannot, however, be used to support Balibar's interpretation. Let us note first that the word *mode* is frequently used by Marx in the sense of *manner* or *fashion*.[12] That it appears in this sense in Balibar's first quotation is made clear in the sentence that follows it. 'It [the production of absolute surplus-value] was not less active in the old-fashioned bakeries than in the modern cotton factories' (*Capital*, I, p. 310). Thus *mode of production* in the quoted passage refers to the *manner* of producing, that is, to the technical organisation of the labour process. The production of absolute surplus-value does not depend on one specific form of labour process, for example, on modern industry rather than old-fashioned manufacture.

If the production of absolute surplus-value does not depend directly on the technical character of the labour process, what does it depend on? Essentially on the activity of capital 'as a producer of the activity of others, as a pumper-out of surplus-labour and exploiter of labour-power' (*ibid.*, pp. 309–10). If we consider the process of production from the point of view of the labour process then the formal subsumption of labour under capital appears to involve no immediate change.

> But it is different as soon as we deal with the process of production from the point of view of the process of creation of surplus-value. The means of production are at once changed into means for the absorption of the labour of others (p. 310).

This change marks the real break that inaugurates the capitalist mode of production and makes possible the specifically capitalist forms of development and transformation of the productive forces. This is the import of Balibar's second quotation. The production of relative surplus-value which revolutionises the technical process of labour *presupposes* the capitalist mode of production. In its absence the conditions of the capitalist transformations of the labour process cannot be realised. It is not the formal subjection of labour to the 'capital' of the merchant or usurer but rather its subordination to capital in the production of absolute and relative surplus-value that constitutes the capitalist mode of production.

> It will suffice to refer to certain intermediate forms, in which surplus-labour is not extorted by direct compulsion from the producer, nor the producer himself yet formally subjected to capital. In such forms capital has not yet acquired the direct control of the labour process. By the side of independent producers who carry on their handicrafts and agriculture in the traditional old-fashioned way, there stands the usurer or the merchant, with his usurer's or merchant's capital, feeding on them like a parasite. The predominance, in a society, of this form of exploitation excludes the capitalist mode of production (p. 540).

Here intermediate forms precede the formal subsumption of labour under capital. In these remarks *capital* must be taken in its strictest sense, not in the sense of merchant's capital or usurer's capital. It does not suffice for the merchant or usurer to employ a few labourers himself for labour to be formally subjected to capital. The capitalist mode of production cannot be defined at the level of the organisation of the individual unit of production. It is Dobb's failure to recognise this point that allows him to treat trade as something which is external to feudalism and which intensifies its internal contradictions.[13] We have seen that the production of commodities on the basis of wage-labour may well develop within the ancient or the feudal modes of production. What is crucial here is that capital should function as an instrument of production of surplus-value and its realisation for a class of capitalists. This functioning cannot be determined at the level of the labour process in individual units of production. Private ownership of the means of production is *capitalist*, in the strict sense, if and only if surplus-value is realised in a capitalist system of commodity circulation by means of the exchange of commodities between the capitalists and labourers of the two departments of production. The capitalist production of surplus-value takes place through commodity production by means of commodities (i.e. labour-power and means of production) and is realised through the exchange of equivalents. A unit of production that is capitalist in form is capitalist in the strict sense only on condition of its integration within a system of capitalist commodity circulation.[14]

The formal subsumption of labour under capital, then, must not be confused with the mere appearance of the wage–labour relation in connection with commodity production. Whether or not manufacturing is capitalist depends not on the form of organisation of the labour process but on its articulation within the system of social production as a whole. If the process of social production as a whole is not dominated by the capitalist mode of production then the revenues of the 'capitalist' and of his labourers are dependent on the level and conditions of appropriation of surplus-labour by non-capitalist means – on, for example, appropriation by ancient or feudal mechanisms. We shall see that this point is of the greatest importance for the analysis of the absolutist state in the period of transition from feudalism to capitalism.

The difference of absolute and relative surplus-value is not, as Balibar suggests, a difference between two modes of production, capitalism and manufacture, but between two capitalist forms of extraction of surplus-value. Both forms of surplus-value are realised as commodities. Under capitalism both forms of extraction of surplus-value may co-exist but there is a tendency towards the domination of relative over absolute surplus-value since there is a tendency towards the increasing organic composition of capital (the relative proportions of constant to variable capital). If this tendency appears accidental at the level of the individual unit of production it is a necessary effect of capitalist domination of the economy as a whole, and, in particular, of the competition that functions as a mechanism for the equalisation of the rate of profit in the different branches of production. In this sense the movement towards the transformation of productive forces in the real subsumption of labour under capital is conditional not on the private ownership of the means of production alone but on the installation of the capitalist mode of production.

2 Teleological causality and material causality in the analysis of transition

We can now return to the question of how precisely the period of transition is to be conceived. So far we have used the term 'transition' rather loosely to refer to a condition in which a dominant mode of production is subject to transformation and to the non-reproduction of its political, ideological and economic conditions of existence. We have argued that the period of transition must be conceived neither as a moment of destructuration nor as a linear or evolutionary progression – although many Marxist theorists of the transition from feudalism to capitalism have analysed it in precisely these terms. In particular, then, the concept of the period of transition cannot be defined by its end points in terms of, for example, a transitional mode of production in which elements of what is to come are combined with elements of what has been, or a formalist non-correspondence of relations and forces of production as a result of which the action of one effects a transformation of the other. All conceptions in which a structure is defined in the future anterior, by the future results of present phenomena, involve a collapse into idealist and teleological theories of history.

If, on pain of teleology, transition is not to be defined in terms of the combination of a past and a future then it is necessary to consider the status of, say, 'the transition from feudalism to capitalism' as an object of scientific investigation. In what sense is 'the transition from *one mode of production to another*' a legitimate object of scientific inquiry? Can there, for example, be a general theory of transition such that each specific transition appears to exemplify the same general structure? These questions must be posed in all seriousness; they are all the more important in that even those who explicitly reject all teleology nevertheless tend to pose the problem of transition in such terms. The attempt by the authors of *Reading Capital* to displace Hegelian and teleological interpretations of Marxism is particularly instructive in this respect since it raises in an acute form the problem of the mode of causality operative in the theory of modes of production and the transition from one mode of production to another.

(i) THE TELEOLOGY OF STRUCTURAL CAUSALITY

We have just seen that Balibar's conception of manufacture as a transitional mode of production is teleological. Now consider Althusser's formulation of the problem:

> the theoretical problems posed by the process of the constitution of a mode of production (in other words, the problems of the transformation of one mode of production into another) are directly a function of the theory of the modes of production concerned. That is why we can say that Marx did give us enough to think this theoretically and practically decisive problem: knowledge of the modes of production considered provides the basis for posing and solving the problems of transition (*Reading Capital*, p. 198).

Quite so. The conception of the transition from one mode of production to another is a rigorous effect of the concepts of the modes of production in question. A teleological theory of transition must therefore be considered as the effect of an idealist concept of mode of production.

In *Reading Capital* the concept of a (non-transitional) mode of production is represented as the concept of an eternity in Spinoza's sense (e.g. *Reading Capital*, pp. 107, 189). This is defined in the first part of Spinoza's *Ethic*, definition VIII, as follows:

> By eternity, I understand existence itself, so far as it is conceived necessarily to follow from the definition alone of the eternal thing.
>
> *Explanation* – For such existence, like the essence of the thing, is conceived as an eternal truth. It cannot therefore be explained by duration or time, even if the duration be conceived without beginning or end.

The Spinozist conception of mode of production as an eternity entails what Althusser calls a relation of structural causality between a structure and its effects, between a structure and its subordinate structures. If the structure is an eternity then neither the structure itself nor its elements and substructures can be subject to a cause external to itself. This means that the structure is conceived

> as a cause immanent in its effects in the Spinozist sense of the term, that *the whole existence of the structure consists of its effects*, in short that the structure, which is merely a specific combination of its peculiar elements, is nothing outside its effects (*Reading Capital*, p. 189).

One further consequence must be noted. If the structure is an eternity then its conditions of existence must be conceived as effects of the structure itself. Otherwise the structure would be subject to external determination and therefore finite; it could not then be conceived as eternal. If mode of production is conceived as an eternity then its existence must entail its conditions of existence.

While he makes no explicit reference to Spinoza it is clear that Balibar's text in *Reading Capital* represents the (non-transitional) mode of production as an eternity in this sense.[15] We have seen, for example, that his conception of the correspondence between relations and forces of production in a non-transitional mode of production requires that each be conceived as an effect of the correspondence that unites them. This correspondence is therefore a cause immanent in its effects and is nothing outside its effects.

This Spinozist conception involves the authors of *Reading Capital* in a curious dilemma since the conceptualisation of the mode of production in the mode of structural causality precludes any conception of transition from one mode of production to another. On the one hand, in opposition to Hegelian interpretations of Marxism, Althusser and Balibar insist that there is nothing in the concept of mode of production that necessarily entails its supersession. For example, many Marxist theorists of the transition from feudalism to capitalism represent the development of feudal money-rent as a form containing the most intense contradictions and therefore as leading to the supersession of feudalism.[16] In such conceptions transition is the necessary result of the full development of the contradictions internal to a given mode of production, so that e.g. the historical tendency of the capitalist mode of production may be seen as leading inexorably to the final crisis and thence to socialism in linear progression. As against this position Balibar argues (*Reading Capital*, pp. 283f) that the specific contradictions of the capitalist mode of production involve a tendency, not towards its dissolution, but precisely to the reproduction of these contradictions. 'The development of the structure according to a tendency . . . therefore means that *the definition of the specific internal temporality* of the structure is part of the analysis of that structure itself' (p. 288).

To the Hegelian conception of the mode of production whose very reproduction is also a moment of its dissolution *Reading Capital* opposes the Spinozist conception of mode of production as eternity. In the one conception the structure produces its dissolution as a necessary effect, in the other it produces as effects its own conditions of existence. Nothing in the latter concept can entail its dissolution.

On the other hand *Reading Capital* also insists that, at least in the case of certain modes of production, the transition from one mode of production to another is possible. The dilemma is stark: if each mode of production is an eternity, then how is transition to be conceived, if transition is to be possible then how can each mode of production be conceived as an eternity? If, say, the feudal mode of production reproduces its own conditions of existence and if transition from feudalism to capitalism requires the non-reproduction of those conditions then how is this transition conceivable? It is clear that the combination of a Spinozist conception of mode of production with the possibility of transition can only lead to theoretical incoherence.

As we have seen Balibar recognises that 'the transition from one mode of production to another can never appear in our understanding as an irrational hiatus between two "periods" which are subject to the functioning of a structure, i.e., which have their specified concept' (*Reading Capital*, p. 273). For this reason Balibar proposes the concept of a transitional mode of production which differs from non-transitional modes in the non-correspondence of relations and forces of production. Transition is then conceived in the mode of a teleological causality in which forces of production are transformed by the action of relations of production so as to bring the period of non-correspondence to an end. We therefore have two types of mode of production – the one an eternity, the other not – and corresponding to these what appear to be two distinct forms of causality. Corresponding to mode of production as eternity we have structural causality: the functioning of the structure reproduces the conditions of its existence as effects. Corresponding to finite, non-eternal, modes of production we have teleological causality: the functioning of the structure produces the conditions of its dissolution as effects.

We shall see that these causalities are not as different as they might appear but first we must take the analysis of Balibar's concept of transition a little further. The introduction of transitional modes of production allows Balibar to combine the concept of (non-transitional) mode of production as eternity with a patently teleological analysis of the movement from transition to non-transition. However any theory of the transition from one mode of production to another requires a concept of the correlative movement from non-transition to transition, from eternity to finitude. It is precisely this movement that is unthinkable in Balibar's problematic. It is one thing to explain why any period of transition must come to an end; it is another to explain how periods of transition are possible. There is nothing in Balibar's theory of transitional and non-transitional modes of production to account for the movement from a mode of production that perpetually reproduces its conditions of existence to one that does not. This movement, and therefore the transition from one mode of production to another, is strictly unthinkable within *Reading Capital*'s Spinozist conception of the (non-transitional) mode of production. If transition is nevertheless to occur it can do so only at the price of theoretical incoherence. Even if transition is conceived as theoretically contingent, the result of accident, the effect of causes external to what *Reading Capital* represents as the Marxist theory of modes of production, it is clear that the very possibility of such contingency must be anathema to any Spinozist eternity.

Thus Althusser's and Balibar's attempt to construct a theory of history combining a Spinozist conception of mode of production with the possibility in certain cases of transition from one mode of production to another requires the incoherent combination of three apparently distinct causalities: structural causality, in which the whole existence of the structure consists of its effects which are also its conditions of existence; teleological causality in which the existence of the structure consists of its effects which are the conditions of its supersession; accident, the effect of causes foreign to Marxist theory.

In fact the first two causalities are not as different as the explicit rejection of teleology in *Reading Capital* would suggest. Both may be subsumed under Althusser's category of expressive causality which deals with the effectivity of a whole on its elements by means of the Liebnizian notion of expression.

> This is the model that dominates all Hegel's thought. But it presupposes in principle that the whole in question be reducible to an *inner essence*, of which the elements of the whole are then no more than the phenomenal forms of expression, the inner principle of the essence being present at each point in the whole, such that at each moment it is possible to write the immediately adequate equation: *such and such an element* (economic, political, legal, literary, religious, etc., in Hegel) = *the inner essence of the whole* (*Reading Capital*, pp. 186–7).

At this point we need only recall Althusser's formula for structural causality in which the structure is to be conceived 'as a cause immanent in its effects in the Spinozist sense of the term' (p. 189). If we write *structure* (in the Spinozist sense) for *inner essence of the whole* then it is clear that structural causality is precisely an expressive causality in the sense of Althusser's definition. The same is true, as we have seen, of the teleological causality of Balibar's concept of transitional mode of production.

There is indeed a distinction to be drawn between structural causality and the expressive and teleological causality of Hegel and of Balibar's theory of transition. However, the distinction does not consist, as Althusser suggests, in a difference at the level of the respective modes of causation. On the contrary it consists solely in the character of the inner essence of the whole whose several expressions constitute the elements of the structure. In one case the inner essence contains the principle of its own transformation: the contradictions of Hegel's philosophy of history, Balibar's non-correspondence of relations and forces of production. In the other case the inner essence contains no such principle; it is therefore the inner essence of an eternity.

We may therefore conclude that the attempt in *Reading Capital* to construct a non-teleological system of concepts which would displace Hegelian interpretations of Marxism by means of Spinozist conceptions of mode of production and of structural causality must fail in its objective. At best it achieves the partial displacement of one form of teleology by another – of an overt, transformative teleology by the stationary, repetitive teleology of structural causality. The result is to introduce further incoherence into what remains an essentially Hegelian theory of history. Where Hegel elaborates a relatively consistent teleological conception of history the combination of Spinozist eternities and transition results in an inconsistent and incoherent conception in which two forms of teleology must be supplemented by contingency.

In effect the explicitly anti-teleological constructions of *Reading Capital* involve the identification of teleological and expressive causality with problematics of perpetual transformation such as Hegel's. As a result of this identification the stationary, repetitive teleology of structural causality is misrecognised and appears to provide a non-teleological principle for analysis of the relation between a structure and it elements. In fact the two causalities are identical since they both involve the expression of an inner essence. It is only with respect to their conception of this inner essence that Hegelian and Spinozist interpretations differ. The contradictory inner essence of the former induces a problematic of perpetual transformation; the inner essence of the latter renders transformation unthinkable. Both interpretations are idealist and lead to idealist analyses of social formations under the dominance of determinate modes of production and in transition.

This extended analysis of the effects of the Spinozist conception of mode of production and the correlative form of structural causality has demonstrated that the break with idealist and teleological deformations of Marxism cannot be restricted to the denegation of the necessity of transition. We have seen that such a denegation is quite compatible with a teleological but non-transformative concept of mode of production. The problem of teleology must be confronted not at the level of its effects in the necessity or otherwise of transition – since these effects depend solely on the character of the inner essence of the whole – but at the level of the mode of causality that is operative.

Balibar has since criticised his conceptions of mode of production as eternity and of transition in the following terms:

> Behind this 'argument' there is an old *philosophical* representation, and it is no accident that throughout this work I was guided approximately by certain reminiscences of Spinozist *formulae*. There is the idea that identity with itself, persistence (including in the form of the persistence of *relations* implied in a cyclical process) needs no explanation *since it explains itself by itself*, needs no cause (or production) *since it is its own cause*. Only 'change', as 'real' change, i.e.,

> abolition-transformation of the essence, could need a cause and an explanation. Let me say that this is a survival of the philosophy of the 'principle of inertia', of substance and the ontological argument ('Self-criticism – an answer to questions from *Theoretical Practice*', p. 65).

So much for structural causality. In this passage Balibar admits the crucial distinction between a structure and its conditions of existence so that the mere existence of the structure does not in and of itself entail the reproduction of its conditions of existence – since these latter are no longer internalised within the concept of the structure itself. The existence of a mode of production cannot ensure the reproduction of its political, economic and ideological conditions of existence. With this distinction the ideological forms of teleological causality are shattered – at least in principle – since it is no longer possible to represent either the reproduction or the transformation of a mode of production as the realisation of an inner principle of identity (in the case of eternal reproduction) or of contradiction (in the case of transformation). On the contrary both the reproduction and the transformation of a mode of production must be analysed in terms of a determinate material causality, as the definite effects of specific real relations.

(ii) THE CONCEPT OF TRANSITIONAL CONJUNCTURE AND THE ROLE OF THE CLASS STRUGGLE

We have used the term 'transition' to refer to a condition in which a specific dominant mode of production is subject to transformation and to the non-reproduction of its political, ideological and economic conditions of existence. This condition can now be specified more precisely. In particular we must insist that transition (and non-transition) can only be understood in terms of certain determinate conditions of the class struggle and as a possible outcome of that struggle. 'Transitional conjuncture' refers to a condition of the social formation such that the transformation of the dominant mode of production is a possible outcome of the class struggle. It is distinguished from non-transitional conjunctures not by the *fact* of class struggle (which is necessarily present in all class societies) but by the specific conditions of that struggle which determine what is and what is not a possible outcome. These conditions ensure that transition is a possible outcome; they do not make it necessary.

It should be noted that this conception of transitional conjuncture is possible only on condition that the reproduction of the political, ideological and economic conditions of existence of a determinate mode of production are not conceived as necessary effects of the existence of that mode of production. In Balibar's conception, for example, the conditions of transition and those of the dominance of a (non-transitional) mode of production are quite incompatible. The period of transition is inaugurated by the destruction of the dominance of the preceding mode of production. On the basis of such concepts, as we have seen, the initial act of destruction of dominance must remain unthinkable.

If the mode of production is not conceived as reproducing its conditions of existence in and of itself then there is no necessary contradiction between the conditions of transition and those of the dominance of a determinate mode of production. There is nothing in the concept of, say, the feudal or the capitalist modes of production to preclude the possibility, under definite conditions, of forms of class struggle capable of effecting a transformation of the dominant relations of production. This point is of the greatest importance. It follows, as we shall see, that there can be no general theory of transition in the sense of a specification of the general structure or process that must be followed in all particular cases of transition from one mode of production to another. Any such general structure or process must denegate the effectivity of the class struggle and the specificity of the concrete conditions in which it takes place. We return to this question below.

If we are to think of the possibility of transition as the outcome of determinate transformations of definite structures of social relations – as the outcome, that is to say, of a determinate material causation and not as the teleological realisation of some inner principle or idea – then it is necessary to consider the specific forms and conditions of class struggle as they appear in determinate social formations dominated by determinate modes of production. The concept of the dominant mode of production and of its possible variant forms specifies the primary forms and certain general characteristics of the class struggle that may appear in the social formation and it governs the possible effects of such struggle with regard to the modification or transformation of the dominant relations of production. In the preceding chapter, for example, we have shown that only certain specific transformations of feudal relations of production are conceivable as the outcome of the class struggle in social formations dominated by the feudal mode of production.

However, to say that certain transformations are conceivable is not to say that they are necessary. Nothing in the concept of the feudal mode of production ensures that it must be transformed into capitalism either by means of a peasant-bourgeois revolution or by means of a landlord-bourgeois revolution. Such transformations can appear only as the outcome of concrete class struggles conducted under determinate real conditions. Not only is the outcome of a specific class struggle always problematic – since it cannot be conceived as the effect of a teleological process of realisation – but the concrete forms and modalities of struggle are the effect of real conditions in the structure of the social formation in question. Both the 'American' and the 'Prussian' roads to capitalism, i.e. the peasant-bourgeois and the landlord-bourgeois transitions, are predicated on the extensive development of commodity relations in the social formation, while the 'Prussian' road also requires the development of specifically capitalist forms of exchange relations.

It must be emphasised that the possibility of transition cannot be determined solely at the economic level. Class struggle is conducted at all levels of the social formation – political and ideological as well as economic. It is never reducible to the purely economic struggles, for wages, ground-rent, etc., generated by the antagonistic structure of the dominant relations of production.[17] The possibility or otherwise of transition depends upon the specific forms of class struggle, its concrete objectives and the forces that can be mobilised in support of these objectives. The particular political, ideological and economic conditions that determine these forms of struggle, these objectives and forces, are never reducible to or deducible from the structure of the dominant mode of production alone. In that respect the existence or otherwise of a transitional conjuncture, the possibility or otherwise of specific transformations, can only be established by an analysis of the real conditions of the class struggle in the social formation in question.

The importance of this requirement cannot be emphasised too strongly. In his *Letters on Tactics. First Letter: Assessment of the Present Situation* Lenin states the necessity for the concrete analysis of the current situation in the following terms.

> Marxism requires of us a strictly exact and objectively verifiable analysis of the relations of classes and of the concrete features peculiar to each historical situation. We Bolsheviks have always tried to meet this requirement, which

is absolutely essential for giving a scientific foundation to policy.

'Our theory is not a dogma, but a guide to action', Marx and Engels always said, rightly ridiculing the mere memorising and repetition of 'formulas', that at best are capable only of marking out *general* tasks, which are necessarily modifiable by the *concrete* economic and political conditions of each particular period of the historical process (*Collected Works*, 24, p. 43).

Lenin's own analyses are exemplary in this respect. We have already referred to the important text, *The Agrarian Programme of Social Democracy in the First Russian Revolution* (*Collected Works*, 13, pp. 217–431),[18] in which Lenin examines the specific conditions of the class struggle in the Russian countryside and concludes that what is at stake in the struggle is the choice between two forms of capitalist transformation.

We have seen that the 'pivot' of the agrarian struggle in our revolution is the feudal latifundia. The peasants' struggle for the land is, first and foremost, a struggle for the abolition of these latifundia. Their abolition and their complete transfer to the peasantry undoubtedly coincide with the line of the capitalist evolution of Russian agriculture. Such a path of this evolution would mean the most rapid development of productive forces, the best conditions of labour for the mass of the population, and the most rapid development of capitalism, with the conversion of the free peasants into farmers. But another path of bourgeois evolution of agriculture is possible, viz. the preservation of the landlord farms and latifundia and their slow conversion from farms based on serfdom and bondage into Junker farms. It is these two types of possible bourgeois evolution that form the basis of the two types of agrarian programmes proposed by different classes in the Russian revolution (pp. 254–5).

Lenin's theory of the two roads of capitalist development and its basis in the structure of the feudal mode of production has been examined in the preceding chapter. What must be emphasised here is that, while the possibility in principle of these distinct forms of transition to capitalism has its basis in the antagonistic structure of feudal relations of production, nevertheless Lenin's conclusion, that what is concretely at stake in the agrarian class struggle is precisely the choice between one road and the other, cannot be deduced from the concept of the feudal mode of production. Nor can it be deduced from any general structure or process of transition from feudalism to capitalism – from, say, the Menshevik 'general abstract stereotyped conception of the bourgeois revolution' (p. 352) as a steady procession through a predetermined and invariant sequence of historical stages. On the contrary, far from proceeding from a general theory of transition, Lenin's first chapter establishes what is at stake in the agrarian class struggle by means of the analysis of Russian agrarian statistics. In this way he establishes what would be the result of a redistribution of the land through the break-up of the feudal latifundia.

> This revolution does not and cannot in any way affect the system of small *production* in agriculture, the domination of the *market* over the producer and, consequently, the domination also of *commodity production*, since the struggle for the *redistribution* of the land cannot alter the relations of production in the farming of this land. And we have seen that a feature of this struggle is the strong development of small-scale farming on the feudal latifundia (p. 234).

However, the structure of the conjuncture, the concrete conditions of the class struggle, cannot be defined at the economic level alone. Lenin clearly asserts the incompleteness of a concrete analysis restricted to the economic level: 'No statistics in the world can assess whether the elements of a peasant bourgeoisie in a given country have "hardened" sufficiently to enable the system of landownership to be adapted to the system of farming' (p. 290). The statistics represent economic conditions, the forms of agriculture and the distribution of landholdings. They do not and cannot represent political and ideological conditions. 'Without the experience of a mass – indeed, more than that – of a nation-wide peasant movement, the programme of the Social-Democratic Labour Party could not become concrete' (p. 256).

More quotations are unnecessary. The essential point here concerns the irreducibility of the political and ideological levels to the economic: the political and ideological conditions in the Russian countryside cannot be deduced from the structure of the economy. The analysis of the conjuncture requires an investigation of the political and ideological conditions of the class struggle. (Lenin analyses the programmes and demands of the peasant movements, speeches of peasant representatives in the Duma, and so on.[19])

We have said that a transitional conjuncture exists when the political, economic and ideological conditions of the class struggle are such that determinate transformations of relations of production and the non-reproduction of the political, economic and ideological conditions of existence of the dominant mode of production are possible as the outcome of that struggle. Further comments are necessary here.

In the first place a transitional conjuncture has a dominant mode of production but one which is subject to transformation and the non-reproduction of its political, ideological and economic conditions of existence. However, economic reproduction takes place throughout a transitional period. If relations of production are not transformed, that is, if transition is not effected, then economic reproduction takes place under the existing relations of production or modified forms of them. If relations of production are transformed then reproduction takes place under the dominance of the new relations. Under certain conditions it is possible that economic reproduction may not take place but in that case the social formation is finished.

Second, transition is not a given necessity. It is possible as the outcome of determinate transformations effected by the class struggle under conditions of a determinate conjuncture. The transitional conjuncture itself is not an accident but has definite conditions of existence in the structure of the dominant mode of production or certain of its variants and a definite causation in determinate transformations in the structure of the preceding non-transitional conjuncture. Thus the economic class struggle may help to create conditions in which transition is a real possibility. For example, the resistance of direct producers under feudalism or the economic struggle of wage-labourers under capitalism may have significant effects in transforming the political and ideological conditions of future struggle.

Third, it should be clear that transition cannot take place solely at the economic level but that it must involve definite transformations at all levels of the social formation. For example, feudal relations of production have definite political, ideological and economic conditions of existence which are quite distinct from those of the capitalist mode of production. In addition the dominance of the feudal mode of production presupposes that the political level is dominant in the social formation. Capitalism, on the other hand, presupposes the dominance of the economic level. Some of these differences are examined in the following section of this chapter. For the moment it is sufficient to notice that any transition from feudalism to capitalism involves a displacement of the dominant level from the political to the economic. The effect of this displacement is to transform the conditions of class struggle and its principal forms. In the course of transition, then, there must be specific displacements in the dominant level and in the dominant forms of class struggle.

Finally, perhaps, we should add that the transition from one mode of production to another must involve a whole period of transition and a number of transitional conjunctures. Here, for example, are Lenin's comments from *Economics and Politics in the Era of the Dictatorship of the Proletariat*:

> Theoretically, there can be no doubt that between capitalism and communism there lies a definite transition period which must combine the features and properties of both these forms of social economy. The transition period has to be a period of struggle between dying capitalism and nascent communism – or, in other words, between capitalism which has been defeated but not destroyed and communism which has been born but is still very feeble. The necessity for a whole historical era distinguished by these transitional features should be obvious (*Collected Works*, 30, p. 107).

In a given transitional conjuncture the immediate outcome must be certain specific transformations and displacements which, depending on the conditions, result either in the closure of the transition period (i.e. restoration or a completed transformation) or in a new transitional conjuncture in which, despite changes in the conditions of struggle, the final outcome is still uncertain. At no point in the transition period is the final outcome a pre-given certainty. In particular, the seizure of state power or the transformation of the relations of production (e.g. from the dominance of feudal relations to capitalist relations) cannot, in themselves, bring the period of transition to a close. The period of transition comes to an end only when the political, economic and ideological conditions are such that the dominant relations of production are no longer subject to transformation. Until that point is reached movement either towards restoration or towards completed transition is a possible outcome of the class struggle.

(iii) THE DENEGATION OF THE CLASS STRUGGLE IN TELEOLOGICAL THEORIES OF TRANSITION

The first chapter of *The Manifesto of the Communist Party* opens with the following words:

> The history of all hitherto existing society is the history of class struggles.
>
> Freeman and slave, patrician and plebeian, lord and serf, guild-master and journeyman, in a word, oppressor and oppressed, stood in constant opposition to one another, carried on an uninterrupted, now hidden, now open fight, a fight that each time ended either in a revolutionary reconstitution of society at large, or in the common ruin of the contending parties (pp. 35–6).

Marxism has always insisted on the primacy of the class struggle and this has been emphasised in our discussion of the transitional conjuncture as a specific form of the conditions of class struggle. In addition we have insisted on the analysis of the social formation in terms of a determinate material causality with real relations producing certain definite effects. In this conception the period of transition appears as a number of specific transformations and displacements – in the relations of production and in the political, ideological and economic conditions of existence of the dominant mode of production – produced as the outcome of specific class struggles in certain definite conditions. For these reasons there can be no general structure or general process of transition. The transitional conjuncture is a specific form of the conditions of class struggle in a social formation dominated by a determinate mode of production. It is a form of the conditions of class struggle which is possible but not necessary. This possibility has its conditions in the structure of the dominant mode of production or of its variant forms and in the specific conditions and tendencies that are compatible with that dominance. The transitional conjuncture has no necessity in the concept of the dominant mode of production. Nor, however, is it accidental. It has its own material causation in specific transformations of the conditions of class struggle in the social formation in question.

In contrast teleological conceptions of mode of production and of transition denegate both the crucial role of the class struggle and the necessity for the concrete analysis of the current situation. In

Reading Capital (pp. 302f), for example, Balibar represents transition as resulting from the transformation of the forces of production through the action of the relations of production. Transition is therefore a given necessity: its necessity is given in the structure of the transitional mode of production as governed by the non-correspondence of relations and forces of production. The movement of transition is the expression of an inner principle. It is not the outcome of the class struggle.

These consequences are not accidental. They are the necessary effects of a mode of analysis imposed by teleological conceptions of causality. The conditions of transition or of non-transition are conceived as the expression of a determinate inner principle, the expression, for example, of the correspondence or non-correspondence between relations and forces of production. It follows that the particular conditions of the political, economic or ideological class struggle can only be conceived as the expression of these same inner principles. They do not have their own specific effectivity. These struggles and their results must alike be conceived as mere expressions of the present stage of a teleological movement.

If the period of transition is conceived in evolutionist terms as a steady progression through a predetermined sequence of historical stages then no further theoretical analysis of the current situation is strictly necessary once the present stage has been correctly identified. Any remaining features of the situation must then appear to operate at the level of accident or contingency with respect to what is thought to be the underlying movement. The existence of apparently contingent features of this kind must give an a-theoretical, pragmatic character to evolutionist political analysis. It is on these grounds that Lenin criticises his Menshevik and divisionist opponents in the dispute over the agrarian programme. On the one hand he observes that a grave fault in the Social-Democratic press and in the Stockholm debate on agrarian questions 'is that practical considerations prevail over theoretical and political considerations over economic' (*Collected Works*, 13, p. 294). On the other hand he refers to 'the glaring historical tactlessness' of the divisionists which reveals an 'inability to take stock of the concrete historical situation' (*ibid.*, p. 291).

The fundamental error is the same in both cases: 'a general, abstract, stereotyped conception of the bourgeois revolution' (*ibid.*, p. 352), derived from a teleological mode of analysis. In consequence the concrete analysis of the current situation demanded by Lenin is replaced by an a-theoretical pragmatism and opportunism which effectively denegates the decisive role of the class struggle in history.

3 The transition from feudalism to capitalism

If, in spite of the preceding discussion, we now proceed to the discussion of that old favourite of Marxist and neo-Marxist historiography 'the transition from feudalism to capitalism' it is absolutely essential that we pose the question of the theoretical status of those essentially retrospective analyses devoted to the historical transition from feudalism to capitalism in Western Europe and Japan. What, to put it bluntly, is the value of an analysis in which the end result of a development appears to govern the definition of the object of investigation so that the development is represented, in effect, as the process of constitution of its pre-given conclusion?

Once the question is posed in such terms the answer must be apparent. The concept of the result can serve to specify, at most, what effects must have been produced if this given result is indeed to appear. If the period of transition is defined in its concept as the process of production of these given effects then the analysis must be teleological. The specification of these effects cannot therefore constitute a scientific analysis of the transition period. It has at best a critical and polemical value – but only on condition that its object is not represented as the theory of the transition from feudalism to capitalism. At worst it is nothing but more or less sophisticated ideology.

Consider, in this respect, Marx's chapters in part VIII of *Capital*, volume I.

> The starting-point of the development that gave rise to the wage-labourer as well as to the capitalist, was the servitude of the labourer. The advance consisted in a change of form of this servitude, in the transformation of feudal exploitation into capitalist exploitation. . . . The expropriation of the agricultural producer, the peasant, from the soil, is the basis of the whole process. The history of this expropriation, in different countries, assumes different aspects, and runs through its various phases in different orders of succession, and at different periods. In England alone, which we take as our example, has it the classic form (pp. 715–16).

It is more than a little misleading to refer to 'the classic form' in this context. It is impossible to maintain that in England a certain object, 'the transition from feudalism to capitalism', appeared in all its purity or that all other cases are impure deviations. In fact Marx's chapters in this part of *Capital* use England as the source of examples and illustrations and they certainly do not constitute a theory of the transition from feudalism to capitalism in general. Indeed these chapters do not even give us a theory of the transition from feudalism to capitalism in England. They have a quite different objective, stated clearly enough in the title, 'The So-Called Primitive Accumulation', and in the opening chapter of this part. This objective is to demonstrate the absurdity of the bourgeois myths of primitive accumulation – a myth that is told and retold in contemporary theories of economic development and especially in those deriving from Weber's *The Protestant Ethic and the Spirit of Capitalism*, according to which certain varieties of protestantism are said to have induced primitive accumulation of an exemplary kind.[20] Marx gives us what can only be called a genealogy or pre-history, a series of chapters in which various features of modern capitalism are shown to have emerged out of a variety of economic, political and legal transformations but not by any means from the thrift and probity of the farmer and manufacturer. A pre-history is no history at all. For all the polemical value of these chapters they do not and cannot provide a scientific knowledge of the transition from feudalism to capitalism in England.

The character of the period of transition as consisting of a number of transitional conjunctures precludes the possibility of a theory of transition 'in general'. Still less can there be a general theory of transition from mode of production x to mode of production y. The object of the theory of transition is the transitional conjuncture and its transformation. Each concrete transition consists of a determinate sequence of transitional conjunctures and the theory of that transition consists in the analysis of these conjunctures and of the displacements and transformations involved in the movement from one conjuncture to the next.

Nevertheless it is possible to draw a number of negative conclusions with regard to existing approaches to the analyses of, say, the transition from feudalism to capitalism. Since transition is always effected by means of a number of displacements in the movements from one conjuncture to another no transition from one mode of production to another can be conceived as a unitary event, the singular effect of a single cause or sequence of causes. There can be no question, then, of explaining the origins of European capitalism as the result, say, of the influx of American bullion or the expansion of maritime commerce. Nor, since there is no necessary sequence of transitional conjunctures, can there be a single general pattern or structure of transition from feudalism to capitalism to which all particular transitions must conform. More particularly the theories of the feudal and the capitalist modes of production enable us to specify what transformations of each of the levels and of the relations of dominance and subordination between levels must be effected if transition is to take place. For example, the conditions of existence of feudal ground-rent on the one hand and of the appropriation of surplus-value for a capitalist class on the other specify that any concrete transition from feudalism to capitalism must effect the displacement of dominance from the political to the economic levels together with certain determinate transformations in these levels.

It must be emphasised, however, that such an analysis merely specifies which effects must have been produced in the course of the transition period. The analysis of these effects is far from constituting a knowledge of the concrete transformations and displacements whose effects these are. This qualification should be borne in mind in the following essentially retrospective examination of the transition from feudalism to capitalism. We shall be particularly concerned with the instituting of a certain 'separation' of the labourer from his means of production, with the transformations in the place and function of commodity relations in the structure of the economy as a whole, and with the elimination of feudal ground-rent as the dominant relation of production. The remainder of this chapter attempts no more than to identify certain of the effects which must have been produced and to specify some of the conditions necessary to produce them.

(i) THE SEPARATION OF THE LABOURER FROM HIS MEANS OF PRODUCTION

The capitalist mode of extraction of surplus-labour involves the production and appropriation of surplus-value by means of mechanisms which work through a system of commodity exchange. These mechanisms require, in particular, that both labour-power and means of production should enter the production process in the form of commodities. The revenues of the labourers are received in payment for their labour-power and are used to purchase commodities in the form of means of personal consumption. Capitalist production must therefore be divided between Department I which produces means of production for sale to capitalists and Department II which produces means of personal consumption for sale to labourers, capitalists and their functionaries. The extraction of surplus-value is realised in the circulation of commodities between and within the labourers and capitalists of these two Departments. Notice, in particular, that the realisation of surplus-value does not require the intervention of any markets outside this system of commodity circulation.[21] These two Departments must exist in one form or another in all social formations. What is peculiar to capitalism is not merely the exchange of products in the form of commodities but the crucial function of the system of commodity circulation in the mechanism of extraction of surplus-labour.

It is not our concern in the present text to analyse this system of commodity circulation.[22] The remarks above are necessary as an introduction to the discussion of the capitalist separation of the labourer from his means of production. If labour-power is to enter the production process as a commodity it must first be sold to the owner of suitable means of production. Thus the capitalist mode of production requires that the mass of labourers have no means of production of their own (they cannot produce commodities on their own account) and no means of livelihood other than through the sale of their labour-power. It is in this sense that the labourers must be separated from their means of production. This state of separation is reproduced in the system of exchange of commodities. Once the labourers have bought and consumed their means of personal consumption they are ready to sell their labour-power for a further period. The capitalist mode of production therefore reproduces and maintains this state of separation of the labourers from their means of production. In the period of transition, however, the situation is not so clear.

> In the ordinary run of things the labourer can be left to the 'natural laws of production', i.e., to his dependence on capital, a dependence springing from, and guaranteed in perpetuity by, the conditions of production themselves. It is otherwise during the historic genesis of capitalist production (*Capital*, I, p. 737).

Notice first that the state of separation cannot be identified with an event or process that happens to direct producers. It is not to be confused with the historical process of expropriation of direct producers in the transition period. Separation from his means of production is the condition of the labourer in the capitalist mode of production. It is not sufficient that there be a mass of impoverished and propertyless individuals. We have seen that strata of this kind develop under conditions of the feudal and of the ancient modes of production. What is required is that the mass of the direct producers are themselves propertyless, that is, without effective property in means of production. The laws of capitalist production continually reproduce this separation. The accumulation of capital and the concentration and centralisation of capital constantly increase the dependence of the workers on the capitalist class.

The expropriation of the feudal peasantry may produce an impoverished and propertyless mass. What it cannot do is ensure that this propertyless mass will become propertyless wage-labourers. The mere presence of such a propertyless mass does not mean either that they will sell their labour-power or that capitalists will be available to buy it. On the first point it is clear that several other conditions are required to ensure that the propertyless sell their labour-power. If productive property is available for the taking then the supply of labourers cannot be taken for granted. It will be recalled that Marx gives the example of a Mr Peel who discovered this fact to his cost.

> Mr. Peel took with him from England to Swan River, West Australia, means of subsistence and of production to the amount of £50,000. Mr. Peel had the foresight to bring with him, besides, 3,000 persons of the working class, men, women and children. Once arrived at his destination, 'Mr. Peel was left without a servant to make his bed or fetch him water from the river'. Unhappy Mr. Peel who provided for everything except the export of English modes of production to Swan River (*ibid.*, p. 766).

In the colonies the system of indentures provided a means of counteracting the worst effects of the freely available productive property. For the rest, even when free property is not readily available, the mechanisms of economic compulsion of the capitalist mode of production (which are not without their own peculiar legal and ideological conditions) cannot be relied on in the transition period to produce an appropriate propensity to wage-labour on the part of the propertyless. The same applies of course to others who are unable to prodece commodities on their own account, for example, the skilled artisans who may possess productive property in their instruments of production but lack the raw materials and other necessary conditions of production. In the transition period especially, therefore,

> The bourgeoisie wants and uses the power of the state to 'regulate' wages, i.e., to force them within the limits suitable for surplus-value making, to lengthen the working-day and to keep the labourer himself in the normal degree of dependence. This is an essential element of the so-called primitive accumulation (*ibid.*, p. 737).

It need hardly be added that this intervention of state power, whatever form it should take, on behalf of the emergent bourgeoisie is not simply theirs for the asking. It has its own definite conditions of existence in the representation of the different classes in the political level of the social formation in transition. If the capitalist class has yet to capture state power it must nevertheless be represented through determinate political mechanisms and alliances. In this respect it is clear that displacements and transformations at the level of the state apparatus are also 'essential elements of the so-called primitive accumulation'.

Second, in addition to the expropriation of the peasantry, the development of a class of propertyless wage-labourers requires the correlative growth of a class of purchasers of labour-power. Thus the historical process of formation of the capitalist mode of production involves a complete transformation of the place of commodity relations in the structure of the economy as a whole. In particular it involves the formation of a market for capitalist production in the shape of means of personal consumption to be bought by wage-labourers and capitalists and of means of production for labourers to work on. This formation of the 'home' market is an imperative condition of successful transition to capitalism. Notice, however, that more is involved here than the simple expansion of commodity production or even of commodity production by means of wage-labour. This last is entirely possible on the basis of a non-capitalist commodity production. It might, for example, rely on the production of means of personal consumption and of raw materials on the allotments of feudal peasants and estates of feudal lords. In such conditions the system of exchange relations is not that required for the realisation of surplus-value for a capitalist class. In this respect the formation of capitalist relations of production requires both the expansion of commodity production and the transformation of the place of commodity relations in the process of social production as a whole. In instituting a mechanism of appropriation of surplus-labour working through commodity relations these transformations must also effect the displacement of dominance from the political to the economic level. As we have seen the content and precise sequence of the requisite displacements is a matter for the concrete analysis of determinate social formations. We will return to these considerations in the closing sections of this chapter which consider the place of the absolutist state and of the commercial revolution of the sixteenth and seventeenth centuries in the development of European capitalism.

(ii) THE ELIMINATION OF FEUDAL GROUND-RENT

Feudal ground-rent refers to the mechanism of the feudal appropriation of surplus-labour by a class of feudal landowners. It is extracted in the variant forms of labour-rent, rent-in-kind, and money-rent each of which has its own specific economic and political conditions of existence. The mechanism of feudal ground-rent is not to be confused with the variant forms in which it is realised. Nor must it be confused with the payment of rent by a tenant of some kind to a landowner of some kind. The mere presence of rent-payments by direct producers is no more and no less a symptom of the feudal mode of production than the production of commodities by means of wage-labour is a symptom of capitalism. The existence of feudal relations of production is not reducible to the presence of rent-payments. What matters is the precise place and function of these payments in the structure of the economy as a whole. Under feudal conditions rent, in various forms, functions as the primary mechanism of extraction of surplus-labour. Capitalist rent, on the other hand, is articulated within an economy that is structured by a very different mechanism of extraction of surplus-labour. If feudal ground-rent functions as a mechanism of appropriation, capitalist ground-rent is a relation that intervenes in the distribution of surplus-value. The forms of capitalist and pre-capitalist ground-rent have been examined in another chapter. Here it is only necessary to outline the two basic forms of capitalist ground-rent, differential rent and absolute rent.

The first is a necessary relation of distribution under the capitalist mode of production and is quite independent of the existence of private property in land. It arises from the following characteristic of agricultural production: the application of equal quantities of capital will yield differential total products because of the unequal fertility of different soils. Thus on unequal soils the same product will have different costs of production per unit. The significance of these differences is apparent if we consider the tendency towards equalisation of the rate of profit so that equal capitals yield equal returns. Under conditions of the free movement of capital an excess profit in a given sector will attract the entry of further capital into that sector and thus lead to the elimination of the excess. There is therefore a tendency for products to be sold at their price of production which is made up of the costs of production together with profit at the average rate. In agriculture the price of production is determined by the costs prevailing on the least fertile soil in production. The effect of unequal fertility is therefore to produce a differential surplus-profit on the more fertile soils. This differential rent is an effect of unequal natural conditions of production on different soils. Its existence and quantity is therefore independent of whether it is pocketed by a landowner, by a capitalist farmer who is also a landowner, or by the state.[23]

If differential rent is independent of the conditions of ownership of the land, absolute rent by contrast is the product of the existence of private property in land. In the case of differential rent private property in land governs only the appropriation of rent by the owner. The condition of existence of differential ground-rent ensures that production price and market price are equal on the least fertile land in production. There is then no rent on that land. If there were no other form of rent this land would yield no rent at all. Under conditions of private property in land the owners of this land cannot extract rent and cannot therefore maintain their economic conditions of existence.

This point has theoretical effects that are of the greatest importance for the theory of capitalist rent in general, and, in particular, for the analysis of the transition from feudalism to capitalism. In the first place while private property in the means of production is an invariant of the capitalist mode of production, the private ownership of land is not. Agricultural production under capitalism is perfectly conceivable without private property in land. Land may be nationalised, in which case differential rent is realised in the form of a tax on agricultural production. If private property in land is not an invariant condition under capitalism, then the economic conditions of existence of a landowning class require a definite legal and political intervention in the economy. Absolute rent is realised on the least fertile soil in production by means of this intervention. Thus absolute rent is conditional on the existence of a landowning class which depends precisely on the extraction of absolute ground-rent. Private ownership of land is therefore a legal relation with economic effects and an economic realisation in the form of rent within the capitalist mode of production. The level of this rent depends in part on the ability of the landowner to withhold his land from cultivation.

> The mere legal ownership of land does not create any ground-rent for the owner. But it does, indeed, give him the power to withdraw his land from exploitation until economic conditions permit him to utilise it in such a manner as to yield him a surplus, be it used for actual agricultural or other production purposes such as buildings, etc. He cannot increase or decrease the absolute magnitude of this sphere, but he can change the quantity of land placed on the market. Hence, as Fourier already observed, it is a characteristic fact that in all advanced countries a comparatively appreciable portion of land always remains uncultivated (*Capital*, III, p. 757).

On the other hand the legal existence of private landed property is itself the effect of a politico-juridical intervention in the economic. It depends on the conditions of representation of the landowning class at the level of the state apparatus.[24] For this reason the primary determination of their revenues does not lie in their ability to withhold land from production but in the partial determination of the level of the market price for agricultural products by the political intervention of the state.[25] A detailed analysis of this question would involve an examination of the conditions of representation of the landowning class in determinate conjunctures, for example, the struggle over the Corn Laws in England, the alliance of Junkers and large industrialists in Prussia, etc.

To the extent that they both depend on a politico-juridical intervention in the economic, the conditions of existence of absolute ground-rent are analogous to those of feudal ground-rent. It is essential that the limits to this analogy be clearly recognised; otherwise there is a real danger of confusing the two economic forms so that absolute rent appears as the form that feudal ground-rent takes under capitalist conditions. P.-P. Rey does precisely this in interpreting the transition to capitalism as a necessary effect of the reproduction of feudal ground-rent. 'It is the reproduction on an extended scale of the fundamental relation of production, ground-rent, which creates the conditions for the development of the capitalist mode of production' ('Sur l'articulation des modes de production',

p. 55). In Rey's conception it is a fundamental tendency of the feudal mode of production to produce a separation of the direct producers from their means of production in the transition period. This tendency leads to the transformation of the form of ground-rent as a result of the class alliance which it induces between capitalists and landowners.

> The transitional phase appears as the phase of a double necessity: a necessity of capitalist development for landed proprietors, since it is this development that assures the development of their rents; a necessity to maintain landed property ownership (under a new form specific to the transition to capitalism) for capitalists, since only this ensures the provision of labour-power on the one hand and commodities (of agricultural origin) on the other (*ibid.*, p. 56).

Here feudalism itself is thought to induce the transition to capitalism as a result of the lords' interest in increasing their rents, and the original formation of capitalist relations of production is thought to be possible only on the basis of feudal relations of production. Once capitalism appears on the world scene the conditions of transition in other social formations are quite different from those of the transition in England. Thus, as a result of his misrecognition of the character of absolute ground-rent and his treatment of it as a transformed form of feudal relations of production, Rey falls into a linear and evolutionist conception of transition, in which each moment of the reproduction of a mode of production is also a moment of its supersession. We have already seen that such a conception of transition is untenable.[26]

In the preceding chapters we have shown that while absolute rent and feudal ground-rent both require a politico-juridical intervention in the economy, the two interventions are nevertheless of an entirely different character. In one case it plays a crucial role in the constitution of feudal relations of production in establishing the conditions of the feudal mechanism of extraction of surplus-labour. In the other case the politico-juridical intervention has no effect at the level of relations of production; it merely effects a certain distribution of the surplus-value extracted by the economic mechanisms of capitalism.

> When the capitalist tenant farmer steps in between landlord and actual tiller of the soil, all relations which arose out of the old rural mode of production are torn asunder. The farmer becomes the actual commander of these agricultural labourers and the

> actual exploiter of their surplus-labour, whereas the landlord maintains a direct relationship, and indeed simply a money and contractual relationship, solely with this capitalist tenant. Thus, the nature of rent is also transformed, not merely in fact and by chance, as occurred in part even under earlier forms, but normally, in its recognised and prevailing form. From the normal form of surplus-value and surplus-labour, it descends to a mere excess of this surplus-labour over that portion of it appropriated by the exploiting capitalist in the form of profit (*Capital*, III, p. 799).

If a landowning class should persist throughout the period of transition, if, that is to say, the landowners are not expropriated *en masse*,[27] the political, legal and economic conditions of their landownership must nevertheless be utterly transformed. In particular, then, the transition period must effect a transformation of the political level involving, at the very least, a displacement of the relative positions of the bourgeoisie and of the landowning class with respect to the state apparatus. The appearance of continuity in, for example, the survival of landowning families from the feudal period, must not be allowed to mask the fact of this transformation. If the separation of the peasants from their means of production is effected through the intervention of such a landowning class then the bourgeoisie achieves these conditions on the basis of an alliance with this class. However, such an alliance is only one of the possible mechanisms of political representation of the emergent bourgeoisie in the transition period. In treating the landowning class as an invariant of the transition to capitalism Rey reduces the problem of the conditions of political representation of the bourgeoisie to the conditions of a class alliance with the feudal nobility on the basis of shared economic interests. This reduction must have grave effects for the analysis of the political struggles in the period of transition.

(iii) THE ABSOLUTIST STATE AND THE WORLD MARKET IN THE TRANSITION TO CAPITALISM

It should be clear from these discussions that there is nothing in the concept of the capitalist mode of production that requires that it be preceded by feudalism. We have just seen that the failure of Rey's attempt to establish such a requirement rests on the erroneous reduction of the conditions of bourgeois political representation in the transition period to an essentially economic alliance with the feudal nobility. Nor, conversely, does the concept of the feudal mode of production ensure that it must be succeeded by capitalism. Everything depends on the conditions in which transition takes place and on the character of the transitional conjunctures. There is no necessary sequence of modes of production. Such a necessity is conceivable only within an historicist problematic since it depends on the condition that each mode of production has a unilineal tendency to decay – with its beginnings in the entrails of the previous mode and its end in the conditions of emergence of the next.[28] Balibar has shown that such a conception of the tendency of a mode of production is entirely foreign to historical materialism.[29]

Nevertheless if the transition from feudalism to capitalism is to take place it is clear that certain necessary conditions must have been created under the dominance of the feudal mode of production. In particular it is necessary that conditions exist within which the so-called primitive accumulation may take place. This requires the extensive development of commodity production and trade with the consequent development of usurer's capital and merchant's capital. This is not yet *capital* in the strict sense – we have seen that that requires a certain structure of commodity relations in the economy as a whole – but in the sense of the capital required for the formation of economic units that are capitalist in form. This condition of extensive commodity production is sufficient to preclude the transition from primitive communism to capitalism.

Given the dominance of the feudal mode of production the extensive development of trade and commodity production has definite legal and political conditions of existence. On the one hand regular and systematic commodity circulation on an extensive scale presupposes some degree of legal guarantee of contracts and a legally guaranteed 'equality' of buyer and seller in respect of certain contracts. There must therefore be a legal and political apparatus capable, at least at a minimal level, of enforcing such guarantees. On the other hand regular commerce presupposes the pacification of the countryside (i.e. it should be relatively free of robber bands and of irregular warfare between feudal lords) and it requires that commerce be relatively free from arbitrary interferences. In these respects the extensive development of trade and commodity production is dependent on a centralised state political and legal apparatus capable of enforcing its decisions against the wishes of individual feudal lords. It presupposes, in other words, the 'absolutist' form of feudal state.

This implies not so much that the absolutist state is itself a transitional phenomenon but rather that the transition from feudalism to capitalism is possible only from the absolutist variant of feudalism. It is for this reason that the absolutist state is such a significant feature of the period of the development of capitalism in Europe. In addition it is well known that the intervention of the state played a major role in the struggle among European powers for the control of the world market opened up in the sixteenth and seventeenth centuries. Thus the question of the absolutist state and its connection with the development of capitalism is of the greatest importance for the whole of modern history.

Any extensive examination of this question would require a concrete analysis of the social formations of sixteenth- and seventeenth-century Europe which would be out of place in the present context. Instead we shall proceed to our discussion of the absolutist state and the world market by means of a critique of the following positions: (i) the 'statist' conception of the role of the absolutist state in the rise of the bourgeoisie; (ii) the theory of the general economic crisis of the seventeenth century and of the role of the world market in overcoming the obstacles to capitalist development.

(a) THE ABSOLUTIST STATE

By the 'statist' conception of the role of the absolutist state in the rise of the bourgeoisie we refer to a position that is widely held among historians, notably by Mousnier whom we take as our example here.[30] This conception emphasises the creative and regulatory role of the absolute monarch in the creation and development of classes and in their struggle. The sovereigns created the class struggle between privileged strata, and directed its course in their own interest. Thus Mousnier:

> Dividing the functions between the two classes, but offering the most important of them to the lesser class, that is, the bourgeoisie, systematically raising it and setting it off against the nobility, the king brought the struggle of the classes to such an equilibrium that he could strengthen his own personal power and ensure in the government and in the state unity, order and hierarchy (*Les XVI et XVII siècles. Le progrès de la civilisation européene et le déclin de l'Orient*, p. 236).

In this conception the struggle of classes is one of the means employed by the sovereign to increase and consolidate his power. While emphasising the importance of other factors, especially foreign wars, in the rise of absolutism these authors advance what is effectively a linear political theory of the transition to capitalism, in which the rise to power of the bourgeoisie is an effect of the will of the absolute monarch.

> Absolute monarchy and large-scale capitalism seemed to be functions of one another. With its own lands, with taxes which were levied largely from agriculture, with its own trade monopolies, absolute monarchy was changed into a capitalist enterprise, in which financiers were the executors, the participants and the suppliers (*ibid.*, pp. 53–4).

Lublinskaya has shown that these conclusions are produced on the basis of two related methodological positions.[31] In the first place Mousnier takes the opinions of contemporaries as his criterion in determining social class – in effect by the status ranking of the members of the society in question. This position ignores the problems of ideology and of conflicting class interests and it presupposes that social divisions are the product of the consciousness of members of the society – or at least that their consciousness is some kind of index of the real relations. Second, Mousnier in common with many historians fails to work with a developed theoretical conception of the structure of the social formation under investigation. It is only on this condition that the opinions of contemporaries can be substituted for a scientific definition of the historian's own problem. This failure to specify clearly the structure of the social formation leads to serious errors in the analysis of absolutism and its characterisation as a form of state.

In particular those strata which Mousnier identified as bourgeois derive their incomes largely from feudal ground-rent and only to a very limited extent from forms transitional to capitalist rent.[32] Despite their bourgeois origin, and public opinion notwithstanding, Mousnier's high-ranking bourgeoisie is clearly a nobility. Thus what is represented as the struggle of competing classes in fact represents the rivalry of two factions of the aristocracy for power and profitable position in the absolutist state apparatus. It is this incorrect analysis of the conditions of this rivalry that allows Mousnier to represent the absolutist state as the independent arbiter and orchestrator of the class struggle between the 'high-ranking bourgeoisie' on the one hand and the nobility on the other.

In this conception of the period of absolutism the position of the real bourgeoisie, the manufacturers and merchants, with respect to the state apparatus is necessarily misrepresented. The development and the transformations of the absolutist state apparatus are therefore analysed primarily in terms of the fiscal and financial difficulties of the state, the need for an efficient decision-making apparatus, and so on.[33] The transformations of the state apparatus with regard to the conditions of political representation of the bourgeoisie and the landowning class which we have shown to play an essential role in the transition from the domination of feudal relations of production to those of capitalism are ignored in this conception.

(b) THE THEORY OF THE GENERAL ECONOMIC CRISIS OF THE SEVENTEENTH CENTURY[34]

In his paper on 'The Crisis of the Seventeenth Century' Hobsbawm argues that there was a general crisis of the European economy in the early part of this period. The crisis constituted 'the last phase of the general transition from a feudal to a capitalist economy' (p. 5). After presenting a number of indices of this supposed crisis Hobsbawm poses the problem of explanation in the following terms: 'Why did the expansion of the late 15th and 16th centuries not lead straight into the epoch of the 18th and 19th century Industrial Revolution? What, in other words, were the obstacles in the way of capitalist expansion?' (p. 14). The crisis of the European economy is here seen as the result of obstacles to capitalist development, it is a crisis of capitalism. Hobsbawm therefore looks only for obstacles to the teleological development of capitalism. He does not consider the concrete economies of the different European countries. These obstacles are, in Hobsbawm's view, to be found in the social structure of feudal society, the difficulties involved in mastering overseas and colonial markets, and the narrowness of the home market. These come down to a lack of effective demand for the products of capitalist manufacture. In order to overcome this crisis and to inaugurate the development leading to the industrial revolution capitalism 'had to find ways of creating its own expanding markets' (p. 43). 'If there was to be an industrial revolution, a number of countries or industries therefore had to operate within a sort of "forced draught", which fanned the entrepreneurs' cupidity to the point of spontaneous combustion' (p. 44). This 'forced draught' is provided by the concentration of trade into the hands of the most industrially advanced countries, the expanding home markets in these countries and especially through the new colonial system and the plantation economies which were 'probably decisive for the British cotton industry, the real industrial pioneer' (p. 44). While Hobsbawm appears to emphasise the purely economic aspects of the crisis and the economic mechanisms by which it is overcome it is clear that the mercantilist policy of the absolutist state must play a crucial role in providing conditions in which the 'forced draught' may operate.

A systematic critique of Hobsbawm's thesis is hardly necessary in the present context. It will be sufficient to consider the function which he assigns to foreign markets in the last phase of the general transition from feudalism to capitalism. For the rest a few comments may suffice. We have argued that the difficulties facing manufacture in the period of formation of capitalist relations of production cannot be overcome merely by increasing the size of the market, and that political intervention in the economy is essential if it is to move towards capitalism. Hobsbawm fails to consider the conditions of this intervention. Lublinskaya has provided a systematic critique of the various notions of the 'general crisis of the seventeenth century' (*French Absolutism*, chapters 1 and 2). The various upheavals usually cited as evidence of the effects of a general economic crisis cannot be accounted for in this way since there is no evidence to support the existence of an integrated European economy at this time. On the contrary, what characterised Europe in this transitional period was precisely the very different political and economic conditions in the different states. Thus the many political upheavals of this period did not have the same causes and were in no way equivalent in character. In each case it is necessary to examine the specific political and economic conditions in the country concerned. In his article 'Problems in the formation of capitalism' Vilar has provided a critique of the related thesis which seeks to account for the growth of capitalism in terms of the influx of American bullion. In this case the analysis is clearly anachronistic since it works in terms of economic categories which specify conditions and facts more pertinent to developed capitalist societies.

Hobsbawm's invocation of the foreign market to supply a 'forced draught' raises the vexed question of the place of foreign trade in the formation of the capitalist mode of production. Both Dobb and Sweezy, in rather different fashions, assign to international trade a fundamental role in the dissolution of feudalism and the formation of capitalism; other positions of this kind are commonplace. Marx himself suggests that the opening up of the world market in the seventeenth century is crucial to the process of primitive accumulation.

> The discovery of gold and silver in America, the extirpation, enslavement and entombment in mines of the aboriginal population, the beginning of the conquest and looting of the East Indies, the turning of Africa into a warren for the commercial hunting of black-skins, signalised the rosy dawn of the era of capitalist production. These idyllic proceedings are the chief momenta of primitive accumulation. On their heels treads the commercial war of the European nations, with the globe for a theatre. It begins with the revolt of the Netherlands from Spain, assumes giant dimensions in England's Anti-Jacobin War, and is still going on in the opium wars against China, etc.
>
> The different momenta of primitive accumulation distribute themselves now, more or less in chronological order, particularly over Spain, Portugal, Holland, France, and England. In England at the end of the 17th century, they arrive at a systematical combination, embracing the colonies, the national debt, the modern mode of taxation, and the protectionist system. These methods depend in part on brute force, e.g., the colonial system. But they all employ the power of the State, the concentrated and organised force of society, to hasten, hothouse fashion, the process of transformation of the feudal mode of production into the capitalist mode, and to shorten the transition. Force is the midwife of every society pregnant with a new one. It is itself an economic power (*Capital*, I, p. 751).

Our problem here concerns the precise nature of this apparent necessity of a foreign market in the transition. Why is it that the commercial wars and the struggle of the European powers for control of the newly created world market play such a fundamental role in the period of the formation of capitalism?

It must be emphasised that the foreign market is not essential to the concept of the capitalist mode of production. There is no necessary insufficiency of effective demand in the home market, as Hobsbawm appears to suggest and the underconsumptionist economists argue,[35] that forces capitalists to find buyers abroad. The capitalist mode of extraction and realisation of surplus-value works through the exchange of commodities between the labourers and capitalists of the two departments of production. In this system of commodity exchange, where labour-power and means of production enter the production process as commodities and the labourer is separated from his means of production and must purchase means of personal consumption, the market for the products of capitalism is created by the development of capitalism itself. The realisation of surplus-value through this system of commodity circulation requires no reference to purchasers external to capitalism. While the capitalist system of commodity circulation may cross national boundaries there is no necessity for it to do so. The foreign market is therefore not an invariant of the capitalist mode of production and capitalist production is conceivable in principle in the complete absence of foreign trade.

In his analysis of the mistakes of the underconsumptionists Lenin gives three reasons of a 'historical order' to account for the importance of foreign markets to capitalism (*The Development of Capitalism in Russia*, *Collected Works*, 3, pp. 64–7). These are: first, that capitalism emerges on the basis of extensive commodity production and is therefore integrated within a system of international trade from the very beginning. Second, the fact that capitalists produce on the whole for markets that are not fully known means that various imbalances in the supply of certain specific commodities must appear within a given social formation. Foreign trade may ease this problem. Third, the tendency towards the unrestricted growth of capitalist production leads to expansion beyond the confines of a given home market. Whatever weight may be attached to reasons of this kind it is clear that they cannot account for the importance of the commercial wars in the period of formation of capitalism.

These conclusions mean that the commercial wars and the struggle for control of the world market during this period cannot be explained away by reference to a necessity inherent in the concept of the capitalist mode of production. If we are to account for the specifically commercial conflicts of this period we must do so in terms of the concrete political and economic conditions of the transitional conjunctures in the different European states. We will try to indicate what characteristics of the structure of the economy in transition from feudalism to capitalism are involved in such an analysis.

We have seen that the extensive development of commodity production under the absolutist form of feudal state provides conditions in which certain forms of 'capitalist' production can develop. The qualification here is essential. It is not wage-labour and commodity production as such which define capitalism but the production and extraction of surplus-value as the dominant mode of appropriation of surplus-labour. We have seen that this condition is not defined at the level of the individual unit of production. It requires not only the presence of economic units which employ wage-labour to produce commodities but that these units be articulated on a reproduction cycle that is internalised within the capitalist sector.

The development of manufacture under the dominance of feudalism however involves a reproduction cycle that cannot be internalised within the capitalist sector. The raw materials of the production process and consumption goods for the labourers are largely supplied from the dominant non-capitalist sector. For this reason prices of production and wage-levels in manufacture are not and cannot be determined by mechanisms specific to the capitalist mode of production. We have shown above that the revenue of the 'capitalist' under these conditions is derived primarily from revenues generated within the feudal mode of production rather than from the extraction of surplus-value through the mechanisms of commodity exchange. At the same time manufacture under these conditions depends principally on non-capitalist markets provided by the feudal revenues of the lords, by state expenditures and by the consumption funds of the peasants. It follows that the market for manufactures is severely limited in scope and that its size depends largely on the level and forms of feudal exploitation. It is true that an internal market for means of production and other manufactures develops within the capitalist sector but this is still dependent on and subordinated to the feudal sector.

The transition to capitalism involves not only the expansion of commodity production but also the displacement of this internal 'capitalist' market into the position of dominance in the structure of the economy as a whole. In particular, then, it is imperative that agricultural production which provides both raw materials and the bulk of the means of personal consumption be internalised within the capitalist sector. The effect of this displacement is completely to transform the articulation of commodity relations within the structure of the economy and thereby to create the conditions of the realisation of surplus-value for a capitalist class.

In the period of transition itself while this displacement is at most only partially effected, the development of manufacturing is dependent on political conditions in a number of respects. In the first place the commodity market depends on the conditions of the feudal class struggle which determine the level and form of ground-rent extraction and therefore govern the revenues available to the state.

For example, an increase in the level of feudal exploitation, either in the form of taxation or of direct rent extraction, may have a considerable effect on the size of the market for certain types of manufactured goods provided by the more prosperous peasants.

In addition the condition of manufacturing in a given society depends on the level of protectionism carried out by the state as against other manufacturing countries, on the ability of the state through war or diplomacy to reduce the level of foreign protectionism and on the availability of captive markets in the colonies. The tendency of English and Dutch manufacturers to benefit at the expense of the French in the early part of the seventeenth century depends in part on the failure of the French government to provide a level of protection for her manufacturers comparable to that provided in England or Holland.[36]

Conversely the development of a commercial and manufacturing bourgeoisie provides an additional source of income for the state. It might seem then that the interests of the state and of the bourgeoisie must coincide: the state needing to develop trade and manufacture to boost its revenues and the bourgeoisie needing the assistance of state power. However, the situation is more complex for both sides of this apparently natural alliance.

On the one hand the bourgeoisie certainly need the assistance of state power and the military and diplomatic policy of the state may well further the expansion of the capitalist sector at the expense of foreign competitors. However, the conditions of this assistance may, while providing sections of the bourgeoisie with lucrative sources of revenue, in fact hinder the growth of capitalist production. To return to the example of France it is clear that the fiscal problems of the state in the early seventeenth century forced it to rely heavily on loans from the bourgeoisie. This situation promoted the development of a specifically financial section of the bourgeoisie closely involved with state finances and increasingly divorced from commerce and manufacture. Here there is direct competition between productive investment and other forms of investment in, for example, the purchase of estates and offices, in tax-farming, and other ventures. The divorce of important sections of the bourgeoisie from productive capitalist investment under these conditions and the accumulation of funds for non-productive purposes by the state machine restricted the rate of capitalist accumulation in France.

On the other hand if the state may use the development of trade and manufacture to boost its revenues there are other sources of revenues – including forced loans and expropriations from the bourgeoisie. More important is the point that to advance commercial and manufacturing interests requires the political intervention of a state still largely feudal with its own political and diplomatic objectives. For the state to impose protectionist policies or to act against other protectionisms would have diplomatic effects which may well run counter to other policy objectives. Again, in the case of the founding or defence of colonies or the organisation of existing colonies the feudal or semi-feudal state is hardly governed solely by the interests of the bourgeoisie. The commercial interests of the bourgeoisie are not in themselves sufficient to ensure that the state will conduct an aggressive military and diplomatic policy to advance those interests. Similarly with regard to internal policies, such as control over wages or the movement of labour, the mere presence of certain interests does not force the state to respond to them.

In all these cases it is clear that the political intervention of the state on behalf of commercial or manufacturing interests must depend on the representation of those interests within the state apparatus. In this respect it is quite misleading to write of the bourgeoisie and its interests on the one hand and of the state and its interests on the other. We have already argued that the transition period is characterised by a double transformation: in conditions of representation of the bourgeoisie and the landowning class at the political level; in the articulation of commodity relations in the structure of the economy as a whole. (There are also certain necessary transformations at the ideological level but these cannot be discussed here.) It is precisely in this double transformation that the displacement of dominance from the political to the economic level is effected. It follows that the commercial wars and struggles for control of the world market between the manufacturing states in the period of transition cannot be analysed without reference to the specific political transformations of the various states in this period. Success in these struggles has the effect of reducing the dependence of the capitalist sector on revenues generated in the feudal sector of the successful economy. In this respect control of the world market not only provides a larger market for commodity production but it also transforms the relative positions of the capitalist and feudal sectors in the structure of the economy.

Conclusion

Concepts and history

We have no doubt that this book will appear to many people, historians and others, to be a contradictory enterprise. How can a book about pre-capitalist modes of production be abstract and anti-historical? Surely, the sole value of the concepts of the pre-capitalist modes of production is to serve as tools or research devices for the investigation of concrete historical societies? What purpose do these concepts have if they are not used as guides to historical research?

Our answer to these questions is simple. They are based on a misrecognition, not only of the nature of our book, but of the nature of Marxist theory: a misrecognition which engenders a cosy conflation between Marxist theoretical work and the historian's practice, a misrecognition which reduces Marxist theory to historical method and to a philosophy of history. Marxism is not a 'science of history' and Marxist theoretical work has no necessary connection with the practice of the historian.

What does the notion of Marxism as a 'science of history' entail? It supposes that Marxism provides a systematic and accurate interpretation of all hitherto existing societies, their development, their events and their struggles. It involves constituting the hitherto existing as a possible field of investigation and explanation, as the coherent object of a distinct knowledge. In this respect the Marxist 'science of history' differs only in its substantive explanations from other histories – those histories also conceive the hitherto existing as the object of a knowledge. Doubtless, history appears to be the 'obvious' object of a knowledge – history 'obviously' exists and it is 'obviously' vital to Marxist theory and to Marxist political practice. This obviousness is nothing of the kind. Historical writing, still more history as an object of research, are not universal and necessary phenomena. The absence in many literate societies of the writing of history and of history as an object of knowledge should indicate that history is not a given, that it is an object constituted within knowledge. It is neither an inevitable nor a necessary object. Why should the hitherto existing appear as a unity, as the possible object of a knowledge? What is the pertinence of this investigation of the hitherto existing?

The object of history

Let us investigate this object which the Marxist science of history shares with other histories, and, having determined the nature of this object, ask by what right this investigation of history calls itself a science. What is the object of history? It is quite simply, despite all the elaborations, equivocations and qualifications of historians and philosophers, whatever is past. History conceives the past as such as a possible object of investigation. Periods, the different regional histories – of the economy, of technology, of art, etc. – are merely divisions within this unity. And yet, by definition, all that is past does not exist. To be accurate the object of history is whatever is *represented* as having hitherto existed. The essence of this representation is preserved records and documents. History's object, the hitherto existing, does not exist except in the modality of its current existence, as representations. It is present as its opposite and absent as itself. Historical practice refuses to recognise this identity of opposites, it conceives its object as a real concrete object, as the given conditions of the past. This real object is accessible *through* its representations.

The problem of reading through the representations to the real is common to all the main conceptions of the historian's practice and of historical method. The idealist historical school conceives the method of interpretation of historical texts as understanding, the recreation of the spirit or cultural essence of a period or society through the meanings present in the representations of it which are still extant. Interpretation, the grasping of the reality of history beyond the record, is possible because that reality is *spiritual*. The historian, because he is a subject, can recognise the meanings of past subjects and re-create or re-live their spiritual life. Positivist historical method interprets representations by means of rules and procedures intended to determine the veracity of the record, to eliminate distortion and to read back through the record to the real conditions of which it is a representation. For the idealist representations are a medium through which spirit is recorded. For the positivist the representations are records of the real through the medium of experience. All empiricist knowledges give rise to the philosophical problem of knowledge, and to scepticism. Certain historians, recognising the unt certainties involved in interpretation, take an extreme nominaliss position and argue that history is nothing but the more or lesr systematic study of documents. Scepticist historians such as Piete-Geyl recognise that all historical writing uses documents and representations as the medium of action of political and social ideology. History, it is argued, is the record of its own time in the guise of the analysis of the past; in *Napoleon For and Against* Geyl shows that the different conceptions of Napoleon held by historians are a function of their differing political ideologies and *Weltanschauungen.*

The historian's conception of his object and his method of knowing is necessarily an empiricist one. The object of history is an object already given to knowledge. It is a given body of representations and a given finite body of real events which underlies those representations. This body of events and representations exists prior to any theory of it, its existence gives to the theory the object it must explain. The historian's theories are developed to account for this given. Theory and hypothesis must rationalise and explain this given object. A *scientific* history is the most complete and accurate saving of the phenomena. The given, the facts of history, is the measure of the explanations of it. Historical knowledge is limited to sifting the essential from the inessential among the facts, events and records given to it, and presenting an account which corresponds to the essential.

History is condemned by the nature of its object to empiricism. Its object, the past, cannot be other than given, and given in one definite and unalterable modality. This object is supposed to have pre-existed its investigation and, as it no longer exists, it can in no way be transformed by this investigation. The double givenness of the object puts it beyond any modification of its conditions of existence, any variation of its forms by the operations of a knowledge. The given real object has a finite and necessary character, definite events which no longer exist, and it exists in the mode of representation. No operation on the given representations can transform the real object of history for it is not present in them. Explanation is limited to finding reasons for what appears in the form of the representation. Despite the empiricist claims of historical practice the real object of history is inaccessible to knowledge. Even within empiricist philosophical epistemology it is recognised that historical knowledge is subject to severe limits. Positivist critics of the notion that history is a science have made much of these limitations. Even within the empiricist canons of knowledge it is recognised that there cannot be experimentation in history, that historical explanations are *post hoc* rationalisations, and that as historical phenomena are finite and unrepeatable they cannot give rise to general laws.

There can be no escape from this empiricism. The object of history cannot be conceived as a theoretically constituted object, as an object not limited by what is given. Such a non-given object cannot be part of history; in being constituted theoretically it is constituted independently of the hitherto existing. History must conceive the object of its knowledge as a given object or cease to be historical. But this given real object, far from being real and given prior to investigation, is constituted by definite social and political ideologies. What the past *is* is determined by the content of the various ideological forms which operate within the parameters of historical knowledge. The content of the past, its nature, its periods and problems is determined by the character of a particular ideological form. The particular modes of writing history invest this or that body of representations with the status of a record. Artefacts, washing lists, court rolls, kitchen middens, memoirs, are converted into *texts* – representations through which the real may be read. The text, constituted as a text by its reading, is at the mercy of this reading. Far from working on the *past*, the ostensible object of history, historical knowledge works on a body of *texts*. These texts are a product of historical knowledge. The writing of history is the production of texts which interpret these texts.

The limitations of history are widely recognised, not least by sceptical historians. History is a potentially infinite text, constantly doubling back on itself, constantly being re-written. Marxist history in no sense escapes from these limitations. It cannot transform the conditions of the historian's practice without ceasing to be history, and if it respects these conditions then it must be merely another form of rationalising an object which it constitutes as the given. If Marxism gives us another history, if it recognises new representations as pertinent (the record of the class struggle, the aspirations of the masses, the evolution of material production, etc.), if it brings new ideological concerns to create, select and order the facts it will take as a given, then it merely gives us *another* history – a novel history, perhaps, but a history like all other histories.

It is the notion of a Marxist history, of a Marxism confined within the conditions of the historian's practice, which is the contradictory enterprise. Marxism, as a theoretical and a political practice, gains nothing from its association with historical writing and historical research. The study of history is not only scientifically but also politically valueless. The object of history, the past, no matter how it is conceived, cannot affect present conditions. Historical events do not exist and can have no material effectivity in the present. The conditions of existence of present social relations necessarily exist in and are constantly reproduced in the present. It is not the 'present', what the past has vouchsafed to allow us, but the 'current situation' which it is the object of Marxist theory to elucidate and of Marxist political practice to act upon. All Marxist theory, however abstract it may be, however general its field of application, exists to make possible the analysis of the current situation.

The notion that the past does have a definite effectivity, that the genealogy of the present is the key to the understanding of the present, has definite theoretical conditions of existence. To deny that the conditions of existence of present social relations are necessarily reproduced in the present is only possible on the basis of a teleological conception of history and a conception of the social totality as a spiritual totality. In teleological conceptions of history historical time is a continuum, its successive moments necessarily linked by the development of an essence. In the conception of social relations as spiritual relations, or spiritually determined relations, the past, although it has no material existence, has a spiritual effectivity, that is, it exists through its influence on the minds and souls of currently existing subjects. Spirit is supra-historical, time is subordinate to it, and the subject which is the carrier of spirit transcends the moments of time. Humanity as a collective subject, or God, existing outside of time, ensures the transmission of spirit and subsumes its particular subjective incarnations. Teleology and spirituality abolish current existence except as a moment of a continuous historical time, as a stage in an evolution, as a form of the becoming of the is-to-be. Teleology and spirituality assign an effectivity to the past, they save it and rationalise it, assuring it a necessary relation to the present. Teleology and spirituality are essential mechanisms of all philosophies of history. And, save for mindless antiquarianism or utter scepticism, there can be no history without a philosophy of history. It is in the philosophy of history that the past becomes a possible and rational object of knowledge. It is through the conception of historical time as a continuum that the past becomes a coherent object.

A historical analysis of the 'current situation' is impossible.

History subordinates the current situation to its teleology. It is explicable only in so far as it is no longer current, that it is subject to a law which transcends it. The currency of the 'current situation' is obliterated by the action of a trans-historical cause. History renders unrecognisable that which is the primary object of Marxist theoretical and political practice. It dislocates that necessary connection between theoretical analysis and politics which is the very core of Marxism. It reduces theory to the role of a rationalisation of the real and the politics based on such rationalisation to an abstract shadow politics of gesture. Beneath this rationalisation and this gestural politics pragmatism is the form in which the 'current situation' is recognised and coped with. The 'current situation', despite all history, refuses to disappear; it is this situation in its currency which always confronts political practice.

Althusser's proposal for a 'science of history'

The rigorous idealism of the philosophy of history, or the speculative empiricism of the historian's practice which suppresses its idealist theoretical conditions of existence, this is the choice facing those who wish to consider Marxism a 'science of history'. There is no other history – no scientific history free of these limitations and which transcends this opposition. But, the reader may ask, is it not a *science of history* that Althusser offers us in *Reading Capital*? Is it not the object of that text to free Marxism, the science of history, from the epistemological obstacles of humanism and historicism?

Althusser argues that the condition of such a science is the rigorous separation of the thought object, history, and the real object, history: 'the concept of history can no longer be empirical, i.e., *historical*' (*Reading Capital*, p. 105). The object of history as a knowledge is not historical. A scientific history is only possible on the condition that it constructs a *concept* of its object, that its object is constituted within knowledge. The object of a science of history is not historical in the sense that it is not a reproduction of 'empirical' history, of a linear and homogeneous time.

Althusser's object in the chapter 'An Outline of the Concept of Historical Time' is twofold: to criticise historicist interpretations of *Capital* and to outline the concept of an anti-historicist theory of history and of time. Althusser argues that the different conceptions of historical time are necessarily coupled with definite conceptions of the nature of the social totality and the form of its causality:

> . . . *the structure of the social whole* must be strictly interrogated in order to find in it the secret of the conception of history in which the 'development' of this social whole is thought; once we know the structure of the social whole we can understand the apparently 'problem-less' relationship between it and the conception of historical time in which this conception is reflected (*Reading Capital*, p. 97).

The structure of the social whole provides the key to the concept of history associated with it. This is because the different totalities entail different forms of causality. Althusser differentiates what he argues is the Marxist concept of totality from the Hegelian 'spiritual' totality and the 'expressive' causality corresponding to it. The Marxist social totality is a complex whole of relatively autonomous levels structured in a hierarchy of causal efficacy and determined 'in the last instance' by the economic level. This totality corresponds to a form of causality Althusser calls 'structural causality'. In this form of causality the structure is present in and as its effects, it does not exist apart from its effects, and the conditions of existence of the structure are secured by its own action. Structural causality gives rise to, and is a property of, self-conditioning totalities – the action of the structure secures its own conditions of existence. Such totalities are self-determining and independent of external causes. Althusser calls this totality an 'eternity', in the Spinozist sense of the word: it is the cause of itself, it is infinite in its kind, and as itself it must necessarily exist.

History must, therefore, be conceived in terms of these eternities and the concept of time which is pertinent corresponds to the times which these eternities engender:

> It needs to be said that, just as there is no production in general, there is no history in general, but only specific structures of historicity, based in the last resort on the specific structures of the different modes of production, specific structures of historicity which, since they are merely the existence of determinate social formations (arising from specific modes of production), articulated as social wholes, have no meaning except as a function of the essence of those totalities, i.e., of the essence of their peculiar complexity (*Reading Capital*, pp. 108–9).

The theory of history is the theory of these eternities. History, as theory, has as its function the determination of the distinct synchronic wholes (this function is exercised entirely within knowledge):

> The synchronic is then nothing but *the conception* of the specific relations that exist between the different elements and the different structures of the structure of the whole, it is *the knowledge* of the relations of dependence and articulation which make it an organic whole, a system (*ibid.*, p. 107).

This concept of synchrony displaces its ideological coupling with the notion of diachrony:

> Indeed, by what miracle could an empty time and momentary events induce de- and re-structurations of the synchronic? Once synchrony has been correctly located, diachrony loses its 'concrete' sense and nothing is left of it either but its epistemological use, on the condition that it undergoes a theoretical conversion and is considered in the true sense as a category not of the concrete but of knowing (*ibid.*, p. 108).

'Diachrony' becomes the relation of theoretical forms within the process of production of knowledge, their successive appearence in the order of discourse.

The complex totalities, as eternities, have no necessary evolution or succession in the real, they exist wholly within knowledge. The concept of time reflects the complexity of the structure of the totality, just as there is no general historical *process* so there is no uniform and continuous *time*:

> We can and must say: for each mode of production there is a peculiar time and history, punctuated in a specific way by the development of the productive forces; the relations of production have their peculiar time and history, punctuated in a specific way; the political superstructure has its own history . . . philosophy has its own time and history (*ibid.*, p. 99).

Times are entirely relative to the totalities considered as eternities. The existence of differential times in the levels which comprise the whole is an effect of the differential nature of the articulation of these levels into the whole:

> The fact that each of these times and each of these histories is *relatively autonomous* does not make them so many domains which are *independent* of the whole: the specificity of each of these times and of each of these histories – in other words, their relative autonomy and independence – is based on a certain type of articulation in the whole, and therefore a certain type of *dependence* with respect to the whole (*ibid.*, p. 100).

These times are *differential* – determined by the differential articulation of the levels to which they pertain into the whole.

The theory of history that Althusser establishes is a theory of the distinct eternities/totalities that are possible and a theory of the complex internal temporalities of these totalities. Thus Althusser's position leads directly to Balibar's attempt to create a necessary and differential series of modes of production in 'The Fundamental Concepts of Historical Materialism'. History as a time continuum and as a teleological process, in the real, is superseded by history as a series of totalities considered as eternities, within knowledge. These eternities have no necessary succession, they do not form a historical progression, rather, the eternities have a necessary connection within knowledge, they form a logical series. Linear and continuous time is dispensed with; the times of the distinct eternities are incommensurable, these times are distinct effects of different structures and they relate to no uniform or base time.

In constructing his theory of history Althusser certainly avoids the Hegelian variant of teleology, a process with a purpose, but only at the price of falling into another, a structure whose end is its existence. Althusser remarks somewhere that Hegel is Spinoza set in motion – Althusser comes very close to being Spinoza once again at rest. In the analysis in *Reading Capital* the complexity of the structure Althusser attempts to establish is contradicted and negated by the structural causality he couples with it. Complexity is negated by the conception of the totality as an eternity. The structure, no matter how internally complex it is, is its own condition of existence – each of the levels of this complexity must be subject to the 'law' of this eternity. No element can escape the place assigned to it by the structure of the whole. The differential times are an effect of the structure, of the differential articulation of the levels into the whole, The whole, although it only exists as the articulation of its parts, governs, as the necessary structure of that articulation, each of its levels and the time of each of its levels. The structure of articulation becomes its own essence: structural causality necessarily engenders a certain structuration, which determines its elements, and this structuration persists through its action on its elements. Structural causality secures the conditions of existence of the totality through its determination of the articulation of the elements, their place and function. Structural causality converts the complex totality into a simple totality: a whole each of the parts of which is necessary to its existence and each of the parts of which the whole, as an eternity, must ensure is in existence. Each part is subordinate to the whole, to the logic which requires the structure to persist through its own action.

Structural causality excludes the determinate material causality of concrete social struggles and practices. Far from designating a general concept which specifies relations the effects of which vary with the outcome of the real struggles and activities that take place within them, structural causality designates a form of causation in which the logical connection of the elements of a concept becomes a real causal connection. Structural causality assigns to the structure an effectivity in itself, an effectivity as a concept. The conception of the structure as present in its effects is negated by the conception of it as an eternity. It is conceived as an eternity *within knowledge*, but these totalities conceived of as within knowledge are so conceived that they are capable of being taken as concrete totalities and treated as functioning real wholes, within knowledge. The rational becomes the real. The causality of logic displaces the causality of real struggles and practices. The class struggle is reduced to an effect, the visible sign, of a causality of logical connection. There can be no doubt that this is not Althusser's object or intention. It is the kind of problem his distinction between the real concrete and the concrete in thought is designed to avoid; yet, as we shall see, it is the very problem that this distinction engenders.

So Althusser's 'science of history' is a general theory of modes of production. But why should this general theory be called a theory *of history*? What is historical about it? Althusser's distinction of the real concrete and the concrete in thought problematises the notion of an 'empirical' history. However, the use of this couple, real object/thought object, and the continued use of the notion of history have definite theoretical effects. To say that *the object of history is not historical* is to make use of a play on the word 'history' and on the word 'object'. What is called a science of history is not a history. The object of history as a science is not only non-historical, there is no object, real or conceptual, 'history'. What is called a 'history' is something quite different, a general theory of modes of production. The radical conclusion to Althusser's argument would be that the supposed real object, 'history', which the thought object is not, is not a real object. There is no real object 'history', the notion that there is a *real* history is the product of empiricism. The word 'history' should be confined to designating the ideological non-object constituted by philosophies of history and the practice of the writing of history.

Althusser fails to break with the notion of history at the very moment of splitting from it. The means of destruction of the empiricist conception of history and of the philosophy of history engender a reprise in which history reasserts itself. Althusser does not say that there is no real object 'history', that the notion of a real concrete history is an illusion. He differentiates the thought object from the real object, but he does not deny the existence of the real object. Indeed, the effect of this distinction is to affirm it, to assign it a definite place in the Althusserian theory of knowledge. History in thought becomes an anti-historicist general theory of modes of production. But history as the real concrete, this survives untheorised and uncriticised. History is not therefore transformed. In the Althusserian theory of knowledge the knowledge effect is the appropriation of the concrete in thought. The thought object is the means of appropriation of the real object. This appropriation is certainly not the direct correspondence of thought and the real. However, the distinction of the objects poses the question of the mode of their correspondence, for both are held to exist, the concrete existing prior to and independently of thought, and thought being the form in which the concrete is known. Althusser's epistemology does not escape the problem of the relation of knowledge and being. The continued and uncriticised existence of the real object allows a shadow 'history' to emerge parallel to the theoretical history, a shadow which reproduces the outlines of the history which Althusser has criticised. The very notion of a real object, history, the object theory appropriates, is an index of this reprise. History is not a real object, an object prior to and independent of thought, it is an object constituted within definite ideologies and discourses. Althusser's general theory of modes of production is the thought object through which the real object, history, unchanged in its conception, is appropriated in thought. By retaining the two objects Althusser creates the possibility of an 'Althusserian' philosophy of history. The science of history, different in character from the empirical appearances of history, appropriates it in thought – it explains and rationalises what is essential behind these appearances.

The general theory of modes of production re-duplicates previous attempts to explain history considered as a coherent object. Balibar, following Althusser, does not conceive the unity of the object, history, as the unity of a teleological process or of a time continuum. The unity of the Balibarian history is the unity of a *series*. History is conceived as a finite series of eternities within the homogeneous space of the general theory of modes of production. This general theory of modes of production has, as a theory of *history*, three possibilities before it. First, it can remain a series of pure concepts, confined within thought – a history *within knowledge* but not a means of appropriation of the real concrete. Second, the concepts may be applied in historical research as interpretations of given historical events – this necessarily implies a capitulation to the conditions of the historian's practice. Both of these options involve a breach of the epistemological protocols of the theory. In the first the problem of the relation of knowledge to being is simply *evaded* – there can be no knowledge effect and the concepts lose their *raison d'être*. In the second the very substance of the Althusserian critique is abandoned in favour of empiricism. The third possibility is the only one which corresponds to the protocols of the theory. It is to regard the concepts of the modes as substantial entities – to ascribe to the *concept* of mode of production the attributes of a functioning structure. The eternities become realities and structural causality an effectivity in the real. Structural causality as we have seen makes this conflation of the real and knowledge possible. These substantialised concepts are then inserted within the fabric of a history and are conceived as the essence of the successive epochs of the past. What appears as a process is shown not to have the structure of a process but to reveal, appropriated in thought, its essence – a series of social formations dominated by specific modes of production. The past should become, if structural causality is respected, a series of structures functioning as eternities and persisting through their own action.

There should be as many histories as there are distinct eternities, distinct modes of production. History would be the parallel existence of auto-determining structures. But this is absurd: history, the 'real' history, which this general theory seeks to rationalise simply does not correspond to this conception. Even if it were claimed that this is the true appropriation of the real object and that all conceptions of that object as a process are false, this theory would still suppose that any given mode of production existed *ad infinitum*. Balibar is neither mad enough nor brazen enough to do that. Balibar introduces a necessary contradiction into the general theory of modes of production. As we have seen in the chapter on transition, the general theory of modes of production is not in fact purely serial. Structural causality, supposing as it does the persistence of the structure through its own action, must generate modes of production which are eternal, which do not change, and which are independent of any other mode of production.

Yet Balibar, while upholding structural causality, introduces the contradictory notion of a transitional mode of production. Structural causality explicitly prohibits the transformation of the structure and the overturning of the hierarchy of its determinations. Transition is arbitrarily introduced into a problematic which should exclude it as a problem. Why? Because in 'real' history transitions do occur. The untransformed notion of history enters here. In order to meet its conditions Balibar is condemned to posit the absurd and contradictory notion of a transitional mode of production. This incoherence reveals Balibar's general theory of modes of production to be a speculative history – to be a rationalisation and reconstruction of what it takes to be a real object.

Concepts and the concrete

We have argued that there can be no *general* theory of modes of production. There are, however, general concepts which serve as a means of formation and of proof of concepts of specific modes of production. The concepts of the specific modes of production outlined here are not the elements of a history. They do not function as the concepts of a science of history or as the means of constitution of history as a thought object. These concepts are not about the *past* and they do not pertain to stages in a teleological process. The idea that the concepts of pre-capitalist modes, the ancient or the slave modes, for example, relate to the past is an effect of the teleological histories which have dominated Marxist theory. The conception of pre-capitalist modes of production used here does not require that, as part of their concept, such modes exist prior to capitalism or that they are necessarily succeeded by capitalism.

The term 'pre-capitalist' is retained here not in its historicist sense, but in a quite different sense. Pre-capitalist modes of production are less developed *as modes of production* than is the capitalist mode. They are less developed in the terms of their concept. 'Development' refers here to the level of productivity of the forces of production specified by the concept of a mode of production, to the extent to which the relations of production and the process of production do or do not depend on non-economic conditions of existence, and to the nature of the relation between the mode of appropriation of the product and the process of reproduction. Thus the concept of the CMP designates a mode of production with a higher level of social productivity than any other mode, in which the relations of production – the division of the classes and the form of exploitation – are reproduced by the process of production of commodities, and in which the form of appropriation of the surplus-product – capitalist accumulation – creates certain of the crucial conditions of existence of the reproduction of the forces and relations of production. Development refers to the attributes of a structure designated by a concept and not to a developmental process. It is not supposed that more developed modes (in our sense of the term) succeed less developed ones, or that there are *any* necessary relations of succession between modes of production. Thus, although socialism is more developed as a mode of production than capitalism according to the above criteria, it is not supposed that capitalism is succeeded by socialism or by any mode at all. The concepts of the modes of production developed here do not form a history in thought, mirroring in their succession the evolution of the real.

The field of application of these concepts is not history. We reject the notion of history as a coherent and worthwhile object of study. These concepts are abstract,their value is not limited by the analysis of the concrete. As concepts they can have a theoretical function even if concrete conditions to which they are pertinent do not exist, have not existed and will not exist. Concepts which are not used in the analysis of concrete conditions are not therefore speculative and empty. It is empiricism which conceives the necessary field of application of all concepts as the real. In fact concepts have a valid field of application *within theory*.

The value of the concepts elaborated here is, indeed, predominantly *within theory*. There are certain concrete situations in which the concepts of the FMP, of primitive communism, and the proof that there is no valid concept of AMP may be useful. For example, the proof that there is no concept of AMP may have value in demonstrating the illusions and the absurd political consequences which would follow from the attempt to use such a concept to analyse the social formations of contemporary Asia. This is a secondary matter. The primary value of the concepts elaborated here is in the rectification, elaboration and development of the concept of mode of production, and in clarifying the procedures by which the concepts of specific modes of production may be formed and proved. In particular we hope that this work will be of value in contributing to the formation of an anti-historicist theory of modes of production, a theory which avoids the pitfalls of Balibar's general theory. The urgent tasks of such a theory are the development of a concept of a capitalism dominated by finance capital, a concept which builds on and goes beyond Marx's concept of the CMP in which industrial capital is dominant, and the development of a rigorous concept of the socialist mode of production. If this work is of service in clarifying the way to these tasks then it will have justified itself.

Having defined what we consider to be the theoretical value of the concepts presented here we will attempt to specify what it is that it is the object of Marxist theory to analyse, the 'current situation'. All Marxist theory, however abstract and general, exists to make possible the analysis of the current situation. This situation must not be conceived as an object given in the real, social reality at a given moment in time. The analysis of the current situation is not a state description of the social formation. The current situation does not exist independently of the political practice which constitutes it as an object. The current situation exists for Marxist theory only in so far as it is given a definite form by Marxist political practice, and in so far as definite problems are designated as objects of analysis or criticism within that practice. These problems are problems of political practice and are specified in political terms. *What* the 'current situation' is cannot be specified in the same way that the object of an empiricist knowledge is specified. The current situation is not a definite substance, a specific unitary element of being. The analysis of the current situation is not a relation between knowledge and being, between entities. One has only to consider the situations 'current' in the works of Lenin, the objects of Lenin's analyses in different conjunctures, to see that the current situation is not one thing. These current situations do not form a unity. They do not have a single essence, a common mode of being which unifies them. The situation 'current' is now the relations between factions in the RSDLP, now the relation of the political lines of the parties in the Duma to the autocracy, now the revolutionary crisis of October 1917, and so on.

Consider for a moment Lenin's *The Development of Capitalism in Russia*. Is this a history of the Russian economy? Is it a state description of the given conditions of late nineteenth-century Russia? No, it is not. The *problem* of this, Lenin's first great work, is a problem constituted within a definite political practice. This problem is engendered by the political competition of Narodnism and Marxism – it is the necessity of differentiating the programmes of Narodnism and Marxism, and at the same time challenging economist and evolutionist variants of Marxism, that defines this book. The problem – why will the capitalist system destroy the conditions of existence of the pre-capitalist forms of production and dominate them, what are the potential modalities of this dominance and what forms of capitalism do they imply? – does not specify a given set of observables to be described. It is for this reason that Lenin insisted that 'no statistics in the world' could settle the questions he had asked. Lenin's analysis concerned the future of Russia, not as the next stage in a teleological process, but as a question to be settled, within definite structural limits, but *settled* nevertheless, by concrete social struggles, by political practice, by programmes, by analysis. Lenin's book is not a description of Russia in the 1890s, it is not even a set of 'predictions' about the future extrapolated from such a description. Lenin's book is a theoretical demolition of the arguments and evidence of Narodnism and evolutionism. 'Empirical' material – in fact, statistics and information, collected according to definite problems, by definite techniques, and within definite political and social purposes, Lenin had no illusions or fetishes about their purity – functions in this book as the object of criticism or as a source of illustration of a theoretical point.*

To say that the object of Marxist theoretical analysis, the current situation, is constituted within political practice is not to surrender to the dictates of pragmatism. Marxist politics is only possible on the condition that it is based on theory, that its problems, programmes and practice are defined by and subject to the criticism of theory. This relation between theory and political practice is the essence of Marxism. Opportunism, abstraction from the current situation, sloganising, all indicate that Marxist theory is absent or displaced by essentialist and teleological conceptions of politics. It is the central role of theory in Marxist politics which makes the substance of theoretical differences so important. It is the central role of theory in Marxist politics which makes the criticism and development of theory, and the attempt to struggle with essentialist and teleological conceptions and positions, of the first political importance. It is in the light of this that we consider the abstractions and generalities in this book to be pertinent to the present.

* This is not to say that Lenin's anti-empiricist practice in this book was coupled with an anti-empiricist epistemology; far from it, Lenin takes a positivist position.

Notes

Introduction

1 See the analysis of the empiricist conception of knowledge in Althusser and Balibar, *Reading Capital*, pp. 34–40, and also in Hindess, 'Models and masks: empiricist conceptions of the conditions of scientific knowledge'.
2 See Hobsbawm's survey of Marxist discussions of pre-capitalist social formations in his Introduction to Marx's *Pre-Capitalist Economic Formations*.
3 Cf. *Reading Capital*, p. 233f. Balibar's conception of manufacture as a transitional mode of production is examined in chapter 6.
4 On this point see Cutler, 'Response to Balibar's "Self-Criticism" '.
5 See, for example, Weber's comments on 'the economic interpretation of history' in *The Methodology of the Social Sciences*, pp. 69–79, 103.

One Primitive communism, politics and the state

1 E. Balibar, 'The Basic Concepts of Historical Materialism' in *Reading Capital*. See also the discussion of manufacture in chapter 6.
2 Baran does indeed recognise that his concept is different from that of Marx but he interprets this difference entirely in terms of the quantity of total output that is counted as surplus.
3 See especially 'The Economy as Instituted Process', in K. Polanyi *et al.*, *Trade and Market in the Early Empires*.
4 Part I, 'The Growth of Intelligence through Inventions and Discoveries'. See also the editor's Introduction by E. B. Leacock, and the commentary on Morgan's text in E. Terray, *Marxism and 'Primitive' Societies*.
5 On these points see Leacock, *op. cit.*, and Terray, *op. cit.*
6 See L. Krader, *Formation of the State*, for a discussion of such positions.
7 Talcott Parsons, 'The distribution of power in American society'. Strictly speaking, Parsons does not deny that differential interests may be vested in the state. However, such differential investment of interests presupposes and is subordinated to a universality at the level of values.
8 M. Fortes and E. E. Evans-Pritchard (eds), *African Political Systems*.
9 N. Poulantzas, *Political Power and Social Classes*. For an analysis of Poulantzas's position see A. J. Cutler, 'Fascism and political theory'.
10 L. Krader, *op. cit.*, chapter 6, and *Social Organisation of the Mongol-Turkic Pastoral Nomads*.

11 Here Marx quotes a passage from *The Civil War in France*, p. 288. The whole of that text together with Engels's Introduction is of the greatest importance for the theory of the state and the political level. See also Lenin's commentary in *The State and Revolution*, chapter 3.
12 See Lenin, *op. cit.*, especially chapter 6.
13 This follows the definition given by Althusser in *For Marx*, p. 116.
14 It may be noted that Poulantzas's definition of practice (p. 41) follows that given by Althusser (see note 13 above), to which he refers, with one crucial exception: there is no mention of the *means* of practice. This omission vitiates his whole analysis of politics since it precludes the definition of political structures as the means or instruments of the political practice of classes.
15 On these points see Cutler, 'Fascism and political theory'.
16 On these points see Marx, *Critique of the Gotha Programme*, Engels, *Anti-Duhring*, and C. Bettelheim, *Calcul économique et formes de propriété* (1970), especially part 1.
17 The definitions of *klala* and *bo* are Meillassoux's: they are taken from p. 183 and p. 176 respectively.
18 In the chapter on co-operation in *Capital*, I, Marx makes a distinction between simple and complex co-operation in his analysis of the labour process of capitalist manufacture. The contrast refers to forms of co-operation of labourers who are separated from the means of production and must therefore work under the direction of a capitalist or his agent. In this respect simple and complex co-operation are distinct forms of capitalist labour process. The same concepts cannot be transferred to the analysis of the labour process of primitive communism. When the labourers are not separated from their means of production the separation of productive labour from the tasks of supervision does not take its antagonistic capitalist form. On this point see the analysis of the labour process under slavery in chapter 3. In the present chapter the terms 'simple' and 'complex' co-operation are used very loosely and descriptively. Terray attempts to carry over into the analysis of the Gouro a contrast that is pertinent to the analysis of the capitalist mode of production.
19 Durkheim's *Elementary Forms of Religious Life* established a set of problems concerning ritual, religion and collective representations which have dominated French idealist sociology and anthropology. Meillassoux's treatment of the hunt as a ritual generating social solidarity belongs to that tradition.
20 C. Meillassoux, 'Recherche d'un niveau de détermination dans la société cynégetique' and Meillassoux, 'From reproduction to production'.
21 See chapter 6 for a critique of this concept of correspondence.
22 For the following argument see also Cutler's 'Response' to Balibar's 'Self-Criticism'.
23 Cf. Meillassoux, 'Essai d'interprétation du phénomène économique dans les sociétés traditionnelles d'autosubsistance'.
24 See G. Dupré and P.-P. Rey, 'Reflections on the pertinence of a theory of the history of exchange' and P.-P. Rey, *Colonialisme, néo-colonialisme et transition au capitalisme*.

25 For this and the following section see the useful discussion in Terray, *op. cit.*, especially the section on kinship, pp. 137f, and the conclusion, pp. 177f.
26 The expressive totality 'presupposes in principle the whole in question to be reducible to an *inner essence*, of which the elements of the whole are then no more than the phenomenal forms of expression, the inner principle of the essence being present at each point in the whole, such that at each moment it is possible to write the immediately adequate equation: *such and such an element* (economic, political, legal, literary, religious, etc., in Hegel) = *the inner essence of the whole*'. *Reading Capital*, pp. 186–7.
27 See Lévi-Strauss, 1952 and 1968, chapter 16.
28 Terray's position is perhaps the most astonishing since his *Marxism and 'Primitive' Societies* includes a discussion of Morgan in addition to the analysis of Meillassoux's work referred to above. Nevertheless he proceeds to examine the social organisation of the Gouro without reference to Morgan's fundamental work.
29 *Ancient Society*, part II, chapter 2, and Engels, *The Origin . . .*, chapter 3.
30 Cf. Leacock's Introduction to *Ancient Society*, pp. II, iii–II, vii.

Two The ancient mode of production

1 See chapter 5 for further discussion of this passage.
2 For an analysis of the ideological notion of despotism see the discussion of Wittfogel, *Oriental Despotism*, in chapter 4.
3 On the first point see Balibar, 'The Basic Concepts of Historical Materialism', pp. 276f. The ideological character of the latter problem consists in its representation of appearances as given by the structure and not, therefore, as products of determinate practices at the ideological level of the social formation. The passages on the 'Asiatic' mode are particularly striking in this respect. The reduction of ideology to what is given by the structure is generated by a 'structuralist' variant of the empiricist concept of knowledge in which the subject is opposed to the structure. In this case, since knowledge is an effect of the structure itself, the possibility of a scientific practice of production of knowledge is precluded.
4 See the following chapter for further discussion of the place of slavery in the ancient world.
5 See chapter 6.
6 See chapter 3.
7 The following account of Sparta is rather simplified and it avoids a number of problematic issues. See H. Michell, *Sparta*.
8 See the discussion in F. W. Walbank, *The Awful Revolution*.
9 See *Reading Capital*, pp. 283f.
10 See E. Badian, *Publicans and Sinners*, on the part played by 'private enterprise' in the administration of the late Republic.
11 E. Badian, *Foreign Clientelae*.
12 The political representation of class interests is the product of a deter-

minate political *practice* with determinate conditions of existence in the structure of the political level and in the forms of intervention of the economic and the ideological levels within the political. The effect of reducing representation to a form of *expression* is the identification of the concept of representation in general with certain 'representative' institutional forms, the vote, popular assemblies, etc. The effect of exclusion from these 'representative' institutions is not the absence of political representation but a transformation of the conditions of political practice and of the forms of intervention in political struggle. To say that patron–client relations function as mechanisms of representation of non-citizen communities is to give an index of the different conditions of representation and different forms of political practice generated by the structure of the Roman state at this time as a political unity embracing Italy and several overseas domains. This state is not reducible to the Roman state in the narrow sense as the union of the citizens of Rome. Failure to make this distinction vitiates most discussions of politics in the Roman Republic.

If we have indicated the site of a problem, that of the theory of the political level of the Roman Republic, it should be clear that the following discussion represents no more than the beginnings of a solution.

13 Some of the materials required for such an analysis may be found in E. Badian, *Foreign Clientelae*, and the references cited in that text.

14 Brunt emphasises the demand for the *ius suffragii* in direct opposition to Sherwin-White, see 'Italian aims at the time of the Social War'. For other references see H. H. Scullard, *From the Gracchi to Nero*, p. 407, note 8.

15 A similar position on the general character of the conflicts of this period is taken in P. A. Brunt, *Social Conflicts in the Roman Republic.*

16 For example, E. Gelzer, *The Roman Nobility*, R. Syme, *The Roman Revolution*, and, for an earlier period, H. H. Scullard, *Roman Politics, 220–150 B.C.*

17 E. Badian, *Publicans and Sinners.*

18 On the decline of 'freedom' see Syme, *op. cit.*

19 On the transformation of the administration of the state see Rostovtzeff, *op. cit.*, chapter 2, Scullard, *From the Gracchi to Nero*, and Sherwin-White, *op. cit.*

20 The contributions of Polanyi are particularly important. See also the critique of his position in Dupré and Rey, 'Reflections on the pertinence of a theory of the history of exchange'.

21 We have inserted in brackets two passages which Pearson omits from his quotation. The first of these clearly changes the meaning of the sentence in which it belongs.

22 Reciprocity, redistribution and exchange are the three patterns identified in *Trade and Market*. . ., a fourth pattern, householding, appears in *Dahomey and the Slave Trade.*

23 Cf. the following passage: 'But the ancients never thought of transforming the surplus product into capital. Or at least only to a very limited extent. (The fact that the hoarding of treasure in the narrow sense was widespread among them shows how much the surplus

product lay completely idle.) They used a large part of the surplus product for unproductive expenditure on art, religious works and public works. Still less was their production directed to the release and development of the material productive forces – division of labour, machinery, the application of the powers of nature and science to private production. In fact, by and large, they never went beyond handicraft labour. The wealth which they produced for private consumption was therefore relatively small and only appears great because it was amassed in the hands of a few persons, who, incidentally, did not know what to do with it' (*Theories of Surplus Value*, II, p. 528).

24 For these developments in the later Empire see the works of Jones, Rostovtzeff and Walbank cited above.

Three Slavery

1 Slavery predates the development of private property. Slaves are held in advanced pre-state societies (societies organised on the basis of kinship or lineage groups and confederacies of such groups) either as the property of the community as a whole or by the elders as kin property which they administer. Slavery probably originates in the first instance from the taking of captives in war. It is only as the institution of private property develops, extending from personal possessions to the ownership of land, the instruments of production and complex forms of mobile wealth, that slaves become the property of individuals. The development of the institution of slavery, as a *form* of property, merely parallels and is part of the development of property, the law and the state; see F. Engels, *The Origin of the Family, Private Property and the State*, for an analysis of the development of property.

In societies with and without developed private property, slavery plays a very different role in the economy. In the former, the ancient world and the modern slave plantation producing for the capitalist world market, slavery is a form of labour system, a means of exploitation of labour, and at the same time a form of capital. In the latter, slaves held by the community merely augment its own labour-power, or slaves are incorporated as *members* of the lineage or clan in order to reproduce or to extend the members' force of labour-power. See, for example, G. Dupré and P.-P. Rey, 'Reflections . . .'.

2 The later legal forms of Anglo-Saxon slavery grew out of a largely non-Roman legal context, they were not more developed *as law*, although they do correspond to the necessities of a highly developed form of exploitation of slave labour and grant the slave precious few rights as a person. For the difference between the slave laws of the Anglo-Saxon colonies and the Latin forms derived from Roman law see S. M. Elkins, *Slavery*. Elkins states the thesis, developed by Frank Tannenbaum in *Slave and Citizen*, that the Latin systems by recognising the personality of the slave avoided the harsher and more barbarous treatment of the Northern Americas and prevented the absolute separation and antagonism of the races that occurred in the Anglo-Saxon colonies. Davis,

The Problem of Slavery in Western Culture, chapter 8, considers the evidence for and against this thesis in a clear and succinct way. See also E. Genovese, *The World the Slaveholders Made*, part 1, chapter 2 for a penetrating reassessment of the evidence and critique of this thesis.

3 See A. M. Pritchard (ed.), *Leage's Roman Private Law*, parts 2 and 3, section 1. On the law of slavery in particular see W. W. Buckland, *The Roman Law of Slavery*, 1908.

4 Clearly, such categories appear only when the various particular and circumstantial laws are rationalised into a system with a principle of unity and a superstructure of theoretical reflection which enables discrepant elements, contradictions and points of dispute to be resolved by an appeal to rational principles which are supposed to underlie the particular laws of the code and the judgments of the courts. Sir Henry Maine (*Ancient Law*, pp. 95–6) emphasised that the Greeks and Roman jurists appealed to such a theoretical rationalisation to justify slavery, the Greeks pointing to the naturally servile condition of some races and the Romans arguing that slavery derives from the compact between victor and vanquished.

5 Hegel in particular was scandalised by this abstraction of the Roman conception of the legal person precisely *because* it is not identical with the human subject, and he attributes the Roman failure to develop any conception of Man *as such* to their bad conscience about slavery:

> In Roman law, a man is reckoned a person only when he is treated as possessing a certain status. Hence in Roman law even personality itself is only a certain standing or status contrasted with slavery [and] Thus in Roman law . . . there could be no definition of 'man', since 'slave' could not be brought under it – the very status of slave indeed is an outrage on the conception of man (*Philosophy of Right*, p. 39 and p. 15).

This position is a function of Hegel's essentially humanist philosophy; he takes for a *failing* what is most *advanced* in this legal form. Roman law provides the basis for an abstract concept of the legal personality; a personality which exists in the sphere of law alone and which is attributable to non-human entities, corporations, etc. This development of Roman law is a function of post-Roman analytic jurisprudence. Hegel attributes this abstraction to the fact of slavery, it can equally be viewed as an achievement of Roman legal practice, a form necessary to the development of the law as such.

6 That is, without such subjects there could be no disputes and no infractions of the law. The combined notions of autonomy and responsibility on the part of the subjects of law are necessary for the existence of a specifically *legal* process, without them there can only be command and coercion. The legal concept of *person* is not a simple abstraction from the attributes of human subject; it is a concept which is the product of the legal system and is specific to the legal sphere. The legal concept of person *predates* the modern one which identifies the person and the human subject. So the legal personality, far from being a grotesque abstraction from the 'real' person, is prior to it. The modern conception of the human subject is an invention of the

seventeenth century, an abstraction developed from legal theory and philosophy.

7 This contradiction between man as subject and man as chattel is the subject of David Brion Davis's *The Problem of Slavery in Western Culture*. Davis, however, conceives this contradiction in an essentialist and humanist form, men are 'obviously' human and as humans essentially free: 'The inherent contradiction of slavery lay not in its cruelty or economic exploitation, but in the underlying conception of man as a conveyable possession with no more autonomy and consciousness than a domestic animal' (p. 78). Davis's text is a history of 'ideas'. Its object is the contradiction in Western civilisation between the ideas of freedom and slavery. Despite this idealist method, which abstracts these themes and treats them as a continuing debate in the realm of 'ideas', the book is a useful compendium of the various positions on slavery.

8 In Greek law and in the code of Hammurabi the slave was considered as property, but in the Hittite code the slave was regarded as a person – see W. L. Westermann, 'Ancient Slavery'. In China (after about 400 B.C.) slaves were 'legally like domestic animals and property', see Eberhard, *Conquerors and Rulers*, p. 22.

9 See Buckland, *The Roman Law of Slavery*, pp. 3–6.

10 Kenneth Stampp, in *The Peculiar Institution*, argues that laws against the murder and maltreatment of slaves were necessarily ineffective because so large a measure of abuse was still permitted to masters within the law that a slave might die as an 'accidental' consequence of punishment and also because these laws were simply not enforced. It was very rare for a master to be punished for killing or cruelly treating his own slaves. Slaves and free Negroes were more harshly punished than whites who committed similar offences. Frederick Douglass, in *My Bondage and My Freedom*, recalls numerous instances of unpunished murder and ill-treatment of slaves by whites from his personal experience as a slave.

11 Clearly, some forms of slavery have existed without legal systems or the state, but even in the case of communal ownership by a lineage group this still supposes customs regulating the conduct of the slaves and their use by lineage members. Developed systems of slave property presuppose the laws and their enforcement by the state, without these institutional supports the status of human chattels as property would be wholly ambiguous and possession would depend on constant control. No slave markets and no holding of slaves as capital could develop in the absence of legal sanction and support of the institution.

12 On the views of Grotius and Hobbes on slavery see Davis, *op. cit.*, pp. 133–7. It should be noted that not all natural law theorists or absolutist political theorists were in favour of slavery; Jean Bodin, although an absolutist, opposed slavery, see Davis, *op. cit.*, pp. 129–33.

13 For the passage in *The Phenomenology of Mind*, see pp. 228–40 of the translation by J. B. Baillie. For an example of such a reading see E. Genovese, *The Political Economy of Slavery*, pp. 38, 71.

14 It should be noted that Mill argues that at an early stage of social

development a more advanced society may aid the development of primitive and barbarous peoples by placing them in a condition of servitude.

15 Slavery in Greece was not a single legal status, but rather had at least four gradations of degree of unfreedom, the worst being chattel slavery. However, there appears to be no evidence that the 'independent' slaves were generally of a more emancipated legal status than the slaves in the mines – they could be and often were chattel slaves. For examples of highly independent slave workers and for the Greek system of slave law and its varied statuses see W. L. Westermann, 'Slavery and the Elements of Freedom in Ancient Greece', in M. I. Finley (ed.), *Slavery in Classical Antiquity*. For other aspects of slave labour, slave numbers, the cost of slaves, etc., in Ancient Greece see the papers of A. H. M. Jones and M. I. Finley in the same volume.

16 For the organisation of the Laurium mines and labour conditions in them, see Mossé, *The Ancient World at Work*, pp. 80–5, and Jones in Finley, *op. cit.*, pp. 4–5.

17 We will only consider certain themes from Elkins's text and ignore completely his treatment of the effect of slavery on American culture and intellectual life.

18 E. Genovese criticises this conception of unrestrained capitalism, although his own conception of the South as a non-capitalist society is open to question, as we shall see later – see 'Rebelliousness and Docility in the Slave: A Critique of the Elkins' Thesis', in *In Red and Black*.

19 Goffman develops this notion in his book *Asylums*.

20 Stampp's book was written in 1956, some considerable time before Elkins's.

21 Eugène Genovese's criticisms of the Elkins thesis are generally sound and telling but in certain respects the cure appears to be rather worse than the disease: 'on close inspection the Sambo personality turns out to be neither more nor less than the slavish personality; wherever slavery has existed Sambo has also' (*In Red and Black*, pp. 77–8). Genovese certainly does show that the elements of the 'sambo' *stereotype* are not confined to the USA, but he does not prove the universality of 'sambo' himself. It should be noted that as Elkins's analysis can be assimilated to wider sociological conceptions of the social processes involved (slave plantation = concentration camp = total institutions) then no definite consequences follow in his analysis from slavery *as such* or the master–slave relationship *as such*.

22 Elkins recognises that 'sambo' was capable of violent outbursts but Elkins's Negro is not the type of personality of whom a Spartacus and a Toussaint are made.

23 For the First Sicilian Slave War see Green, 'The First Sicilian Slave War'; for a short account of the Spartacus uprising see Michael Grant, *Gladiators*, pp. 19–26; for the Zanj see E. A. Belyaev, *Arabs, Islam and the Arab Caliphate*, pp. 239–47, and Bernard Lewis, *The Arabs in History*, pp. 103–6; for the Haitian revolution see C. L. R. James, *The Black Jacobins*.

24 Belyaev confirms that the Zanj, like the Sicilian slaves, had no interest in the suppression of slavery as an institution (*op. cit.*, 1969, p. 245):

> These former slaves, freed from oppression and exploitation, by no means abolished slavery; as we have seen, 'Ali ibn-Muhammad had promised them, at the very start of the uprising, that they themselves would be rich slave owners. Indeed, as the rebellion spread over more and more territory, the number of slaves increased as captives and even part of the free population were enslaved.

25 Helots were not chattel slaves, they were the direct producers of Sparta, of a hereditarily subordinate status, and forming a separate legally-defined social group. Thus they were more like serfs than slaves.

26 Stampp makes this point with some force.

27 See M. I. Finley, 'Was Greek Civilisation based on Slave Labour?', in Finley, *op. cit.*

28 See I. M. Lapidus, *Muslim Cities of the Later Middle Ages*, pp. 6, 44–8, 68–9, etc.; S. Lane-Poole, *A History of Egypt in the Middle Ages*, pp. 242–50; and W. Muir, *The Mameluke or Slave Dynasty of Egypt, 1260–1517 AD.*

29 Bernard Lewis, in P. M. Holt *et al.*, *The Cambridge History of Islam*, vol. I, p. 227, contends that *all* adult Mamelukes were freedmen, the other sources do not confirm this or contend the opposite.

30 Greek mercenaries played such a role in the Persian Empire.

31 Slavery as a *legal status* persisted in those parts of feudal Europe subject to Roman law – see Davis, *The Problem of Slavery in Western Culture*, pp. 53–6.

32 Obviously, the slave is mortal, just as machines may rust, stocks of wood, cotton, etc., may rot – this is not the point, the slave remains a form of property and a saleable commodity as long as he *exists*; labour-power in the wage-form is not alienated by the labourer, rather he *gives* it for a definite period.

33 See Cairnes, *The Slave Power*, pp. 46–7. Cairnes is a serious analyst of slavery in general and in the USA; his Utilitarian position does not prevent him from presenting a radical democratic case against the Slave Power as we shall see below.

34 Here we see a rational explanation of the notorious tendency of slave-owners to argue that slaves are lazy, helpless, childlike, incompetent, etc., 'unable to do anything without their owner'. The owner takes as an attribute of the slave's nature the specific inability forced upon slaves by the slave mode's labour process, the inability to set the means of production in motion.

35 In the case of the free peasant proprietor (and to a lesser extent the feudal serf) the functions of labourer and co-ordinator *do* coincide: 'The peasant proprietor, appropriating the whole produce of his soil, needs no other stimulus to exertion. Superintendence is here completely dispensed with' (Cairnes, *op. cit.*, pp. 48–9).

36

> Considerations of economy, moreover, which, under a natural system, afford some security for humane treatment by identifying

> the master's interest with the slave's preservation, when once trading in slaves is practised, become reasons for racking to the uttermost the toil of the slave; for when his place can at once be supplied from foreign preserves, the duration of his life becomes a matter of less moment than its productiveness while it lasts. It is accordingly a maxim of slave management, in slave-importing countries, that the most effective economy is that which takes out of the human chattel in the shortest space of time the utmost exertion it is capable of putting forth (Cairnes, *op. cit.*, p. 122).

37 This does not mean that the labour of supervision must be wage-labour – the costs of supervision are still entailed even if the supervisors are slaves, the cost of their maintenance must be deducted from the product of the labourers they supervise.

38 As we have seen, in Athens slavery was not a simple and single legal status – certain categories of slave had extensive property rights. Slave artisans might well own their tools, working capital, etc.

39 These presuppositions are not *causes* of the CMP or the SMP; in themselves they are not sufficient to constitute the mode, they are merely forms which must be present if it is to exist.

40 The point being made here was that the state *guarantees* the security and legal title of slave property. As in capitalism it guarantees the forms of property, but it does not directly determine them or the distribution of property. That is, there must be an effective separation of the *public* and *private* domains, and the creation of the political and legal freedom necessary for the distribution of property to take place within the private sphere.

41
> In the same way, the slave-holder considers a negro, which he has purchased, as his property, not because the institution of slavery entitles him to that negro, but because he acquired him like any other commodity through sale and purchase. But the title itself is simply transferred and not created by the sale. A title must exist before it can be sold, and a series of sales can no more create this title through continued repetition than a single sale can. What created it in the first place were the production relations (*Capital*, III, p. 757).

42 See chapter 2 for a discussion of the Spartan social formation.

43 See Marx, *Pre-Capitalist Economic Formations*, pp. 77–80, for a discussion of the 'Teutonic' mode of production.

44 Some anti-slavery reformers and abolitionists hoped that the abolition of the slave trade (apart from ending an evil in itself) would deal a death blow to slavery; however, slavery could not be damaged at all seriously unless the internal trade in slaves could be stopped.

45 Such tendencies to the conservation of labour-power do not, of course, appear irrespective of the given conditions. In the later Roman Empire there were few systematic attempts to raise the productivity of slave-labour by the introduction of new techniques or methods of working. Other labour systems were available as substitutes, the switch from slaves to *coloni* in agricultural production and the intervention of the state (especially during and following the reign of Diocletian) in

compelling artisans and others to remain in their occupations, establishing state enterprises, etc., led to a decline in the relative importance of slave production. See M. I. Finley, 'Technical innovation and economic progress in the ancient world'. These substitute labour systems were, in general, less efficient than slave production. Weber, 'The Social Causes of the Decay of Ancient Civilisation' (in Kahl, *Studies in Explanation*) identifies this use of *coloni* and state enterprises with the decline of the ancient world's economic and social relations.

46 Genovese minimises the relation of his argument to that of Cairnes, referring to the 'simplistic and mechanistic notions of Cairnes', *The Political Economy of Slavery*, p. 243. However, their general positions are very similar.

47 These theses are drawn from Cairnes, *The Slave Power* and Genovese, *The Political Economy of Slavery*.

48 We have seen above that the SMP sets no inherent limits to generalised commodity production; slave production cannot in itself constitute such limits to demand.

49 See M. Weber, *The Theory of Social and Economic Organisation*, 1964, pp. 275–8.

50 Genovese, *op. cit.*, p. 16.

51 This political/economic position has its origin in the work of Freidrich Lizt who argued for a policy of economic autarchy for the German nation, based upon protectionism and the encouragement of industry.

52 Genovese does argue (*op. cit.*, pp. 135–6) that the *plantation* autarchy favoured by Southern reformers would have weakened the South's economic position still further by restricting the commodity market to an even greater extent. This does not contradict but rather reinforces the centrality of the concept of economic backwardness in Genovese's work.

53 See Genovese, *op. cit.*, pp. 284–5.

54 See Genovese, *The World the Slaveholders Made*, part 2.

55 On the African slave trade and the central role of merchants' capital see Eric Williams, *Capitalism and Slavery*.

56 On agrarian commodity production in the West Indies, etc., see Ramiro Guerra y Sanchez, *Sugar and Society in the Caribbean*, which deals with Cuba.

57 In Malaya there was no suitable indigenous labour force and as the form of production, rubber plantations, prohibited peasant cultivation, indentured labourers were imported on a large scale.

58 Edward Gibbon Wakefield, *England and America*, vol. II, p. 33, cited in *Capital*, I, p. 766.

59 On the reasons for higher labour costs in the USA and the resulting search for labour-saving techniques see H. J. Habakkuk, *American and British Technology in the Nineteenth Century*.

60 See Cairnes, *The Slave Power*, chapter 2.

61 And to a limited extent the fortunes of Manchester were affected by the South, the Northern blockade in the Civil War cut off cotton supplies and led to heavy unemployment in the cotton industry. Unemployment the workers appear to have been prepared to shoulder in the interests of

principle, see Marx and Engels, *The Civil War in the United States*, pp. 139–43.

62 See F. H. Bradley, *Ethical Studies*, and Marx, *Capital*, I, pp. 609–10n.

63 On the agronomic treatises of antiquity and the economic conditions they suppose see C. Mossé, *The Ancient World at Work*, pp. 31–8, 62–7. M. I. Finley in *The Ancient Economy*, strongly attacks the notion that slavery retarded production in the ancient world, see ch. II. Mossé advances the argument that peasant agriculture and handicraft production were the main limits to productivity in the ancient world.

64 See Mossé, *op. cit.*, pp. 67–71, and for the rising price of slaves, see Jones in Finley (ed.), *op. cit.*

65 For Marx's analysis of the dependence of the productivity of the labourer and the character of the labourer on the nature of the labour process and of the means of labour see *Capital*, I, ch. XV, 'Machinery and Modern Industry'.

66 Cairnes is not *only* a Utilitarian philistine, he is also a radical democrat and a principled anti-racialist opponent of slavery.

67 Genovese, *op. cit.*, p. 99.

68 On the relation of rent to the differential fertility of the soil, see the exposition of Marx's concept of differential rent in chapter 4.

69 See Douglass, *op. cit.*

70 This war involved considerable expense to the Federal government and was the product of lobbying by Southern interests.

Four The 'Asiatic' mode of production

1 For discussions of the AMP and the debates surrounding it, see Eberhard, *Conquerors and Rulers*, pp. 48–60, 66–74; Carrere d'Encausse and Schram, *Marxism and Asia*, pp. 7–9, 92–7; Godelier, 'La notion de "mode de production asiatique". . .', pp. 37–100; Hobsbawm, 'Introduction', Lichtheim, 'Marx and the "Asiatic Mode of Production" '; and Wittfogel, *Oriental Despotism*, ch. 9.

2 See Eberhard, *op. cit.*, pp. 66–74, and Wittfogel, *op. cit.*, particularly the (biased) account of the Leningrad 1931 discussion.

3 See Lichtheim, *op. cit.*, and Wittfogel, *op. cit.*, ch. 9.

4 Wittfogel, *op. cit.*, p. 380.

5 Wittfogel, *op. cit.*, pp. 402–4.

6 Fertility can only be understood relative to technique and social relations. Soils may be extremely 'fertile' in the sense of being capable of supporting large crops, but unusable because they cannot be cultivated with existing ploughs (for example, the English heavy clays in the early feudal period), or because they require drainage and water control which is impossible without combination and division of labour and therefore they cannot be worked by independent peasant proprietors.

7 See Lenin, *Collected Works*, vol. 3, pp. 191–3.

8 This is discussed in greater detail in chapter 6.

9 No concept of a mode of production can make its geographical location necessary; *where* (or if) a mode of production exists is a

contingent and not a necessary matter. It is only, in the last instance, in the form of 'Spirit' that geography can be made necessity, and in the form of the Hegelian dialectic which works by exclusion and contradiction. Thus if there were an AMP there would be no reason why it should not occur in Africa, Europe, Australia or the North Pole, its existence *in Asia* would be contingent. For Hegel it is no accident that *this* land and *this* people play a particular role in world history.

10 Weber was clearly an exponent of this ideology. His 'Social Psychology of the World Religions' is little more than an attempt to sociologise and empiricise Hegel's *Philosophy of History* – for Weber, as for Hegel, it is the absence of the subject which explains the stasis of the East.

11 For a study of Montesquieu's political thought see L. Althusser, *Politics and History* – see pp. 75–86 on Montesquieu's concept of despotism. For his discussion of despotism, see *The Spirit of the Laws*, pp. 18, 25–8, 57–66, 122, 129.

12 See A. D. Lublinskaya, 'The contemporary bourgeois conception of absolute monarchy', pp. 83–8.

13 Thus the decisive advance of Adam Ferguson's *An Essay on the History of Civil Society* is the recognition that *all* forms of state have their social-structural conditions and limitations.

14 E. Leach, 'Hydraulic society in Ceylon'.

15 See Eberhard, *Conquerors and Rulers: Social Forces in Medieval China*, pp. 74–88.

16 For an example of the use of 'operational' techniques in the administration of a pre-literate society see K. Polanyi, *Dahomey and the Slave Trade*, ch. 3 – particularly pp. 40–4.

17 See Eberhard, *op. cit.*, pp. 56–7.

18 Eberhard, *op. cit.*, suggests a completely different interpretation of medieval Chinese social relations from that of Wittfogel – see chs. II and III of his text. Barrington Moore also presents a very different picture of the power systems of two of the important cases Wittfogel discusses, the Chin dynasty in China and the Maurya empire in India, in his paper, 'Totalitarian Elements in Pre-Industrial Societies', in *Political Power and Social Theory*, pp. 40–59. While in both cases there are relatively centralised bureaucracies neither is 'agromanagerial' nor particularly concerned with 'hydraulic' agriculture; furthermore, in the case of the Maurya bureaucracy it 'rested heavily on the army' and 'the state encouraged and protected merchants and artizans' (p. 55).

19 Wittfogel often takes very emphatic positions of interpretation in respect of cases where *all* the evidence is vague and weak, e.g. pre-imperial China, Inca Peru, prehistoric Mesopotamia, etc. Similarly, he uses sources like the *Arthashastra* and *The Book of Lord Shang* (which play a vital role in his illustrations concerning India and China) as if they were an objective description rather than 'manuals for princes' similar to those of Renaissance Italy. These texts systematically overestimate the power and effect of the prince and of government.

20 See M. Weber, *Economy and Society*, vol. III, ch. XI.

21 See M. Weber, *The Religion of China*, chs II and V.

22 *NYDT*, 1 July 1853, in Marx and Engels, *On Colonialism*, pp. 31–8, and, Marx to Engels 14 June 1853, in Marx and Engels, *Selected Correspondence*, pp. 101–4.
23 See Wittfogel, *op. cit.*, ch. 9, pp. 372–7.

Five The feudal mode of production

1 In the chapter on the AMP we used the concept of feudal rent as presented in *Capital* to contrast it with tax/rent. For the purposes of that chapter this concept was adequate. Our criticisms of the concept of feudal rent do not weaken but rather *reinforce* the criticisms made of the AMP.
2 See E. A. Kosminsky, *Studies in the Agrarian History of England in the Thirteenth Century*.
3 Except, that is, for *métayage* – a form which Marx argues is transitional 'from the original form of rent to capitalist rent' (*Capital*, III, p. 783). In this form:

> The manager (farmer) furnishes labour (his own or another's), and also a portion of working capital, and the landlord furnishes, aside from land, another portion of working capital (e.g., cattle) and the product is divided between tenant and landlord in definite proportions which vary from country to country. On the one hand, the farmer here lacks sufficient capital required for capitalist management. On the other hand, the share here appropriated by the landlord does not bear the pure form of rent (*ibid.*).

4 See P. Vinogradoff, *Villainage in England*, first essay – 'The Peasantry of the Feudal Age', chs V, VI and VII.
5 See M. M. Postan, *Essays on Medieval Agriculture . . .*, ch. 8, 'The Charters of the Villeins'.
6 These terms, 'demesne' and 'manor', do not imply the given institutional and legal forms of the European Middle Ages.
7 See Vinogradoff, *op. cit.*, pp. 148–9 and Kosminsky, *op. cit.*, pp. 296–303, 315–18.
8 Vinogradoff, *op. cit.*, mentions that a common unit of tenure, the *virgate*, 'being the fourth part of the hide corresponds to one-fourth part of the plough, that is two oxen, contributed by the holder to the full plough-team' (p. 238). The unit of tenure here corresponds to part of the necessary means of production which must be combined (in fact, the full eight ox team was by no means universally or even commonly used). Vinogradoff argues that this is evidence of the existence of communal institutions prior to feudalism.
9 Absolute rent *can* exist under pre-capitalist conditions, but only where the mechanisms of the market and competition exist.
10 Thus in Russia the growth of centralised state power in the sixteenth and seventeenth centuries was accompanied by the reduction of the direct producers to a servile status, and the loss of political autonomy of the nobility was accompanied by an increase in their power and control over the serfs. See J. Blum, *Lord and Peasant in Russia*, especially chapters 12 and 13.

11 See Lublinskaya, *French Absolutism*, and 'The contemporary bourgeois conception . . .'.
12 See Vinogradoff, *op. cit.*, second essay, ch. V.
13 Vinogradoff, *op. cit.*, argued that the English feudal system showed strong evidence of the preceding communal institutions of Saxon England. While arguing that the regime of tillage, crop rotation, pasturage, and so on, were strictly controlled by the village community (p. 230), that the forms of land distribution show evidence of communal ownership and attempts to equalise holdings (pp. 237–8), he does not deny that holdings, tenures, rents and production were individual. The communal forms are at best *vestiges* – tenure is not communal and the village community does not distribute the labour of its members.
14 By 'appears' we mean that the structure of the mode of production makes a certain mode of calculation of the relation NL/SL possible. This calculation is not necessarily made – calculation supposes *means* of calculation which are not given in the concept of the mode of production. It is not supposed here that 'appearances' are given to the perceiving subject by the structure of the mode of production – we have criticised this notion earlier in the chapter on slavery. Concrete ideological forms which create representation effects for the subject may interdict or suppress this calculation or serve as a support for it. Conflict between ideological forms is possible; we have only to think of Christian religious ideology – 'Render unto Caesar' *versus* 'when Adam delved and Eve span, who was then the gentleman?'
15 For a criticism of this view of commutation as leading to a dissolution of feudal economic relations see Postan, *op. cit.*, ch. 7, 'The Chronology of Labour Services'.
16 Lenin points out this difference between 'giving the economic struggle itself a political character' and 'social democratic politics', between the political defence of the economic class struggle *within* capitalism and the political struggle for socialism *against* capitalism, in *What is to be Done?*, *Collected Works*, 5.
17 See Rodney Hilton, *The Decline of Serfdom in Medieval England*, pp. 25–6.
18 See Vinogradoff, *op. cit.*, pp. 77–86; see also Hilton, *op. cit.*, pp. 17–31.
19 Vinogradoff, *op. cit.*, argues that such collective controls were a limitation on the productivity of the individual tenant: 'The passage toward more efficient modes of cultivation was very much obstructed by these customary rules as to rotation of crops, which flow not from the will and interest of single owners but from the decision of communities' (p. 231).
20 See W. Hinton, *Fanshen*, part I, chs 2 and 3, and R. H. Tawney, *Land and Labour in China*.
21 See Postan, *op. cit.*, ch. 8.
22 It is the class struggle, a concrete and definite cause, which determines the predominance of one variant form or another. The structure of the mode defines the variants, their limits and their possible combinations, it does not cause one or the other of them to predominate. The class struggle is operative within the structure of the FMP, it is no empirically

external 'modifying factor'. Only a structuralist teleological causality would suppose that the structure assigns its own variants their places as effects.

23 Lenin argues that these forms are combined in *The Agrarian Programme of Social Democracy in the First Russian Revolution, Collected Works*, 13, pp. 239–41.

24 We have used the term Junker economy to refer to *feudal* conditions; Lenin uses 'Junker' to refer both to the feudal landlord and to a certain form of landed estate in transition to capitalism.

Six The transition from feudalism to capitalism

1 E. Balibar, 'The Basic Concepts of Historical Materialism'. Balibar's account is not without its errors. Some of the most important of these are discussed in the present chapter.

2 For a critique of this idealist position see Dupré and Rey, 'Reflections on the pertinence of a theory of the history of exchange', especially part one.

3 For example, 'The most important opponent with which the spirit of capitalism, in the sense of a definite standard of life claiming ethical sanction, has had to struggle, was that type of attitude and reaction to new situations which we may designate as traditionalism' (*The Protestant Ethic and the Spirit of Capitalism*, p. 58).

4 See M. Dobb, *Studies in the Development of Capitalism*, and the *Science and Society* symposium, *The Transition from Feudalism to Capitalism*.

5 See their papers in *The Transition* . . ., and Dobb, *op. cit.*, ch. 2.

6 In Sweezy's view the growth of international trade, which he sees as *external* to feudalism, is primarily responsible for its downfall. Sweezy borrows this position from the non-Marxist work of Pirenne. Were it not for trade, it seems, feudalism might have gone on for ever. However, Sweezy regards capitalism as transitional in its concept since its dissolution is the effect of its internal development.

7 On p. 304 he insists that both correspondence and non-correspondence must be analysed 'only in terms of an effectivity and a mode of effectivity'.

8 In his later work Bettelheim rejects the notion of a transitional *mode* of production for the reasons given in (i) above. He replaces it by transitional *form*. See Bettelheim, *Calcul économique et formes de propriété*, 1970. While he retains the terminology 'correspondence', 'non-correspondence', his conception of the transition period effectively rejects the teleology implicit in Balibar's transitional mode of production.

9 Weber treats Marx's concepts in precisely this sense (*The Methodology of the Social Sciences*, p. 103):

> The eminent, indeed unique, *heuristic* significance of these ideal types when they are used for the *assessment* of reality is known to everyone who has ever employed Marxian concepts and hypotheses. Similarly, their perniciousness, as soon as they are

thought of as empirically valid or as real (i.e. truly metaphysical) 'effective forces', 'tendencies', etc., is likewise known to those who have used them.

Notice how in this empiricism concepts function merely as useful tools for organising our perceptions. Weber therefore rejects the possibility of an objective knowledge of the world.

10 A particularly clear example of this tendency may be found in E. Terray's 'Historical Materialism and Segmentary Societies', discussed in ch. 1. Terray uses the organisation of the labour process, in particular, different forms of co-operation, as a means of identifying modes of production.

11 We quote the wording given in Balibar, *op. cit.*, p. 236, which is a retranslation from Marx-Engels *Werke*, Bd XXIII, pp. 532–3.

12 *Reading Capital*, pp. 209–10.

13 *In Studies . . .*, ch. 2, and his paper in *The Transition. . . .*

14 This point is of the greatest importance in the analysis of the transition from capitalism to socialism. See Bettelheim, *op. cit.*, or his 'State property and socialism', together with the Introduction by Hindess.

15 But see the first edition *Lire le Capital*, vol. 2, 1965, pp. 250–1, where Balibar constructs an explicit analogy between Marx and Spinoza. That passage does not appear in subsequent editions.

16 See note 4 to this chapter.

17 On this point see especially Lenin's discussion of the theoretical and political effects of economism in *What is to be Done?*, *Collected Works*, 5.

18 For an extended discussion of the following points see the commentary on this text in Hindess, 'Lenin and the agrarian question in the First Russian Revolution'.

19 Ibid.

20 See also Weber's myth of the putter-out and the spirit of capitalism in *The Protestant Ethic*, pp. 66f, in which the idyllic state of traditionalism collapses under the impact of the spirit of capitalism. 'The question of the motive forces in the expansion of modern capitalism is not in the first instance a question of the origin of the capital sums which were available for capitalistic uses, but, above all, of the development of the spirit of capitalism. Where it appears and is able to work itself out, it produces its own capital and monetary supplies as the means to its ends, but the reverse is not true' (pp. 68–9).

21 See below for the importance of this point in connection with the transition to capitalism. For a concise refutation of the under-consumptionist argument of the necessity for a foreign market see Lenin, *The Development of Capitalism in Russia*, *Collected Works*, 3, ch. 1.

22 See *Capital*, I, ch. xxiii, *Capital* II, part iii, Lenin, *op. cit.*

23 It should be noted that differential rent is not reducible to the effect of fertility, location, and so on. The effects of different applications of capital allow for the appearance of differential rent on what is otherwise the least fertile land. On this point see Marx's analysis of the forms of differential rent in *Capital*, III, part viii.

24 For this reason theoretical errors with respect to ground-rent may have

crucial political effects. To reduce capitalist ground-rent to differential rent under conditions of private landed property is to preclude the analysis of the political effects of the representation of the landowning class at the level of the state. It follows that there can be no recognition of the significance of the question of land nationalisation (i.e. expropriation of the landowning class) for the development of capitalism in agriculture. See especially Lenin, *The Agrarian Programme of Social Democracy in the First Russian Revolution, Collected Works*, 13, in particular ch. 3, pp. 294–325, and also the commentary on this important text in Hindess, 'Lenin and the agrarian question in the First Russian Revolution'.

25 Rey has shown that there is a nascent economism in Marx's own analysis of this question in his tendency to provide a purely economic explanation of the level of absolute rent in spite of the fact that, as Marx clearly demonstrates, it is an effect of politico-juridical intervention in the economy. See P.-P. Rey, 'Sur l'articulation des modes de production', and the review of this work in A. J. Cutler and J. Taylor, 'Theoretical remarks on the theory of the transition from feudalism to capitalism'.

26 See also Cutler and Taylor, *op. cit.*

27 For a concise statement of the effects of this expropriation see the preface to the second edition of Lenin's *The Development of Capitalism in Russia, Collected Works*, 3, pp. 31–4.

28 This appears to be Dobb's position. It is shared by the other participants in the *Science and Society* debate.

29 See the analysis of the tendency of the rate of profit to fall in the capitalist mode of production in *Reading Capital*, pp. 283f.

30 Mousnier's conception of absolutism in this and other texts is examined in A. D. Lublinskaya, 'The contemporary bourgeois conception of absolute monarchy'.

31 *Ibid.* See also G. M. Littlejohn's Introduction to this article.

32 Mousnier himself supplies evidence of this in *La vénalité des offices en France sous Henri IV et Louis XIII.*

33 Trevor-Roper uses a rather different, and ill-informed, variant of this position to argue for a general political crisis in seventeenth-century Europe brought on by the excessive development of the state bureaucracy. See his article and the debate on it in Trevor Aston (ed.), *Crisis in Europe 1560–1660: Essays from Past and Present*. Lublinskaya discusses the theory of a political crisis in *French Absolutism*, ch. 2.

34 The literature on this supposed crisis is considerable. See, for example, the papers of Hobsbawn and Trevor-Roper in Aston, *op. cit.*, Mousnier, *Les XVI et XVII siècles*, book IV, and the discussions in Lublinskaya, *French Absolutism*, ch. 1, and P. Vilar, 'Problems in the formation of capitalism'.

35 Examples of the underconsumptionist thesis in various forms may be found in R. Luxembourg, *The Accumulation of Capital*, J. Robinson, *An Essay on Marxian Economics*, P. Baran and P. Sweezy, *Monopoly Capital*. For an excellent short analysis of this question see Lenin, *The Development of Capitalism in Russia, Collected Works*, 3, ch. 1.

36 See Lublinskaya, *French Absolutism*, ch. 3.

Bibliography

ALTHUSSER, LOUIS, *For Marx*, London: Allen Lane, 1969.

ALTHUSSER, LOUIS, *Lenin and Philosophy*, London: New Left Books, 1971.

ALTHUSSER, LOUIS, *Politics and History*, London: New Left Books, 1972.

ALTHUSSER, LOUIS and BALIBAR, ÉTIENNE, *Reading Capital*, London: New Left Books, 1970.

ALTHUSSER, LOUIS, BALIBAR, ÉTIENNE, and ESTABLET, ROGER, *Lire le Capital*, vol. 2, Paris: Maspero, 1965.

APTHEKER, HERBERT, *American Negro Slave Revolts*, New York: International Publishers, 1969.

ASTON, TREVOR (ed.), *Crisis in Europe 1560–1660: Essays from Past and Present*, London: Routledge & Kegan Paul, 1970.

BADIAN, ERNST, *Foreign Clientelae*, Oxford: Clarendon Press, 1958.

BADIAN, ERNST, *Publicans and Sinners*, Oxford: Basil Blackwell, 1973.

BALIBAR, ÉTIENNE, 'The Basic Concepts of Historical Materialism', in Althusser and Balibar, *Reading Capital*.

BARAN, PAUL A., *The Political Economy of Growth*, New York: Monthly Review, 1957.

BARAN, PAUL A., and SWEEZY, P., *Monopoly Capital*, Harmondsworth: Penguin, 1966.

BELYAEV, E. A., *Arabs, Islam and the Arab Caliphate*, New York and London: Praeger and Pall Mall, 1969.

BETTELHEIM, CHARLES, *La Transition vers l'économie socialiste*, Paris: Maspero, 1968.

BETTELHEIM, CHARLES, *Calcul économique et formes de propriété*, Paris: Maspero, 1970.

BETTELHEIM, CHARLES, 'State property and socialism', *Economy and Society*, vol. 2, no. 4, 1973 (a translation of Bettelheim, 1970, part II, ch. I).

BLUM, J., *Lord and Peasant in Russia*, New Jersey: Princeton University Press, 1961.

BRADLEY, F. H., *Ethical Studies*, New York: Bobbs-Merrill, 1951.

BRUNT, P. A., 'Italian aims at the time of the Social War', *Journal of Roman Studies*, 55, 1965, pp. 90–109.

BRUNT, P. A., *Social Conflicts in the Roman Republic*, London: Chatto & Windus, 1971.

BUCHER, C., *Industrial Evolution*, New York: H. Holt, 1912.

BUCKLAND, W. W., *The Roman Law of Slavery*, Cambridge University Press, 1908.

CAIRNES, JOHN E., *The Slave Power* (1863) – reprinted 1968 by David & Charles, Newton Abbot.

CARRERE D'ENCAUSSE, HÉLÈNE and SCHRAM, STUART, *Marxism and Asia*, London: Allen Lane, 1969.

CHILDE, V. G., 'The birth of civilisation', *Past and Present*, II, 1952.

CUTLER, ANTONY, 'Fascism and political theory', *Theoretical Practice*, no. 2, 1971.

CUTLER, ANTONY, 'Letter to Étienne Balibar . . .', *Theoretical Practice*, no. 7/8, 1973.

CUTLER, ANTONY and TAYLOR, JOHN, 'Theoretical remarks on the theory of the transition from feudalism to capitalism', *Theoretical Practice*, no. 6, 1972.

DAVIS, DAVID BRION, *The Problem of Slavery in Western Culture*, Harmondsworth: Penguin, 1970.

DOBB, MAURICE, *Studies in the Development of Capitalism*, Routledge & Kegan Paul, 1963.

DOUGLASS, FREDERICK, *My Bondage and My Freedom* (1855), reprinted 1969 by Dover Books, New York.

DUPRÉ, G. and REY, P.-P., 'Reflections on the pertinence of a theory of the history of exchange', *Economy and Society*, vol. 2, no. 2, 1973.

DURKHEIM, ÉMILE, *The Elementary Forms of Religious Life*, London: Allen & Unwin, 1915.

EBERHARD, WOLFRAM, *Conquerors and Rulers: Social Forces in Medieval China*, Leiden: E. E. Brill, 1970.

ELKINS, STANLEY M., *Slavery: A Problem in American Institutional and Intellectual Life*, Chicago University Press, 1969.

ENGELS, FREDERICK, *The Origin of the Family, Private Property and the State*, in K. Marx and F. Engels, *Selected Works*, One Volume, London: Lawrence & Wishart, 1968.

ENGELS, FREDERICK, *Anti-Duhring*, London: Lawrence & Wishart, 1969.

FERGUSON, ADAM, *An Essay on the History of Civil Society* (1767) – reprinted 1966 by Edinburgh University Press.

FINLEY, M. I. (ed.), *Slavery in Classical Antiquity*, Cambridge: Heffer, 1968.

FINLEY, M. I., 'Technical innovation and economic progress in the ancient world', *Economic History Review*, 18 (2nd series), 1965.

FINLEY, M. I., *The Ancient Economy*, London: Chatto & Windus, 1973.

FORTES, M. and EVANS-PRITCHARD, E. E. (eds), *African Political Systems*, London: Oxford University Press, 1961.

GELZER, E., *The Roman Nobility*, Oxford: Basil Blackwell, 1969.

GENOVESE, EUGÈNE, *The Political Economy of Slavery*, New York: Vintage, 1967.

GENOVESE, EUGÈNE, *The World the Slaveholders Made*, New York: Vintage, 1971.

GENOVESE, EUGÈNE, *In Red and Black*, London: Allen Lane, 1971.

GODELIER, MAURICE, 'La notion de "mode de production asiatique" . . .', in CERM, *Sur le 'Mode de production asiatique'*, Paris: Éditions Sociales, 1969.

GOFFMAN, ERVING, *Asylums*, New York: Doubleday, 1961.

GRANT, MICHAEL, *Gladiators*, Harmondsworth: Penguin, 1971.

GREEN, PETER, 'The First Sicilian Slave War', *Past and Present*, 20, 1961.

GUERRA Y SANCHEZ, RAMIRO, *Sugar and Society in the Caribbean*, Yale University Press, 1964.

HABAKKUK, H. J., *American and British Technology in the Nineteenth Century*, Cambridge University Press, 1967.

HEGEL, G. W. F., *The Philosophy of History*, New York: Dover, 1956.

HEGEL, G. W. F., *The Phenomenology of Mind*, London: Allen & Unwin, 1966.

HEGEL, G. W. F., *Philosophy of Right*, London: Oxford University Press, 1969.

HERSKOVITS, MELVILLE J., *Economic Anthropology*, New York: Knopf, 1953.

HILTON, RODNEY, *The Decline of Serfdom in Medieval England*, London: Macmillan, 1969.

HINDESS, BARRY, 'Lenin and the agrarian question in the First Russian Revolution', *Theoretical Practice*, no. 6, 1972.

HINDESS, BARRY, 'Models and masks . . .', *Economy and Society*, vol. 2, no. 2, 1973.

HINTON, WILLIAM, *Fanshen*, New York: Vintage, 1968.

HOBSBAWM, E. J., 'Introduction', to K. Marx, *Pre-Capitalist Economic Formations*, London: Lawrence & Wishart, 1964.

HOLT, P. M., LAMBTON, A. K. S., and LEWIS, B., *The Cambridge History of Islam*, vol. I, Cambridge University Press, 1970.

JAMES, C. L. R., *The Black Jacobins*, New York: Vintage, 1963.

JONES, A. H. M., *The Later Roman Empire*, vol. II, Oxford: Basil Blackwell, 1964.

KAHL, R. (ed.), *Studies in Explanation*, New Jersey: Prentice-Hall, 1963.

KOSMINSKY, E. A., *Studies in the Agrarian History of England in the Thirteenth Century*, Oxford: Basil Blackwell, 1956.

KRADER, LAWRENCE, *Social Organisation of the Mongol-Turkic Pastoral Nomads*, New York: Humanities Press, 1963.

KRADER, LAWRENCE, *Formation of the State*, New Jersey: Prentice-Hall, 1968.

LANE-POOLE, S., *A History of Egypt in the Middle Ages*, London: Methuen, 1901.

LAPIDUS, I. M., *Muslim Cities of the Later Middle Ages*, Cambridge, Mass.: Harvard University Press, 1967.

LEACH, EDMUND, 'Hydraulic society in Ceylon', *Past and Present*, 15, 1959.

LENIN, V. I., *The Development of Capitalism in Russia, Collected Works*, vol. 3, 1899.

LENIN, V. I., *What is to be Done?*, *Collected Works*, vol. 5, Moscow: FLPH, 1905.

LENIN, V. I., *The Agrarian Programme of Social Democracy in the First Russian Revolution, Collected Works*, vol. 13, 1907.

LENIN, V. I., *The State and Revolution, Collected Works*, vol. 25, 1917.

LEONTYEV, L., *A Short Course of Political Economy*, Moscow: Progress Publishers, 1968.

LÉVI-STRAUSS, CLAUDE, *Race and History*, Paris: UNESCO, 1952.

LÉVI-STRAUSS, CLAUDE, *Tristes Tropiques*, New York: Atheneum, 1963.

LÉVI-STRAUSS, CLAUDE, *Structural Anthropology*, London: Allen Lane, 1968.

LÉVI-STRAUSS, CLAUDE, *The Elementary Structures of Kinship*, London: Eyre & Spottiswoode, 1969.

LEWIS, BERNARD, *The Arabs in History*, London: Hutchinson, 1970.

LICHTHEIM, GEORGE, 'Marx and the "Asiatic Mode of Production" ', *St Antony's Papers*, no. 14, 1963.

LOWIE, R., *The Origin of the State*, New York: Russell & Russell, 1961.

LUBLINSKAYA, A. D., *French Absolutism: The Crucial Phase 1620–1629*, Cambridge University Press, 1968.

LUBLINSKAYA, A. D., 'The contemporary bourgeois conception of absolute monarchy', *Economy and Society*, vol. 1, no. 1, 1972.

LUXEMBOURG, R., *The Accumulation of Capital*, London: Routledge & Kegan Paul, 1951.

MAINE, SIR HENRY, *Ancient Law* (1861), London: Dent, 1954.

MALINOWSKI, BRONISLAW, *A Scientific Theory of Culture and Other Essays*, Chapel Hill: North Carolina University Press, 1944.

MARX, KARL, *Capital* I, Moscow: Progress Publishers, 1965 (for chapters 3, 4 and 5), London: Lawrence & Wishart, 1967 (for chapters 1, 2 and 6); *Capital* II, Moscow: FLPH, 1957 (for chapters 1, 2 and 6), Moscow: FLPH, 1961 (for chapters 3, 4 and 5); *Capital* III, Moscow: FLPH, 1962 (for chapters 3, 4 and 5), Moscow: Progress Publishers, 1966 (for chapters 1, 2 and 6).*

MARX, KARL, *Pre-Capitalist Economic Formations*, London: Lawrence & Wishart, 1964.

MARX, KARL, *The Civil War in France*, in K. Marx and F. Engels, *Selected Works*, one volume, London: Lawrence & Wishart, 1968.

MARX, KARL, *Theories of Surplus Value*, vol. II, London: Lawrence & Wishart, 1969.

MARX, KARL, *A Contribution to the Critique of Political Economy*, London: Lawrence & Wishart, 1971.

MARX, KARL, *The Critique of the Gotha Programme*, in *Selected Works* (see above).

MARX, KARL and ENGELS, FREDERICK, *The Communist Manifesto*, in *Selected Works* (see above).

MARX, KARL and ENGELS, FREDERICK, *On Colonialism*, Moscow: FLPH, n.d.

MARX, KARL and ENGELS, FREDERICK, *Selected Correspondence*, Moscow: FLPH, n.d.

MARX, KARL and ENGELS, FREDERICK, *The Civil War in the United States*, New York: International Publishers, 1971.

MEILLASSOUX, CLAUDE, 'Essai d'interprétation du phénomène économique dans les sociétés traditionnelles d'autosubsistance', *Cahiers d'Études Africaines*, 4, 1960.

MEILLASSOUX, CLAUDE, *Anthropologie économique des Gouro de Côte d'Ivoire*, Paris/The Hague: Mouton, 1964.

MEILLASSOUX, CLAUDE, 'Recherche d'un niveau de détermination dans la société cynégetique', *L'Homme et la Société*, 6, 1967.

* Different printings of the Soviet edition of *Capital* vary as to pagination, the different printings have been listed to make it possible to check references.

MEILLASSOUX, CLAUDE, 'From reproduction to production', *Economy and Society*, vol. 1, no. 1, 1972.

MICHELL, H., *Sparta*, Cambridge University Press, 1952.

MILL, J. S., *Utilitarianism, Liberty, Representative Government*, London: Dent, 1962.

MONTESQUIEU, BARON DE, *The Spirit of the Laws*, New York: Haffner, 1949.

MOORE, J. M. BARRINGTON, *Political Power and Social Theory*, New York: Harper, 1962.

MORGAN, LEWIS HENRY, *Ancient Society* (1877), New York: Meridian Books, 1967.

MOSSÉ, CLAUDE, *The Ancient World at Work*, London: Chatto & Windus, 1969.

MOUSNIER, ROLAND, *La Vénalité des offices en France sous Henri IV et Louis XIII*, Rouen: Maugard, 1945.

MOUSNIER, ROLAND, *Les XVI et XVII siècles. Le progrès de la civilisation européenne et le déclin de l'Orient (1492–1715)*, Paris: Presses Universitaires de France, 1954.

MUIR, W., *The Mameluke or Slave Dynasty of Egypt, 1260–1517 AD*, London: Smith, Elder & Co, 1896.

PARSONS, TALCOTT, *The Social System*, London: Routledge & Kegan Paul, 1951.

PARSONS, TALCOTT, 'The distribution of power in American society', *World Politics*, no. 1, 1957.

PEARSON, H. W., 'The Economy has no Surplus', in Polanyi *et al.* (eds), *Trade and Market in the Early Empires.*

PEARSON, H. W., 'The Secular Debate on Economic Primitivism', in Polanyi *et al.* (eds), *Trade and Market in the Early Empires.*

POLANYI, KARL, 'Aristotle Discovers the Economy', in Polanyi *et al.* (eds), *Trade and Market in the Early Empires.*

POLANYI, KARL, 'The Economy as Instituted Process', in Polanyi *et al.* (eds), *Trade and Market in the Early Empires.*

POLANYI, KARL, *Dahomey and the Slave Trade*, Seattle: Washington University Press, 1966.

POLANYI, K., ARENSBURG, C. M. and PEARSON, H. W. (eds), *Trade and Market in the Early Empires*, Chicago: Free Press, 1957.

POSTAN, M. M., 'Revisions in economic history: the 15th century', *Economic History Review* (1st series), 1939.

POSTAN, M. M., *Essays on Medieval Agriculture and General Problems of the Medieval Economy*, Cambridge University Press, 1973.

POULANTZAS, NICOS, *Political Power and Social Classes*, London: New Left Books, 1973.

POULANTZAS, NICOS, *Fascism and Dictatorship*, London: New Left Books, 1974.

PRITCHARD, A. M. (ed.), *Leage's Roman Private Law*, London: Macmillan, 1964.

REY, PIERRE-PHILIPPE, *Colonialisme, néo-colonialisme et transition au capitalisme*, Paris: Maspero, 1971.

REY, PIERRE-PHILIPPE, 'Sur l'articulation des modes de production', *Problèmes de Planification*, nos 13, 14, 1971.

ROBINSON, J., *An Essay on Marxian Economics*, London: Macmillan, 1963.
ROSTOVTZEFF, M., *Social and Economic History of the Roman Empire*, 2nd ed. Oxford: Clarendon Press, 1957.
ROUSSEAU, JEAN-JACQUES, *A Discourse on the Origin of Inequality Among Men*, in *The Social Contract and Discourses*, ed. G. D. H. Cole, London: Dent, 1961.
SCIENCE AND SOCIETY, *The Transition from Feudalism to Capitalism*, 1954.
SCULLARD, H. H., *Roman Politics, 220–150 B.C.*, Oxford: Clarendon Press, 1951.
SCULLARD, H. H., *From the Gracchi to Nero*, London: Methuen, 1963.
SHERWIN-WHITE, A. N., *The Roman Citizenship*, Oxford: Clarendon Press, 1939.
STAMPP, K. M., *The Peculiar Institution*, London: Eyre & Spottiswoode, 1964.
SYME, R., *The Roman Revolution*, Oxford: Clarendon Press, 1939.
TANNENBAUM, FRANK, *Slave and Citizen*, New York: Random House, 1947.
TAWNEY, R. H., *Land and Labour in China*, London: Allen & Unwin, 1964.
TERRAY, EMMANUEL, 'Historical Materialism and Segmentary Societies', in *Marxism and 'Primitive' Societies*.
TERRAY, EMMANUEL, *Marxism and 'Primitive' Societies*, New York: Monthly Review, 1972.
THOMSON, GEORGE, *Aeschylus and Athens*, London: Lawrence & Wishart, 1966.
VILAR, PIERRE, 'Problems in the formation of capitalism', *Past and Present*, 10, 1956.
VINOGRADOFF, PAUL, *Villainage in England*, Oxford: Clarendon Press, 1968.
WALBANK, F. W., *The Awful Revolution*, Liverpool University Press, 1969.
WEBER, MAX, *The Methodology of the Social Sciences*, Chicago: Free Press, 1949.
WEBER, MAX, *The Religion of China*, Chicago: Free Press, 1951.
WEBER, MAX, *General Economic History*, New York: Collier Books, 1961.
WEBER, MAX, *The Theory of Social and Economic Organisation*, New York: Free Press, 1964.
WEBER, MAX, *The Protestant Ethic and the Spirit of Capitalism*, London: Allen & Unwin, 1965.
WEBER, MAX, *Economy and Society*, vol. III, New York: Bedminster, 1969.
WESTERMANN, W. L., 'Ancient Slavery', *Encyclopaedia of the Social Sciences*, New York: Macmillan, 1934.
WILLIAMS, ERIC, *Capitalism and Slavery*, London: André Deutsch, 1964.
WITTFOGEL, K. A., *Oriental Despotism*, New Haven: Yale University Press, 1963.

[illegible] London, Hutchinson & [illegible] 1969.

[illegible]

[illegible]

Index